Studies in Penderecki

Vol. II

Penderecki and the Avant Garde

Prestige Publications, Inc.
Princeton, New Jersey

ISBN 0-911009-11-6

ISSN 1097-5977

Studies in Penderecki

PENDERECKI AND THE AVANT GARDE

Prestige Publications, Inc. Volume II, 2003

PENDERECKI'S WORKS: ANALYSES

REVIEWS

BOOKS

Editor's Column

With this issue, Studies in Penderecki honors not only Krzysztof Penderecki, on the occasion of his seventieth year, and other important Polish composers in the 1950s and 1960s, but also the musical contributions of those from other countries who labored, often under extremely difficult circumstances in the post-World War II period, to reach their audiences with a distinctive and original musical message. This was a difficult time for artists, especially those in Eastern Europe; it was a period when the world was divided politically and the work of composers in one country was often unknown to those in another. Some were fortunate and benefited not only from freedom of expression in their native land, but also from governmental subsidies, festival performances, regular radio and television broadcasts, and recordings of their works; while others worked in isolation, in repressive societies, fearful that they were exceeding the guidelines of governmental policies in the arts. In some situations composers were not allowed to travel and meet at venues like the Warsaw Autumn Festival to share ideas and new directions in their work. Even today, many who labored faithfully and brilliantly during these years are unknown in the west and their stories have never been told in the English language.

Because it was difficult to secure information about musical life in Europe in the period after the war, the American periodical *The Musical Quarterly* devoted an entire issue in 1965 to the topic of new developments in Europe in the mid-twentieth century: "Contemporary Music in Europe" [Volume 51:1]. It was in this way that many in the west first learned about their colleagues behind the Iron Curtain. It was then at the three main festivals of contemporary music – Darmstadt, Donaueschingen and Warsaw – that the works of these composers was heard for the first time in public. Krzysztof Penderecki and the Polish composers of this period are a case in point. It was the performances of their works at these events that brought their art to the attention of respected American composers and writers like Elliott Carter (b. 1908) and Everett Helm (b. 1913), who then wrote reviews of their new works in such English language periodicals as *Musical America, The Musical Quarterly* and *The Musical Times*. It is the desire of the editorial board of Studies in Penderecki that the articles contained herein will similarly shed further light on the work of composers hitherto unknown in the west and thereby contribute to a more complete picture of this important period of musical history.

In planning the contents of *Studies in Penderecki II,* it was the decision of the editorial board that the most effective way to place the work of Krzysztof Penderecki in context was to devote the entire volume to a survey of musical composition in Eastern and Western Europe and the United States in the twenty-year period 1950 to 1970. It was deemed necessary not only to survey the work of avant garde composers in these countries but to commission articles as well from outstanding Polish scholars in the fields of art, literature and aesthetics and thereby place these years in their broader cultural context. The editorial board is deeply appreciative to each author who has taken the time and made the effort to contribute in this way.

Finally, the editor wishes to offer special thanks to co-editor Regina Chłopicka. Without her knowledge of this period and her ability to conceptualize how all the pieces would fit together appropriately, the publication of this volume would not have been possible.

The Editorial Board wishes to express appreciation to a number of individuals who provided assistance in the preparation and completion of this volume. Acknowledgment is due, first and foremost, to the composer and his wife, Elżbieta Penderecki, for their continued assistance and cooperation in so many ways, not the least of which was finding time in their busy schedules to answer questions and supply needed information which only they have in their possession. Without the help of Magdalena Chrenkoff in proofreading, research and correspondence with the authors and Kazimierz Płoskoń in typesetting and technical matters this project would have never been completed. Deep appreciation is expressed to them.

Special acknowledgment is due Katja Riepl at Schott International and Sabine Hasse-Moeck, Moeck Verlag, for their assistance in so many ways, but primarily with copyright matters and the permission to print musical examples of works under copyright by their firms.

Finally, the Board would like to thank Eleanor Doverspike, a music lover in Indiana, Pennsylvania (USA), for her generous financial support of this project. Her assistance is most deeply appreciated.

Ray Robinson
West Palm Beach, Florida

Krzysztof Penderecki
An Address from *Labyrinth of Time*

THE TREE INSIDE[1]

The outstanding political commentator and critic Julian Klaczko said, paraphrasing Goethe, that "just as in literature, so also in the life-story of every eminent human being, we can see the epoch of the Iliad and the epoch of the Odyssey." The first is the "period of youthful heroism," "the epic of struggle," and the second is the "period of manliness and the search for the return," the "epic of tired age and nostalgia for home."[2]

I also have my Iliad and my Odyssey. For me, Troy was the avant garde, the era of youthful rebellion and faith in the possibility of changing the way of the world through art. The avant garde offered the illusion of universality. We young composers - hampered by the aesthetics of socialist realism that prevailed in Poland - regarded the musical world of Stockhausen, Nono, Boulez and Cage as liberation. I began my career at a time when there was still much left to discover. A new vision of art and the world were opening before me. Quickly, however, I realized that there was more of destruction than of building anew in the innovation that boiled down mainly to formal experiments and speculation; the Promethean tone of those days was a Utopia. The escape from the avant-garde trap of formalism enabled me to turn back towards tradition. I was even called "the Trojan horse of the avant garde." Not until *Cosmogony*, at the beginning of the seventies, however, did I manage to free myself of that Utopian faith in the possibility of building "one great family of man," which was an equally important element in the avant-garde doctrine.

Of course, it was hardly my intention – even as I sought inspiration in tradition - to become a traditionalist. I can identify with the words that Joseph addresses to Amenhotep IV in Thomas Mann's novel:

---

[1] This article is taken from the English version of *Labyrinth of Time* (Princeton, 1998), pp.15–19; there are also Polish and French versions of this book (editor).

[2] From an address delivered in 1868 and quoted by Stanisław Tarnowski in *Julian Klaczko*, Vol. 2 (Kraków, 1909), p. 69.

> The example of tradition comes from the depths, from what lies at the bottom, and that is what binds us together. But the "I" comes from God, and appertains to a spirit that is free.[3]

This is the moment where my Ulyssean adventure begins, which "through travails, dangers and pain travels towards the lost Ithaca," my Odyssey, in other words, the creation of my own way, the search for the center.

I was guided by a longing for synthesis, a desire to integrate the welter of experience that is the lot of contemporary man. Each past age has left behind its own recognizable language. Bach or Mozart knew for whom they were writing, and knew that they would be understood. The contemporary artist, despite his longing for universality, is fragmented and alienated. For me, the conscious use of tradition became an opportunity for overcoming this dissonance between the artist and the audience. I look back feelingly on my *Passion According to St Luke,* which constituted a turning point in my artistic journey. I reached for the archetype of the Passion – and thus for a theme 2,000 years old – in order to express not only the sufferings and death of Christ, but also the cruelty of our own century, the martyrdom of Auschwitz and, today, I would add: the martyrdom of Sarajevo. I wanted the spectator to be drawn by the tension and drama of the music into the very heart of what was happening – as in a medieval mystery play, at which no one viewed it from a distance. Each spectator can be drawn into that *Passion* crowd, the *turba,* which demands that Christ be crucified. Similarly, each spectator finds salvation. The old theme was brought up to date by new means of expression.

Malicious critics accused me of eclecticism, which was the opposite of what I had intended. Synthesis cannot depend on the mechanical connecting of elements, but must rather be a homogenous alloy resulting from a unifying experience. I do not deny that I always felt tempted by many styles. Polystylistics – so fashionable now – was already present in the *Passion* and Matins [*Utrenia*], not to speak of my more recent works, such as *The Black Mask* and *King Ubu,* which result, each in their own way, from the deliberately accepted aesthetics of post-modernism. I am a hybrid. My family comes from the Eastern Marches of Poland. My paternal grandmother was Armenian, and my grandfather German. I have always felt, for example, attracted to Orthodox liturgy, while at

[3] Thomas Mann, *Joseph und seine Brüder* [Joseph and His Brethren], Vol. III (*Joseph, der Ernährer*) (Stockholm, 1948), p. 170.

the same time being fascinated by Western culture and its rationalism, and also by its capacity for expressing the most complex states and feelings. After all, Mediterranean culture - which is my home in the broadest of senses - arose precisely out of that fruitful linking of the most varied elements and influences.

I feel within myself the need for variety, and some ascribe to me the traits of the mythical Proteus, who kept constantly changing his appearance. The acute critic will perceive an inherent logic here. I am tempted by both the *sacrum* and the *profanum*, God and the devil, the sublime and its violation. Sublime works of the *sacra rappresentatione* type must find their counterpoint in iconoclastic or buffo forms. I cannot be sure that I have not sinned too much, especially towards the free "I," in yielding to the imperatives of power and the national ethos. Works like the *Polish Requiem,* or the earlier *Threnody to the Victims of Hiroshima,* while they may possess an autonomous artistic existence, are liable to be read as journalism. I fear the mixing of orders; I would not want that music, written in particular times, to be background for something else, subject to the same simplification.

Today, after passing through a lesson in late romanticism and utilizing the possibilities of post-modernistic thinking, I see my artistic ideal in *claritas.* I am returning to chamber music, for I realize that more can be said in a hushed voice condensed in the sound of three or four instruments. That escape into musical privacy is its own sort of answer to our *fin de siècle,* this speeding up of the historical clock, this confusion associated with the reshuffling of the norms in culture, ethics and politics. Might not this escape from a world turning sour, this surrounding oneself with the wall of a *cordon sanitaire,* not be desertion, some sort of symptom of a new Biedermeier? *Musica domestica* instead of great oratorios involved in the renewal of the world, planting trees instead of struggle and conquest? My attitude is best defined by the words of a poet of the last *fin de siècle,* Rainer Maria Rilke:

> And I, who want to grow,
> Look inside, and in me grows a tree.[4]

The alchemists supposed that the perfection of the self must be accompanied by the regeneration of nature. Planting trees in Lusławice, where I have found the haven of my Odyssey, my Ithaca, I feel as if I am purifying

---

[4] Rainer Maria Rilke, *Wiersze* [Poems] (Wrocław, 1976), p. 126.

myself, approaching the essence of myself and the essence of music. According to the esoteric teachings, that *materia prima* of which the alchemists built their *opus magnum* was accessible through inquiry into nature. Seeking the most concentrated and economical of forms, I too am thinking of such a synthesis. It is precisely chamber music that is the source of the approach to the *materia prima* of music for me. Will this stage lead me to the anticipated Grand Synthesis, the *opus magnum*? It seems to me that the recovery of the genuine and natural, the universal language of music, is possible only through such a purification and transmutation of everything that already exists.

PENDERECKI'S WORK: AN OVERVIEW

Mieczysław Tomaszewski
Cracow

Listening to Penderecki

THE ELEMENTARY FORCE

It is difficult to remain detached while listening to the music by Krzysztof Penderecki, especially if it is the composer himself who imparts on it its final shape. His music is engaging, moving, bewildering, at times shocking and offensive, always – stimulating. Its first impression connotes with words such as exuberance, flamboyance, vitality, liberated energy, dynamic chain of sound phenomena, emergence of primary elements. The nature of the sound that reaches the audience is more than that of an object; it is "alive," resonant, vibrant, tone-colorful, articulated and intoned-like speech, that flows from man to man, rather than like a text on paper. Penderecki constructs his compositions painstakingly; his scores exhibit a confident hand, leading the various parts according to contrapuntal rules. All this somehow backs off at the very end before the directness of the "speech": how typical it has become for him to begin a work by pre-setting the audience's mood through long-lasting sounds of bass instruments. This is particularly discernible in his "dialogue with the rediscovered past" phase (i.e. since *Paradise Lost*), but has been one of Pende-recki's characteristic idioms well before that.

The liberation of sound energy began in the earliest scores. This kinetic energy was a product of the sound of speech, split into its primary elements (*Dimensions of Time and Silence*), and of the sonorism of traditional instruments, liberated by an almost barbarian hand (*Threnody, Polymorphia*) or of instruments only introduced into concert halls. Penderecki made his violins play the tailpiece, the bridge and in-between; hit the strings, the sound-box, even the music-stand – with the bow, the heel; with fingers, with an open palm. He attacked the audience with the aggressive sound of the siren and the whip (lastra), of the hammer against pieces of iron (*un pezzo di ferro*), shaking metal sheets (flexaton) or chains (catena), sawing (sega) and grinding, shrill whistles (fischetti) or softer whistles and humming accompanying the instrumentalist's own play,

K. Penderecki, *Threnody to the Victims of Hiroshima*, sketch.

with the rattle of a typewriter. At the time, it seemed that Penderecki was carried away by the wave of *avant-garde*-ism, that he released the elements like a sorcerer's apprentice. As we know, he was able to restrain the effervescent sonority of *Fluorescences* as he later did with the raging emotions of *Dies irae* or, still later, with the unfettered eloquence of the First Violin Concerto. Kinetic energy gave way to potential energy, pure sonority to musicality, pure emotionality to controlled expression, extensive form to intensive form.

The discovery of the elementary force went hand in hand with a return to sources, to archetypes. In Penderecki, the man of nature yields to the man of nurture; the temperament to the consciousness of belonging to a specific tradition. He placed himself there quite clearly at the very beginning with *Psalms of David* (1958) and *Strophes* (1959), respectively an interpretation of selected verses of the Psalmist, calling *de profundis* to God, and with texts by philosophers, poets and prophets pondering human existence. He could well echo Norwid's "David's key opened my mouth, Rome called me man."[1]

INTO THE DEPTH, TO THE TOP, TO THE BRIM

Since his earliest works, Penderecki has used, among his many other notation marks, two pointers, which might symbolize his way of thinking and creative action: they indicate the highest and the lowest possible sounds. One is reminded here of Andrzej Hiolski's voice in the aria *Deus meus*, climbing towards the topmost sound, only to fall two octaves down, or of the ecstatic *Velichaniye*, ascending towards the upper barrier in *Utrenia I*. How often the voice of the violins in *Paradise Lost* rises from the darkest depths towards the upper and lightsome registers! Penderecki's music is that of the extremities; his experience is that of the extreme, which, within the thematic sphere, results in eschatological tendencies, in the interest in the beginning (*Paradise Lost*) and the end (*Requiem*, *Dies irae*). At the same time, his music is that of completeness, richness, excess.

Some aesthetics limit the assortment of constituent elements of a work of art in a rigorous selection: all classicisms only tolerate the presence of some well-defined type of beauty in a work; sentimentalism goes as far as

[1] Cyprian Kamil Norwid, *Moja Ojczyzna* [My country], ll. 15–16.

allowing exclusively "the most beautiful scenes of the most beautiful nature, the sweetest moments of the best of people."[2]

Penderecki's position is at the other extremity. He is interested in the good and the evil, the beautiful and the ugly – in fullness. This is a fullness of the material that can house both harmony and noise, all vocal textures and all instruments, homo- and heterogeneous sound, sound subtle and brutal. This is a fullness of the means, collected from throughout the last millennium of music, used as a generalized principle of construction rather than in imitation or stylization. This function might be served, in Penderecki, by choral and organ textures, that of the hoquetus and that of the motet, a Dutch or a Venetian style, a post-Romantic or an idiom of expression, all side by side with techniques adapted from dodecaphony and post-serialist pointillism, with aleatoric and sonoric procedures. What might have been an eclectic conglomerate becomes, in the heightened creative temperature, a new quality on a higher plane, leading from coexistence to integration.

Richness often borders on excess, extremities might usher in monumentalism, not valued too highly by our century. Yet Penderecki does not fear the path of the rise and fall, one experienced by Handel and Hasse; Berlioz and Meyerbeer; Wagner, Bruckner and Mahler. He fears neither sweeping themes nor sweeping emotions, nor sweeping forms.

BETWEEN *SACRUM* AND *PROFANUM*

The preponderance of sacral subjects in Penderecki is visible at first sight. It seems obvious that his creative path is denominated by works inspired by the Old and the New Testament: *Psalms of David* and *Stabat Mater, Passion* and *Utrenia, Canticum canticorum* and *Magnificat, Paradise Lost, Te Deum, Polish Requiem, Seven Gates of Jerusalem* and *Credo.* All these are supplemented by *Strophes, Dies irae, The Devils of Loudun, Cosmogony,* and *The Black Mask,* i.e. works dealing with philosophical and moral issues clearly related to religion. On the other hand, the numerous and varied group of purely instrumental compositions seems to create a magnificent, multihued background, from which vocal-instrumental works emerge. It is, at the same time, a laboratory for means later used in sacral forms. Or vice versa: at times, instrumental compositions appear on the

[2] A principle of Classicist poetics formulated – after N. Boileau and J.P. Richter – by K. Brodziński in his treatise *O idylli pod względem moralnym* [On the idyll in terms of morality], Warszawa 1823.

margin, as it were, of material shaped in those other ones. And yet: *Threnody to the Victims of Hiroshima, De natura sonoris,* First Symphony, *The Awakening of Jacob,* Violin Concerto, Symphony No. 2 ("*Christmas Eve*"), *Cello Concerto* – all show that Penderecki's "pure" music can well do without word, plot or scene.

One might conjecture that the composer's fascination with the *sacrum* and his constant lingering within that sphere stem from the mystery of human existence in both of its parallel and complementary perspectives: the metaphysical and the ethical. Penderecki's choices of his subject vary, yet quite meaningful is his preference for those that lie in-between the two: crime and punishment, pain and death; issues at the borderline between the human and the divine and, at the same time, issues of a universal dimension and significance. One might suspect at times that the composer is interested solely in their humanist aspect: injustice, enslavement, intolerance, inhumanity; and yet, as when his music becomes pure contemplation, ecstasy and ardor – this happens particularly in oases of *a cappella* choruses – another perspective seems to appear. That Penderecki's inherent strong feeling of independence drives him to adopt unorthodox, or even quasi-heretical approaches, is still another matter.

Reverting to "the *sacrum*-based tradition, lost or discarded at a certain point" became, for Penderecki, an act of conscious choice and, at the same time, as he states in the well-known Poznań text,[3] "a major turning point" in his artistic biography.

THE THICK BLACK LINE

Penderecki's themes, while still *in statu nascendi,* are characteristic in their specific and heightened mode of expression. The primitive reactions of the mob in the *Passion,* the Apocalyptic orgy of evil in *Dies irae,* the lamentations, painful concentration and ecstasy of *Utrenia,* the scenes of demoniac possession and auto-da-fé in *The Devils of Loudun,* the exalted and ecstatic moments of *Magnificat,* the intense prayer of *Te Deum,* the horror and the frenzy in *The Black Mask,* the heavenly *Song of Cherubim* – how could anyone react to this with musical neutrality?

[3] From the lecture at the University of Poznań, during the ceremony of Penderecki's honorary degree there. The text published by *Tygodnik Powszechny* (1988, 1, p. 3); the most significant and the most outspoken fragments were deleted by the censorship at the time.

Penderecki reacts to the emotional content of his texts with no fear of transgressing barriers imagined by a couple of critics. His reaction is extreme and intensely concentrated. A lament becomes a lament, a frenzy a frenzy, an euphoria an euphoria. He is close to expressionism – the more so as he highlights the expression of negative, resentimental emotions. He does not shrink from garishness or brutality, from the art of the poster rather than of painting (*Death Brigade, Dies irae,* the *Paradise Lost* finale). Yet there are also scenes there of an exceptional subtlety; one might even speak of Penderecki's other, lyrical strand, of his lyricism of lyricism (entire parts in *Canticum canticorum* and in *Paradise Lost*) and religion (the contemplative moments in *Passion, Utrenia, Te Deum, Polish Requiem*). The more aggressive their sound context, the stronger is their impact.

The heightened expression is determined by the choice of expressive means themselves. All kinds of singing and all modes of speech are possible, as are shouting and whispers, crying and laughter, whistling or even the sound of breathing. Melodic motives carrying words of particular import are drawn with utmost intensity; it is then impossible to forget the expression of the second sequences in *Deus Meus* or *Agnus Dei,* or in the diminished sixth's leap in *Lacrimosa.* The moments in which Penderecki works through a tonal explicitness are delineated with equal clarity: the luminous E-flat major at the word "Gloria" explodes in a full *tutti* in the *Magnificat;* the expression of A-flat major at "Dominus" in *Te Deum* is unmistakable. It really does seem as if Penderecki marked the bass line with a thick, black pen; his music, often open "upwards," is firmly based on the ground.

RHETORICAL GESTURE

And yet: is the expression of Penderecki's works a manifestation of his own emotions? As often as not, it is a theatre of expression, an expression performed.

The borderline between the stage and the bandstand is often indistinct in Penderecki. A devotee and connoisseur of the Antique, he is close to the concept of the threefold chorea, where the word and the sound, together with the movement (the dance and stage gesture) used to be one. His music develops in an imaginary space as well as in time. Its aplomb and gesture, "the slow movement of musical images,"[4] akin to the Baroque idiom, have been observed.

[4] As stated by Alexander Ivashkin: *Krzysztof Penderecki, Monographicheskiy ocherk.* Moskva, 1983.

When, in *Magnificat*, the bass begins to chant "Fecit potentiam," and the kettledrums and the brass join in with the low strings, the passion of this moment is perceived as a Baroque *teatrum*. The same happens in *Te Deum*, when the elevated "Tu, rex gloriae" resounds, interspersed with the exclamations of the choir ("Christe!") as the music leads us into a dramatic space. Many other scores (especially in *Dies irae* and the *Requiem*) contain that theatrical gesture, a mode of expression in which a particular convention prevails over the directness of the expression, a theatrical pretence over psychological or realistic truth.

In a way that is not conventionalized, as in the Baroque, yet certainly with much resemblance to the poetics of that time, and, it is certain, unconsciously, Penderecki employs techniques and tropes in which one could find the *exclamatio, abruptio, anabasis, gradatio* and *climax* of old. Thus he restrains the elemental expression with conventional forms. The effect is paradoxical: the use of figures of musical rhetoric enhances the power of expression.

This play of forces might become dangerous in bad performances: loftiness neighbors on pompousness, passion on pathos. It seems that the occasional highly negative criticism of some of Penderecki's works, e.g. of the *Dies irae* oratorio or of certain parts of *Polish Requiem*, has one of its sources in faulty conducting interpretations. There is neither pompousness nor pathos in the performances conducted by the composer himself; the categories of loftiness and passion ring true as essential expressive qualities.

Pure Play

Penderecki's early scores were combinatorial, much in the spirit of dodecaphony and serialism, supplemented with the composer's own exploration. The original version of *Dimensions of Time and Silence* was based on the old magical square – an attempt at a musical adaptation of Paul Klee's postulates. Specific series of numbers regulated the rhythmic flow of *Anaklasis*. Strict permutations of a few articulation modes defined the structure of the *First Quartet*, and *Threnody*'s middle part was made up of an intricate, 36-voice canon of punctualist texture.

In the most general terms, this idea of searching for a possibly most precise form for the sound material remained with Penderecki until today

("I do not believe in open form"[5]). It only discarded external automatisms and became thoroughly internalized. Even those early combinatorial choices of the mind were accompanied by those of the ear; later on, experience with sounds and direct intuition began to dominate over pure play. At the same time, contrapuntal logic started to prevail over permutation procedures; and the vindication of timeless formal principles - those of the refrain and the reprise, modification and development, stratification and stretto, was a consequence of personal experience. "I think," he said in 1976, "that new form cannot be created. A number of forms have been around since the beginnings of music - and all attempts at their destruction have been futile."[6]

Obviously, these words should not be understood in their literal sense. None of Penderecki's *passacaglia* resembles old forms in all but the most general structural idea. Even what we still call counterpoint is now a far cry from its original cast; only the elementary principles have been preserved. Dodecaphonic thinking has left an indelible mark on the way Penderecki shapes the melodic line, even that born of a post-Romantic aura; the stratification method has led to the emergence of counterpoint-square.

It is equally obvious that conservative thinking underlies each score by Penderecki; the question is whether it is a manifestation of pure play, or whether it serves a particular expression. In this sense there is a difference between e.g. the halftone pitch alteration of the second violin in *Emanations* (1958), and basing the tonal structure of *The Black Mask* (1986) on two halftone-removed fifth environments. In the former, the sound image becomes slightly off-focus and, to a point, accidental; in the latter, the structure of sounds is sharpened, while their more discernible dissonance increases the dynamics of the musical narration.

There are other sanctuaries of pure play in Penderecki. These include, to some extent, concerto works for the violin, the viola, the cello, the harpsichord. His tendency to play with form is manifest in the occasional re-emergence of the cycle of capriccios — for Wanda Wiłkomirska's violin, Heinz Holiger's oboe, Siegfried Palm's cello or Zdzisław Piernik's tuba. This is the Penderecki *buffo* of provocative interviews, the same Penderecki as in his following opera *Ubu Rex*.[7]

[5] Krzysztof Penderecki, discussion during a session on his *oeuvre*, Cracow, January 1975. C.f. *Muzyka*, 1976, 2.

[6] Ibid.

[7] The opera, in an obviously *buffo* style, was finally realised in 1991. (Now Penderecki is working on the opera *Fedra* - editor).

Clashing Contrasts

Serialism is confronted with sonorism in *Threnody;* singing in the spirit of the choral and dodecaphonic technique combine in the sound matter of the *Passion.*[8] In *Dies irae,* the sacral vision of St John is interrupted with the profane madness of Aeschylus' Eumenides.[9] Religion and eroticism, contemplation and frenzy clash in *The Devils of Loudun.* In *Paradise Lost,* the universe of God confronts the universe of Satan in the language of music.[10] Dozens of similar examples could still be given. As stated by Władysław Stróżewski, "Penderecki's *oeuvre* is an immense musical realization of dialectics, of dialectics stretched between extremes, somehow coping with them and, at the same time, keeping them alive."[11]

Just as in Ecclesiastes, where the various antitheses are clearly identified and succinctly, speaking of "a time to be born, and a time to die; a time to weep, and a time to laugh; a time to mourn, and a time to dance; a time to keep silence, and a time to speak"; as Ecclesiastes, then, does Penderecki clearly set contrary universes against each other. His mastery of the varied wealth of modes of expression permits him to articulate through musical structures and to clash such categories as joy and pain, love and hate, good and evil, the heavenly and the infernal, the human and the inhuman.[12]

With the course of time, authenticity is joined in Penderecki by complementation, contrast by concord. In the climax of *Te Deum,* the pleading melisma of the soprano's "Salvum fac populum Tuum, Domine" harmonizes with the contemplative texture of the unexpected *Boże, coś Polskę.* In the climax of *Polish Requiem,* the poignant "Święty Boże, Święty, Mocny" [Holy God, Holy, Powerful] of the choir is contrapuntally commented upon by the solo "Recordare Jesu Pie." Thus the national is in agreement with the universal.

Penderecki was accused of betraying the avant-garde after his *St Luke Passion* – as if tradition and modernity were incompatible. Pascal

---

8 C.f. Ray Robinson and Allen Winold, *Die Lukaspassion von Krzysztof Penderecki* ['St Luke Passion' by Krzysztof Penderecki]. Celle: Moeck Verlag, 1983.

9 C.f. Teresa Malecka, "*Dies irae*". In *Festival... 1988,* Kraków 1988, pp. 55–56.

10 C.f. Joanna Wnuk-Nazarowa, "Postać szatana w *Raju utraconym*" [The character of devil in 'Paradise Lost']. In *Współczesność i tradycja...,* 1983, pp. 221–235.

11 Władysław Stróżewski, final discussion during a session on Penderecki, Cracow, January 1975.

12 C.f. Regina Chłopicka, "Problem dobra i zła w twórczości scenicznej Krzysztofa Pendereckiego" [The Problem of Good and Evil in the Scenic Works of Krzysztof Penderecki]. In Anna Oberc (ed.), *Muzyka, słowo, sens.* Kraków: Akademia Muzyczna, 1994, pp. 113–134.

noted: "We do not display greatness by going to one extreme, but in touching both at once, and filling all the intervening space."[13]

OBSESSIONS

Penderecki likes returns and repetitions, even though he follows Picasso's and Stravinsky's example by going ever forward, changing his external expression modes from time to time. He likes, then, to repeat words, motet-like (*Agnus Dei*) or aria-like (*Deus Meus*); he likes reprises, even allusive ones (the ocarinas in *The Awakening of Jacob*); he likes refrains of all kinds. Their presence in *The Black Mask* makes it possible to listen to the opera with eyes closed – the music is autonomous structurally.

The Black Mask seems to be a work the composer has been unconsciously building up for many years; one that brings together a number of earlier tendencies. Writing the Catholic-Protestant *Passion*, and then, in turn, the Eastern Orthodox *Utrenia*, the Old Testament *Canticum canticorum Salomonis* and the New Testament *Magnificat*, Penderecki might have been realizing a hidden ecumenical agenda of his own. The plot of *The Black Mask* gathers at a table representatives of almost all creeds. The theme of *Dies irae*, ominously resounding in one of the opera's culminations, has been tormenting Penderecki for years; we remember it from the Auschwitz oratorio, from the final scenes of *Paradise Lost*, even from *Te Deum*, obviously from the *Requiem*. The catastrophic finale of *The Black Mask* has also had its own anticipations.

It can be said that Penderecki has been treading around dark subjects: death, the Holocaust, the Apocalypse, the Inferno. The works that deal with these also include projects as yet not realized: Dante's *Inferno* and *The Last Judgement*.

THROUGH WORD, THROUGH SOUND AND BEYOND SOUND

Krzysztof Penderecki's music is undoubtedly that of the semiotic age. It has discarded the tradition of art for art's sake together with the rejected Hanslick's paradigm. It has rediscovered the long-lost functions of music, eliminated by the domination or the monopoly of the aesthetic function – expressive and appellative, phatic and symbolic. A composition can again express things, appeal, help to establish a relationship and

[13] Blaise Pascal, *Pensées*, translated by W. F. Trotter. New York, 1941.

carry a message; yet it can do so only if it meets the highest criteria in itself, in its sound matter and formal structure.

Obviously, the message is easiest to read in works carrying words. These are never accidental in Penderecki; their choice and distribution is usually determined by the composer himself. One glimpse at the texts of the *Psalms* or the *Strophes* is enough to see that he uses "foreign" words to express his own program. Although, to avoid a too literal impact of the text, he has long used textures and techniques preventing the direct reception of its content, he always makes an exception from this rule for the significant, sense-bearing words and phrases; these are invariably emphasized in a specific way which further enhances their expression. Lacos Peris,[14] who stresses Penderecki's dependence on the word, observes that "it is often the word moving one to the core, the word described by Heidegger as the 'home of Being', the word treated by the composer as liberating". Penderecki himself has said in 1976, that all one need to compose is "just a single book, the Holy Writ."[15]

Penderecki's parallel message is transmitted by the musical text. For the composer, this is a category that may be called "meaningful form." A differentiating system is set in place. To make a long story short: positive connotations are carried by clear sound, not by hums and noise; *cantabile* or *espressivo* melodies more than any other variety; chords (mostly elliptic) or unisons are positive too, but not so dissonant multiple chords or clusters. It is by no means a coincidence that works such as *Stabat Mater, Passion* or *Magnificat* resound in D, E, and C, respectively. If such moments are endowed with the force of expression, it is also because they serve, at the same time, as vantage points: surrounded and preceded by music from the other extremity, one that can connote chaos and danger.

Relatively recently, a new, sense-conveying means of expression has appeared in Penderecki: culminations created by the "revelation,"[16] in the work, (unexpected yet well-prepared) of music endowed with deeply symbolic meaning. The Bach choral *O grosse Lieb'* in *Paradise Lost, Boże, coś Polskę* in *Te Deum, Święty Boże* in the *Requiem, Silent Night* in the Second Symphony, the choral *Aus tiefer Not* in *The Black Mask* – these are only apparent quotations. In fact, these moments are an organic part of the

[14] Presenting Penderecki for a honorary degree in Madrid, 1987; fragment of lecture.

[15] Penderecki in the mentioned discussion, Cracow, January 1975. C.f. *Muzyka*, 1976, 2.

[16] Beethoven's term (*Offenbarung*), introduced into the system of musical aesthetics by Kurt Huber, *Musikästjetik*. Ettal 1954.

work, its heart rather than an addition, a *cantus prius factus* of sorts. The type of their musical material highly determines the other themes of the work, just as *cantus firmus* used to determine the counterpoints it produced. As word-music entities, these "revealing" themes carry meanings which might be described as a vindication and a justification of foolishly squandered values.

Translated by Jan Rybicki

Tadeusz A. Zieliński
Warsaw

The Penderecki Controversy

The Penderecki Festival held in Cracow in 1998 not only provided an occasion to listen to an abundant portion of the work of a renowned artist, but also prompted reflections on the special and, in its way, extraordinary phenomenon of the work of the 65-year-old composer of the *Passion* and the *Polish Requiem*. I am using this circumstance as a pretext. In the end, there would be a great deal to think about even without such a festive occasion, for the Penderecki phenomenon continues to be a feature of our musical scene (and indeed, is an increasingly prominent feature of it). For decades, this phenomenon has been stirring varied emotions and controversies, delight and opposition, animosity and admiration, amazement and uneasiness.

In the common view, Krzysztof Penderecki is linked with three catchphrases: first, shocking avant-gardism (the early works); second, a colossal career, honors, and fortune; and third, a new apotheosis of neo-romanticism or, as some would have it, the stylistic reanimation of neo-romanticism. Seen in schematic simplicity, these three elements look logically incongruous. For anyone used to conceiving of art (and the world) in easy, simple formulas, they might give rise to irritation and a sense of having to do with something freakish.

I do not feel, however, that it would be proper to paste together an image of Penderecki the composer from just these elements. The first of them – the purely "sonoristic" works like *Threnody, Dimensions of Time and Silence* and the First String Quartet – is a chapter that was closed long ago (despite the fact that these works were once counted among the most highly regarded accomplishments of the avant garde) and that they are no basis for claims to Penderecki's stature or to his present position in music. Similarly, the second element is irrelevant to what is worth knowing about Penderecki's art (or, in any case, lies outside my sphere of interests, no matter how many people get excited about it). We are left, then, with the third element, which is again simplified and trivialized in the formula: Penderecki as a rebel against "modernity," who places the ideal of neo-romantic poetics and the sorts of experiences associated with the great composers of centuries past above the invention of ever-new sounds and structures. This is indeed a great and weighty theme, over which we should pause and reflect.

1.

For more than a quarter of a century, Penderecki has manifested a distinct distance toward the philosophy and practice of the avant garde by creating music that is stylistically new (because it is his own) but rooted in certain past aesthetic examples, especially those of late-romanticism, and that is quite different to what other composers are writing. Although it is always accepted by the public and eagerly performed, Penderecki's work often arouses objections or, at best, expressions of discomfort, unease, and awkwardness among composers, musicologists and critics. It is easy to see why. These works shake up the carefully arranged concepts and the simple image of the development of music - and the simple concept of the contemporary - that have been accepted for several decades. Not many people like seeing their view of the world destroyed, especially when they have put no small effort into forming that view. The view, in this case, holds that contemporary is the radical undermining and rejection of tradition, and not an appeal to tradition. On the other hand, the format of Penderecki's art somehow makes it impossible to dismiss. This leads to an axiological discomfort, or even a certain embarrassment felt by many - as if an outstanding composer were leading us into the kabala.

Such conflicting feelings, rather typical in our circles, are revealed in Andrzej Chłopecki's long article on Penderecki titled "Leaving the Door Open Behind Oneself,"[1] which combines respect with unconcealed consternation and embarrassment. Chłopecki feels that Penderecki "has been, for a long time, the most alienated composer of our modernity. His music increasingly resembles an isolated island not linked by any means of aesthetic communication with modern music. Or to put it differently: contemporary music is an isolated, alienated island that is losing its communication links with the music and aesthetics of the Polish composer." This second idea, interesting as it is, remains only a glittering stylistic ornament that the author does not develop.

In itself - taken out of context - the opinion cited above is one of the greatest and most serious compliments that can be paid to a creative artist.

[1] Andrzej Chłopecki, *Tygodnik Powszechny*, March 8, 1998.

Nothing testifies to greatness like distinctness of imagination and independence of the myths and stereotypes of one's own epoch. As we read Chłopecki's article, however, we become convinced that the dissonance between "contemporary music" as personified by the "main actors on the musical stage in the second half of the twentieth century: Boulez, Xenakis, Ligeti, Kagel, Kurtág, Lachenmann, and Schnittke," and the independent Penderecki, is hardly to the credit of the latter. Rather the converse. As Chłopecki sees it, Boulez, Xenakis, Kagel, and Lachenmann are clearly in the right, while it is Penderecki who raises obvious reservations.

However, this anxiety is grounded in not any sort of inability on the part of Penderecki, or the quality of his work, but solely in his attitude - his very rejection of *the contemporary*. Chłopecki understands this concept unambiguously, and it is crucial in his article. We therefore read that Penderecki "does not pay homage to the contemporary," that he makes a spectacle of his "flight from the contemporary"; we also read about the "motif of Penderecki's turning away from the contemporary" and his "skepticism in regard to his own times."

I am not citing these words in order to argue with what is, after all, an interesting article by Chłopecki. His position and way of understanding things are typical of our circles, and he uses the concepts mentioned above in the way that they are universally understood. However, I would like to consider the real ambivalence and slipperiness of these very concepts, which are so often - erroneously - made into absolutes and appropriated by a certain tendency in the art of our times.

What, really, is the contemporary? What defines any epoch in the history of art? What, in fact, is the time that is filled with radically different composers?

Today, thinking back on the first half of the nineteenth century, it is difficult not to call it the age of Beethoven, but in the eyes of those alive at the time it was rather the era of the *brillante* style and of Paganini (not to mention the new Italian operas). The composer of the *Eroica* and the sixteen quartets was an alien body in "the contemporary," thus understood. And how does Johann Sebastian Bach square up against what was regarded as the only "contemporary" tendency at the time he was composing his fugues? Please bear in mind as well the sort of tendency and poetics that were referred to as "new music" in the latter half of the nineteenth century, which was, after all, if not above all, the time of Brahms, who opposed such tendencies. It is also hard to think of a wider gap than the one between Shostakovich and the radical avant-gardism that was at its most aggressive in his creative years. Yet perhaps, in the final reckoning, those years may be the "epoch of Shostakovich." The present (and surely, to an even greater degree, the future) fate of his work seem increasingly to point in this direction.

History should not, of course, be simplified by associating specific epochs with a single chosen artistic option. The face of each epoch is multifaceted. Yet it is a natural thing that, when mentioning a given epoch, we associate it above all with the greatest artists who were then alive.

2.

I regard Penderecki as the foremost living composer. Not, of course, because he chose one poetics over another or because he uses a certain set of techniques, but because he has created an individual, recognizable style of great power, and within this style has composed works and concepts that remain deeper in the musical memory and feelings than the works of other composers of our day. The criterion accepted here (and expressed in brief form) is not arbitrary, for it has been the ultimate determinant of the distinctions and honors and the existence in the concert hall of the composers named above, who have apparently been working against the grain of their age. It is, after all, what distinguishes all the historical "greats." In the final reckoning, it is always a matter of the power of the individual message, and not of the language used. Although it is the sounds that most rapidly arrest the attention of the listener, and despite the fact that superficial criticism often fails to go beyond these sounds, the true and final judgment is about what they convey, and thus about the weightiness of the expression. An expression that, after all conveys experiences rather than sensations, and which carves out a vestige in our minds and our memory.

Chłopecki is, of course, correct when he writes in his article that Penderecki is "one of the most powerful, but at the same time one of the most self-assured personalities among the composers of our time." Such a personality, in my opinion, also becomes apparent in the fact that it feels under no obligation - not in the smallest degree - to submit to the current schemes, imperatives, and prejudices that prevail in its epoch. In the formation of its vision of contemporary music, it is guided *exclusively* by its own sense of its hidden potentials and perspectives and its most fully private, personal taste. The second thing includes Penderecki's love of Wagnerian neo-romanticism. The first, on the other hand, is the very fact of forging creative bonds with "pre-avant-garde music and its hastily discarded ideals – that is, what the composer has beautifully and accurately defined as "leaving the door open behind oneself."[2]

Such a stance undercuts some simple images of the contemporary, based on the allegedly irreversible acts of the postwar avant garde and the axioms it accepted. But treating those acts and axioms outside their own dimensions and borders is an intellectual abuse. Why should the character and position of some composers be obligatory for anyone else? Even assuming that they are individually worthwhile? Such demands are senseless. Therefore, even if the above-mentioned "leaving the door open" were only a peculiar caprice of Penderecki's individual imagination, it would still – in view of the results achieved – have sufficient reason for being, and immense artistic significance.

3.

It does not, however, seem that this "leaving the door open" was merely an exceptional and perverse whim. On the contrary: it accords with the objective rationale of the further development of music, which is deprived on the current path not only of perspectives, but even of any chance of survival. Postwar avant-gardism, whatever we might think of the value of its particular products, has done colossal harm to contemporary music, isolating it behind an artificially erected wall – a sort of iron curtain – that separates it from all musical tradition and continuity, endeavoring to sever its links with history and from the feeling of melody, harmony, form and, in general, musical sense, as they have developed over the centuries. A situation has arisen from which there is no way out, because music cannot and has not been able to live and develop on the "zero" foundations from which an effort to begin was made – and certainly not for longer than the lifespan of one generation. It has been threatened with being stunted, with artistic minimalization or the reduction of art to technology and spiritual vacuity.

The only possible salvation was to smash as quickly as possible through that unfortunate wall and, into the artificially sterilized atmosphere of that mad ("Huxleyan") laboratory, to admit authentic air, a breeze that restores contact with the world of the past and, with it, the possibility of normal feeling. The necessity of such a breach ("leaving the door open behind oneself") in contemporary music is something that Penderecki recognized sooner than anyone else, and although he is not alone in this attitude today,

[2] Krzysztof Penderecki, *Labirynt czasu* [Labyrinth of Time]. Warszawa, 1997, p. 22.

he has provided the most convincing example so far of the restoration of "forgotten" ideals in what is now a new style.

Such behavior naturally meets with a reactionary, disapproving response from the conservative elements that are attached to the received image of the contemporary, and the ideology that underpins it. From this point of view, the restoration of contact between the composer and tradition is equivalent to taking the soft option in artistic terms and churning out non-creative works . . . after all, they are stylistically derivative.

Such a judgment may, however, attest to nothing more than the total disorientation of its authors in the real problems of contemporary music and the condition of that music, as a result of which their accusations miss the mark by 180 degrees. The situation is, after all, the precise opposite. The soft option for composers today is the comfortable and secure reproduction of the stylistic ideas of the postwar avant garde, petrified in new conventions of patterns and techniques, taught for years in the music schools and mechanically assimilated by no less than three generations of composers. While these models may have been attractive thirty or forty years ago because of their freshness and oddity, if not their internal vitality, all of that is long gone today. All of the present (broadly conceived) "post-avant-garde" mainstream is distinctly redolent of decline, non-creative, shopworn, and marked by all the symptoms of academic ossification ("avant-gardism").

The rejection of this dead model and the search for a way out of it are precisely what talent, boldness and creative imagination demand. Leaving the door open behind oneself, in order to be able in a natural way (no longer pretending) to open the doors in front of oneself as well, represents not only an historical necessity, but also the greatest of artistic challenges. How to do this? No one can tell the composer how to do it. The recipe is not provided by any learned technique, or any copied example. Received musical techniques make it possible to compose a new symphony in the style of Mozart (a renowned Polish composer played such a joke for us a few years back) or to come up with a splendid baroque jingle for the Second Program of Polish Radio, or a famous romantic piece for a film, or even, indeed—for, after all, there is not the slightest difference in the method! - yet another post-avant-garde work, just like hundreds, or even thousands, of others. But to transpose old ideals and experiences to the ground of contemporary craft and today's sensitivity - that involves authentic innovation, fantasy, and artistic risk. This is what it means to invent and shape music through individual intuition and inspiration. In my opinion, Penderecki's works, and especially his most recent symphonies and

and especially his most recent symphonies and concertos, occupy a place that is especially important, and perhaps downright exceptional, on the most creative paths of our time.

4.

To the degree that the demolition of the artificial wall separating the contemporary from the traditions of past epochs is an objective requirement of our time, so Penderecki's late-romantic turning must now be explained through the composer's personal taste. And perhaps by broader factors as well, since nineteenth-century romanticism in general seems to be a particularly valuable and exceptionally wealthy model that is still capable of supplying many more spurs to the contemporary musical imagination. Nevertheless, such a distinct turning by the composer in the direction of the "Wagnerian" current is clearly an expression of his individual likings and taste, and furthermore features a certain provocative character in view of the fact that it is precisely this tradition that clashes particularly with the feeling and understanding of modernity in (almost) all of the twentieth century.

When speaking of Penderecki's neo-romantic affiliations, however, it is necessary to add certain caveats without which it is easy to mix things up and fall into error. Above all, this is not the composer's only link to tradition (near or remote); the roots of his new style also extend elsewhere. If the attention of the listener is dominated by that one selectively apprehended model, then it is precisely because it is such an unexpected (paradoxical) phenomenon in our epoch.

We doubtlessly sense the presence of the neo-romantic spirit in the Second Symphony and the Third Symphony, in the Second Violin Concerto, to a somewhat smaller degree in the Clarinet Quartet and the Fifth Symphony (although it also announced itself earlier in the opera *Paradise Lost* and in the First Violin Concerto). It must, however, be noted that even in these examples it never defines the style of the work as a whole, but rather certain of its characteristics and places in the process. As much as the beginning of the Fourth Symphony and the development of its melodic themes, as well as certain of its dramatic traits, evoke strong associations with that tradition, it would be hard to say the same thing about many other parts of the work, especially the two rapid segments with their captivatingly acute rhythms and sounds.

However – and this is the fundamental thing! – even where these associations are the greatest, we are dealing in reality with something entirely different from the reconstruction of a model from the past. Penderecki does not bring back the historical style and language or don a costume from the theatrical wardrobe – as has occurred in the examples given above of the work of other composers. The conviction that Penderecki does indeed compose in a post-Wagnerian style can only be the result of the illusion produced by the contrast between his poetics and the "typical" phenomena of contemporary music. Against the background of these phenomena, any *resemblance* to a model that is so unexpected today is bound to seem identical to that model. Yet such an illusion could arise only in someone who is content with general, superficial impressions, without going into the details or the process of the music.

5.

In reality, the musical language and the style of these "neo-romantic" works of Penderecki's are completely different from the century-old model with which they are associated. If for no other reason than the fact that this model was organically associated with the major-minor tonal system. Even in the most remote regions and peripheries of nineteenth-century romanticism, the basis of harmonic thinking was precisely this model and its farthest-reaching consequences. Yet there is not the slightest trace of this system in Penderecki's music. His harmony grows out of the most radical accomplishments of the twentieth century, and the melodic basis is the chromatic scale in a tight configuration, in a form that rules out any association with major and minor modes. Yet – and this is extraordinarily important – even though we are dealing here with the autonomous sense of each of the twelve tones of the scale, this language is also radically different from the Schoenbergian total twelve-tone system (which I am so tempted to refer to as the "freakish bastard of Tristanian chromatism").

In his concept and treatment of the scale, Penderecki is closest to the model of Bartók (in such works as *Music for Strings, Percussion and Celesta*, the *Sonata for Two Pianos and Percussion*, and the Fourth and Fifth Quartets). The strict chromatic scale is treated in such a way that its individual stops form a certain hierarchy and have a varied significance: some of them are clearly displayed and return repeatedly, so that a certain arrangement of melodic tension arises, within which one point plays the main role, as if it were a tonic. This "tonic," however, results from the arbitrary picking out of its place in a given melody by the composer, and not from the construction of a scale (as in major and minor); the old tonal key is completely useless here. The theme of the passacaglia in the Fifth Symphony is, of course, some sort of F, but it is neither F major nor F minor, since such concepts have no meaning within this music. Similarly, the main theme in the Fourth Symphony and its series of segments lean first towards C (the main note of the work), and then towards A and F.

In this language, the chromatic scale in a tight arrangement plays a role analogous to that once played by the twelve-tone scale. Thus the most elementary move in sound (and, at the same time, the key to the logical sense of this language) is the stepping of half tones across the chromatic scale – just as, among the classics, the simplest, most elementary move is striding up and down the major or minor scales. Larger, selected intervals (including Penderecki's beloved sixth) "break away from" these small half-tone progressions to define the motive. By highlighting and emphatically repeating these intervals and the selected sounds, the phrase takes on its individual musical and expressive sense. The melodic calm between these intervalistic "gestures," a return to the logical base, as it were, is usually this most simple of movements along the chromatic scale.

Brought to life by Penderecki's talent, the language thus conceived overwhelms the listener with its naturalness, which may strike some as traditional even though it is not; it is built, after all, on a completely different principle. In fact, not a single page of these "neo-romantic" works fits into either the major-minor scale, or the style that these works apparently evoke.

This is also true of the forms and means of developing the process. Although we are struck in the building of dramatic tension, in the culminations, and in the "adagio" musings by the resemblance to the expressive gestures of late romanticism, the very architectonic conception, together with the microform (the detailed course and succession of ideas), are completely different, a-typical of, and alien to this model. Let us also add the difference in the manner of treating the orchestra: despite a similar solemn monumentalism, the sound of Penderecki's orchestra is significantly more transparent and variegated, and the autonomous role of the individual instruments or groups of instruments is so strongly underscored that the symphony resembles a modern orchestra concerto.

6.

The most succinct thing that can be said about Penderecki's links with late-romanticism is this: these are associations, and not allusions. Even where a specific composer is recalled for a moment, such as Wagner in the Tetralogy (*Der Ring des Nibelungen*), Bruckner, Mahler or Karłowicz. Listening to Penderecki's most recent symphonies, I am aware that the particular charm of this music does not displace the style of any of the above named composers for me, just as – despite certain associations – no baroque concerto displaces the separate beauty of Stravinsky's Violin Concerto.

Let us note in closing that Penderecki's individual style also has other sources, such as the vitalism of Bartók, Prokofiev and Stravinsky (from *The Rite of Spring*), or Bartók's polyphony with its highly condensed tension (from the first part of *Music*), or finally, to a special degree, Shostakovich's expressiveness, especially in the mobile, highly emotional passages and in the specifically sarcastic grimaces (by the way, this composer, formerly regarded as a stylistic conservative, in fact composed works that are gold mines of ideas and forward-looking potential – far more, for example, than the self-enclosed, aesthetically limited Webern). Penderecki follows this "dynamic" Shostakovich in the acutely pulsating passages of his works, with their somewhat perverse and piquant melodics, as in the quick passages of the Viola Concerto or in the (polyphonic) final sections of the *Sinfonietta for Strings*.

All these instances, of course, have to do with the phenomenon of rootedness that is so well known in the history of music, which was present until recently in all great compositions, and which has been stifled only by the ideology of avant-gardism. If we are encountering it again today in the work of the composer of our time, this simply means that contemporary music is returning to normalcy. "Without roots, there can be no creativity," Penderecki wrote in his "Elegy for a Dying Forest."[3]

7.

The multiplicity and variety of roots is naturally connected with the dimensions of the phenomenon that we might refer to as the "Penderecki style," with the multiplicity of types of expression that it contains. This style is also an aura of mystery and a harsh, dark-toned seriousness (as, for example, in the opening segment of the Fourth Symphony or the passacaglia of the Fifth Symphony), as well as the powerful emotions and drama that have such a powerful sway over the listener in all the symphonic and oratorical works. Yet it is also the delicate lyricism, expressed through the extraordinarily economical interval means and the equally economical texture that, in the Clarinet Quartet and often in the symphonies, appears in

[3] K. Penderecki, *Labyrinth...*, p. 40.

a slender pair of instrumental voices, or even in the long line of the individual voice. At times, this style may also be a colorful, piquant grotesque that evokes scenes from a mime ballet (the characteristic episode in the Fifth Symphony), at other times a virtuoso flash, dazzling sophisticated figures and showy details (especially in the concertos), and yet again a fantastic aural strangeness (the episode in the Viola Concerto). But above all, there is the splendid, enrapturing, nonpareil category of the high-energy "demonic scherzo" that is a special attraction in almost every large-scale instrumental or oratorical work, to name only the *Polish Requiem* and *The Seven Gates of Jerusalem*.

8.

The odds are stacked in favor of a long life for Penderecki's music in the concert halls and in the aural memory of future generations of listeners, above all, beside its expressive virtues, by its clear motives and the clarity of every tiny detail in the process. In Penderecki's symphonies and concertos (I am no longer speaking of the oratorical works), there are no "empty" places filled with mere technique. Nor is there the situation that is common today, in which the structural considerations outweigh Krzysztof Penderecki, *Labyrinth of Time* – or simply shoulder out – the attractiveness to the listener of certain segments. Penderecki knows how to look after his listeners all the time – not only in the main theme-ideas, but literally in every succeeding segment, even those that are essentially transitional or linking. The vitality and shapeliness of the detail are always attention-riveting.

Obviously, melody plays a great role in this music. There is no lack of ideas of grand beauty, especially in the Second Violin Concerto as well as the Fourth Symphony, where perhaps the most enchanting thing is the cantilena (I call it the second theme), which occurs first in the cellos and brims with great feeling and a romantic sound, even though there is no way to assign it to any tonality. Equally lovely is the lilting French horn theme that returns several times in the Fifth Symphony (with its final motive that seems to be "in B minor"). Extraordinarily spiritual, melodic lyricism mark the slow parts of the radical Clarinet Quartet (where the only thing that gets on my nerves is the third part of the *serenade*, which calls Schoenberg somewhat to mind). An important element in the charm of all these melodies is their economy of sound, the cautious balancing of each tone and interval, and the expressive concentration and moderation of the external gesture, which distinguishes them from the nineteenth-century melodic style.

When speaking of Penderecki's style, there can be no forgetting the varied colors of the harmonics. As distinguished from the typical image of contemporary music, which is essentially indifferent to harmony and based on balanced, equably dissonant resonance (the remains of the bad tradition of the Vienna school), Penderecki's harmonic language is very broad and diverse in terms of sound. Depending on the expressive sense of the various places in the work, we found a variety of types, both gestures and multiple sounds, chords that sound almost rustling, as well as others that are harmonically bright, subtle, and soft, of which an example can be found, at least, in the affecting episode with the strings *con sordino* in the Fourth Symphony.

Finally, let us also mention the great role of polyphony, even in forms approximating to the fugue (Fourth Symphony and *Sinfonietta for Strings*), but also in the unfettered, slow, and transparent conduct of two or three melodies, and at the same time in the interweaving of voices under enormous tension (as, for example, in the introductory part of the Viola Concerto).

By returning the emphasis to the main elements of music, Penderecki gave new birth at once to musical themes, which are of fundamental importance to the sense and action of his instrumental works. The fact that certain ideas and motives return in the compositions in a special way and are fixed in the memory is something that gives his music a human dimension – to put it succinctly, because there would be a great deal to say about all the psychological, formal, expressive, and downright philosophical aspects of this phenomenon, which has been developing for centuries. I think that, in general, this "human" – in the broadest meaning of the word – characteristic of Penderecki's art, its vitality and extroversion, its defiance of all speculative ideas and sonoric alchemy, contrasted with a faith in the natural feeling of music, is one of the essential ingredients in the value of his work. The talent, strong individuality, and virtuoso craftsmanship that have grown into this attitude work together to create a phenomenon that, as I foresee it, will determine the further fate of the music of the world, or at least leave an important, lasting influence.

Translated by William Brand

THE MUSIC SCENE IN THE 1950s AND 1960s

WESTERN EUROPE AND UNITED STATES

Thomas Service
London

The Avant Garde in the West in the 1950s and 1960s: Innovation and Consolidation

CRITICISING "THE AVANT GARDE"

"The Western avant garde" is a term so familiar that it has become almost invisible. In conventional histories of music, the "avant garde," in its incarnations on both sides of the Atlantic, is reduced to a series of key figures and historical moments, and made part of the onward march of the larger narrative of the history of music. It is as if the avant garde of the fifties and sixties was made up of a homogeneous group of composers who were mere vessels through whom flowed the developments of aleatoricism, serialism, sonorism, and the whole catalogue of modernist "isms." Their challenges to tradition, their achievements in charting new and unfamiliar areas of musical expression, and their social and political consciousness are now contained in a tightly knit historical package. There has become, in effect, orthodoxy of the avant garde. The diversity of the music of the decades following the Second World War has been squashed into a one-size-fits-all musicological corset.

Even when more specific definitions are essayed beyond the blanket term "avant garde," they are often executed along geographical lines, so that France's avant garde is reduced to Pierre Boulez, Germany's to Karlheinz Stockhausen, Italy's to Luigi Nono and Luciano Berio, and America's to John Cage and Milton Babbitt. These kinds of characterization employ a crude nationalism to describe and define the advances of particular composers. On the largest scale, Europe is associated with system and serialism, and America with indeterminacy and university-based theory. On a more localized scale, specific places have become associated with particular figures and movements: New York and John Cage are indelibly associated with chance procedures, graphic scores and performative indeterminacy; Cologne is the crucible of Stockhausen's development of electronics; and, looming like a vast, dark monolith at the centre of the picture of international modernism, both geographically and metaphorically, is Darmstadt and its Summer Courses for New Music.

The association of Darmstadt with narrow technical developments is only the most damaging of the caricatures to which the summer school, and the composers who visited it – have been subjected. Recent accounts tell a different story.[1] Far from being a laboratory of coolly objective reflection, or agreeable debate over the future of music, the competing ideologies of composers like Boulez, Stockhausen, Nono, and Sylvano Bussotti, produced a hothouse of conflicting egos and personalities. In an extreme form, it is possible to argue that the history of Darmstadt is not so much a history of musical progression, in which the biographies of individual composers are merely circumstantial contributing elements; but rather a story of social one-upmanship, in which the music that was produced was a way of moving within social hierarchies of Darmstadt. On that view, the works composed at, for, or in the wake of Darmstadt represent composers' contributions to that special social system, rather than the closed, autonomous systems of historical imagination.

Yet Darmstadt remains defined by, in the eyes of many historians, the move towards and reaction against total serialism (the expansion of Schoenberg's serial approach to pitch to the other parameters of musical composition and construction). But as Paul Griffiths suggests, in the titles of two of his chapters in *Modern Music and After*, total serialism was in fact a "moment" rather than a movement; a brief snapshot of time and technique rather than a culmination of post-war compositional development.[2] In historical terms, it certainly was: Messiaen's *Mode de valeurs et d'intensités*, the precursor of a heightened pre-compositional control, dates from 1949-50, and Stockhausen's *Kreuzspiel* was written in 1951. Boulez's *Structures Ia*, the infamous high-watermarks of total serialism,

[1] Especially significant are Paul Attinello, "The Interpretation of Chaos: a Critical Analysis of Meaning in European Avant Garde Vocal Music, 1958-68." Dissertation: UCLA, 1997; and M.J. Grant, *Serial music, serial aesthetics: Compositional theory in post-war Europe*. Cambridge: Cambridge University Press, 2001.

[2] See Paul Griffiths, *Modern Music and After*. Oxford: Oxford University Press, 1995, pp. 29–49.

was completed in 1951, when the composer was in his mid-twenties, and no other subsequent pieces by Boulez adopted the same approach. (*Structures Ia* had an extremely significant analysis by György Ligeti in the fourth issue of *Die Reihe*,[3] the journal founded to enshrine the languages and values of serial music, whose eight volumes appeared from 1955-1962.)

Not just in terms of the small number of pieces composed under its strictures, but also because of the short few years when this approach had any kind of dominance in the minds of composers, "the moment of total serialism" is precisely that: a passing phase in the development of the avant garde, a comet in the constellation of techniques of the post-war decades in central Europe. That Darmstadt came almost exclusively to be linked with the progress of this elusive total serialism is rather an expedient of the telling of music history than a consequence of the works produced by the composers at the forefront of the avant garde; still less is it a reflection of the diversity and energy of the music of the period.

To focus on a variety of compositional approaches - encompassing electronics, music theatre, graphic notation, political engagement, open and modular forms, to name merely a few of the key areas developed by these composers - would be a much more accurate way to represent the music of the fifties and sixties in Europe and America. Yet it also messier and more problematic than the simplistic narratives under which this music is often subsumed. Instead of a story of single-minded discovery and colonization of particular musical fields, this is a history of cross-fertilization and competition, of negotiation and contingency. In effect, this is a postmodern narrative of the developments of high modernism.

BOULEZ, CAGE, AND THE INTENTION OF NON-INTENTION

It is one of the commonest parodies of the avant garde to split the "systems" of Darmstadt and Central Europe apart from the "indeterminacy" - both performative and compositional - of America. As suggested above, the two figureheads of either "school" are usually thought to be Pierre Boulez and John Cage. Yet, as their correspondence (collected and edited by Jean-Jacques Nattiez),[4] and Cage's hugely influential visit as lecturer to Darmstadt

[3] György Ligeti, Pierre Boulez: "Entscheidung und Automatik in der Struktur Ia," *Die Reihe* vol. 4, pp. 38–63.

[4] Jean-Jacques Nattiez, *The Boulez-Cage Correspondence*. Cambridge: Cambridge University Press, 1993.

in 1958 demonstrate, these divisions are more arbitrary than real. Instead of comprising antagonistic arguments over ideology and method, the correspondence charts two composers seeking different means towards similar ends. The roots of what was to become - albeit briefly - a close friendship lie in Cage's visit to Paris in 1949. Boulez himself introduced the American iconoclast at Suzanne Tézenas's salon, in which Cage performed his *Sonatas and Interludes for Prepared Piano* (1946-8). Boulez's affectionate words are full of admiration for Cage, and suggest points of contact between what he saw and heard in Cage's work and the preoccupations of his own music:

> Cage uses the idea of constant invention, which avoids the idea of classical development, since in this way everything becomes development, or, if you like, everything is thematic. This freedom of invention thus operates in contrast to the invariant factors, the rhythmic structure and the musical scale.[5]

The analogy scarcely needs spelling out: Boulez's use of serial methods to generate means of "constant invention" underpins the explorations of his first major works, like the *Sonatine* for Flute and Piano (1946), or the Second Piano Sonata (1947-8).

And there are other points of contact as well: both Cage and Boulez were interested in shattering conventional notions of historical, musical and temporal linearity. Boulez's early works are testament to his attempt to challenge tradition from within; Cage's music seems to bypass tradition entirely. The suspension involved in Boulez's Second Piano Sonata and Cage's *Sonatas and Interludes* is not simply a musical one - the hectic, moment-to-moment energy of the former, or the durational rigour of the latter - but a historical one too. Boulez's work deconstructs the musical forms of the Western tradition - sonata form, fugue and scherzo; and Cage's music replaces them with a durational scheme and timbral universe that owes as much to Eastern traditions as it does to any Western models or techniques.

However, important differences between Boulez and Cage seem to be demonstrated in another pair of works: the former's *Structures Ia* for two pianos and the latter's *Music of Changes* for solo piano. These contemporaneous pieces (both composed in 1951) are created through apparently oppositional processes: Cage's by consulting the Chinese *I Ching* (or *Book of Changes*), and Boulez through using a matrix by which every aspect of musical construction is controlled according to a pre-determined system.

[5] J.-J. Nattiez, *The Boulez-Cage Correspondence*, p. 31.

This seems to be an opposition of total indeterminacy with total control. And yet the result, in both pieces, is a sonic surface of radically unpredictable musical motion, in which the conventional continuities of musical structure are effaced. Along with this striking sonic resemblance, there is a deep-seated aesthetic similarity between the two pieces. Both approaches – "system" and "chance" – have the same effect of distancing the composer from the sound of the music. Compositional intention and subjectivity are eschewed in favour of external, objective forces.

Karlheinz Stockhausen's series of *Klavierstücke*, begun in 1952, exhibit another approach to the same idea. Stockhausen's attraction to the systematisation of Messiaen's *Mode de valeurs et d'intensités* was, as Paul Griffiths has suggested, based on what he saw as a radical way of bypassing human subjectivity in favor of a theoretically "pure" musical object: this was a music that offered a vision of how to create "sound structures which would have nothing human in their composition, which would be images of divine unity."[6] The sixteen bars of *Klavierstück III* (actually the first of the series to be written) have posed an analytical conundrum ever since the piece was first published. The work apparently obeys some kind of compositional system, yet attempts to derive it, or to account for the resulting form of the music have proved as various as their authors.[7]

This radical distancing of composer from sounding result, common both to Cage and Boulez – and connecting, therefore both Atlantic sides of the avant garde – contradicts many critical approaches to the period. For Susan McClary, writing as recently as 2000, "the serialists found a way of ensuring the continual presence of centered subjectivity. . . ." In pieces by Schoenberg, Boulez or Babbitt we know (because we are told, because we know how to analyze scores) that an idiosyncratic but rigorously integrated subject controls the events, however incoherent they may sound; thus the urgency of set theory and analysis. To the ear the works of John Cage may not sound all that different from those rigorously ordered by means of combinatorial sets. Yet this is precisely why Cage posed such a threat, for he presented the possibility that beneath that discontinuous surface there "lurks . . . nothing at all."[8] But this "integrated subject" she hears in the three serialists she mentions is an invention of the analysis she knows so well rather than a product of the works themselves. This is

[6] P. Griffiths, *Modern Music...*, p. 32.

[7] For a concise summary of these approaches, see Griffiths, *Modern Music*, pp. 71–76.

[8] Susan McClary, *Conventional Wisdom: The Content of Musical Form*. Berkeley: California University Press, 2000, p. 136.

a radical misprision of the achievements of these composers, based on believing the conclusions of set-theoretical analysis rather than the sound of the music. In fact, Stockhausen's call for the creation of sound structures composed seemingly without human intervention chimes with Cage's use of chance procedures, and his own desire for music free of the traces of compositional subjectivity. The avant garde of the early fifties is defined, in a sense, by the explosion of composer from sounding result, of a radical rupturing of compositional intention from the features of the musical work.

In that sense, the developments of serialism in the early fifties by Stockhausen and Boulez (and others) could be encapsulated as a move towards perceptual and aesthetic openness - just like Cage's compositional advances. M.J. Grant, in her recent book *Serial Music, Serial Aesthetics* - one of the first seriously to challenge the hegemonies of the conventional narrations of the avant garde - encapsulates the imminent aleatoricism of serial music:

> Serial music, unlike thematic music, is not defined by foreseeability; it is surprising, unforeseeable; it is not closed, but open. Aesthetic rather than semantic; statistic.[9]

These conclusions come in the wake of a discussion of *Structures Ia*, usually conceived as a totem of aesthetic autonomy and closed, systematic control.

Faced with the chasm they had opened up between compositional process - of whatever (in) determinacy - and sonic result, composers had to decide how to continue; or, indeed, if continuation were possible. For Boulez and Stockhausen, the choice was to investigate open or modular forms in pieces like Boulez's Third Piano Sonata and Stockhausen's *Klavierstück XI*, but for Cage the path was even more radical. For all the self-effacement in the *Music of Changes*, there was still an interplay between freedom and control in Cage's compositional process. Just as Boulez had to decide on what series was to form the basis of *Structures Ia* (although his solution was, in a sense, another form of distancing himself from his material, since the row he chose was the same as the one Messiaen had used in the *Mode de valeurs et d'intensités*), Cage decided what pitches would be fed into the random generator of the *I Ching*. But in *4'33"*, composed in 1952 and first performed by David Tudor, he extended his durational approach to composition, and the distancing of his

---

[9] M.J. Grant, *Serial music, serial aesthetics: Compositional theory in post-war Europe*. Cambridge: Cambridge University Press, 2001, p. 164.

compositional ego to the ultimate extreme. Cage's famous "silent" piece, *4'33"* has become an icon of American experimentalism and musical indeterminacy. What could be more indeterminate than a piece in which no sound is notated, and in which the emphasis is on transforming listeners' relationship to their surroundings, and removing them from the realm of the musically aesthetic to the environmentally aware? And yet, in the context of the rest of his work, there is nothing indeterminate about Cage's compositional approach in *4'33"*. The piece is one of the most rigorous and uncompromising investigations of the dislocation of composer from sounding artefact. Far from compositional anarchy, the piece embodies Cage's compositional focus and single-mindedness.

BODIES DISEMBODIED: ELECTRONICS AND VOCAL MUSIC

The openness that serialism engendered in musical thinking opened up questions of the material of sound itself; this investigation became the focus of the research and development of electro-acoustic and electronic music. Electronics offered the possibility of creating new worlds of sounds; the uncharted realms dreamed of by Edgard Varèse in the early 50s. However, manipulating pre-recorded sounds also meant reconfiguring the relationship between the composer, the listener and the sonic environment. Pierre Schaeffer's *musique concrète* created music from recorded sounds, transforming fragments of everyday life into aesthetic material. Electronics and electroacoustic techniques thus offered an opportunity for composers: to manipulate hitherto unavailable areas of sound. Stockhausen's *Gesang der Jünglinge* traverses the gamut of expressive possibilities offered by the tape manipulation and electronic sound generation techniques of the period (1955-56). Based on the opposition of electronic sounds and a boy's recorded singing of a text from one of the Apocrypha to the Book of Daniel, the piece negotiates a host of extremes: from pure electronic sound to the "acoustic" sounds of vocal music; from transparent comprehensibility of the text to total incomprehensibility.

The relationship between electronics and the voice was further developed by Berio, in his *Thema – omaggio a Joyce* and *Visage*; in the latter piece, the voice of his wife, the soprano Cathy Berberian, is layered with different versions of itself and electronic sounds, creating an interplay between a personal character and inhuman mechanisms, between embodiment and disembodiment. Cage's works of the period also demonstrated his interest in the burgeoning technology of electronics in works like *Fontana Mix* (1958), *Music for The Marrying Maiden* (1960), and *Rozart Mix* (1965). There is another direct point of contact here between Cage and the European avant gardes: Cage was invited to compose *Fontana Mix*, at the request of Berio, in the Studio Fonologia in Milan. For Cage, the medium was another mechanism for compositional distancing; a different approach from the dialectic of corporeality and non-corporeality investigated by some European and American composers. Cage himself criticised American composers who used tape technology:

> The works for magnetic tape by [Otto] Luening and [Vladimir] Ussachevsky, Louis and Bebe Barron, are not properly termed avant garde, since they maintain conventions and accepted values.[10]

As well as his engagement with electronics, Cage engaged directly with the problems of writing for the human voice in *Aria* (1958), another work for Cathy Berberian. Boulez similarly developed his fascination with the voice throughout the fifties and sixties. After the *Le Visage nuptial* (originally written in 1946; but revised on multiple occasions, like so many of Boulez's works) setting the poetry of René Char, and *Soleil des Eaux* (originally composed in 1948), another Char setting, Boulez composed what would prove to be one of the most important word settings of the avant garde: the nine-movement *Le Marteau sans maître* (a further setting of René Char's poems), for alto voice, and an ensemble of six players. The soundworld of the piece owes as much to Debussy and Eastern musics as it does to Webern; the combination of alto flute, viola, xylorimba, vibraphone, and unpitched percussion produces a hallucinogenic effect. The piece does not offer itself up to the kind of systematic, serial analysis that Ligeti attempted on *Structures Ia*, and Boulez's word setting similarly obscures direct, semantic meaning. The whole piece is caught in a musical and poetic limbo, creating an allusive and elusive world. Boulez would extend these ideas in his *Pli Selon Pli* (originally 1957-1962), settings of Mallarmé's poems for soprano and ensemble.

Distorted Bodies: Performers and Performing

Boulez's symbolic staging of the voice, of the body, and of a confrontation between musical and poetic meaning, finds explicit manifestation in other pieces of the period. The works of Sylvano Bussotti of the late-fifties are

---

[10] John Cage, *Silence*. London: Marion Boyars, 1978, p. 25.

tokens of his conception of musical performance as erotic, sensual, even disturbing. His works sometimes thematise that eroticism, for example in his *Passion selon Sade* (1965), but in a broader sense, he makes the performers of say, the elaborate and beautiful graphic notations of the *Sette Fogli* (1959) participants in a mysterious theatre.

For Bussotti, the consequences of his graphic notation were the creation of an elusive interaction between the performers and the work; for American composers like Earle Brown, Christian Wolff, and Morton Feldman, and John Cage, explorations in new kinds of notation were ways of developing new but concrete relationships with performers. The proportional notation of Feldman and Brown's early works might specify duration, register but not precise pitches or rhythms. Cage's own graphic notations, such as in the Concert for Piano and Orchestra (1958) are often described as evidence of the total freedom he gives to performers. In fact, each element of a Cage graphic notation is designed to be interpreted in specific ways by the players, such that each individual element of a score - horizontal lines, say, as opposed to wavy lines - should denote a particular musical parameter, and be consistently interpreted in that way. In the same sense, the apparently "open," infinitely interpretable score of Brown's *December 1952*, with its apparently random placement of rectangles, in which no musical parameter is specified at all, nevertheless encodes a kind of fixity: the geometric precision with which the rectangles are rendered implies a similarly rigorous approach on the part of the performer. Feldman's early scores go as far as creating recognisable "works" in performance: the graph-like notations specify time, register, instrumentation, and number of events precisely. His notation is simply the most efficient way for him to achieve the soundworld he wants to create.

Cage was the catalyst for a series of happenings at Black Mountain College, beginning in the early fifties. For all their use of different performance practices, improvisation - always strongly resisted by Cage - was never part of the ideology of these events. Incorporating performance practices from theatre, dance, the visual arts and music, these happenings were part of an emergent practice of performance art, a movement that would flourish in the experimental explosion of the Fluxus movement in New York in the sixties. The works and instructions for action of composers like George Brecht (whose background was in the visual arts), Takehisa Kosugi and LaMonte Young typified the freedom of performance as it had developed in the late fifties and sixties. In a piece like George Brecht's

Three Telephone Events (whose entire score reads: "When the telephone rings, it is allowed to continue ringing, until it stops./When the telephone rings, the receiver is lifted, then replaced./When the telephone rings, it is answered."[11]), the work of music is reconfigured as an instruction for action, and extends into realms other than the auditory as a consequence. Theatre, literature and the visual arts all form part of the background for this kind of performance art.

The diversity of notational approaches in the contemporary musical scene as a whole was celebrated by Cage's collection of *Notations*.[12] Pages of conventional notation appear alongside more radical and unconventional systems; the collection is a snapshot of the diversity of musical notation and its functions as artefact, instruction and programme for radical performance. Nam June Paik, whose compositional career had been catalysed by Cage's Darmstadt lectures in 1958, was represented in *Notations* by his *Danger Music for Dick Higgins*: a photocopied page with the handwritten words: "Climb inside the vagina of a living whale."

THE POLITICS OF PERFORMANCE

The performance art of America in the fifties and sixties, and the mix of influences from theatre, the visual arts, film and technology on musical practices would have an important influence on the first generation of musical minimalists. The four major figures - Steve Reich, Philip Glass, LaMonte Young, and Terry Riley - were all affected by this fusion of creative approaches. The sense of freedom, from conventional musical practices, and from the weight of tradition and history, that such practices celebrated was not an option for composers in Europe, or for those composers who moved to work there. Berio's series of *Sequenzas* for solo instruments, a series begun in 1958 with the *Sequenza* for flute, stages individual performers in a dialogue with the repertoires of the instrument, and the grammar of their own performance. The third in the sequence, for solo female voice (composed in 1965-6, and another work composed for Cathy Berberian) analyses the minutiae of a specially written "modular" text by Markus Kutter, investigates the mechanics

[11] For further discussion of some of the musical consequences of Fluxus, and for an insight into the diversity of a wider musical experimentalism, see Michael Nyman, *Experimental Music: Cage and Beyond*. Cambridge: Cambridge University Press, 1974; 2nd edition, 1999.

[12] John Cage and Alison Knowles, *Notations*. New York: Something Else, 1969.

and semiotics of vocal sounds: from the production of individual phonemes to gestures like laughter and coughing, and singing. There is a desperate character about this piece, as if the singer were coming close to a psychological as well as musical collapse. Berio would extend this forensic interest in the preparation of musical performance in *Recital* (1971, again for Berberian), in which the singer's personal and musical lives are subjected to a devastating, surgical scrutiny.

For Mauricio Kagel, like Berio, musical performance is always an act of theatre, and therefore inserted into discourses that go beyond the purely sonic. In *Match*, (1964) for two cellists and percussionist, for example, the two cellists are competitors in an obscure game, with the percussionist acting as referee. Kagel would develop these ideas: *Tremens* (1963-5) uses the situation of a hospital cubicle to investigate the effects of distorted sounds on the performer, a metaphor for the psychological distortion undergone in any performance.

The politics implicit in Berio and Kagel's investigations of the theatre of performance are explicit in the music of Luigi Nono. The subject matter of Nono's works, like his 1956 *Il canto sospeso* or his 1961 opera, *Intolleranza*, both deal with the themes of personal and political oppression. Nono's serialism is the mechanism through which he expresses his sympathy for the political prisoners whose words form the basis *Il canto sospeso*, or the refugee at the heart of *Intolleranza*. He makes no attempt to negate the strength of his feelings for this emotive subject matter: for all its radicalism of language, the effect of Nono's music is uncompromisingly direct. As M.J. Grant has put it, discussing the music of *Il canto sospeso*, "the music is utterly sad."[13] The act of composing, for Nono, was explicitly to engage in political work, and his music had therefore to function as an active part of society, as an attempt to mobilise the consciousness of its audiences. The relative conservatism of some aspects of Nono's approaches to form – *Intolleranza*, for Paul Griffiths, was "the first opera by one who had not fled the ranks of the avant garde"[14] – was offset by Nono's attempts to make avant garde practices and aesthetics part of the expression of political radicalism in society. He performed his works in prisons, and other unconventional arenas, in conjunction with performers such as Maurizio Pollini and Claudio Abbado.

[13] M.J. Grant, *Serial music...*, p. 203.

[14] P. Griffiths, *Modern Music...*, p. 146.

THE LATE SIXTIES: CONSOLIDATION AND RENEWAL

The change wrought to musical languages and musical practices in the fifties and early sixties encompassed all of the parameters of musical thinking, from composition to performance, and listening. After so much experimentation, succeeding decades brought a consolidation of techniques and languages, and a synthesis of influences and practices. For those composers at the centre of developments of the fifties, like Boulez and Stockhausen, the next decade brought a subtle change of priorities. Stockhausen, heavily influenced by Eastern musics and techniques, saw his music as contributing to a new consciousness of global unity, expressed in pieces like *Telemusik* (1966) and *Hymen* (1966-7); Boulez, on the other hand, explored more conventional kinds of musical continuity than that exhibited by his earlier works in pieces like *Eclat* (originally 1965) and *Domaines* (1968).

Berio's 1968-9 *Sinfonia* symbolises the effect of this consolidation of languages, and the new expressive areas it could reveal. The piece is defined by commentary: on itself, on history and on performance. The central, third movement is based on the second movement of Mahler's Second Symphony, and allusions to repertoire ranging from Stockhausen to Debussy are overlaid on Mahler's original music, so much so that it often disappears behind the screen of these quotations and references. These fissures through the music are glimpses of the network of connections between past, present, and future that lies beneath the skein of every artwork, every piece of music. As Edoardo Sanguineti, poet and collaborator of Berio's, puts it: history is "the mud all over our shoulders." The third movement of *Sinfonia* simply writes in the "mud" of Berio's interpretation of the Mahler movement. In the final, fifth movement, Berio visits a similar process to the other movements of *Sinfonia* as he does to the Mahler in the third movement: the piece has become its own commentary.

But then the mud was over everyone's shoulders by the mid-1960s; and modernism itself had become part of that history, even the achievements of the fifties themselves. Milton Babbitt's use of serialism as the basis of a transparent, classical, aesthetic is one manifestation of this phenomenon in America; Igor Stravinsky's late adoption of Webernian serialism is another. Synthesis became a creative modus operandi for composers; in retrospect, it is possible to account for an emergent postmodernism in this period (even though another way of thinking about the "postmodern" in music is that the features usually associated with the idea are already latently present within modernism itself). But this was not a fading of idealism, or a failure of creative nerve: using and developing the languages of the fifties and early sixties allowed composers to create new creative paths, and find new musical solutions. Elliott Carter's 1969 *Concerto for Orchestra* is one example of this synthesising tendency: a rich, complex work created from the interactions of a multi-layered musical texture. The heterogeneity that had always defined the avant garde as a whole - whether European or American, post-serial or experimental - now came to define the outputs of individual composers as well. Composition, for the artists who had come to maturity in the decades of the fifties and sixties on both side of the Atlantic, was now about ways of dealing with that diversity, of negotiating their relationships with the history of musical modernism, and the history of their own creative past, while exploring the need for innovation and renewal.

Niall O'Loughlin
Loughborough

The Avant Garde in Germany in the 1950s and 1960s

THE BACKGROUND

Music in Germany after the Second World War was changing very rapidly because of a number of factors. Many composers, but notably Hindemith (1895-1963), Kurt Weill (1900-50), Hanns Eisler (1898-1962), and Bertold Goldschmidt (1903-1996), had left Germany during the 1930s as a result of Nazi persecution and threats. A number of composers such as Karl Amadeus Hartmann (1905-1963) deliberately maintained an artistic silence until creative freedom was re-established. This also affected composers in what had been occupied Austria. Arnold Schoenberg (1874-1951), whose presence might have influenced music in the late- 1940s, stayed in the United States and Anton Webern (1883-1945), who was posthumously to influence a whole generation of composers, retreated into his music during the Second World War, but was accidentally killed in the re-occupation process in 1945. Two German composers of the earlier generation, Richard Strauss (1864-1949) and Hans Pfitzner (1869-1949), were both active after World War Two, but with their deaths in 1949, German music had reached the end of an era. One of the most gifted of younger composers, Hans Werner Henze (b.1926), who might have been expected to be one of the leaders of the avant garde in Germany, left the country in 1953 to take up residence in Italy.

Politically, Germany became subdivided with the sector occupied by France, Britain and the United States coming together and forming in 1949 the Federal Republic of Germany or West Germany (Bundesrepublik Deutschland - BRD), while the Soviet sector became the German Democratic Republic or East Germany (Deutsche Democratische Republik - DDR). This political division was reflected in the New Music. In East Germany, there was a move to stay within traditional values. With the return to (East) Germany of Hanns Eisler in 1948, after his expulsion from the United States as a Communist sympathizer, a link with the past was established. Eisler's music of this period was mainly incidental music to plays and films,[1] excellent in its way but not trailblazing in the manner that now occurred in West Germany. After Eisler's death in 1962, the continuity was maintained by the work of Paul Dessau (1894-1979), who had earlier worked with Bertolt Brecht. It was then in West Germany that the avant garde flourished. With the deaths of Richard Strauss, Pfitzner, Kurt Weill, and Schoenberg and the absence of Hindemith from Germany, there was little continuity with the past. The Hindemithian idea of *Gebrauchsmusik* was of course continued by Carl Orff (1895-1982), but his music was totally irrelevant to the avant garde. Karl Amadeus Hartmann returned to composing after the war and maintained a fairly central orientation, while Boris Blacher (1903-1975) did some experimentation in twelve-tone techniques, but did not become associated with the avant garde. In a sense the slate had been wiped clean and a fresh start seemed inevitable.

NEW DEVELOPMENTS

It is very interesting to note that in volume IV of *Die Reihe*,[2] which was devoted to the discussion of the work of ten young composers, there were only four Germans, and of these, Hans Werner Henze had already left Germany. This left Giselher Klebe (b. 1925) and Bernd Alois Zimmermann (1918-1970) and one other. Klebe has not made much headway outside Germany, while Zimmermann has gained some familiarity with such works as his opera *Die Soldaten*, which had its first performance in Cologne in 1965. Neither can be considered to be leading composers of the European or even German avant garde nor have either composer's reputations matched that of the tenth composer discussed in the book. The post-war avant garde in Germany was in effect created as a result of the efforts of this one man who had the foresight and brilliance to explore new ideas and the determination and clarity of vision to see them develop into a coherent musical philosophy. He gathered around him a number of like-minded composers, mostly from abroad, and produced large numbers of revolutionary works and a considerable amount of commentary to explain his ideas and creations at every stage. His name is Karlheinz Stockhausen (b. 1928).

---

[1] Albrecht Betz: *Hanns Eisler: Political Musician*, translated by Bill Hopkins. Cambridge: Cambridge University Press, 1982, pp. 208–41; Theodor Adorno and Hanns Eisler: *Composing for the films*. London: Athlone, 1994.

[2] Vienna, 1958. English edition, Bryn Mawr PA, 1960.

Strangely, the seeds of this revival took place in France. Stockhausen had been studying in Cologne in the years 1947-50 and gradually started to establish himself as a composer. In early 1952 he traveled to Paris, studying with Olivier Messiaen (1908-1992) whose influence on the organizational aspects of his composition was seminal and with Pierre Schaeffer (1910-1995) whose work drove him to electronic music *per se*, rather than the *musique concrète* that Schaeffer was advocating. It cannot be stressed enough how much this was to affect the development of the music of the avant garde in Europe in the next two decades.

The first development on which Stockhausen embarked was that of electronic music, with the first serious work in this direction being made possible in 1951 by the founding of the Studio for Electronic Music of Westdeutscher Rundfunk in Cologne. The director, Herbert Eimert, invited a number of composers to work there, but it was particularly the invitation to Stockhausen that was important. He produced his two electronic pieces (*Studie I* and *Studie II*) here, working with the production and manipulation of sine tones. Unlike in the work of Schaeffer, all the sounds in these pieces were actually produced electronically and everything was calculated in elaborate detail: scrupulous organization was considered an essential part of the composition. In contrast, Schaeffer had always advocated some form of improvisation, something at this stage Stockhausen studiously avoided. The first German electronic music concert in October 1954 included works by Eimert, Goeyvaerts, Gredinger, the Frenchman Henri Pousseur and Stockhausen. It was a later concert in 1956, however, with first performances of works by Eimert, Koenig, Křenek and Stockhausen, whose *Gesang der Jünglinge* broke new ground by combining recordings of children's voices with electronic sounds, that real progress was made.[3] In this work Stockhausen used a sliding scale of sounds ("mutual sound-continuum"[4]) from sung sounds to those produced electronically. Because he believed that it was only possible to do this electronically, Stockhausen made recordings of the sound of a boy's voice and then created a full range of the transformed sounds for use in the piece. At many points in the composition the composer aimed for a high level of homogeneity of sound so that sung sounds and electronic sounds are not clearly distinguishable by the

[3] See Stockhausen's article "Actualia." In *Die Reihe II*. German edition Vienna: Universal, 1955; English edition Bryn Mawr, PA, Theodore Presser, 1958, pp. 45–51; and: "Music and Speech." In *Die Reihe* VI, pp. 57–64.

[4] Stockhausen, "Music and Speech" (see note 3), p, 58.

listener, if at all. A very elaborate ambiguity between comprehensible words and pure sounds was achieved in this way. This was the first step by Stockhausen to achieve a synthesis of electronic and traditional sounds, a process that involved a number of other composers at the time.[5] To see how important this was to Eimert and his followers one need only read the first volume, entitled "Electronische Musik", of a new periodical called *Die Reihe,* edited by Eimert and published by what was to become the leading producer of the scores of the avant garde in Europe, Universal Edition, A.G. of Vienna.[6] Clearly Eimert's priority was to ensure that electronic music was understood and appreciated. This series was soon translated into English and published by Theodore Presser in the United States.[7] Stockhausen's interest in electronic music was extended in an elaborate work entitled *Kontakte* [Contacts] of 1959-60, which combined electronic sounds with live piano and percussion. The publication of the score with extensive and detailed notes by the composer of his working methods was a landmark in the development of electronic music.[8] *Kontakte* was noteworthy for a number of reasons: it focused on a number of areas as follows: timbre, use of space and compositional organization. It is no coincidence that Stockhausen gave a series of lectures in American universities in November 1958 on the topics: "Electronic and Instrumental Music" and "Music in Space," the very issues that *Kontakte* addressed.

In the first place Stockhausen approached the question of sound quality or timbre. By producing a commercial recording[9] of the four-track electronic only form of *Kontakte,* he confirmed the possibility of an independent existence. The greater perspective that he produced with the creation of the parts for piano and percussion, however, is enormous. Six types of timbre produced by the percussionist, both sound and noise from each of metal, skin and wooden instruments are united or separated by the piano. Stockhausen devised in the electronic sound varying degrees of fusion with and departure from the instrumental sound. One can note the obvious way that the timbre of instruments and electronic

---

[5] This is discussed in some detail in my article: Niall O'Loughlin, "The European synthesis of electronic and traditional music." In *Glasba v tehničnem svetu - Musica in machina,* P. Kuret (ed.), Festival Ljubljana, Ljubljana, Slovenia , 1995, pp. 86–103.

[6] Published in 8 volumes from 1955-1962.

[7] Published in 8 volumes by Theodore Presser from 1958-1968.

[8] Karlheinz Stockhausen, *Kontakte,* realization and performing scores, Universal Edition, London, 1968. The rights are now owned by the composer.

[9] Deutsche Grammophon LP 138811, Hamburg, 1968, and on CD Stockhausen 3, Kürten, 1992.

sounds is matched in some passages, one with its short drum-like electronic sounds, bongos and tom-toms, and another with the use of marimbaphone and the electronic wooden-sounding notes. Throughout the work, however, one observes that Stockhausen is constantly adjusting the nature of the relationship between the live piano and percussion on the one hand and the electronic sounds on the other.

To create the effect of music moving in space in *Kontakte*, Stockhausen originally used a rotating loudspeaker with a number - usually four - microphones. However, it is relatively easy today to produce this apparent movement on most multi-channel tape recorders. Movement of sound here is strictly speaking also an illusion, as the volume level is simply decreased in one loudspeaker and at the same as it is increased in another, but the ear interprets this as movement of the sound source. *Kontakte* produces both illusion and reality: it creates an illusion of movement in its use of shared material between the static pianist and percussionist, as well as with the tape, but it produces perceptible "movement" of sound between the different loudspeakers. The composer identified five forms of movement in space: rotation, looping movements, alternation, separation of fixed sources, linking of fixed spaces. All five can be applied to the electronic sources, but only the last two can be used by the live instrumentalists. He further emphasized the point very directly when he said, "the instrumentalists represent spatially rigid sources of sound."[10]

Stockhausen used what has become known as moment-form, in that the sections of a work appear as experiential units, normally addressing different parameters. These sections can be connected in succession by common characteristics or they are more normally clearly distinguished from each other by changing the parameters. There is no obligation to employ any forms of repeat or reprise. The procedure allowed him the flexibility to move instantly from one relationship to another, which is done either within the moment itself or from one moment to the next. In effect, he modified the parameters of his electronic change on a sliding scale. On the other hand he also changed the relationships or contacts, from one moment to the next, between the electronic and instrumental sounds with sudden and dramatic effect. It is these features which give the work its kaleidoscopic or rather its "kaleidophonic" effect.

His later electronic works developed these ideas further. *Mikrophonie I* (1964) for instruments, voices and electronic manipulation and *Mikrophonie II*

---

[10] In Karl. H. Wörner, *Stockhausen Life and Work*, London, 1973, p. 46.

(1965) with the addition of voices, both explored the use of live instruments with electronic sounds or electronic modifications of live sounds. *Telemusik* (1966) used electronic sounds exclusively, but with imitations of live sounds, and *Hymnen* (1966-1967) used electronic sounds and concrete sounds, notably national anthems. In the latter there is also the optional addition of orchestra in one part. It was this series of works which established the medium of electronic music as a vital part of the range of the European avant garde.

LIVE MUSIC

The same kind of development took place in live music for instruments and voices. It is no coincidence that Eimert's second volume in the series *Die Reihe* was devoted to detailed studies of the music of Anton Webern.[11] This composer was presented as the founding figure of the European avant garde with his techniques now being extrapolated to justify the use of serial organization. Eimert's introduction to the book stands almost as a manifesto statement of the avant garde. Referring to Webern's creative career, Eimert said: "Nothing in it foretells the leading position that must be accorded his work today [1955]."[12] The analyses explain the positions taken by leading composers to Webern's work, the Germans, Eimert, Stockhausen, Metzger, Spinner and Armin Klammer and the Frenchmen Pierre Boulez and Henri Pousseur. These studies investigated the tone rows, the interval structures, the time patterns and phrase structures that were not previously considered in any explicit way. But more important, these determining features were now to be applied to all compositions that were to be taken seriously.

In almost every work that Stockhausen composed, he used a new technique and in doing so created a wide range of procedures that were to involve the avant garde in Germany and further afield for at least two decades. The importance of this can hardly be overstated. Even early on, Stockhausen's *Kreuzspiel* of 1951 employed serial procedures that were suggested by the techniques used by Messiaen in his piano piece *Modes de valeurs et d'intensités*. The pointillist serial techniques found in *Kontrapunkte* of 1953 were developed in the earlier Piano Pieces, especially 1-4, and in the elaborate *Gruppen* for three orchestras of 1955-57, in which an

[11] *Die Reihe* II ...
[12] *Die Reihe* II, English edition, p. 29.

extensive and complex system of time relationships is explored.[13] Independent tempos were employed for the three orchestras for much of the work and spatial techniques were extensively used, with mirroring, echoing and dialog between the three groups. The large-scale *Carré* for four orchestras and choirs from 1959-60 extended moment-form. One aspect of this work was very influential: the use of textural sound masses. Boulez, and to a greater extent, György Ligeti and Penderecki developed these techniques. *Momente* of 1961-64 for voices and instrumentalists explored a wide range of relationships between words and music, but also presented the concept of "open-endedness" that was to appear in numerous works that followed. In this connection, *Momente* itself was subjected to wholesale revisions in 1964 and 1972, but neither constituted a "definitive" version.

POST-SERIALISM

Total serialism and its elaborate organizational techniques led in many musicians' eyes into an impossible impasse, from which there was no obvious escape without a complete change of method. This was manifest in a number of developments that went in a completely different direction from that of total serialism. These were flexibility in performance, indeterminacy, aleatory techniques, improvisation and theatrical performances (not necessarily on stage).

Flexibility of performance was introduced by, for example, inviting the performer to create works according to detailed instructions. Stockhausen's *Zyklus* of 1959 for percussion used an elaborate system of graphic signs. In a number of pieces the order of sections was not predetermined as, for example, in Stockhausen's *Mixtur*, while his *Plus-Minus* of 1963 presented the performer(s) with an extensive series of instructions for processes from which these performers could create a performing version. This became a common method for many pieces in the 1960s, but was only a small departure from highly organized structures, as the processes were still the same.

The second important idea that affected music in the musical centers of the German avant garde was indeterminacy. A catalytic occasion must

[13] See particularly: Karlheinz Stockhausen: "...how time passes...", *Die Reihe III Musical Craftsmanship*, English edition (Bryn Mawr, PA: Theodore Presser, 1958) pp. 10–40; Stockhausen, "Structure and Experiential Time," *Die Reihe II*, 64-74; Roger Smalley, Stockhausen's *Gruppen, The Musical Times*, vol 108 (1967), pp. 794–97; and Norman Del Mar, "On Co-conducting Stockhausen's *Gruppen*," *Tempo* 59 (1961), pp. 15–23.

have been the appearance of John Cage at the 1958 Darmstadt Summer Course (see below). He had already toured Europe in 1954, visiting Cologne, Milan and Paris, and, with his colleague David Tudor, had presented his prepared piano at Donaueschingen. But in 1958 his course called 'Composition as Process' laid the ground for a complete change of approach from the avant garde. His ideas about indeterminacy had been current for some years, but now they took on a new relevance. It was impossible for the avant garde in Germany at this time to change its approach completely and abandon all its detailed micro- and macro-planning, but equally Cage's ideas could not be ignored.

Improvisation took on a number of forms. In some cases, for example, in Stockhausen's *Plus-Minus* mentioned above, the process was completely mapped out for the performer(s), and in others a simple plan might be laid out in symbols. This reached its ultimate form in the work of Stockhausen's performing group which operated in ways that flew in the face of the serial orthodoxy that had been the norm in the previous decade. The players would isolate themselves for hours and sometimes days, trying to achieve a detachment and a trance state. Some of the performances would simply be intuitive in that ideas were created spontaneously and built on by the rest of the group, but in many performances and recordings, verbal texts, rather than musical scores, were used to stimulate the players to create musical material. The most famous work of this type is Stockhausen's *Aus den sieben Tagen* of 1968, a collection of fifteen texts. They were used for group improvisation, taking the performers almost as far away as possible from the exactly notated and precisely determined "finished" score that Stockhausen was aiming at only ten years previously. This was followed in 1969-70 by another group of seventeen texts called *Für kommende Zeiten*.

There was inevitably some kind of theatrical element in the work of Stockhausen's performing group, but this was far more in evidence in the work of two foreign musicians who had settled, at least temporarily, in Germany, the Argentine-born Mauricio Kagel and the French-born Slovene composer and trombonist, Vinko Globokar. Kagel is perhaps the more important in this respect. His *Match* for two cellos and percussionist of 1964 is typical of this musico-theatrical performance in which the two cellists are involved in a musical contest with the percussionist the referee. Although a sound-only version conveys much of the drama, the brilliant film version shows what Kagel had in mind, a bizarre and almost mad theatrical entertainment. Other kinds of musical theater by Kagel are more ambitious, a notable example being his *Staatstheater*, composed between 1967 and 1970, an all-embracing piece of social comment, satire and grotesque entertainment. Globokar's theatrical pieces are mostly concert works that are staged in a way that enhances and in many cases exaggerates the musical features of the piece. In many cases they are aligned to a new virtuosity in the first instance of the composer's own instrument but by extension in any instrument.

The move away from the intellectual was also advocated in a new wide-ranging avant garde movement called *Fluxus* that was born in the 1960s. Founded by the Lithuanian artist and architect, George Maciunas, it was formally inaugurated in 1962 in Wuppertal. The musical activities were led by numerous, mostly foreign composers and performers, including La Monte Young. Its aim was to "purge the world of bourgeois intellectuals, commercialized culture and institutionalized art."[14] One of the most important aspects of its activities was to bring together like-minded artists of different disciplines.

FESTIVALS AND COURSES

While much of Stockhausen's work took place in or near Cologne, there was a great deal of activity elsewhere. The Musica Viva concerts in Munich were famous for introducing new works to audiences that were more used to hearing traditional music, but the new music was more likely to be performed in a specialized context. Across West Germany there were various pockets of activity in which the avant garde thrived.

For example, in the central German city of Darmstadt, Wolfgang Steinecke founded the Darmstadt Summer Courses (Internationale Ferienkurse für Neue Musik) in 1946 and created the Städtishes Fachinstitut für Neue Musik in 1948. The courses (held annually until 1970) and institute attracted many avant garde composers from both Germany and abroad. Their music was played to receptive audiences, while the composers themselves lectured extensively on the new ideas and techniques. German composers who appeared included Fortner, Adorno, Rehfuss, Henze, Rihm and Stockhausen, but foreign musicians were also greatly in evidence, e.g. Messiaen, Berio, Boulez, Cage, Ligeti, Maderna, Nono, Pousseur and Xenakis. The main trend, especially in the 1950s, was the development of serial methods in composition, notably following the

---

[14] David W. Bernstein, Fluxus. In *The New Grove Dictionary of Music and Musicians*, ed. Stanley Sadie, London: Macmillan, 2002, vol. 9, p. 48.

ideas of Luigi Nono, who championed the idea of total serialism. There developed some very strong ideas among the composers of what has become known as the Darmstadt school, especially Boulez, Nono, Maderna and Stockhausen himself. The techniques advocated were considered essential for composing in any modern idiom. Inevitably, though, there were disagreements as the composers gradually retreated from the extreme position of total serialism.

A much more moderate, tolerant and practical development occurred in parallel with this in the southern German town of Donaueschingen. Its contemporary music festival, called Donaueschinger Musiktage für Zeitgenössischer Tonkunst, was revived in 1950 as a platform for contemporary music in a collaboration between the town and Südwestfunk in Baden-Baden. Under the direction of the conductors Hans Rosbaud and Ernest Bour a large number of important premieres were given here, notably by Fortner, Henze and Stockhausen and many foreign composers active in Germany, e.g. Boulez, Berio, Nono, Penderecki and Xenakis. It was the practice of the festival to make a large number of commissions for new orchestral works.

THE IMPLICATIONS

Because of the unique circumstances of the avant garde in Germany, a whole range of new techniques were developed quickly and without much reference to tradition. Composers such as Stockhausen were given free rein, and were enthusiastically joined by the foreigners Luciano Berio, Bruno Maderna, Pierre Boulez, Luigi Nono and Iannis Xenakis. What developed was an authoritarian approach to serious musical developments in Europe. The elaborate organizational techniques that were advocated by this group became the *sine qua non* of serious musical composition. Composers not following these techniques were ignored and their music was considered irrelevant. However, the dead-end of total serialism was a difficult situation for the avant garde composers, because they had left behind all but a small proportion of their audience. To re-establish musical communication with the listening public at large meant a retreat from this advanced position and something that was reckoned to be akin to treason.

After the collapse in confidence in total serialism the German avant garde went in many directions. Its pluralism spread far beyond the borders of West Germany and has developed into a wide range of techniques that collectively make up "postmodernism."

However, we always seem to come back to the ideas of Stockhausen. His use of improvisation within his performing group, influenced as it was by Cage, did create a new way forward, but, like everything else that was initiated in this period, it became only one part of the many-faceted techniques of musical composition in the next forty years. The theatrical work of Kagel and others led a new way forward that engaged the audiences more strongly and moved the center of music away from the cerebral. But in all this we can agree with a headline in *The European* newspaper: "Blame it all on Stockhausen."[15]

[15] *The European*, no.192 (14-20 January 1994) section 3 *Élan*, p. 1.

Michelle Biget-Mainfroy
Tours

Music in France 1950-1970

Since 1950, French music has evolved in symbiosis with an international movement, and it seems receptive to, among others, German, Italian, and American influences. Moreover, figures - if this designation still bears any meaning in this end of 20th century - of foreign origin are not exceptional in French musical structures, as Xenakis or Parmegiani for instance. The stylistic quest of composers has been dominated either by serial language, which results from a constructivist choice, or by pure instrumental research - and in particular, the quest of percussive resonances. Some people have also attempted to express large global phenomena, natural cataclysms or human manifestations: the music of Iannis Xenakis strives to organize these phenomena through sophisticated probability calculation. Lastly - and this holds true in most countries - the collective is promoted, rhythm takes precedence over melody, the parameter of tone takes on a new importance.

There is still no getting away from one personality: that of Olivier Messiaen, who taught Pierre Boulez, Jean Barraqué, Karlheinz Stockhausen. Most certainly, in 1950 Messiaen had already conceived a large part of his works and his theoretical writings in *Technique de mon langage musical* [Technique of my musical language], published in 1944. But it can be claimed that Messiaen's experiences are at the origin of all the elements that should conquer their autonomy in serial harmony and in electronics. The composer works mainly in modal circuit, where modality provides him an acoustic universe referring to cultures, which associate music and religion. Likewise, the synesthesis of color/sound, which he readily convokes, have a theological value in the Orient. Messiaen's music expresses a theological vocation, as poetics open for the Divine, and to which sounds of the Far East, as well as birds' songs convey a substance free from any corruption from civilization.

Modes de valeur et d'intensité [Mode of value and intensity] for the piano submits as early as 1949 a version of what will later be called integral serialism. By establishing new rhythms emancipated from bar, inspired by Hindu metrics, in particular those famed "non retrogressive rhythms" totally independent from any sound levels, Messiaen had already increased the musical community's awareness of the irreducible property of rhythm, and drawn attention to something else than sound levels - which were in the center of the Viennese serial techniques, which were in fashion at the time. Messiaen will renounce integral serialism, just as he will *music concrète*, after a brief episode at the RTF studio.

The *Catalogue d'oiseaux* [Catalogue of birds] (1956-58), for the piano, should indeed be understood as more than a "concert of noises." If it does depart from clearly identified trends, the influence of Messiaen on young composers of the two decades considered (1950s and 1960s) is nevertheless capital, as much on the level of musical writing - notably with this predilection for the rhythmic dimension - as on that of a spiritual heritage.

It is worthwhile delving into the vocal field, where in France a certain tendency towards conservatism may be observed. Lyricism and the return to voice are often at odds with an avant garde language and form (serial technique, quartertones, complex rhythmical values, multi-phonic sounds, forms bearing the appearance of improvisation): as if the voice remained the shelter of the *espressivo*, the area of sensuality.

The Boulez of the *Le Marteau sans maître* [Hammer without a master] (1954), or of *Pli selon pli* [Fold as per fold] (1969), is not that of the *Deuxième sonate* [Second Sonata] or of the *Structures* for the piano. It will take until 1965 to witness a burst of music and text in parallel. The scale of phonemes expands to all kinds of parasite noises and voice blends intimately with the musical ensemble, and even with the electro-acoustic system.

For Jean Barraqué, *Séquence* (as early as in 1950-55), arisen from three poems of Nietzsche, or *La Mort de Virgile* [The death of virgil] (1956), after a work of Hermann Broch, bear witness to an unlimited exploration of the textual and musical material, based on a proliferous series. In Boulez's *Le Marteau sans maître*, René Char's text is assumed to be known beforehand; we do not need to grasp the significance to appreciate its poetic substance. The instrumental comment announces or prepares the text, the voice emerges and vanishes. Later, Charles Chaynes or Paul Méfano will constantly play on those effects of emergence/disappearance of voice, not any more as impudent soloist, but as a component of an indissociably vocal and instrumental Whole.

The notion of *objet sonoré* [resounding object] is one of the post-war period's novelties. In 1948, Pierre Schaeffer created the Groupe de Musique Concrète [Concrete Music Group] in RTF (French Radio and Television). Musical research is led in a radio station in collaboration with sound engineers – not an exception in those times. The purpose is to negate any preconception, to offer raw sound as a precondition to any musical construction.

The traditional instrumentation soon seems too narrow. Moreover, the arrival of the tape recorder in 1951 allows one to manipulate sounds. In 1950, Pierre Schaeffer and Pierre Henry display the *Symphonie pour un homme seul* [Symphony for a man alone], for noises, notes bursting from spoken or sung text. This work, which derives from the disc recording techniques, is considered as the first "electronic" work played in public. Two texts by Schaeffer present his concepts: *A la cherche d'une musique concrète* [Searching for a concrete music] (1952), and the *Traité des objets musicaux* [Treatise on musical objects] (1966). Michel Philippot, Olivier Messiaen *Timbre-durée* [Timbre-duration] (1952) and Pierre Boulez' *Symphonie mécanique* [Mechanical Symphony] (1956) will be among the guests of the RTF studio.

Pierre Henry leaves the RTF to create the studio Apsome, and the birth of the Group for Musical Research [GRM] (1958) inaugurated in France the reign of the electro-acoustic. Luc Ferrari, François-Bernard Mâche, François Bayle, Bernard Parmegiani, Ivo Malec work in team over the constitution of a real catalogue of examples. A first collective concert is played at the Ranelagh in 1962. An example of all possible manipulations is found in Parmegiani's *Capture éphémère* [Ephemeral capture] (1968).

It seems that the French specificity resides in the live association of magnetic tape and music: Ivo Malec's *Cantate pour elle* [Cantata for her] for soprano, harp and band (1966) or François-Bernard Mache's *Volume* for twelve tracks, seven drums, two pianos and percussion (1960).

Faced with this sonorial greediness, serial technique comes across as a stronghold of functional organization. Pierre Boulez is the one who cherished the hope of seeing the ***serial system*** called upon to reform not only the musical system, but also its rhetorics and its poetics. The serial principle was primarily thought as decisive in the evolution of western music after 1945, in France as well as in other countries. The essential benchmark was represented by Webern's works.

According to Boulez, a reflective and logical theory is necessarily a prelude to any compositive practice. In *Penser la musique d'aujourd'hui* [Boulez on music today] – the title itself is revealing – Boulez retains from serialism an organizational principle and stretches it to all sounding parameters. In *Structures* for two pianos (1955: the year of Stockhausen's *Kreuzspiel*), series is extended to timbres and intensities. We may notice Boulez's concern – in conformity with the French tradition – to find support for musical ideas in literary references: Mallarmé or Joyce. The serial arbitrary is in fact associated with a taste for improvisation: in that sense, it may be claimed that the problematic of the mobile work is a logical extension of serialism. The mobile work rethinks the too exclusive principle of authority and reconsiders the relation of the composer to the interpreter and the public. Thus, Boulez's *Troisième Sonate* [Third Sonata] for piano (1957) offers to the pianist – through its five "formatives" – some itineraries, and a chart of initiatives. One cannot assimilate Boulez's concept of openness to John Cage's random concept (the same remark would be valid for André Boucourechliev). At last, Boulez's intense institutional activity must be mentioned: in the foundation of concerts of the *Domaine Musical* in 1954, and during the 1970s in the Institut de Recherche et de Création Acoustique/Musique – IRCAM – [Institute for Research and Acoustic/Musical Creation].

Serial determinism is only a particular case of a more general logic. The application to the composition of *règles mathématiques* [mathematical rules] is advocated by Iannis Xenakis, in order to solve the "problems of continuity and discontinuity of composed sound beings."[1] In *Metastasis* (1953), Xenakis organizes masses and densities according to Boltzmann's and Maxwell's laws; in *Pithoprakta* (1956), the arrangement of the speed of *glissandi* depends on stochastic formulas according to Gauss' and Poisson's laws. But soon will Xenakis perceive a need to use electronic brains. He invents a programme designed for the IBM 7090 computer of the Scientific Research Centre of IBM France.

Xenakis considers composition under the angle of fundamental relations, independent of time: a privilege is granted to the sounding area in this algebra of "in-time" and "out-of-time." This insistence on the necessity to formalize composition, for which mathematics are an ideal model, is based on a rational conception of music, which, despite proclamation of

[1] Cf. Iannis Xenakis, *Musique. Architecture.* Paris: Casterman, 1971.

intention, is not very distant from Boulez's ideas. Again, one shall moderate this weight of exact sciences on the musical act. In Xenakis' works there is also what one may call an order of the sensitive. This composer, while making a very singular use of the "computer machine," keeps an open ear. He creates techniques in order to vary, propel and mix the sound, and the new generation of the 1970's will not neglect to imitate it.

It sometimes happens in Xenakis' work that sounds produced by traditional instruments sound as if electronic: his material appears before his research in Schaeffer's studio, as early as in *Metastasis*. The most calculated works explore sound clouds as well as rarefied densities of sounding events. At last, one must mention three important pages hardly related to mathematics and bearing witness to this sonorial research, which, in post-1945 France was an alternative to rationality in music: *Polla Ta Dhina* (1962) for children's reciting voices and orchestra, *Nuits* (1967) for twelve voices a cappella, and *Cendrées* (1974) for mix choirs and orchestra. The voices adopt a sometimes quasi-instrumental style of emission.

We notice thus in French music composed between 1950 and 1970 a large pendular movement between the strict organization of sound and the autonomy of sound research. After the Liberation, a modernizing will derives from the struggles of the Résistance. There is an aspiration to redefine European unity based on rationality, and Hugues Dufourt[2] makes sure that serialism is part of this modernization.

Prior to René Leibovitz' work dedicated in 1944 to "Schoenberg and his School," few people in France had heard of serial technique. Pierre Boulez, who had frequented Darmstadt, appeared as its standard bearer. The new order established through series seemed to be meant to dominate the musical scene for long; in reality, its reign - in the strict sense - was brief. Deviations from series soon arose: indeterminate, electro-acoustics - which truly fractured boundaries of what distinguished the musical from the non-musical - and above all, all those larval efforts, a very French tradition since Debussy, at practicing the sensual exploration of the universe of sound.

Computer-assisted composition offers a good example of this search for sound. For Xenakis or Pierre Barbaud, the computer initially helped

---

[2] Hugues Dufourt, *Musique, Pouvoir, Ecriture* [Music, Power, Writing]. Paris: Christian Bourgois, 1991.

musicians to solve their compositive problems; it gave a score to decipher and then to transpose into musical signs more usual for interpreters.

But it was put in charge of the sound realization in all its details. Jean-Claude Risset thus composed in 1969 his catalogue of registered synthetic sounds, with their numerical description. This medium, which can be transmitted from one research centre to another, ensures a sharpness of control over the production of sound and a complexity of sources, greater than what can be obtained in electronic music studios. The "scientific accuracy" a computer programme can offer is by no means heterogeneous with a curiosity towards the sensitive effect: this constitutes, from Rameau's orchestrations through Berlioz and so-called impressionist composers, an inclination quite natural to French music.

Translated by Agatha Collin

Pierre Albert Castanet
Paris

Musical Idioms in Italy in the Years 1950-1960

> Music will always remain a historical presence, a legacy of men who consciously withstand the historical movement, and who take decisions at each stage of that movement, in full control of their intuition and logical consciousness, and act in order to open new paths to the vital need of new structures.
>
> Luigi Nono, 1959

Forever a land of conquests, Italy may be symbolized by the following tripartition, which rests on the phenomenon of Religiosity / Vocality / Theatricality:[1] from codices linking the *laudario di Cortona* of the XIIIth century to the arrangement of the rap opera (1996) of young Andréa Liberovici, through Monteverdi's madrigals, Vivaldi's cantatas, Verdi's, Rossini's, Puccini's and others' operas. In fact, the diverse bonds which link the ins and outs of this Trinitarian symbolism probably have their roots in the Word (whether intelligible or not), as vehicle of thoughts – possibly of ideologies – as exhibitionistic medium of emotions, of belief, of abstraction, or as winged support of poetry, theatre, or simply of the resounding object. Therefore, owing to his wife Cathy Berberian, Luciano Berio was a distinguished specialist of verbal and paratextual compositions, displaying thus a vast horizon, from the vocalized word to the diverse forms of the Theatre of the Absurd.

Thus, for more than seven centuries, the destiny and vocation of Italian composers seem indeed to have been directed towards the arts of spectacle (and for epochs closer to us, towards acusmatic diffusion modes). Thus, although it has faced the sometimes audacious assaults of the avant garde, the music of the 1930's-1960's has not been able to liberate itself from those atavistic idioms, which form the Italian particularity.

[1] See attached, as indication, several compositions related with this "trihedral" mirror of Italian musical art: around muses inspiring religiosity, vocalism, and theatricality.

A EUROPEAN GROUP SPIRIT

Although religiosity was not a major preoccupation for composers of the generation of 1925, the European intermingling of modernistic ideas reached its climax, most notably during the annual rendezvous of Darmstadt[2] summer classes. It is indeed in this German temple of the avant garde that the Italians Luciano Berio, Bruno Maderna, Luigi Nono and Niccolo Castiglioni have mixed uninhibitedly with the aesthetics of such composers as John Cage, Earle Brown, Pierre Boulez, Karlheinz Stockhausen, Henri Pousseur, André Boucourechliev, Francis Miroglio, Hans Werner Henze, Dieter Schnebel, Mauricio Kagel, Jean Barraqué, and so forth . . .

For most of those creators, compositional utopia aspired to the conquest of a salutary serial totalitarism. After the end of the Second World War, history recorded the existence of that multidisciplinary melting pot, where disciplines such as aesthetics (represented by Theodor Adorno, Hans Heinz Stuckenschmidt and Heinrich Strobel), or acoustics (with Herbert Eimert, Werner Meyer Eppler, among others) met; notwithstanding the presence of instrumental classes (with David Tudor, Alois Kontarsky on the piano, Christoph Caskel on percussion, Siegfried Palm on cello, Séverino Gazzelloni playing the flute - eager creator of Berio, Maderna, Boulez . . .) and composition classes (with the aforementioned). In 1992, André Boucourechliev regretted (as did Luigi Nono in his time), the progressive institutionalization of Darmstadt's meetings. This institutionalization seems to have increased at the end of the 1960's. The fertile epoch of that international "School" beamed during some twenty years (1946-1966).

We should also mention the dawn of the Florentine School,[3] which integrated musicians wishing to practice an "unlimited cultural exercise" from currents of modern music. Its founding members: the musicologist Reginald Smith-Brindle, the guitar player Alvaro Company, that specialist of multiple sounds of wind instruments Bruno Bartolozzi, young Sylvano Bussotti, Arrigo Benvenuti and Carlo Prosperi (1920-1990).

In the field of music, which will become "electroacoustic" and then "acousmatic," another fellowship should be mentioned (with the French studio of "concrete music" directed by Pierre Henry and Pierre Schaeffer - from 1948 - and of the electronic studio of Cologne radio with Herbert

[2] The famed summer courses held in Darmstadt, Germany beginning in 1946.

[3] For more information, refer to: Donata Bertoni / Renzo Cresti, *Civiltà Musical.*, p. 269.

Eimert, Fritz Enkel and Karlheinz Stockhausen - from 1950): the studio of Musical Phonology located in the Milanese radio, and founded in 1955. If the material of French "concrete music" was concerned with sound in its "native state" (as Schaeffer said – sound as provided by nature, as fixed by machines and factory instruments, and as transformed by different studio manipulations), the spirit of German "electronic music" as well broadcast on magnetic tape detached from recognizable concrete sources in order to draw on the source of a rising technology with purely abstract references. The aura of artificial sound was then produced by nets of electric generators. In the wake of that research and composition on magnetic support, the Milanese studio tried to assimilate the French and German concrete and electronic experiences, even being able to "learn a double lesson from their reciprocal limitations."[4]

Directed by Luciano Berio (born in 1925) and Bruno Maderna (1920-1973), the Milanese Studio of Phonology did work of quality and specialized, for the better or worse, in the vocal domain (the Italian *bel canto* is a must), even if a good number of aesthetic tendencies have learned their talent on the pulpits and consoles of RAI radio (we may mention for instance *Scambi* by Henri Pousseur, *Fontana Mix* by John Cage, *A Floresta é Jovem e Cheia de Vida* by Luigi Nono, *Divertimento* by Niccolo Castiglioni, or *Partner* by Angelo Paccagnini).

At the time of the foundation of the Italian studio, Luciano Berio was already a renowned serial composer. Nevertheless, the electronic experience boosted his enlargement of acoustic and parametrical conception: the relation to the continuum-discontinuum, unreserved reflections on the articulate and the disarticulate, abstract games with enriched or filtered parameters, the selection of diverse resounding objects, stacking of phonemes treated with a non-representative intention (cf. *Omaggio a Joyce* - 1958, *Visage* -1961 . . .). Later, some commentators will even note the influence of the electronic gesture on the purely vocal and instrumental writing of Berio (refer, for instance, to *Laborintus II* -1965) – as will Iannis Xenakis, György Ligeti or Tristan Murail later on. As to Bruno Maderna, he will be the apostle of mix music, integrating as soon as 1958 live instruments or voices, registered or manipulated, into the solid content of magnetic tape (*Musica su due dimensioni* -1958, *Invenzione su una voce* -

[4] Pierre Schaeffer, *La musique concrète,* p. 85.

1960). His opera *Hyperion* (1964) demonstrated to what extent electrified music could take on and evoke such a dramatic significance.

However, in spite of those grand masses celebrating modernity, some creators dared to go it alone, rejected by the institutional system or preserved by rather introspective intuitions.

THE LONELINESS OF STRONG TEMPERS

A disciple of Arnold Schoenberg's theories, Luigi Dallapiccola (1904-1975) has wanted to insert into his works an intense sound and an audacious technique incorporated into an ascetic architecture. Bearing the marks of the peak of fascism, the themes of captivity and liberty will relentlessly bother him (and eventually inspire him). A Latin man to his fingertips, he knew how to cross dissonance and rhythmic rigor of the serials with the natural consonance and typical *bel canto* of his own country: "Tonality exists and will probably exist still longer" he declared in 1951. The French musicologist Pierre Michel analyses the situation thus: "At a time when some composers - Ligeti, Scelsi, Xenakis, Penderecki, Cerha - radicalized the treatment of timbre(s) to the point that they sometimes became one of the dominant aspects of composition, Dallapiccola pursued his research in a different direction, parallel to post-Weberian attempts of serial organization of timbers."[5]

A committed composer, Luigi Nono (1924-1990) violently reacted against the condemnation of tradition, dictated by Pierre Boulez.[6] Following the example of Luigi Dallapiccola, for whom Nono shared a great admiration with Bruno Maderna and Hermann Scherchen, the composition consisted in recall in the past in order to nourish it with novelties and current affairs of any type (conflicts, slogans, wars, etc.). Moreover, from the time of summer meetings in Germany, Nono has stood firm against the freedom of laisser-faire and of the inaction of a John Cage (and of his absence of creative power), but he also fought against the emergence of a proud academism that took place little by little. In his conference named "Historical presence in today's music," pronounced in 1959, Nono goes even further by saying that Webern had been forged in Darmstadt! At last, Nono, the communist and combatant of every cause, tried to define a Culture as the moment of sudden awareness, of fight,

[5] Pierre Michel, *Luigi Dallapiccola*, p. 116.

[6] See part of the text "Schoenberg est mort" written in 1952, in Pierre Boulez, *Relevés d'apprenti*, Paris: Seuil, 1966.

provocation, discussion, and of participation.[7] It is probably these gestures of a political essence which have isolated him from the numerous converging powers of the international musical movement. In a speech given in Berlin and Munich in 1969, and symptomatically entitled *Music and revolution*, he refused en bloc any Eurocentric concession and vehemently opposed American imperialism. This led him, for instance, to harshly denounce the "demagogical" words of Penderecki "who lets himself be supported by American associations in Berlin . . ."[8]

As to Giacinto Scelsi (1905-1988), dodecaphonism appalled him. Mystical, referring to several gods (Jesus Christ, Buddha, Shiva, Vishnu,[9] etc.), the poet-composer - all the same a great improviser - was influenced by Zen philosophy and by the putting in dilated tense ritual extra-European ceremonies. Focused on the virtues of a unique sound, the quasi-spectral art of Scelsi will remain confidential until the years 1980 (he forbade that his music be broadcast on the national radio in Rome). Having abandoned the live spectacle, he wrote many vocal pieces deliberately transcending the *bel canto* of his ancestors, and adapting it intuitively to Oriental harmonic modes (*Canti del Capricorno* - 1962-1972).

If, at the dawn of the XXth century, Italy had to get down to an artistic renaissance while trying to forget the remains of verism (thanks to composers as Respighi, Malipiero, Casella and Pizetti), the second post-war period would give rise to a renovation of the order of a modernity which does not have to be ashamed in the globally European context. Adapting to the rules and making the best of laws resulting from Viennese dictates, Italy has always kept an immoderate love for studies of phonetic and phonologic order, as it has always had a strong taste for large lyrical gushes.

In 1962, evoking the "three leaders, Nono, Maderna and Berio," the French critic of music wrote: "Italy's relatively disadvantaged position in the international cultural field has not made it yet possible for this new school to be renowned as much as it deserves. However, there are now pieces of music, there are names, which can not be omitted anymore in the chronicle of our epoch's musical destiny."[10]

---

[7] Refer to the chapter "Pour une histoire sociale de la musique contemporaine" in Pierre Albert Castanet, *Tout est bruit pour qui a peur*, pp. 38–104.

[8] Luigi Nono, *Ecrits*, p. 253.

[9] You may study for instance: *Quattro illustrazioni sulla metamorphosi di Visnù* (1953) for the piano, or *Ko-Tha - tre danze de Shiva* (1967) for the guitar alone . . .

[10] Claude Samuel, *Panorama de l'art musical contemporain*, p. 474.

APPENDIX:

ITALIAN PIECES COVERING THE PERIOD 1950-1969

Pieces related with **religiosity**:

Magnificat (1949-1971) by Luciano Berio; *Job, una sacra rappresentazione* (1950), *Noche oscura* (1951) - words by saint Jean de la Croix - by Goffredo Petrassi; *Requiescant* (1957-1958) - after the Gospel according to Saint Matthew - by Luigi Dallapiccola; *Il libro dei Sette Sigilli* (1951) - biblical cantata by Franco Donatoni; *Tre Canti sacri* (1958) by Giacinto Scelsi; *Passagio* (1961-1962) - mass on scene by Luciano Berio; *Parole di San Paolo* (1964) - according to the First Epistle to the Corinthians - by Luigi Dallapiccola; *Julio Organum Julii* (1968) - Liturgy for organs by Sylvano Bussotti.

Pieces related with **vocality**:

Tre liriche di Montale (1951) by Domenico Guaccero; *Nonsense* (1952) by Goffredo Petrassi; *Goethe Lieder* (1953) by Luigi Dallapiccola; *Liebeslied* (1954) by Luigi Nono; *Tre Canti populari* (1958) by Giacinto Scelsi; *Serenata* (1959) by Franco Donatoni; *Circles* (1960) by Luciano Berio; *Tre liriche corali* (1961) by Armando Gentilucci; *Taiagarù* (1962), *Canti del Capricorno* (1962-1972) by Giacinto Scelsi; *Gyro* (1963) by Niccolo Castiglioni; *Lettura di Michelangelo* (1964) by Roman Vlad; *Laborintus II* (1965), *Sequenza III* (1966) by Luciano Berio; *AkaAka to I, II, III* (1967-1968) by Salvatore Sciarrino.

Pieces related with **theatricality**:

Il mio cuore è nel Sud (1950) - radiodrama by Bruno Maderna; *Der rote Mantel* (1953) - ballet by Luigi Nono; *La filia di Jorio* (1954) by Ildebrando Pizetti; *La donna è mobile* (1954) by Riccardo Malipiero; *Mimusique n°2* (1955) - ballet by Luciano Berio; *Una demanda di matrimonio* (1956) - comic opera by Luciano Chailly; *La Lampara* (1957) - ballet by Franco Donatoni; *Intolleranza* (1960-1961) by Luigi Nono; *La sentenza* (1960) by Giacomo Manzoni; *Ulisse* (1960-1968) - opéra according to the Odyssey - by Luigi Dallapiccola; *Don Perlimplin* (1962) - radiophonic opera, *Hyperion* (1964) - opera with electroacoustics by Bruno Maderna; *Aladino e la lampada magica* (1963-1965) - lyrical tale by Nino Rota; *Hyperion* (1964) - lyrics in the form of spectacle by Bruno Maderna; *Clitenestra* (1965) by Ildebrando Pizetti; *La Passion selon Sade* (1965-1966) - chamber mystery with live paintings by Sylvano Bussotti; *Il Gabbiano* (1968) - danced and sung variations by Roman Vlad.

BIBLIOGRAPHIC SUPPLEMENTS:

Baroni Mario/Dalmonte Rossana, *Bruno maderna documenti.* Milano: Suvini Zerboni, 1985.

Bertoni Donata/Cresi Renzo, *Civiltà Musicali.* Firenze: GDB Edizioni, 1994.

Boulez Pierre, *Relevés d'apprenti.* Paris: Seuil, 1966.

Castanet Pierre Albert, Cistemino Nicola, *Giacinto Scelsi, Viaggio al centro del suono.* La Spezia: Lunaeditore, 1993.

Castanet Pierre Albert, *Tout est bruit pour qui a peur. Pour une histoire sociale du son sale.* Paris: Michel de Maule, 1999.

Ferrari Giordano, *Armando Gentilucci.* Lucca: LIM Ricordi, 1998.

Gentilucci Armando, *Guida all'ascolto délla musica contemporanea.* Milano: Feltrinelli, 1983.

Gentilucci Armando, *Introduzione alla musica elettronica.* Milano: Feltrinelli, 1983.

Golbeck Frédérick, *Des compositeurs au XXème siècle.* Paris: Parution, 1988.

Lucioli Alessandra, *Sylvano Bussotti.* Milano: Targa, 1988.

Mazzola Nangeroni Gabriella, *Franco Donatoni.* Milano: Targa, 1989.

Michel Pierre, *Luigi Dallapiccola.* Genève: Contrechamps, 1996.

Mila Massimo, *Maderna, Musicista europeo.* Torino: Einaudi, 1976.

Nono Luigi, *Ecrits* (réunis par L. Feneyrou). Paris: Bourgois, 1993.

Petrassi Goffredo, *Autoritratto.* Roma/Bari: Laterza, 1992.

Samuel Claude, *Panorama de l'art musical contemporain.* Paris: NRF, 1962.

Schaeffer Pierre, *La musique concrète,* Collection Que sais-je? No. 1287. Paris: Presses Universitaires de France, 1973.

Stoïanova Ivanka, *Luciano Berio, Chemins en musique,* La Revue Musicale n° 375–377. Paris: Richard-Masse, 1985.

Vlad Roman, Italian music today, *Twentieth Century Music.* London: John Calder, 1960.

Weid Jean Noël von der. *La musique du XXème siècle.* Paris: Hachette, 1997.

Translated by Agatha Collin

Niall O'Loughlin
Lougborough

Music in Britain 1950-1970

The musical establishment in Britain in the 1950s was in general conservative and unadventurous. There were few platforms for new music but the British Broadcasting Corporation (BBC) provided one, and the opportunities for composers increased with the appointment in 1959 of William Glock as Controller of Music. The many bold programmes that followed set a new tone in serious radio broadcasting and concertgoing in Britain. Performances of Schoenberg, Berg and Webern became almost routine, and broadcasts of music by Nono, Boulez and Stockhausen appeared and were eagerly followed by an increasingly aware musical public. The immediate result was the acceptance of the twelve-tone system as a valid composing technique. There was an increasing number of composers and performers who were interested in following up these developments. Some had studied abroad and were aware of many new developments that they wanted to explore.

The music of the 1950s in Britain, however, as in many other countries in Europe, remained doggedly conservative. There were the final works of one of the century's finest English folk music collectors, Ralph Vaughan Williams (1872-1958). In his serious works, especially his symphonies, he maintained an uneasy and unresolved dichotomy between folk-related sounds and a distant and discordant harmonic idiom. Yet this was easily understood at the time, even if not fully appreciated. Vaughan Williams remained a traditionalist, as did most of his contemporaries, e.g. William Walton, Arthur Bliss, Benjamin Britten and Michael Tippett, some whose works had already achieved classic status in Britain, and to some extent abroad, as well. But two composers were notable exceptions to this trend: Humphrey Searle (b. 1915), who had studied briefly with Anton Webern and Elisabeth Lutyens (b. 1906). Both were already using forms of Schoenberg's twelve-note technique. Searle's symphonies show a use of symmetrical twelve-tone series, and an increasingly spare texture, the effect of his refining of a romantic style under the delayed influence of Webern, with whom he studied in 1937-8. Despite the fact that Searle's First Symphony uses the same note row that Webern used in his String Quartet op. 28, its sound world is more that of Alban Berg. But, in listening to the work today, it is amazing to hear that in 1960 Searle's music was considered "difficult." Lutyens's music is generally thinner in texture than that of Searle, with a fondness for using tone-rows that show symmetries of a Webernian character, and palindromic forms that later became a by-word of the avant garde of the 1960s. Another composer, Matyás Seiber (1905-1960), the Hungarian emigré who had settled in England in 1935 and was tragically killed in a car crash in South Africa in 1960, adopted twelve-tone technique with a distinctive Hungarian sound in the melodic lines. (He was an ardent though not slavish admirer of the music of Bartók.) His excellent music includes the *Quartetto Lirico* (1951) and a number of rigorous but often beautiful chamber works from his last years, notably the sometimes severe wind quintet *Permutazioni a cinque* (1958) and the Violin Sonata (1960).

The idea of total serialism that occupied the minds of Boulez, Nono, Stockhausen and others in the late-1950s did not find much favor in Britain. It was considered an unsatisfactory method of composition. There are three positions or points of view: serial procedures not recognized by the listener, serial procedures recognized unconsciously, and serial procedures explicitly recognized by the listener. The last viewpoint is the only one that would have been acceptable, but even this was deemed to be impossible for most listeners. Hence the feeling that this technique was unsatisfactory.

The new Polish music did not reach Britain to any great extent until the late-1960s. There were, however, performances of such works as Penderecki's *Threnody* and String Quartet No.1 and, in 1967, with much publicity and some controversy, Penderecki's *St Luke Passion*. But in any case these works were merely a small part of the new range of styles that were "on offer." With attitudes such as those just expressed (and this is not in any way extreme), it is hardly surprising that few British composers followed the system to any great extent, the most notable being David Bedford (b. 1937). His *Two Poems* for chorus of 1963 on vivid poems by the American, Kenneth Patchen, employ microtonal textures of many parts. Also with words by Patchen, *Music for Albion Moonlight* of 1965, for soprano and small ensemble, exploits many syllabic manipulations and tonal permutations.

There was the emergence of a new group of young composers, mainly those who had studied together in Manchester: Alexander Goehr (b.1932), Harrison Birtwistle (b.1934) and Peter Maxwell Davies (b.1934). They were all keen to compose for mixed ensembles of various sizes. At this time there were no groups in existence that specialised in contemporary music. A new music ensemble had been formed by the English conductor, John Carewe, for a famous BBC performance in 1960 of Boulez's *Le marteau sans maître,* but it was short-lived. The group that undertook performance of new works by Birtwistle and Maxwell Davies was the London-based Melos ensemble, which was more accustomed to playing the larger ensemble works of Beethoven and Schubert. Their performances, however, were excellent, as recordings still testify.

Davies's intense *Leopardi Fragments* of 1961 for soprano, alto and ensemble, set telegraphic texts by Giacomo Leopardi in disjointed heterophonic lines, a challenge even to performers familiar with the idiom. His *Seven in Nomine* subjected the technique of the 16th and 17th century English *in nomine to* some surprising distortions. Both these works were first performed by the Melos Ensemble, as was Birtwistle's iconoclastic *Tragoedia* (1965), a fifteen-minute score, sometimes of almost unremitting violence. The ensemble consists somewhat surprisingly merely of wind quintet, harp and string quartet. Although the work itself has no explicit programme, it was intended to bridge the gap between "absolute music" and theatre music. It is dramatic, but this drama is purely musical.

The same attitude was held by Peter Maxwell Davies, and in succeeding works of his and of Birtwistle himself, they went one stage further and made the drama more explicit. Clearly the time was ripe for creating an ensemble specially for performing such works. Maxwell Davies found the problems of performance even more pressing in the mid-1960s as he was composing a setting of Trakl's *Offenbarung und Untergang* (to be called *Revelation and Fall* despite the German of the setting), whose technical requirements were going to be of significant difficulty. Davies and Birtwistle accordingly founded in 1967 the Pierrot Players, basically the quintet required to perform Schoenberg's *Pierrot Lunaire,* with a sixth player for percussion and any extra players as required. In the three years of its existence (until 1970, when the ensemble was renamed The Fires of London), the Pierrot Players were responsible for numerous premieres of avant garde British and foreign works. Central to the achievement of the players must be the performances of Maxwell Davies's *Revelation and Fall, Antechrist* (a distorted Medieval motet) and the two stunning parodistic theatre pieces *Eight Songs for a Mad King* for baritone and ensemble and *Vesalii Icones* for cello and ensemble, as well as a handful of smaller works by Birtwistle. The extension of vocal technique in *Eight Songs* to include shrieking and growling over a huge vocal range was similar to but even more vivid than that found in Hans Werner Henze's contemporary *Versuch über Schweine.* Its theatrical element is unusual in that the instrumentalists are all in the drama played by the singer in his mad ravings, and musically there is a stark conflict between the free 'modern' melodic lines and textures and quotations or quasi-quotations from traditional tonal dance music. György Ligeti had used something dramatically similar in his earlier *Aventures* and *Nouvelles Aventures,* but had not integrated the acting into the drama in such a compelling way.

Birtwistle gained less from the existence of the ensemble. His *Verses for Ensembles* , on a much larger scale than *Tragoedia* (30 minutes, 13 players), was first performed by the newly formed London Sinfonietta in 1969. It extended the ideas of the earlier work, making the violent sounds even more obvious. More significant was the bizarre 'dramatic pastoral' *Down by the Greenwood Side,* based on a medieval English mummer's play, which set the tone of his future theatrical and operatic ventures. An even more important work had come earlier. Taking the traditional English puppet entertainment called Punch and Judy, Birtwistle created in 1966-67 what is probably the most original and brilliant opera from an English composer in the second half of the twentieth century, *Punch and Judy* (1968). Its first performance, at the normally staid and delightful Aldeburgh Festival of 1968, horrified the festival director, the composer Benjamin Britten, and caused him to walk out during the first performance.

Orchestral works appeared from Birtwistle and Davies, usually played by the ever versatile BBC Symphony Orchestra. The first British performance of Davies's Dortmund-commissioned *St. Thomas Wake - Foxtrot for Orchestra,* with its incongruous juxtaposition of avant-garde and popular elements, irreverently appeared alongside Beethoven's Fifth Symphony in the eminently traditional Cheltenham Festival of 1969. By 1970 we can see that the situation of 1960 had been changed out of all recognition. Both Birtwistle and Maxwell Davies had contributed considerably to this new position in which audiences' expectations were totally altered.

In Britain the best equipped electronic studio was undoubtedly the BBC's Radiophonic Workshop, but this was almost exclusively used for producing "sound effects" for radio plays rather than for independent musical compositions. One composer who did valuable original creative work in the BBC's studio was the Spanish-born Roberto Gerhard (1896-1970) who had made his home in England after the Spanish civil war.

His death in 1970, at the height of his powers was a great loss to advanced music in Britain at this time. During the 1960s performances of electronic works by Stockhausen and others did take place in London and gramophone records appeared from time to time of electronic music, mainly from Germany and the United States, where there were much better equipped electronic studios. In Britain, despite pockets of enthusiasm and expertise, electronic music remained very much a peripheral activity for many years, pending the establishment of a really well-equipped studio.

Overall, then, we can see that music in Britain had changed out of all recognition between 1950 and 1970. The leading position of the traditionalists had been usurped by the younger composers Maxwell Davies and Birtwistle. Their achievement was enormous and today their works from this period have achieved classic status. The foundation laid proved a fertile ground for the many British composers who were now reaching their maturity.

Erik Christensen
Copenhagen

Danish Music of the Fifties and Sixties: The Transition from Tradition to Modernism

For almost ten years after World War II, the musical tradition remained uninterrupted in Danish music, characterized by tonality and diatonic modality inherited from the Nordic symphonic composers Carl Nielsen (1865-1931) and Jean Sibelius (1865-1957), traditional form, and the influence of Bartók, Hindemith and Stravinsky. The predominant composers of the post-world war II years were Vagn Holmboe (1909-96) and Herman D. Koppel (1908-98), who had established themselves as composers in the 1930s, and Niels Viggo Bentzon (b. 1919), who made his debut as a composer in 1939.

In his large-scale works, Vagn Holmboe remained true to the ideals of musical tradition, unity, coherence and balance. The study of folk music strengthened his conviction that the modal-diatonic melos is the basis of music, and he dissociated himself from expressionism and dodecaphony. He developed a personal metamorphosis technique, in which the musical material was continually being transformed from one state to another, as heard in the piano suite *Suono da Bardo* (1949) and Symphony No. 8 (*Sinfonia Boreal*, 1952).

Herman D. Koppel was strongly influenced by the music of Carl Nielsen. He studied piano at The Royal Danish Academy when Nielsen was director. Also influenced by Bartók, Stravinsky and jazz, Koppel's music is characterized by rhythmic vitality, strong melodic lines and clear-cut form. Born of Jewish parents, Koppel had to flee from Denmark during the German occupation, and, in memory of the victims of the Holocaust, he set Biblical texts to music in *Three Psalms of David* for chorus, tenor solo and orchestra (1949).

Niels Viggo Bentzon is a multi-talented, restless figure in Danish musical life. He is active as a pianist, writer, pictorial artist, and incessantly productive as a composer. He is a talented improviser and composes impulsive music, most often with roots in tonality and such traditional forms as the sonata, partita, toccata, symphony and concerto. In his constant search for new ideas, he has performed the piano works of Arnold Schoenberg and published an introduction to twelve-tone music (1953). This is an indication of a budding interest in dodecaphony, which had been largely neglected in Danish musical life and musical education for thirty years, due to the prevailing anti-romantic and anti-expressionist attitude.

The composer and musicologist Jan Maegaard (b. 1926) discovered Schoenberg's music in 1952. This was a revelation for him, and after a period of self-study he unveiled his first dodecaphonic works in 1955, a Piano Sonata and *Equinox Elegy* for voice, cello and organ. In 1956, Maegaard was elected president of DUT, the Danish ISCM section, and took advantage of this position to present works by Schoenberg, Berg, Webern, Boulez and Stockhausen in concert. A violent debate for and against musical modernism arose in newspapers and periodicals, culminating in a clash when Stockhausen visited Denmark in 1958.

A few Danish composers went abroad in search of new impulses. Gunnar Berg (1909-89) studied in Paris with Honegger and Messiaen. After participating in the Darmstadt summer course in 1952, he applied serial principles to pitch, rhythm and dynamics in *Cosmogonie* for two pianos (1953).This piece remained unperformed until 1967, but Berg's large piano work *Gaffky's* (1958-59), based on a personal version of serialism, aroused attention in Denmark and the Nordic countries.

Poul Rovsing Olsen (1922-82) introduced oriental influences into Danish music. He studied with Boulanger and Messiaen in Paris, and discovered the large collection of ethnic music at the Musée de l'homme. As a musical anthropologist, he collected the music of Arabia and Greenland, and employed elements of oriental rhythm, melody and ornamentation in his own music, notably in the raga-inspired *Alapa-Tarana* for mezzo soprano and percussion (1959).

Axel Borup-Jørgensen (b. 1924) was born in Denmark, but grew up in Sweden. Inspired by the concise concentration of Swedish poetry, he departed from musical tradition in the 1950s, developing a personal lyrical-expressionist style characterized by the predominance of timbre, movement and harmonic color. The experience of the Nordic landscape, light, mood and temperature was rendered in *Somma Suite* for orchestra (1957) and *Winter Pieces* for piano (1959).

By the end of the 1950s, the ground had been prepared for a breakthrough of musical modernism in Denmark. This was late in comparison with developments in Central Europe and Sweden, but Danish music benefited from the non-dogmatic and rapid introduction of a variety of modernist trends and techniques in the 1960s: serialism, sound experiments, Fluxus and happening, pluralism, collage, concretism and minimalism. The radio series *Music of Our Time*, initiated in 1959, was an important source of information.

A new generation of composers was now ready to step forward. Ib Nørholm (b. 1931), Per Nørgård (b. 1932), and Pelle Gudmundsen-Holmgreen (b. 1932) were educated in the musical tradition, but they gradually realized that a new orientation was necessary and inevitable. In 1959, Nørholm composed a Piano Trio employing a serial ordering of pitch, duration and timbre, Gudmundsen-Holmgreen wrote a Webern-influenced String Quartet, and Nørgård introduced his "infinity series" technique in *Fragments I-IV* for piano. A journey together to the ISCM festival 1960 in Cologne was rewarding for these composers, exposing their ears and minds to an abundance of contemporary masterworks, including Kagel's *Anagrama*, Ligeti's *Apparitions*, Stockhausen's *Kontakte* and Boulez's *Pli selon Pli*. They responded with serial works and an exploration of sound. Nørholm's *Fluctuations* for strings and plucked instruments (1961) was based on systematic interval permutation, and *Relief I-II* for chamber orchestra (1963) employed a large variety of untraditional instrumental effects. Gudmundsen-Holmgreen explored time proportions in *Chronos* for 24 instruments (1962), and Nørgård employed the infinity series to create hierarchic structures in *Fragment VI* for 6 orchestral groups (1961). A newcomer, Bent Lorentzen (b. 1935), made his debut as a composer with a serialist opera, *Stalten Mettelil* (1963), and investigated new sounds in *Zyklus I-IV* for strings (1966).

The introduction of serialism in Danish music had an immediate cathartic effect, but serialism soon gave way to other trends. A provocative performance by the Korean anti-artist Nam June Paik in 1961 and a Fluxus Festival of unpredictable happenings in Copenhagen (1962) presented a negation of conventional artistic values that sparked off a furious new public debate on the meaning of art.

Nørholm revolted against the idea of the autonomous work of art in his violin piece *Direction: Inconnue* (1964), which included spoken quotations from music critics and the activation of mechanical toys, and he revolted against orthodox modernism by introducing stylistic pluralism, and integrating serial procedures and noise effects with traditional melody and harmony in his String Quartet No. 3, *From My Green Herbarium* (1966) and the piano piece *Strophes and Fields* (1965).

Henning Christiansen (b. 1932), active as a promoter and performer in the Fluxus Festival, introduced musical concretism in his *Perceptive Constructions* (1964), in which 10-second columns of motionless sound alternate with 10-second intervals of silence. Here, he treated sound as an object deprived of subjective significance. A similar reduction of material was displayed in Pelle Gudmundsen-Holmgreen's *Tricolore IV* (1969), where a string chord, a unison brass tone and a woodwind chord were superimposed in different combinations, focusing attention on sound as a concrete material. A collocation of object-like sounds and incoherent musical fragments was heard in Gudmundsen-Homgreen's *Frère Jacques* for chamber orchestra (1964). *Je ne me tairai jamais. Jamais* for voices and instruments (1966) is an absurdist piece which repeats a Samuel Beckett sentence over and over, accompanied by scratching and rattling sounds, a police whistle and a car horn.

Stylistic pluralism was prominent in Per Nørgård's music of the mid-1960's. The ballet *The Young Man Must Marry* (1964), based on a play by Ionesco, was filled with grotesque quotations and allusions to wedding music and love songs. The stage work *Babel* (1966) for amateur musicians and performers mixed a variety of serious and popular styles, displaying an image of the Babel-like confusion of modern music life. In his subsequent orchestral works *Iris* and *Luna* (both 1967). Nørgård once again went in search of coherence and unity, exploring new sonorities of chromatic textures and interference. *Voyage Into the Golden Screen* (1968) presented the full unfolding of the infinity series that became the organizing principle of Nørgård's works in the 1970s, a technique that permitted a synthesis of systematic structure, melodic flow, harmonic color and organic growth in a hierarchy of simultaneous tempo layers.

For the following generation of composers born in the 1940s, a wide range of possibilities was now open: systematic construction and organic growth; coherence and unity versus collage and pluralism; music as objective material versus music as emotional expression; and the investigation of sound and exploration of time.

For Ole Buck (b. 1945), the simple, clearly perceptible processes of concretism formed a basis for personal lyricism in his *Summer Trio* (1968), and repetitive structures related to American minimalism were heard in *Punctuations* for orchestra (1968). In the light of musical pluralism, Karl Aage Rasmussen (b. 1947) pursued the idea of "music on music." His *Symphony for Young Lovers* (1967) interwove quotations from European music, jazz and popular melodies. The *Symphonie classique* (1969) assembles clichés from Vienna classicism while maintaining an ironic distance to both the musical tradition and system-oriented modernism. As a teenager, Poul Ruders (b. 1949) was struck by the powerful and direct musical expression that he experienced when listening to a recording of Penderecki's *Threnody*. His debut as a composer was the piano piece *Three Letters from the Unknown Soldier* (1967), pervaded by violent contrasts and emotional effects. Strong expression remains the chief concern of his music.

Ole Buck, Karl Aage Rasmussen, Poul Ruders and the slightly younger Hans Abrahamsen (b. 1952) become prominent figures in the 1970s, leading Danish music in new directions.

Ray Robinson
West Palm Beach

The United States in the 1950s and 1960s

A discussion of American music in the 1950s and 1960s is unthinkable without at least some reference to Charles Ives (1874-1954). If there is one composer who blazed the trail for the avant garde movement in the United States, it is Ives. Called by Aaron Copland, "a genius in a wasteland," Ives almost single-handedly established an American musical idiom, actually fore-shadowing many of the new directions usually credited to far more prominent composers. An insurance salesman by day and a composer by night Ives left a truly impressive string of accomplishments. Before he was finished he had explored atonality, quotation and collage composition, free rhythm, quarter-tone harmony, poly-metrics, poly-tonalities and even different kinds of music, employing unconventional combinations of instruments, placing musicians in various acoustic positions, allowing a degree of freedom to the performer, and introducing many of the techniques that challenged composers in the mid-twentieth century. He seems to lurk in the background of every contemporary American style. He had learned early in life from his most important teacher - his father - that there were no rules in music, that the world of sounds was open for experiment and innovative solutions. Ives was America's first "avant garde" composer! It became the task of his followers to build on his trail-blazing experiments.

THE SITUATION AT THE MID-20TH CENTURY

By the mid-century a number of American composers had established themselves as important musical voices. Aaron Copland (1900-1990), Roy Harris (1898-1981) and Louise Talma (1906-1996) were composers who, like Ives, consciously and deliberately based their style on the American folk idiom (including jazz). Samuel Barber (1910-1981) and Walter Piston (1894-1976), widely recognized for their craftsmanship, rooted their compositions in more traditional idioms. Carl Ruggles (1876-1971), Wallingford Riegger (1885-1961), Roger Sessions (1896-1985) and Elliott

Carter (b. 1908) were writing in more advanced styles, including atonal and serial music, without necessarily being thought of as experimental composers. And innovators like Henry Cowell (1897-1965), who invented the prepared piano and composed using cluster chords, his student John Cage (1912-1992), who explored electronic and chance idioms, Henry Brandt (b. 1913), an explorer of spatial music, and Milton Babbitt (b. 1916) were already recognized even in the 1940s as "experimentalists". Of this group of composers, Copland and Sessions would experiment briefly with serial technique, Cage and Babbitt would assume leadership roles in the wider avant garde movement and Carter would gain in respect and stature as he nurtured a long and illustrious career.

SERIALISM AND THE AVANT GARDE MOVEMENT

Arnold Schoenberg's death in Los Angeles at the beginning of the decade of the 1950s (July 13, 1951) might be seen symbolically as the event that passed the torch to a new generation of serialist composers. But it is interesting that the revival of interest in the system, which took place after the war, occurred not in middle Europe, where serialism was conceived, but primarily in France and the United States. There were good reasons for this strange turn of events. First and foremost, the Nazi problem had driven Schoenberg and his pupils out of Germany and Austria, and it was in Paris and America that they settled. But equally significant was the fact that in the period after World War II a new generation of American composers was stimulated by a desire to start afresh and construct new works in this idiom.

While Milton Babbitt (b. 1916) was not a Schoenberg student, he would nevertheless assume an important leadership role in the development of serial composition in the United States. His careful craftsmanship and his brilliant solutions to compositional problems influenced many younger composers, including James K. Randall (b. 1929), Donald Martino (b. 1931), Peter Westergaard (b. 1931) and Fred Lerdahl (b. 1943). Trained as a mathematician, Babbitt set out to investigate the theoretical implications of serial music and arrived at total organization before the European experimentalists. He produced his first serial composition (*Three Compositions for Piano*) in 1947, but his approach was more innovative than that of Boulez and Stockhausen. Applying his mind to the mathematical properties of serialism as a system, Babbitt invented rhythmic serial procedures that had a close affinity with the techniques conventionally used in the twelve-tone method. In contrast to his European colleagues, who had simply used an arithmetical scale of durations from, say, one thirty-second note to twelve (a quarter note), choosing that range because there are twelve notes in the chromatic scale, Babbitt created subtle and ingenious ways of dealing with something at first ignored by the European serialists, namely that pitch has a regular repeating unit, the octave, for which some rhythmic equivalent must be found.[1]

Another American who was attracted by the music and thought of the Second Viennese School is Babbitt's contemporary, George Perle (b. 1915), a brilliant writer as well as an influential composer, teacher and theorist. But his interest was not so much in the 12-tone system itself as in the idea of a creating a generalized systematic approach to dodecaphonic composition. In contrast to Babbitt, who was influenced by Schoenberg and Webern, Perle found his models in Berg and Bartók and his twelve-tone modal system codifies procedures of harmonic incidence that he discovered in their works. His pupil Paul Lansky (b. 1944) describes Perle's system as one that "creates a hierarchy among the notes of the chromatic scale so that they are all referentially related to one or two pitches which then function as a tonic chord or chord in tonality."[2] In opposition to other serialist composers of the period, the sound of Perle's works and the manner in which he unfolds his musical ideas are straightforward and relatively uncomplicated as seen in *Three Movements for Orchestra* (1960) and String Quartet No. 5 (1960, rev. 1967).

George Rochberg (b. 1918), who discovered the expressive potential of dodecaphony after meeting Luigi Dallapiccola in Rome (1950), went through a typical history of post-Schoenbergian and post-Webernian serialism in the 1950s and early 1960s. After the Piano Trio (1963), his last serial piece, he adopted an idiom that mixed abstract chromaticism with tonal idioms and quotation. In *Contra mortem et tempus* (1965) for four instruments, Rochberg quotes from Boulez, Berio, Varèse and Ives. Quotation from the tonal repertory is carried to a higher degree of synthesis in such works as the Third String Quartet (1972), in which he quotes Mahler and later Beethoven.

---

[1] Babbitt's innovations in serialism are discussed in significant detail by Paul Griffiths in *Modern Music and After* (London, 1995), pp. 59–69.

[2] John Lansky, "Perle, George," in: *Dictionary of Twentieth-Century Music*, edited by John Vinton (London, 1974), p. 568.

Among Babbitt's students at Princeton, Peter Westergaard (b. 1931) is recognized for his contributions to serial theory[3] and also for his compositions, in which a Webernian approach to symmetry and mirror relationship is allied to a Babbitt-like regard for the systematic and integrated use of all parameters. These techniques are revealed in the *Quartet 1960* (cl, vib, vln, vc) and the chamber opera *Mr and Mrs Discobbolos* after King Lear (1965).

Other prominent American serialists of the period include Charles Wuorinen (b. 1938), who attracted early attention by winning the New York Philharmonic's Young Composer's award at the age of 16, and Stefan Wolpe (1902-1972), the German-born American composer. Wuorinen's compositional output includes a large number of works that feature a solo instrument, whether alone, appearing within a chamber group, or heard against an orchestra as demonstrated in *Chamber Concerto* for Cello and Ten Players (1963). His setting of abundant and often extravagant imagery within clear forms and calculated contrapuntal textures suggests a peculiarly modern form of neo-classicism which one finds in works like *Politics of Harmony* (1966-67), a theater piece scored for alto, tenor and bass soloists with chamber orchestra. His major electronic composition - *Time's Encomium* (1968) - was awarded the Pulitzer Prize in 1970.

Already a brilliant pianist and formidable conductor, Wuorinen co-founded (with Harvey Sollberger) the Group for Contemporary Music in 1962, an ensemble that set a new performance standard for modern music. Stefan Wolpe's *Piece for Two Instrumental Units* (1962) and *Trio in Two Parts* for Flute, Cello and Piano (1964), works that sought to achieve a synthesis between moment form and integral serialism, were both written for and first performed by the Group.

ELECTRONIC MUSIC

Serialism was not the only force in the music of the 1950s and 1960s: there was also the new medium of electronic music. The invention of the tape recorder presented composers with a flexible, versatile means of recording and storing sounds, of changing them in pitch and rhythm by altering the playback speed, of superimposing them, and of rearranging

[3] See Westergaard's article: "Towards a Twelve-tone Polyphony," in *Perspectives of New Music* 4:2 (1966), pp. 90–112.

them in any order. These few techniques made possible the true birth of electronic music composition. Following the pioneer work of Varèse (*Poème électronique*) and other Europeans like Pierre Schaeffer and Pierre Henry (Paris), Americans could be found working with this new medium in every corner of the country. The Tape Music Studio at Columbia University (later to become the Columbia-Princeton Electronic Music Center) was established in 1951, only three years after the founding of the Paris Studio. Then the Moog synthesizer came on the market in 1964 and made it possible for virtually anyone to become an electronic music composer.[4]

In contrast to Europe where electronic studios were organized primarily around radio stations and industrial companies, the development of the medium in the United States depended on the entrepreneurial ability of individual composers and universities. In addition to the efforts at Columbia University in New York, where Varèse completed work on his *Deserts* tapes (1961), Gordon Mumma (b. 1935) and Robert Ashley (b. 1930) founded the Cooperative Studio for Electronic Music at Ann Arbor, Michigan (1958), Morton Subotnick (b. 1933) and others worked at the San Francisco Tape Music Center (1960), and various universities, notably the University of Illinois at Urbana, organized their own studios.

The Russian-born, American composer Vladimir Ussachevsky (1911-1990) initiated the earliest American experiments in the electronic medium at Columbia University (1951). He is also credited with the initial American demonstration of the new medium's potential in 1952, when he and his teacher Otto Luening (1900-1996), presented a concert of electronic music at the Museum of Modern Art in New York on October 28, 1952. Ussachevsky's *Sonic Contours* (1952), characteristic of Schaeffer's early studies from piano recordings, and Luening's *Fantasy in Space* (1952), which similarly extends the possibilities of the flute, are representative of their efforts, which were eventually to lead to the establishment of the Columbia-Princeton Electronic Music Center in New York (1960).

Whereas Babbitt's point of departure as an electronic composer was Schoenberg's twelve-tone method, John Cage (1912-1992), who had

[4] The Moog Synthesizer, designed by the American inventor Robert A. Moog (b. 1934), in collaboration with the composer Herbert A. Deutsch, was marketed for the first time in 1964. With the success of Walter Carlos's "Switched-on Bach" recording (February 1969), which uses the Moog Synthesizer, Moog's name, perhaps more than any other, became associated with the commercial electronic synthesizer.

studied with Cowell, and for a short time with Schoenberg, began with a re-examination of the raw material of music: sound! Cage's interest in electronic music went back long before the work of Ussachevsky-Luening to a 1937 essay[5] and the works that followed it, like, for example, the pieces for prepared piano, *Bacchanale* (1940) and *Sonatas and Interludes* (1946-48) in which he adjusted the timbres of the piano by placing screws, nuts, bolts and other items to alter the sounds of as many as 45 notes. In contrast to Ussachevsky, Luening and Babbitt, Cage was not affiliated with an academic institution (he worked in the private studio of Louis and Bebe Barron who were responsible in 1956 for the first electronic film music, *Forbidden Planet*); he also differed from the Columbia-Princeton composers in his view of tape as a medium of collage rather than as a distorting mirror. He went on to apply chance methods to the electronic medium in *Imaginary Landscapes No. 5* (1951-52) and *Williams Mix* (1952).

Despite their significantly different approaches, Cage and Babbitt arrived at a common ground in creating music by electronic means. While Babbitt's following in this area was actually very small, for the intellectual discipline he required was so rigorous, Cage was backed by patrons of the visual arts, and by dancers like Merce Cunningham, and relatively soon developed a wide platform for his ideas. Working at the Columbia-Princeton Center, Babbitt's early electronic pieces – *Composition for Synthesizer* (1960-61) and *Ensembles for Synthesizer* (1962-64) – were created on a large synthesizer, an organ-like instrument, with an enormous range of stops. Babbitt utilized the instrument to its fullest potential by employing quasi-orchestral polyphonies within the equal-tempered twelve-tone scale. His most appealing work combining live performance with tape is *Philomel* (1964).

Among the many electronic composers of the era, the Argentinian born Mario Davidovsky (b. 1934), Morton Subotnick and Charles Dodge (b. 1942) should be mentioned. Davidovsky is best known for compositions successfully combining live instrumental performance with recorded electronic sounds, and in particular for the *Synchronisms* nos. 1 (1962), 3

[5] John Cage, "The Future of Music: Credo," in: *Silence* (Middletown, Connecticut, 1961), p. 4. A commentary by the composer on this early reference to electronic music: "The following text was delivered as a talk at a meeting of a Seattle arts society organized by Bonnie Bird in 1937. It was printed in the brochure accompanying George Avakian's recording of my twenty-five-year retrospective concert at Town Hall, New York in 1958."

(1964), 5 (1969) and 6 (1970); while Subotnick used electronic devices, such as the sequencer, which could store a cycle of instructions, in his *Silver Apples of the Moon* (1967) and *The Wild Bull* (1968). The electronic music of Dodge is based on the computer's ability to analyze speech submitted to it and then to use this analysis in the creation of speech sounds, on to which the composer can impose new pitches, timbres and durations. Dodge realizes these possibilities in *The Story of Our Lives* (1974), a miniature opera for one male and one female singer, and *Celebration* (1975).

CHANCE, INDETERMINACY AND IMPROVISATION

Total serialism and electronic music had become the wave of the future in the New Music, reaching their apex in 1951, the year of Boulez's *Structures* and Stockhausen's *Kreuzspiel*. But 1951 also saw the entrance of chance as a critical element in the music of John Cage, and it was through the acceptance of innovations in this area that new fields were to be opened to composers in Europe and America. Cage, who introduced the concept of indeterminacy at a Darmstadt lecture in 1958, soon turned his attention almost completely to chance occurrence.

It was his studies in Eastern philosophies with Gita Sarabhai and of Zen Buddhism with Daisetz T. Suzuki that were decisive in this new direction. Aided further by the formulations of a Hindu philosopher, Amanda K. Coomaraswamy, that "all arts should imitate Nature in her manner of operation," Cage concluded that music, instead of communicating thoughts or feelings, should become an "ending process without any design." At this point he turned to the ancient Chinese Book of *I-Ching* [Book of Changes], whose intricate chance operations from then on directed his choice of sounds. In producing *Music of Changes* for piano (1951), he tossed coins to decide how he should make choices from charts of pitches, durations, intensities and other sound aspects. Similar methods were used in notating the parts for *Imaginary Landscapes No. 4* (1951).

Cage was also fascinated with the relationship between sound and silence; his definition of silence being "sounds not intended." Based on this premise, he created *4′33″* (1952), a piece for piano, composed entirely of not-intended sounds - silence. "Written" in three movements of silence, at its first performance the pianist David Tudor opened and covered the keyboard to indicate the separation of the movements.

By the 1950s Cage had attracted a group of like-minded colleagues in New York, among them the pianist David Tudor (1926-1996), and the composers Earle Brown (b. 1926), Morton Feldman (b. 1926) and Christian Wolff (b. 1934). The group also had associations with visual artists of the period, including Alexander Calder (1898-1976), Mark Rothko (1903-1970), Willem de Kooning (1904-1997) and Jackson Pollock (1912-1956). Brown, who took note of what he called "the creative function of non-control" in their work, introduced indeterminacy at the level of form. He is given credit for pioneering such concepts as graphic notation, time-notation and the element of open form. His "open forms," influenced by Calder's mobiles, are typified in *Available Forms I* (1961), in which each of the score's six unbound pages specifies four or five events; the conductor, who has general control over dynamics and velocity, begins with any event on any page, and creates from the available materials an individually shaped version of the work.

Geometrical means, or "graphic scores," were to be a common working method for Wolff, Brown, and particularly Feldman in the 1960s. The latter's numerous *Projections* and *Intersections,* as well as a large group of other works, are all written in a graphic system. Wolff was interested in China-style socialism, and his *Accompaniments I* (1972), a work for singing pianist, has a text that solemnly praises progress made in sanitation, contraception and infant care under Chairman Mao.

Among other composers interested in the aleatory process are Lukas Foss (b. 1922) and Lou Harrison (1917-2003). Foss, the German-born American composer-conductor, formulated what he called "system and chance music," a kind of controlled improvisation. He subsequently produced a series of highly original works, such as *Time Cycle* (1959-60), *Echoi* (1963), a Cello Concerto (1965) and *Fragments of Archilocos* (1966). Harrison is recognized for his percussion music, experiments with just intonation, and syntheses of Asian and Western Styles. His works employ Chinese, Korean and Indonesian instruments as well as Western instruments and those of his own construction.

QUOTATION, COLLAGE AND MULTI-MEDIA THEATER

Quotation is certainly not a new phenomenon in American music. Composers from Charles Ives to George Crumb (b. 1929) include excerpts from earlier works in their scores. But attempts at bridging the gulf between present and past by juxtaposing current and traditional musical idioms are explored by many American composers in the 1960s. Rochberg's *Contra mortem et tempus* (1965), the orchestral piece *Music for the Magic Theater* (1956), the Third Symphony (1968) and the String Quartet No. 3, which won the Naumberg Chamber Composition Award (1972), are based largely on quotation. George Crumb (b. 1929) uses quotations from Bach, Schubert and Chopin in *Night of the Four Moons* (1969). His *Makrokosmos I* (1972) for amplified piano quotes the middle section of Chopin's *Fantasie-Impromptu* in "Dream Images" (Love-Death Music).

The first fully developed examples of collage are to be found in the works of Ives (although he did not use the term to describe these pieces). While works like *Three Places in New England* (movement 2) and Symphony No. 4 (the second movement and the transcendent spiritual experience in the finale) were originally performed and published between 1927 and 1937, no other American composer became interested in this medium until the 1950s and 1960s. Cage's *Imaginary Landscape no. 5* is a work that might also be characterized as a musical collage.

Cage was influential in one other area of experimental composition in the 1960s. Among the more diverse, less prescriptive and often theatrical "multi-media" activities with which he was associated, *Variations V* (1965) extends the notion of collage in several directions at the same time. Because "theatrical-performance music" has a longer history in the United States than in Europe, it became much more widespread in the 1960s in America, especially on campuses like the Universities of Michigan, Illinois and California. These scores might contain conventional notation, coupled with instructions for movement and similar activities, but more generally they comprise instructions for gestures, speech, movement and free sounds. It is possible that there would be no score in notation, and the essential aspects of performances are lighting effects and the inclusion of films, slides, and taped sounds.

Indeterminacy is often an important factor in Cage's theater; his *Theatre Piece* (1960) can be performed by one to eight performers, including musicians, dancers, singers, "to be used in whole or part in any combination." Eric Salzman's (b. 1933) *The Nude Paper Sermon* (1968-69) is only one of the more clever essays in pastiche, stylistic heterogeneity and deliberate abandonment of linear consequence, where the "sermon," read by an actor, takes a circuitous path through assortments of speech, song and instrumental playing, including a madrigal set in fake 16th-century style as a "ruin."

MINIMALISM AND FLUXUS

The origins of minimal music, which later attracted composers like Górecki, Pärt and Tavener, can be traced to the early works of LaMonte Young (b. 1935). While still a student at the University of California in Berkeley, he showed his *Trio for Strings* (1958) to his composition teacher Seymour Shifrin, who organized its first performance in an unsuccessful attempt to show Young the error of his ways. The *Trio,* composed entirely of long tones and rests, some lasting a minute or more, is now generally recognized as a defining work in the minimalist movement, and Young as its founder. The Americans Terry Riley (b. 1935), Steve Reich (b. 1936), Philip Glass (b. 1937) and Young are widely considered pioneers in the evolution of this genre.

It should be noted in passing that the approach of early minimalist composers in the United States had more in common with the still basically modernist idea of minimalist art than with the post modernist aesthetic in musical composition. Steve Reich's music is a case in point. His polished, patterned surfaces could be compared with those produced in the paintings of Bridget Riley. In *Four Organs* (1970), the mind is mesmerized by repetition, put into such a state that small motifs can leap out of the music with a distinctness quite unrelated to their acoustic dominance.

La Monte Young and George Brecht (b. 1926) were among a limited number of Americans who were attracted to Fluxus, an international art movement that began on June 9, 1962 at the Galerie Parnass in Wuppertal, Germany, and whose American center was New York. This movement flourished in the United States during the period 1960-65. Founded by George Maciunas, a Lithuanian artist and architect, Fluxus composers rejoiced in the musical potential of unconventional sounds, such as smashing a violin in Nam June Paik's *One for Violin Solo*. They pioneered a new genre of performance art called "short forms" or "events", which consisted of brief instructions, actually no longer than a sentence or two, defining a limited activity of some sort to be carried out by one performer. Young's *Composition 1960 no. 10,* for example, instructs a performer to draw a straight line and follow it; while Brecht's *Drip Music* (*Drip Event*) explains simply that: "A source of dripping water and an empty vessel are arranged so that the water falls into the vessel."

THIRD STREAM MUSIC

Gunther Schuller (b. 1925), a professional horn player, conductor and self-taught composer, coined the term "third stream music" in 1957 in a lecture at Brandeis University to describe a type of music which, through improvisation or written composition or both, synthesizes the essential characteristics and techniques of contemporary Western art music and other musical traditions. At the heart of the concept is the idea that any music stands to profit from a confrontation with another; thus Western art music can learn a great deal from the rhythmic vitality and "swing" of jazz, while jazz can find new avenues of development in the large-scale forms and complex tonal systems of classical music.[6]

Schuller's own works in this direction are concerned with bringing principles of twelve-tone composition into jazz, i.e. *Conversations* for jazz quartet and String Quartet (1959). At the same time, he has derived powerful impulses from visual forms, and several of his compositions are intended as musical analogues of paintings or sculpture. In the *Seven Studies on Themes of Paul Klee* (1959), he sought a retranslation into musical terms of the musical elements in certain Klee pictures. His opera, *The Visitation* (1965), based on Kafka's *The Trial*, was received enthusiastically at its Hamburg (Germany) première. Composers associated with the Third Stream Movement in the United States include Larry Austin (*Improvisations for Orchestra and Jazz Soloists*), Milton Babbitt (*All Set*), Ran Blake (*Jim Crow, Silver Fox, Vanguard, Doktor Mabuse, Olivier Messiaen, Sontagism*), Ornette Coleman (*Forms and Sounds*), Don Ellis (*Improvisational Suite No. 1*), J.J. Johnson (*Poem for Brass*), William Russo (*Egdon Heath*), Gunther Schuller (*Variants on a Theme of Thelonius Monk*) and Alec Wilder (*Jazz Suite*).

[6] Gunther Schuller, Third Stream. In *The New Grove Dictionary of American Music,* Vol. IV (London, 1986), p. 377.

Central and Eastern Europe

Andrzej Chłopecki
Warsaw

The New Music of East-Central Europe: Between Thaw and Freeze

We have grown accustomed to perceiving the history of composition in a selective or even an instrumental way. We see the music of the 1950s and 1960s through, above all, the prism of the striking intensification of attitudes that were innovatory, modernistic, and to a large measure avant garde, thus concentrating on a relatively narrow segment of musical reality. The central point in our attention is therefore occupied by the group of phenomena that, on the European scene, we define with the metaphorical term "Darmstadt School," against the background of the enterprises of John Cage and the American artists associated with him – an alternative but, nevertheless, an avant garde alternative. This focusing in an *a priori* way on a selected group of composers and musical centers has elevated them to the rank of phenomena defining the spirit of the age and best embodying historical development. It is worth noting that such chosen concert practices of the period as serialism and aleatorism, happening and graphical music, electroacoustic music and instrumental theatre, and topophonic and stochastic music, intriguing though they may have been, remain nevertheless on the margin of the broad current in which contemporary music flowed. These practices were the alternative gestures of the younger generation of composers, who wanted to use the tones of their new scores and the gestures of their new ideas, both technical and esthetic, to be able to exist in a space symbolized by such names as Shostakovich and Kódaly, Stravinsky and Britten, Hindemith and Martin, to name only a few of the best known creators of twentieth-century music. It was these latter names who set the tone for music in the 1950s.

When looking at the changes that the music of the East-Central European countries went through at a time when the syndrome of the flourishing of avant garde tendencies against the background of the modernistic space of Euro-American music was drawing the special attention of critics and musicologists, it is worth observing carefully the context that accompanied the trends, attitudes, and musical works that were coming into being. The phenomena of contemporary music, too, were divided in the late 1940s, the 1950s, and, to a significant degree, the 1960s as well, by an ideological iron curtain into, on the one hand, the political space subordinated to the Soviet Union and, on the other, the space generally conceived of as the West. There is no room here to characterize the social, civilizational, and cultural differences between these spaces. It is nevertheless worth noting the specifics of this difference exclusively in the area of musical composition. Particularly in the first phase of this period, two ideological doctrines stood facing each other. Naming the first of them causes no problems: it was the doctrine of socialist realism (there is no point going into the ruminations over its essence and form that went on at the time) – the calling card of the East. The other side demands somewhat more extensive discussion, and could be defined using the term "the ideology of anti-ideology."

Let us observe at this point that the International New Music Summer Courses in Darmstadt were called into existence in 1946, right after the conclusion of the war and with the support of the American administration, as an educational facility intended above all to restore the art that had been sentenced as long ago as 1933 to elimination or banishment in the fatherland of the concept of "Degenerate Art" (*entartete Kunst*), the country where the struggle against this art and these artists had been carried out. Germany and that whole part of Europe that had been subjected to Nazi rule for a longer or shorter period of several or more than a dozen years wanted not only to open the doors to the figures and attitudes that had had to take shelter in either an actual or "inner" emigration, and invite them back into normal life. This was more than a matter of posthumous justice for those who were prevented by the barbarity of history from living to see the end of the war. It also had to do with assimilating the values denied by Nazi ideology. Note must be taken of the fact that the prominent figures in German music of the 1960s and 1970s –

composers as well as musicologists and theoreticians - were encountering for the first time in their lives not only the music, but even the names of Webern, Hindemith or Varèse when they traveled as twenty-somethings to Darmstadt in the early 1950s, at almost the same time as their Polish colleagues behind the political iron curtain. The avant garde that arose in and around the Darmstadt circle thus chose, as its ideological slogans, "Down with ideology" or "Down with any sort of ideology." Music means music itself. It is a non-semantic art. Music can serve no ends beyond itself, neither ideology nor worldview. Yet, at the same time, it can and should be politically engaged. A paradox? Yes. The sharp Hegelian edge and persuasive force of the Frankfurt philosophical and esthetic schools, featuring Theodor Wiesengrund Adorno as the bearer of the truth about the morality of musical art? Yes. Antifascism and anti-ideology, as a (paradoxically) leftist and para-communist ideology lie at the basis of the avant garde Western attitude of the time, a basis that resonates to a degree with the party ideology of the East at the same time that it leads to diametrically opposite results in esthetic expression. Art is to be socialist in form and national in expression, proclaimed the doctrine of socialist realism. Art is to be communist in its message, but the concept of subject matter does not apply to it, proclaimed the convoluted thesis of the western avant garde. This avant garde was perceived by the East as degenerate and formalistic art, as a bourgeois product of the "rotten" West.

The process of achieving creative freedom in the East-Central European countries was thus a process of loosening and dismantling the ideological doctrine of socialist realism in order to introduce to the poetics of composition the technical and expressive means formed in the countries of Western Europe and the USA. The avant garde gesture of creating these means was accepted sooner or later in various countries of East-Central Europe as a gesture that was already well-born, borrowed, and therefore eclectic. It was superimposed on local tradition, after all, and did not preserve its innocence in the majority of instances.

It is a paradox all of its own that the group of Russian composers (or, more properly, citizens of the Soviet Union of various ethnic backgrounds) regarded as the Russian avant garde group, as a phenomenon functioning on the boundary of the alternative and dissident movements and symbolized by such names as Andrey Volkonsky (b. 1933, for all intents and purposes the first dodecaphonist in postwar Russian music), and especially Alfred Schnittke (1934-1998), Edison Denisov (1929-1996) and Sofia Gubaidulina (b. 1931) reached for the idiom of the Western avant garde, variously conceived and assimilated, in the 1960s not as a gesture of opposition but out of a feeling of profound esthetic, ideological, and sentimental links with, above all, the work of Dimitri Shostakovich. Despite the fact that Shostakovich had been built up into the leading light of the Soviet music that expressed the idea of the communist Motherland, primarily as a result of at least a part of his cantata-oratorio work, this work - especially but not also the chamber music - became at the same time a tradition to be taken up by the next generation of composers in the Soviet Union and especially, but not only, in Russia. By generations, we might add, that were seeking a new direction in which to grow and opening up to the world of contemporary music in the Western countries while turning away from the esthetics of socialist realism, as a result of which they were relegated to the margins by the mechanisms that controlled the most important centers of musical life.

The respect accorded to Shostakovich and the way he and his music were treated as artistic authorities by the generation of composers that created the particular syndrome of the avant garde in the Soviet Union does not contradict the fact that the "guru" of this generation, above all in Moscow, was the man who introduced this generation to the Viennese School of Arnold Schoenberg and the poetics of Anton Webern as early as the 1950s, Philipp Herschkovitsch, Webern's student of Rumanian-Jewish origins who emigrated from Vienna to Moscow in 1945 and emigrated from the Soviet Union in the late 1980s. Herschkovitsch's private and entirely informal work as a musical educator, consisting of listening at home to recordings and studying and analyzing Vienna School scores that were not officially available in the Soviet Union, can be compared on the one hand to the later efforts of the democratic opposition in other countries of East-Central Europe known as "flying universities." On the other hand, however, Herschkovitsch's influence on the new esthetic consciousness arising in Moscow, thanks to the reception of the achievements of the school of Schoenberg, can, of course, within the strict limits imposed by the communist police-state system, be compared in its own way with the familiarization of Paris circles with the Vienna School thanks to René Leibowitz (1913-1972). Philipp Herschkovitsch's influence ended up being highly important for two generations of composers - the generation born in the late 1920s and early 1930s, and the next, born around 1950 and including Jelena Firssova (b. 1950), Dmitri Smirnov (b.1948) and Nikolai Korndorff (1947-2001), many of whom emigrated from Russia at the same time as their master, thus opening the esthetic perspective of Russian music to other values than those of the avant garde.

The Moscow syndrome described above, the acceptance as one's own of a tradition acknowledged by the authorities (leaving aside here the numerous perturbations that accompanied this acknowledgement and the brutal stamp that it left on the mind and on many pages of the works of Shostakovich), and, as if in equal measure, the acceptance as one's own of a tradition conveyed in the catacomb-like conditions of "secret meetings" and exposed to police harassment, may serve as a metaphorical image of the history of the New Music in almost all of the part of Europe that was subject to Soviet hegemony, although this syndrome, of course, went through numerous local modifications. For Hungarians, including György Ligeti (b. 1923) and György Kurtág (b. 1926), the work of Béla Bartók and, in part, that of Zoltán Kodaly became a starting point on the road to the contemporary in the mid-1950s in a natural way and without being treated in any way as an *à rebours* value. For Poles, it was above all Karol Szymanowski's "middle" period, and for Czechs the microtonic Alois Hába (1893-1973) and, to a certain degree, Bohuslav Martinů (1890-1959) – greats whose modernist creative attitudes were acknowledged as important values in the music of the first half of the twentieth century. It is a paradox that the passage to innovation in the mid-1950s occurred in a more evolutionary manner in these countries than it did in the countries of the West, and especially in German circles. In both places, the reception of the Vienna School provided the main impulse, but it meshed better in the East with local traditions above or off to the side of the doctrine of socialist realism than it did in the West, which was still recovering from the Nazi plague. In the West, paradoxically, it came as more of a shock. That is why the concept of the "avant garde" can be relatively more easily accepted for certain musical phenomena in the West at the beginning of the 1950s, while only with difficulty can it be fitted to the needs of the music of the East during the violent transformation a decade later.

Let us take a generalized, panoramic view of the history of East-Central European music at the time when, after the death of Stalin, and precisely in around 1956, the time of the "thaw" came to the whole eastern bloc. For composers, this was a time of liberalization when it became possible to reject the doctrine of socialist realism. We should remember that Andrey Zhdanov, the main ideologue of the doctrine, died in December 1948, almost immediately after the international conference of composers and musicologists in Prague that made the doctrine obligatory throughout the eastern bloc, but before specific instructions were issued to particular countries in 1949. The second half of the 1950s thus offered a political opportunity above all to music (which did not always require words or music) – a chance to cast off the ideological yoke. Poland seized the chance most effectively by founding the international Warsaw Autumn contemporary music festival (1956), of European significance. When the authorities attacked the festival on political grounds in subsequent years, this was seen as an attack on cultural freedom carried out in full view of European culture. Thanks to its international prestige, this festival could blackmail the authorities. Too violent an attack would have compromised the authorities in European eyes – the last thing the leadership wanted. With its festival, Warsaw became a site for East-West musical dialogue, a place where people from Sofia, Moscow or Prague who were not free to travel to Paris, Cologne or London could exchange experiences and calling cards while meeting informally with people who would not be given a visa to Sofia, Moscow or Prague. One way or another, and after going through cumbersome passport and visa procedures on both sides, it was possible to come to Warsaw on musical business.

It was not the East-Central European musical circles of the day who created an institution like the Warsaw Autumn Festival, which could exert political pressure on local authorities fearful of international disgrace. While the first Festival was underway in October 1956, Władysław Gomułka was released from prison and took up the post of communist party first secretary, Polish Roman Catholic primate Stefan Wyszyński was released from internment, and the Red Army threatened Poland with armed intervention. Poland escaped this threat. Had the invasion occurred, the history of music in the late twentieth century would not have been the same.

Instead of Poland, the tanks struck Budapest several weeks later. Under their gun barrels, neither György Ligeti nor György Kurtág had the conditions they needed for creating new forms of musical expression. Both were soon in the West; the former as an *émigré* who had crossed the open border illegally and the latter on a scholarship to Paris. Kurtág went home to Budapest, and waited longer for artistic recognition than Ligeti. Pál Kadosa saw to it that Hungarian music remained noble in an abject time. Above the gun barrels of the Warsaw Pact tanks, Hungarian music fulfilled its mission in a space not bounded by the state's border posts. Notably, it was the *émigré* Ligeti (like the Greek *émigré* in Paris, Iannis Xenakis, who had been sentenced to death in his homeland and been struck in the face by a shell fragment during the Greek civil war, or like Krzysztof Penderecki, who was a romantic in his sonoristic gestures) who became one of the main schismatics within the western musical avant garde, when his "super-complete" polyphony opened new perspectives for the new music of the West and constituted a polemic with serialism. It would be many years before Europe discovered the Webernian purity of Kurtág's chamber scores, "infected" by the vision embodied in Stockhausen's *Gruppen* - to be present at the 1958 première of which Kurtág stopped in Cologne on his way home from Paris to Budapest.

The Warsaw Pact tanks rolled into Prague in August 1968 to kill off the vision of "socialism with a human face" and bring the "Prague Spring" to an end. What did they kill from among the things born in Czech music since the 1950s? Although Czech new wave work had been presented at the Warsaw Autumn Festival, it was insufficiently recognized as a new tone in that region of Europe. Yet the work of the Czech visionaries, with its "Schweikian" minimalism, experiments with graphic music, contemplative qualities long before these qualities became characteristic of the music of the West in the 1970s, and attempts to transform the experience of the passage of musical time - all these valuable, groundbreaking essays in new expression were brutally denied an international reception as a result of the military aggression. History killed the strange, slightly dadaistic and slightly surrealistic scores, with values waiting to be discovered, of Rudolf Komorous (b. 1931), Jan Rychlík (1916-1964), Josef Berg (1927-1971) and Zbynek Vostřák (1920-1985), to name but a few of those who began shaping Czech avant garde music in the 1960s but, after the invasion, either emigrated into obscurity (like Komorous to Canada), or lived out their lives in oblivion, expelled from the Union of Czechoslovak Composers and making a living in occupations that were strange for people of culture but at least permitted them to maintain their biological existence.

What was happening in East-Central Europe in the period of interest to us, the 1950s and the 1960s, the springtime of the composers of the peoples inhabiting this part of Europe?

The Czechs and a large part of the European cultural space with them realize that the country's *moderne* composers, Czech Germans of Jewish origins, were murdered in the Theresienstadt, Auschwitz or Wüllzburg camps in 1942-44: Erwin Schulhoff (1894-1942), Victor Ullmann (1898-1944), Hans Krasa (1899 - 1944) and Pavel Haas (1899 - 1944). Unaware of this heritage, the road towards the contemporary was followed by Viktor Kalabis (b. 1923), Svatopluk Havelka (b. 1925), Otmar Macha (b. 1922), and Petr Eben (b. 1929), who blazed the trail for Pavel Blatny (b. 1931), Marek Kopelent (b. 1932) and Jan Klusák (b. 1934). The new tone of Czech music, as soon as it emerged from the time of petrification mandated for Czech culture by the gun barrels of the Warsaw Pact tanks, was set by the musical generation born in the mid-1950s: Martin Smolka (b. 1959), Petr Kofroň (b. 1955), and others their age, who only with difficulty can be shoehorned into the syndrome of the avant garde *moderne*: they belong to the post-avant garde post-*moderne*.

Slovak musical culture also had values from which it could benefit on the road towards contemporary late-twentieth-century music, and it did so. The composers were Eugene Suchoň (b. 1908), Alexander Moyzes (1906-1984) and Ján Cikker (b. 1911). The school of composition that coalesced around the latter two made succeeding generations of their pupils comfortable with not only the ideas of the late Stravinsky and the Vienna School, but also the ideas of serialism, aleatorism and even the happening. Slovakia was part of the Czechoslovakia that fell victim to "fraternal aid in the defense of socialism." The initiatives that vanished under military and political repression included the contemporary music seminars in Smolenice, with its ambitions of becoming the Czech Darmstadt, or the Hudba Dněska (Today's Music) group, which had become the center of the Slovak musical avant garde movement and its European ambitions. This idiom of chasing to catch up with Europe and enter into dialogue with Europe was undertaken above all in the scores of Roman Berger (b. 1930), Ilja Zeljenka (b. 1932), Josef Sixta (b. 1940), Juraj Beneš (b. 1940) and Miro Bázlik (b. 1931) who, to a large degree, opened the perspectives of the Slovak modern to postmodern esthetic horizons.

The Baltic countries and the Ukraine constituted a separate chapter when the history of contemporary music was taking shape in the mid-1950s. Incorporated into the Soviet Union, these countries continually demanded cultural autonomy with greater or lesser degrees of determination. The tradition established in Lithuanian music by Antanas Račiūnas (1905-1984), Julius Juzeliūnas (b. 1916) and Eduardas Balsys (b. 1919), but above all by Vytautas Bacevičius (1905-1970) and Balys Dvarionas (1904-1972), was put to innovative or downright groundbreaking use by the generation born in the 1930s: Vytautas Barkauskas (b. 1931), but also Bronius Kutavičius (b. 1932), Feliksas Bajoras (b. 1934), and Osvaldas Balakauskas (b. 1937), who endowed Lithuanian music with a tone that lying between the expression of the *moderne* and signs of post modernism. The same esthetic tension appears between the work of Pauls Dambis (b. 1936) and that of Peteris Vasks (b. 1946) and Peteris Plakidis (b. 1947), and between Arvo Pärt's serial scores of the 1950s and the "new medieval" scores that he wrote in the "bell" technique immediately after emigrating, as opposed to the extraordinarily powerful course of Estonian music, one of the most intriguing phenomena in today's European music, as emblemized by the names of Jaan Rääts (b. 1932) and Lepo Sumera (1950-2000).

Borys Latoszyński (1895-1986) opened the door to new tendencies in Ukrainian music. Those who attended his composition classes included Leonid Hrabovski (b. 1935), the main figure in Ukrainian modernism in the 1960s and 1970s, and Valentin Silvestrov (b. 1937), who created a highly individualistic poetics in the 1960s that assured him a distinctive place of his own in the landscape of post-modern phenomena. Note should also be taken of such composers from this generation as V. Bibik and M. Skorik. In Romania, the generation of composers whose work opened up to new tendencies in the 1960s (Anatol Vieru, Serban Niculescu, Tiberiu Olah, Dan Constantinescu, Aurel Stroe, Cornel Taranu) assumed greater significance only as long as the Ars Nova group could remain active in Cluj. Names worth mentioning in Bulgarian music include Lazar Nikolov, Aleksandr Raichev, Konstantin Iliev, Georgi Tutev, Simon Pironkov and Georgi Minchev. In Belorussia, the name to reckon with was Damian Smolski, who began composing chamber works on a mathematical basis in the 1960s. In Hungarian music of the 1970s, a group of composers associated with the New Music Studio (Laszló Sáry, Zoltan Jeney, Laszló Vidovsky and Peter Eötvös) distanced themselves from the national neo-folk tradition.

The opening of composers in the countries of East-Central Europe to the influence of Western new music, including Polish music, in the 1960s, involved a relatively small number of figures. Their paucity resulted to an ever-lessening degree from the continuation of socialist realist doctrine, and to an ever-increasing degree from conservatism and the defense of the *status quo* by the bureaucrats who dominated composers' lives through the artistic unions. The career of Tichon Chrennikov (b. 1913) is a prime example. President of the Union of Soviet Composers throughout the entire epoch, from 1948 until 1992, when the composers' associations of the various republics broke away from Moscow, Chrennikov exercised enormous influence over the shape of musical life in the area of contemporary music. Such a state of affairs combined with the stifling of democratic movements in various specific countries to freeze the tendencies that arose at the time of the thaw. Before the 1989 "Spring of the Peoples," before the rejection of communism and, even more so, the rejection of the seesaw of succeeding thaws and freezes in the countries of this part of Europe, another sort of esthetics began arising here with increasing intensity, and this is what created the post-modern situation in various ways.

Translated by William Brand

Andrzej Chłopecki
Warsaw

Polish Music 1958-1966: The Syndrome of the Double Opening

For the historian drawing lines of demarcation and undertaking to fix the periods in Polish music, there is perhaps no situation more clear-cut and obvious than the birth of the phenomenon of new music in the mid-1950s. In the early 1960s, this phenomenon was labeled "The Polish Composers' School," which carried echoes of similar definitions in other arts, such as "The Polish Film School," "The Polish Poster School," and "The Polish Jazz School." The moment was identified with the addition of the "Warsaw Autumn" festival to the Polish cultural calendar in 1956, and the addition somewhat later (in 1958) of the Polish Radio Experimental Studio to the ranks of important centers of new music in Europe.

In Poland, it was the political "thaw," which became possible after the death of Josef Stalin in March, 1953, that called to life the phenomenon of new music corresponding to what had begun arising around 1950 in such centers as the International New Music Summer Courses in Darmstadt, the electronic music studio in Cologne, and, even earlier, the concrete music studio of the Paris Radio under Pierre Schaeffer and Pierre Henry. In Poland, the "thaw" led to the political watershed that came to be called the "Polish October of 1956" – the principal events of which occurred during the very days in which a festival, which would soon come to be called the Warsaw Autumn Festival, was taking place. It is symptomatic that the initiative for holding an international festival of contemporary music in Poland came from two young composers, Kazimierz Serocki (1922-1981) and Tadeusz Baird (1928-1981) who were, along with the conductor and composer Jan Krenz (b. 1926) and in collaboration with the musicologist Stefan Jarociński, signatories of the "Grupa 49" [Group of 49] project.

The "Grupa 49" arose during the ill-famed August 1949 congress of Polish composers and musicologists in Łagów Lubuski, during which the doctrine of socialist realism was decreed to be obligatory in music. The manifesto of the "Grupa 49" can be interpreted as a compromise endorsement of imposed guidelines: the signatories announced their readiness to create music that was accessible to a wider audience, with the reservation that they would shun banality and the simplification of compositional methods. This did not happen without gestures of political obeisance – the list of works included such marginal, typically socialist-realist works as Serocki's cantata *Murarz Warszawski* [The Bricklayer of Warsaw] and Baird's *Ballada o żelaznym kubku* [The Ballad of the Iron Cup].

The work of these young composers appeared frequently in the repertoire of the Warsaw Philharmonic (which became the National Philharmonic in 1955). They involved themselves energetically in the structures of the Polish Composers' Union. This lent credibility to their initiative not only in the eyes of the authorities (Bolesław Bierut, then president of Poland and head of the communist party, approved the holding of the first festival), but also in musical circles. Witold Lutosławski, Józef Patkowski and Jan Krenz took part in the creation of the Warsaw Autumn program which, from 1958 on, became an annual event. They turned it into the main artistic undertaking of the Polish Composers' Union, as well as the main venue for new music in east-central Europe, and one of the leading venues of its kind in Europe. The festival has maintained its status to this day.

The establishment of the Warsaw Autumn Festival made possible – and even, to put things emphatically – brought about a radical change in the style of Polish music, seen in a wider perspective. The festival was never based on the personal choices of a single individual. With programming done by a repertoire commission nominated by the leadership of the Polish Composers' Union, it quite rapidly turned into the "joint property" of the musical community, and integrated that community around the basic ideas that inspired the festival. These ideas included, above all, familiarization with the stylistic phenomena in contemporary western music that had been inaccessible or accessible in a drastically limited way during the Stalinist period, when the Iron Curtain had been drawn tight; a broad retrospective of the music from the first half of the twentieth century that had been deprived of a proper reception due to the Second World War, Nazi fascism, and Stalinist ideology; and the creation of a place for dialogue between the musical art of east and west that would be free of ideological pressure.

At the time of this opening-up, Polish music was still under the particularly strong sway of neo-classicist influences as symbolized by the name of Nadia Boulanger, with whom - a few exceptions aside - a whole generation of composers had studied. This is what had set the tone for Polish music after Karol Szymanowski (1882-1937). At the threshold of the stylistic changes symbolized by the birth of the Warsaw Autumn festival, therefore, stood an important group of Polish composers with established positions in their own country and beyond its borders. Responses to the challenges of the new era varied. Grażyna Bacewicz (1909-1969) and Bolesław Szabelski (1896-1979) accepted the experience of dodecaphony and serialism, and turned to the idiomatic. This was read as a spectacular turning in the direction of the contemporary by composers who had clout, and set an example by embracing the new situation. Their neo-aesthetic works (such as Bacewicz's 1958 *Muzyka na smyczki, trąbki I perkusję* [Music for Strings, Trumpet, and Percussion], her 1960 *VI Kwartet smyczkowy* [Sixth String Quartet], and her 1961 *Pensieri notturni* for 24 instruments, or Szabelski's *Sonety* [Sonnets] for orchestra of 1958, his *Wiersze* [Verses] for piano and chamber orchestra, 1969, and his *Aforyzmy "9"* [Aphorisms 9] of 1962) were consonant with the achievements of the younger generation of Polish composers.

Above all, it was the acceptance of the twelve-tone technique, applied in various individual and non-schematic ways that were generally derived from the theoretical ideas of Arnold Schoenberg, and of the pointillist style derived from the musical aesthetics of Anton Webern, that became a sign of liberation from the days of socialist realism, when there had been a danger of being accused of musical formalism. Characteristically enough, this change occurred without the slightest reference to the tradition of the first Polish dodecaphonist, Józef Koffler (1896-1944), or to the dodecaphonic music of the Swiss composer Constantine Regamey (1907-1982), who was active in Poland from 1944 onward. It can thus be said that the syndrome of contemporaneity prevalent in Polish music at the end of the 1950s was a series of experiments under the sway, above all, of the International New Music Summer Courses in Darmstadt, which Polish composers had already begun attending in a sporadic way (Włodzimierz Kotoński and Kazimierz Serocki were the first) and where they were more and more often presenting their work.

The latter half of the 1950s thus marks a profound stylistic break in the creative work of such composers as Baird and Serocki, the founders of the Warsaw Autumn Festival. In each case, as illustrated by the scores of compositions from 1956 (Baird's *Cassazione per orchestra* and Serocki's

Sinfonietta for two string orchestras), they broke with aesthetics largely influenced by late romantic ideas.

The syndrome that might be defined as an innovative period of *Sturm und Drang* - or, simply, as the multifaceted phenomenon of "the Polish composers' school" - has been designated in the title of the present sketch with two dates: 1958 and 1966. These dates are chosen *a priori* to symbolize the beginning and end of something rich in differences and shades. The beginning is preceded by a prelude and the end has not yet played itself out. 1958 is the premiere of Lutosławski's *Muzyka żałobna* [Mourning Music] in Katowice, and 1966 is the premiere in Münster Cathedral of Krzysztof Penderecki's *St Luke Passion*. This choice of historical markers seems accurate if for no other reason than that it indicates works that are outstanding in the history not only of Polish, but also of world music - works that, furthermore, have historical contexts that themselves are turning points.

Witold Lutosławski (1913-1994) treated the *Muzyka żałobna* as the first work that he composed as he wanted to, and not as he was able to. With works in his compositorial dossier that were characterized by an intriguing originality of sound and formal concepts (*Wariacje symfoniczne* 1936-38), as well as those that were accused of formalism (*I Symfonia* 1941-47) or that constituted a crowning of the neoclassical-folklore current (*Koncert na orkiestrę* 1950-54), he created in the *Muzyka żałobna* a language of twelve-tone harmonics and inaugurated an entirely new and autonomous compositorial idiom that gradually coalesced into an integral and recognizable system. It was precisely in this work, which he began in 1954 (and also in the 1957 *Pięć pieśni do słów Kazimiery Iłłakowiczówny* [Five Songs to Words by Kazimiera Iłłakowiczówna]), that he opened a highly serious and significant polemic with the dodecaphonic doctrine of Arnold Schoenberg and its reception in postwar European music.

The *Passion according to St Luke* of Krzysztof Penderecki (b. 1933) led to accusations from the new music community that he had betrayed the ideals of the musical avant garde of the time. In turn, it provoked Penderecki to pronounce his famous diagnosis that it was the avant garde that had betrayed music. There is no room here to explore the arguments of the two sides in this spectacular conflict. Nor is there room to indicate what it was in the *Passion* that carried on the innovative spirit, and what contradicted it. It is nevertheless difficult to deny that it was Krzysztof Penderecki who threw down the gauntlet and challenged the avant garde, opening the musical space of the last half of the twentieth century to postmodernist games with the traditions familiar from new music festivals. The visage of the avant garde proved highly vulnerable to such a blow - clearly, the twilight was descending. Although Penderecki was not the only one to proclaim the end, he was the one who made it all the more painful, since he had until so recently been a participant in and a co-creator of the avant garde - recalcitrant and unpredictable though he may have been.

Krzysztof Penderecki debuted at the Warsaw Autumn Festival in 1959 with *Strofy* [Stanzas]. 1960 saw the premiere of *Wymiary czasu i ciszy* [Dimensions of Time and Silence], which was presented soon afterwards at the Mecca of the German avant garde, the Donauschingen festival. The famous *Tren – Ofiarom Hiroszimy* [To the Victims of Hiroshima: Threnody] was played in 1961, *Polimorfia* [Polymorphia] in 1963, and *Stabat Mater*, composed in 1962, was performed in 1964. Penderecki was one of the "angry young men" who came on the scene simultaneously with the Warsaw Autumn Festival and were unencumbered by the sorts of compromises that composers only a few years older had had to make. He had nothing to be ashamed of, nothing to renounce, and nothing with which to make a break. His music shared a common denominator with the new generation made up of his contemporaries Wojciech Kilar (b. 1932), Henryk Mikołaj Górecki (b. 1933), Bogusław Schaeffer (b. 1929), and the slightly older Andrzej Dobrowolski (b. 1921), Włodzimierz Kotoński (b. 1925) and Witold Szalonek (1927-2001). Not to mention, of course, Szabelski, Bacewicz, Lutosławski, Serocki, Baird and others.

Through the holes in the Iron Curtain, the so-called "Polish school" carried on a dialogue with the avant garde (specifically, serial and post-serial) of western music (we should add that, just as Polish music was licking the wounds of the Second World War, socialist realism, and the concept of "artistic deformation," so western music was still licking the wounds of the Second World War, fascism, and "degenerate art"). This dialogue was a game that looked like a schism. The schism was represented, on the one hand, by Lutosławski's intellectual, rational, and systematic poetics, and on the other hand by the phenomenon of Polish sonorism, the playing with colors, the penetration of traditional instruments by non-traditional means of articulating sound, the liberation of the eruption of wild percussion, and the cascading and wild manipulation of blocks of sound freed of rational rules. Through these gestures, as documented in the 1960s scores of Penderecki, Kilar, Górecki, Szalonek and Schaeffer, Polish music attacked "Darmstadt" post-serialism on its own territory with the force of romantic negation. Although these scores were built to a large degree on a serial plan subordinated to pitch material, the conception of a rational order of rhythmic progression, and at times even of the progression of color, the ultimate expression of these works mocked the faith in a musical aesthetics derived from the iron rules of a musical structuralism that was frigid in its normative rationality.

At the same time as the stochastic achievements of the scores of Iannis Xenakis and the incomplete polyphony of György Ligeti, Polish sonorism attacked the crisis of structural musical thinking simultaneously with the concept of loosening formal rigors by using elements of chance as enunciated by Pierre Boulez, and through the aesthetic somersault of Karlheinz Stockhausen's "intuitive music." The Polish scores of the 1960s became an important contribution to the discussion about where the modern music of Europe in the 1960s could and should be heading. The phenomena of sonorism current in Polish music, which included but were not limited to Penderecki's cluster technique, Witold Szalonek's combined wind instrument sounds, the "riff" expression in the scores of Wojciech Kilar, and the wild, brutal onrush of sound in the works of Henryk Mikołaj Górecki, at once lent flair and attractiveness to the musical *moderne* of the 1960s through its sensual and wholly spontaneous gestures (at times defined as Slavic and romantic, and thus typically Polish), while simultaneously infecting it with the virus of crisis and stripping it of absolute power over the way things were developing. The time for the "end of history" had arrived in the history of music.

There was one more highly significant aspect to Polish music in the 1960s. This had to do with two composers, Zygmunt Krauze (b. 1938) and Tomasz Sikorski (1939-1988). They can be placed within the space of European-American music as the precursors of the minimal movement, which arose simultaneously in the USA and, of all places, in Poland – thus leading to a new situation in European music. Sikorski made his debut as a composer at the Warsaw Autumn Festival in 1963 with *Antyfony* [Antiphones]. Krauze first appeared there in 1965 with *Kwartet smyczkowy nr 1* [String Quartet No. 1] before carving out a name for himself on that stage with the 1968 *Polichromia* [Polychromes] for the Musical Workshop and, finally, the 1970 score of *Piece for orchestra No. 1*.

Although the aesthetic tone of these composers' scores seemed to be something different, it can nevertheless be understood as the swan song of the Polish sonorism school. The handling of colors in the scores, usually formed in contrasted textures, juxtaposed segments, and sound blocks with their own characteristic, individual physiognomies, led in the case of the scores of Tomasz Sikorski to a maximal formal asceticism: with multiple repetitions of gestures concentrating on the same figures and refined sound objects that seemed suspended in space and time, the sonoristically overwrought scores were reduced to the most sensitive asceticism, and the previous extravagance of expression to introverted subtlety. Like the early scores of Penderecki, Kilar and Górecki, and the music of Szalonek, so Sikorski's music does not condemn the play of contrasts, even when they are not dealt with in the course of "impacts" (Górecki's 1960 *Zderzenia na orkiestrę* [Impacts on Orchestra]) can serve as an ideational example here), but rather reveals them in what seems like the contemplation of isolated objects. A different approach to form, and even to the conception of musical time, is introduced in the works of Zygmunt Krauze. He transfers to musical composition the concepts of unism, as formed by the constructivist painter Władysław Strzemiński (1893-1952). The composer uses a conflict-free form and fills the time of the composition with sound material in such a way as to suggest that - lacking culmination and tension - it is, *de facto*, without either a beginning or an end, and is purely a product of chance. Krauze brought into Polish music the concept of "art-exhibition-opening music," which led to a poetics of musical "installation," which was more characteristic of the post-avant garde than of the avant garde itself.

The time period that is arbitrarily restricted here to the years 1958-1966 introduced a significant number of Polish composers in at least three generations, and an impressive number of scores that they composed, into the space of European music, where these composers arrived not as imitators, but as sovereign co-creators of the aesthetics of the musical composition of their time, which we sometimes refer to as the avant garde, and sometimes - and this seems more accurate - as the twentieth-century *moderne*. The expressive inventiveness in the area of Krzysztof Penderecki's use of the string instruments (*Threnody*, *Polymorphia*, and the first two quartets) and voices (*Dimensions of Time and Silence*, *Ecloga*), in Witold Szalonek's use of the wind instruments (*Les Sons*), in Kazimierz Serocki's use of percussion (*Continuum*), in the experience of work in the electroacoustic studio of Polish radio (founded by the musicologist Józef Patkowski) and the experiments in the domain of instrumental theater (Włodzimierz Kotoński, Bogusław Schaeffer) and graphic music

(Schaeffer) - all of this went to make up not only a forceful aesthetic statement at a time when, thanks to the Warsaw Autumn Festival, music was one of the fields in which the Iron Curtain was being parted but had not yet fallen, but also an important contribution to the form of what was then European and contemporary, and which still means something to this day, when we look back on it from a post modern perspective.

Taking a bird's eye view of the romantic moment when Polish music turned towards modernity and of the phenomenon known as the Polish Composers' School, and placing a diversity of aesthetic options over a common denominator for the sake of conceptual ease, we can take comfort in noting that the time at which it occurred saw the second edition of the Warsaw Autumn Festival and its broad look at the school of Arnold Schoenberg and its aftermath, Lutosławski's *Muzyka żałobna,* the opening of the Polish Radio Experimental Studio, and the symbolic debut of the "Generation of 1933." This was also the year when the Polish Radio first took part in the sessions of the International Composers' Tribunal, organized by the International Music Council at UNESCO headquarters in Paris. Marking the endpoint of the phenomenon is not so easy. Although the première of the *St Luke Passion* has been pointed to as something that was unusually spectacular not only in the artistic but also in the political dimension (since it occurred at the time of the propaganda campaign mounted by the Polish authorities against the exchange of letters between the Polish and German Catholic episcopates, featuring the famous request by the Polish bishops for mutual forgiveness), several reservations must be made in a matter that seems to be obvious. If the *Passion* is to be taken as the milestone marking the aesthetic border, it is because the composer used therein almost the entire arsenal of previous experiments in the service of religious music and blended them with elements of compositional technique that traced their pedigree to the European musical tradition, including Gregorian chant - and yet the whole thing was based on dodecaphonic series borrowed from Anton Webern. Yet the road leading to this score included not only the *Stabat Mater,* a work composed in 1962 and incorporated into the *Passion,* but even the *Psalmy Dawida,* composed a further four years earlier and located, in chronological terms, at the beginning of the attainment by Polish music of sovereignty in the second half of the twentieth century.

Thanks to Penderecki, the beginnings of the "Polish Composers' School" were thus marked by the stigmata of its end, although this fact was not recognized at the time. When the triumphal E major chord that closes the *Passion* was still sounding in Münster at the premiere in the presence of Stefan Cardinal Wyszyński, primate of Poland, Polish sonorism - already starting to be minimalist and electronic - was surely innovative even if it was not necessarily avant garde, and the composition scene had not blown the retreat from the beachheads it had established in the new European music. The composing careers of Zbigniew Bujarski (b. 1933), Marek Stachowski (b. 1936), Zbigniew Bargielski (b. 1937), and Krzysztof Meyer (b. 1943) were beginning or continuing. Meyer was the youngest of those who fell within the syndrome of the "Polish Composers' School." Penderecki's *Przebudzenie Jakuba* [The Awakening of Jacob], Górecki's *Ad Matrem,* Kilar's *Upstairs-Downstairs,* Krauze's *Aus aller Welt stammende,* and Kotoński's *Róża wiatrów* [Wind Compass], to name some symptomatic scores from the early 1970s, were harbingers of the paradigmatic shift in the variegated forms of the Polish version of the European-American postmodern. Yet, after all, Lutosławski had not yet said the last word in regard to his compositional idiom and had not opened it, as he would do a decade later, to polystylistic palpitations. Serocki had not yet written his *Pianophonia,* nor Szalonek his series of works on the Medusa. In all these compositions, and in the "new romantic" Penderecki of the *Paradise Lost* period as well as in the early work of the next wave (known as the "Stalowa Wola Generation" or, because it was the year of the birth of Andrzej Krzanowski, Eugeniusz Knapik and Aleksander Lasoń, as the "1951 Generation"), and also in the super-conventional Paweł Szymański (b. 1954), the spirit of the Polish Composers' school remained, in spite of everything, alive. Even while it remained alive, it was dissolving into new spaces - into the space of the post-avant garde, the postmodern, and musical post-history - spaces of which Krzysztof Penderecki became one of the prophets.

Translated by William Brand

Milan Slavický
Prague

The Political Oppression of Music in Bohemia (Czechoslovakia) in the 1950s and 1960s

The oppression of culture was an important part of the communist system, which is why the Soviet model of supervision was quickly established at all levels of social life within months of the communist *coup d'etat* in Czechoslovakia (i.e. after February 1948). The so-called "nomenclature" system was introduced; according to which a clearly defined set of leadership functions at all levels of public life was open exclusively to the communist party members. Leading functions at the state radio, in the press, at the universities, educational institutions, and so on, were reserved for party comrades only, some of whom were devoted pre-war communists, but many of whom were simply post-war opportunists or young people without any experience in such leadership positions, but ambitious to make their way towards success. This was the case with theaters, orchestras and artistic institutions, as well. Many excellent actors, producers, conductors, composers, performers, writers and journalists lost their jobs (and some of them even their freedom), and many others chose exile instead of the tragedy in their homeland.

As for Bohemia (the Czech part of Czechoslovakia) at the time, renowned musicians like Bohuslav Martinů (1890-1959), Rudolf Firkušný (1912-1994) or Rafael Kubelík (1914-1996) remained abroad or left the country. Many artists were imprisoned, such as the conductor Václav Talich (1883-1961), the actors Adina Mandlová and Vlasta Burian and others even as early as May 1945, as punishment for their wartime artistic activity, and many writers, like Jan Zahradníček and his Catholic friends, spent the whole decade of the 1950s in jail, imprisoned and condemned for purely aesthetic and religious reasons. The evil spirit of the late 1940s and 1950s was a musicologist and aesthetician, Prof. Zdeněk Nejedlý, who was responsible for the sphere of culture and education. His tastes and personal antipathies landed literary figures in jail or internal exile. The fate of famous Czech conductor Václav Talich, who was hated by Nejedlý, is typical. Music Director of the Czech Philharmonic Orchestra (1919-1941), the Konzertföreningen in Stockholm (1931-34) and the National Theatre Opera in Prague (1935-45), Talich premiered compositions by such leading Czech composers as Novák, Suk, and Martinů, and was considered to be one of the best European conductors of his time. Talich was deprived of his positions and imprisoned in 1945. After his release from prison, his activities were very limited. In the summer of 1947, Talich was reinstated (by a non-Communist Minister of Culture) as the Music Director of the National Theatre Opera, but shortly after February 1948 he was again forced to resign from this position. Afterwards, he was sent to Bratislava to form the newly founded Slovak Philharmonic Orchestra there (1949-52). After the deaths of Stalin and Gottwald, he was again permitted to conduct in Prague, but he suffered a stroke in 1955 and never recovered fully. The best things of his that remain for us are the recordings he made between 1953-1955 - a typical Czech fate!

The Soviet model of unions was introduced as a means of controlling artists. The pre-war artistic clubs, based on personal friendship and shared aesthetic orientation (Devětsil, Mánes, Umělecká Beseda, Přítomnost, and so on) were either banned or condemned to public inactivity. Newly created unions like the Union of Composers, Union of Writers, Union of Architects, and so on, gained the exclusive power and right to decide about the public presentation of works of art and about the personal position of particular artists. The artists were subsidized by the state - special institutions like the Music Fund and Literary Fund were later established for that reason - but the mighty monopoly of the Unions in a particular field (like music) was absolute. The Union, led by carefully selected party members, decided not only about the programs of its own concerts, including the annual "review" of new compositions, later known as the Weeks of New Music, but about all performances of contemporary music in the country. Composers like Václav Dobiáš (1909–1978) or Jan Seidel (1908–1999) and musicologists like Antonín Sychra, Jan Hořejš, Miroslav Barvík and Jaroslav Jiránek were the key figures during the late 1940s and early 1950s, with some younger composers like Radim Drejsl (1923–1953), Vladimír Sommer (1921-1997) or Ludvík Podéš (1921–1968) following their lead. The imported Zhdanovian idea of "Socialist Realism" (which, unfortunately, found enough domestic adherents to run the whole system for years) was the leading aesthetic principle and all composers and their new works were publicly and very critically examined as to the degree to which they fulfilled the demands of the "new age." The transcripts of discussions from those years are nearly incredible: serious disquisitions about technical details (which chords are still "realistic" and which have already become "decadent"!), acts of self-criticism by old people and the arrogance of their young colleagues, sometimes even their students, who were given the power to decide their careers and fates - all of this went to make up the atmosphere of the Stalinist period in central Europe. The results were not hard to foresee: Czech and Slovak music lost contact with the rest of the world and its spiritual life; new music production was driven into the sphere of clear tonality and festive expressions of joy (with numerous mandatory folk music elements), and only exceptional personalities like Alois Hába (1893-1973), Miloslav Kabeláč (1908-1979), Klement Slavický (1910-1999) or Jan Rychlík (1916–1964) were strong enough to defend at least some vestiges of their own individual music world.

The shadows of Stalinism were rather long in Czechoslovakia. Throughout the 1950s, the screws were loosened only very gradually. Alois Hába was a lonely figure in his continuation of prewar microtonal composition. The first attempts by the younger generation to introduce dodecaphony or elements of New Music came only around 1960, with Jan Klusák (b. 1934), Marek Kopelent (b. 1932), Zbyněk Vostřák (1920-1985) and the Musica Viva Pragensis. As opposed to Poland or Hungary, the oppression was more harsh and contact with the western half of Europe even more limited. Young Czech composers were allowed to spend some months abroad at the turn of the 1960s and 1970s, when Ivana Loudová (b. 1941) went to Paris, Evžen Zámečník (b. 1939) to Munich, and Marek Kopelent to West Berlin, but they had to come back soon and faced somewhat serious problems during the following decades, including interrogation by the secret police, since they were seen as potential spies.

Despite all this oppression, the dynamic developments of the 1960s moved the whole situation forward quickly. Composers who had maintained their own artistic and human identities during the 1950s, such as Alois Hába, Miloslav Kabeláč, Klement Slavický or Jan Rychlík, were joined by some other composers of their generation like Jan Kapr (1914-1988), Vladimír Sommer and others, who continuously updated their style in the direction of more recent music language, and whose attitudes became more personally independent. Composers of the younger generation, born in the late 1920's and the 1930's, like Petr Eben (b.1929), Marek Kopelent, Jan

Klusák or Luboš Fišer, contributed a markedly fresh approach that eroded what remained of the monolithic Stalinist world of the 1950s. Their music featured inspiration by plainchant (Eben), dodecaphonic and serial techniques (Klusák), and elements of New Music (Kopelent, Fišer, and later Ivana Loudová and others). The late 1960's were surely the best and most fruitful time in Czech music between 1945 and 1989. Unfortunately, the second wave of oppression, which started in the early 1970's, (after the 1968 Soviet invasion and the subsequent reestablishment of the totalitarian regime) halted this dynamic development once again.

As I have mentioned, the suppression of creative people and culture in general was much more harsh harder in Czechoslovakia than in, for instance, Poland or Hungary (and probably even more harsh in the Bohemian or ethnically Czech part of the country than in the Slovak part). A comparison of the differing individual fates of the composers Witold Lutosławski (1913-1994) and Miloslav Kabeláč (1908-1979) is very illustrative in this regard. The two had similar personalities (they were interested in mathematics in their youth, and were integral persons with a strong sense of ethical values and of the formation and logical development of their music, an interest in new methods and approaches, and each had a strong influence on the younger generation of composers). Kabeláč (persecuted during the war because of his Jewish wife) spent a post-war decade at Prague Radio as a senior producer, and was allowed to teach at the conservatory for three years in the late 1950's. During this short time he trained some interesting young composers (Loudová, J.Krček, etc.), but was not allowed to continue. During the 1960's, he grew into a remarkable personality with a considerable international reputation, which is why he was one of the most severely persecuted composers after 1968. All his compositions were banned in the country (as were those of Slavický, Kapr, Kopelent, Klusák and many of others). Czech performers were forbidden to play his music at home or abroad, and the composer was not allowed to attend premieres of his compositions abroad. Even foreign performers had serious problems scheduling his music in Czechoslovakia. Kabeláč suffered a stroke in the early 1970s; after a valiant struggle to recover his capacities in order to go on composing, he died in 1979. The official media (including the music monthly *Hudební rozhledy*) neglected to carry any information about his death, and his funeral service became a silent demonstration by the Prague music world against such systematic injustice and the persecution of the best people - another typical Czech *curriculum vitae*!

Ĺubomír Chalupka, CSc.
Bratislava

Slovakian Music after 1945

The sense of the development of Slovakian music in the second half of the twentieth century is a struggle for cultural authenticity and artistic creativity. This struggle came to the fore during the long period of coexistence with aggressive socialist-realist norms in conditions of cultural and social isolation that resulted from Slovakia's place – as a part of the Czechoslovak Republic – in the eastern bloc while Europe was politically divided. Two culture-shaping forces accompanied this struggle: efforts at self-identification and the process of acculturation.

Within the concept of contemporary Slovakian music, self-identification emerged in both a narrower sense related to folklore, and a wider cultural sense. Stylized in various ways, introspection about and the transformation of specific structural elements in Slovakian folk song and dance prevailed over romantic-nationalist tendencies and aspired to artistic expression that would bear witness to the time not only through original means of expression or faithfulness to patriotic ideals, but also through managing to capture the interest of wider audiences rather than merely local ones.

This effort was aided by the inclusion of Slovakian music in processes of acculturation, which meant overcoming a narrow understanding of tradition and accepting impulses from more mature neighboring cultures. Selection and the transformation of impulses from outside moved in the direction of an open national style and renewed efforts at self-identification.

Unfortunately, the changes in the political system in 1948 hampered this process. The ascendancy of a vulgar sociological outlook and the primitive artistic ideas of socialist realism as imported from the Soviet Union interrupted the developmental continuity of the national style and even caused regression, while also imposing an ideologically motivated isolation from almost all of twentieth-century European music. The totalitarian ideological practices of the Czechoslovakian Composers'

Union appeared in musical life with particular strength between 1949 and 1955. This caused a crisis of professional criteria in the prewar generation and deformed the natural tendency towards creative experimentation among younger composers.

The original concept of national music was nullified and replaced by a narrow, codified palette of compositional and technical means, genres and subjects, with a conventional concept of sound. Attempts at breaking out of this regulated system were rare in this period (see Suchoň's opera *Krútňava* and the symphonic *Metamorphoses*).

The mid-1950s saw a growing desire among composers to oppose the destructive limitation of creative freedom. A tendency to reevaluate one's own position emerged. This movement, resulting from the loosening of the most dogmatic aspects of the socialist system, was an inspiration for all of culture and art. Among Slovakian musicians, it led to a renewal of the concepts of self-identification and acculturation, and of the relationship between the two. The result was an idea of openness and a pluralism of styles combined with compositional-technical professionalism and a broadening of horizons. Indeed, this tendency emerged even among the oldest composers (in Suchoň's folklore-inspired synthesis of modality, or the themes from world literature in Cikker's operas). However, the younger composers who came on the scene in the late 1950s and early 1960s were the ones who started the program rolling.

The move towards openness was intended not only to reconstruct, but above all to negate the previously accepted assumptions and signposts. Composers regeneration through a creative attitude towards twentieth-century music, including the impulses coming out of Darmstadt. Twelve-tone music, serialism, aleatorism, and the new ideals of structure and sound that were born in electronic sound studios (the first electronic compositions arose in the Bratislava Television sound studio, the second such facility in the socialist bloc, after the Experimental Studio in Warsaw) - all passed through phases of trial and error on the way to phases of individual transformation and stylistically varied forms of expression.

Composers like Ilja Zeljenka (b. 1932), Roman Berger (b. 1930), Jozef Malovec (b. 1933), Peter Kolman (b. 1937), Miro Bázlik (b. 1931), the self-taught Ladislav Kupkovič (b. 1936), Ivan Parík (b. 1936), and, later, Ivan Hrušovský (b. 1927) Juraj Pospíšil (b. 1931), Pavol Šimai (b. 1930), the Polish-trained Tadeáš Salva (1937-1995), Juraj Hatrík (b. 1941), Jozef Sixta (b. 1940), and Juraj Beneš (b. 1940) represented independent attitudes towards the above-mentioned concepts, techniques and ideas. Nor did they confine themselves exclusively to the sources of the New Music. Rather, in the context of the European avant garde of the 1920s and 1930s, and above all of the inspirational effect of the Polish school of composition, they bestowed upon Slovakian music of the 1960s an unprecedented breadth of means of expression. The enthusiasm of the young composers appeared not only in their music, but also in their writings and the way that they organized musical life. Kupkovič founded the Hudba Dneška (Today's Music) group and took it to renowned contemporary music festivals around Europe. The Smolenic Seminar functioned from 1960 to 1970 as an appendage of the Darmstadt courses. These composers came up with the idea of an international contemporary music festival in Braitslava – although a quarter of a century would pass before the idea became fact in the Melos-Etos Festival.

The younger generation of the 1960's also imbued the development of Slovakian music with dynamism. Their numerous innovations turned out to be historically justified and allowed Slovakian music to join the innovative tendencies in European music. The experience gained in this period served as an important source of strength in the years of "normalization" that followed the invasion by the Warsaw Pact armies in 1968. The methods for limiting artistic freedom that were reintroduced in the wake of the invasion proved insufficient to paralyze the aspiration of Slovakian composers to freedom and authentic creativity.

Primož Kuret
Ljubljana

Slovenian Music of the 1950s and 1960s

In 1948 political decentralization was imposed on Yugoslavia, and the country began the process of separating itself from the Stalinist political, ideological and economic terror of the Eastern Block. The attitude toward art as a political-revolutionary instrument started to thaw as well. In Yugoslavia the period of promoting socialistic-realism in the country was relatively short considering the fact that after the landmark date 1948 new political relationships became possible which meant an easier access for the composer to the advanced technological and aesthetic trends, especially those coming from the West and (after October 1956) from Poland. The result was a broad range of new and interesting artistic ideas and initiatives. Hence the musical scene in Slovenia remained open to all new and interesting tendencies.

For instance, the generation of younger composers sought to renew cooperation with the ISCM (International Society for Contemporary Music), especially after 1957, after the congress of that society was held in Zurich. The members of the Slovenic Section of ISCM founded the organization entitled Collegium Musicum, which for several years enriched the musical life of Ljubljana with presentations of works by Béla Bartók and Paul Hindemith, alongside those of other contemporary musical traditions (e.g. English, Swiss, Slovakian). The Zagreb Biennale, which was established in 1961, added another important impulse to the musical life in the country. The Festival of Contemporary Chamber Music in the Slovakian resort city of Slatina Radenci joined the Zagreb meeting two years later. In the same year there was established the Ensemble Slavko Osterc, which became the leading contemporary music group, not only in Slovenia, but also in the entire Republic as well for many years to come.

It was the Zagreb Biennale that served a function of utmost importance in the resulting development of music in post-war Yugoslavia. In Ljubljana at this time there stepped forward the younger generation of composers. In 1954, these composers joined forces within the Composers'

Club, later renamed (1960), Pro Musica Viva. Their ardent desire was first to evaluate the latest European musical tendencies, to absorb them, and eventually, to create and publish original works of their own.

As the group blossomed, its members included Darijan Božič (b. 1933), Jakob Jež (b. 1928), Lojze Lebič (b. 1934), Ivo Petrić (b. 1931), Alojz Srebotnjak (b. 1931), Milan Stibilj (b. 1929) and shortly thereafter, Igor Štuhec (b. 1932). Ivo Petrić (b. 1931), who founded the above-mentioned ensemble Slavko Osterc in 1963, led it up to its final concert in 1978. Working closely together, the key members of the ensemble kept on leading it alongside their older collegue – the last of Osterc students – and later Casella's student in Rome, Primož Ramovš (1922-1999). His cooperation was of vital importance to the group, since by that time he had already established his firm position as an accomplished composer, also held the title of a "Nestor of Slovenian Music". Ramovš's contributions were multifaceted and far-reaching. Of utmost importance was his visit to the Warsaw Autumn in 1960, which provided the opportunity to pick up new impulses. The same went for his younger colleagues from the group Pro Musica Viva. It was the opinion of some members of the group that Vinko Globokar (b. 1934), who was raised and trained in Ljubljana, should have been a member of the group. However, his support was not unanimous, so the issue remained unresolved. The case of Globokar seems especially noteworthy. He subsequently returned to France (the country of his birth) where he began his amazing rise to the fame as a composer and instrumentalist.

In 1963, at the Warsaw Autumn the Slavko Osterc Ensemble achieved considerable success with works by Ramovš (*Enneaphonia*) and Petrić (*Croquis sonore* for harp and strings; *Impressions* for flute, harp and strings). Since that time the group has toured extensively in and out of the country. The name of Slavko Osterc (1895-1941) may justly serve an example of a prominent representative of Slovakian music at foreign music centers before and after the war. It is necessary to note that the group was not always given a similar and enthusiastic response at home, because there was present a strong promotion of the music of other older, already firmly established, Slovakian composers. Many of them held posts as professors in music at academies, disseminating traditional aesthetic values, mostly neo-classical, expressionistic or neo-romantic.

It is worth noting that even the "great old master" Lucijan Marija Škerjanc (1900-1973), generally recognized as the "gray eminence" of

Slovakian music in the 20th century, a composer and teacher, under whom have studied many Slovakian composers, wrote *Seven Dodecaphonic Pieces* (1958) just to prove, that even he was able to make a decisive turn toward the music of the future.

Some others, e.g. Karol Pahor (1896-1974) and Danilo Švara (1902-1981), both already before the WW II representing a strict avant garde ideology before World War II, wrote pieces after 1945 that continued to reflect socialist realism aesthetics, but then turned toward folk art. As both came from Triest, they began an inquiry into the local folk music traditions, based on the untempered Istrian mode. In 1950, Pahor wrote a cycle of 15 pieces entitled *Istrijanka*. Following his example Švara composed his most famous work *Sinfonia da camera in modo Istriano* (1957). They both strived to rejuvenate their musical language by strengthening ties with their native folklore. Švara also composed five multi-stylistic operas, starting with the atonal *Cleopatra* (1940), through *Veronica Deseniška* (1943) and *Prešeren* (1952), with almost romantic folk overtones, concluding with the dodecaphonic *Ocean* (1969).

Summing up the presentation, one should note that the panorama of Slovakian music in the 1960s was stylistically colorful and varied. There were active at that time both older and younger composers, representing extremely different stylistic approaches that resulted in a rich and musical life, thereafter never to be repeated in any form. In closing, one could mention a few names out of many, e.g. Uroš Krek (b. 1922), Zvonimir Ciglič (b. 1921), Janez Matičič (b. 1926). Special attention should be paid to Dane Škerl (1931-2002) and his symphonic output, as well as to older composers, like Pavel Šivic (1908-1995) and Marijan Lipovšek (1910-1995). All were prominent at the time on the Slovenian music scene.

Translated by Roman Kowal

Rūta Goštautienė
Vilnius

Between Socialist Realism and the Avant Garde: Lithuanian Music of the 1950s and 1960s

The Lithuanian musical landscape looked grim at the beginning of the 1950s. The war and Soviet occupation had taken a heavy toll. In the 1940s, a significant part of the musical community had emigrated or ended up in Soviet camps. The damage done by postwar ideological complications and the notorious attacks on musical formalism by Soviet ideologues was no less severe. Juozas Gruodis (1884-1948), a classical figure in Lithuanian music, died prematurely in the wake of sharp criticism leveled at him publicly; the composer Juozas Pakalnis (1912-1948) died in mysterious circumstances, and Jonas Nabažas (1907-2002), who was only beginning his career as a composer after studying in Paris, fell silent for many long years.

In this situation, both the older generation who had begun composing before the war and the younger generation just coming on the scene – Antanas Račiūnas (1905-1984), Balys Dvarionas (1904-1972), Stasys Vainiūnas (1909-1982), Julius Juzeliūnas (1916-2001), Eduardas Balsys (1919-1984) and others – tried to adapt to the new conditions. The ideal of national music, as formulated at the turn of the nineteenth and twentieth centuries by Mikalojus Konstantinas Čiurlionis (1875-1911), Juozas Naujalis (1869-1934), and Česlovas Sasnauskas (1867-1916), now had to be reconciled with the new normative esthetics. This meant that folk-music motives had to be shoehorned into the norms of socialist realism. The "new values" were reflected in the hierarchy of genres: mass songs stood at the peak, with the lower positions occupied by the cantata, oratorio, stage music, and the large instrumental forms (symphony, symphonic poem, concerto, etc.). Chamber music and light music lay at the bottom of this hierarchy. Political and sociological-cultural changes had an unavoidable influence on composers' output. Despite the fact that the political climate changed in the 1950s and 1960s, a characteristic phenomenon of the period was the special interest shown by composers in the genres of opera and ballet. It seems that Lithuanian composers produced more operas and ballets in this period than during all the later decades of the twentieth century.

At the risk of restating what is universally known, I would like to point out that the conformism of Lithuanian music in the 1950s was not a movement away from apologetics for Pure Music in the direction of propagandistic-political opportunism. That would be too great a simplification of the processes of change. On the other hand, the musical language of the prewar composers still left in the country did not take the form of avant garde experimentation and might even be called a trend towards moderate modernism, based on national ideology (the affirmation of folklore consistently remained the supreme value for the exponents of this direction). The first avant garde generation from the prewar period, headed by Vytautas Bacevičius (1905-1970), Jeronimas Kačinskas (b. 1907), and Julius Gaidelis (1909-1983), faded from musical life and the private tastes.

Although musical creativity did not die out in the 1950s, neither was it flourishing. To use Andrzej Chłopecki's definition: a reconciliation of dialectically divergent values, or even a blank space in the development of the Lithuanian musical tradition. It is worth recalling what may well remain to this day the two most popular stage compositions (judging by their presence in the repertoire) - Vytautas Klova's opera *Pilėnai* (1956) and Eduardas Balsys's ballet *Eglė žalčių karalienė* [Eglė the Queen of Grass-snakes, 1960] date from just this period. Both works, based on national themes, express delight with the idea of the renewal of the musical language within the framework of continuing the national musical tradition. Compositorial ideas of renewal were characterized at the time by the concept of "fresh harmony." In other words, "fresh idiom" and "fresh harmony" were significant terms in the process of modernizing Lithuanian music from 1956 on. The leading exponents of this trend, beginning in the 1960s, are undoubtedly Julius Juzeliūnas and Eduardas Balsys. They laid down the two most important postwar traditions of musical thought in the development of the Lithuanian school. Julius Juzeliūnas's interests developed towards the structural reorganization of the harmonic system, rejecting the sharp-flat system that was alien to ancient Lithuanian folk music. Balsys broke free of the official rhetoric.[1]

[1] It should also be noted that Balsys and Juzeliūnas taught popular composition classes for decades at the Vilnius Conservatory.

The rather restrained experimentation that Juzeliūnas and Balsys carried out in musical language had an influence not only on the reinforcement of the neoclassical tendency in Lithuanian music, but also fostered a far more liberal climate in musical circles in the 1960s. Thanks to this, the first signs of the avant garde, spurred on by the post-war European avant garde, could appear in Lithuanian music. The precursors of this tendency were the composers from the younger generation in the 1960s: Vytautas Barkauskas (b. 1931), Antanas Rekašius (b. 1928), Jurgis Juozapaitis (b. 1942), and Vytautas Montvila (b. 1935).[2] These composers flung themselves into the dodecaphonic, serial, sonoristic and collage currents. The Lithuanian variant of the avant garde opens with characteristic compositions from this period: Barkauskas's *Poezija* [Poetry] for piano (1964), *Intymi kompozicija* [An Intimate Composition] for oboe and twelve string instruments (1968), *Kontrastinė muzika* [Contrastive Music] for flute, cello, and percussion (1969), and *Pro memoria* for flute, bass clarinet, piano, and percussion (1970); there were also Rekašius's four symphonies (1962, 1963, 1969, 1970) and Montvila's *Gotiškoji poema* [Gothic Poem] for symphony orchestra (1970).

Information about new musical phenomena evoked euphoria but was transmitted through unofficial channels. Not one of the avant garde works was performed publicly in Lithuania at the time. The most important source of information was Poland, and above all the Warsaw Autumn festival and Bogusław Schaeffer's books. Vytautas Barkauskas, one of the young Lithuanian composers who managed to attend the Warsaw Autumn in the 1960s, recalls that the music of Witold Lutosławski, Krzysztof Penderecki, and György Ligeti made the biggest impression on him. Barkauskas came home from Warsaw with a recording of Penderecki's *Threnody*. When he played it at the Union of Lithuanian Composers, it unleashed a scandal and brought down the wrath of the ideological "watchdogs." It is worth mentioning that this presentation of *Threnody* was one of the few occasions when avant garde music was played publicly in Lithuania in the 1960s.

I doubt, however, that the music of these composers can be called an "avant garde revolution" in Lithuanian musical life. The way in which Lithuanian composers adapted the avant garde reflects the social and cultural context: avant garde tendencies appeared belatedly in Lithuania,

---

[2] I must note that the first examples of the use of twelve-tone techniques appeared in works by other composers: Benjaminas Gorbulskis's *Concerto for Clarinet and Orchestra* (1961) and Eduardas Balsys's *Dramatinės freskos* for symphonic orchestra (1965).

when the rhetoric of the cult of innovation and technical transformation had already won general acceptance as part of the development of Soviet society. This is shown, for example, by an excerpt from the musical criticism of the day: "caught up in the contemporary whirl, we look for new, up-to-date things, and together with modern furnishings and the fashions of recent years, we usually opt for new melodies."[3]

[3] Algirdas Ambrasas, *Muzika ir dabartis. Šiuolaikinės muzikos etiudai*, Vilnius 1969, p. 5.

Svetlana Savenko
Moscow

The New Soviet Music of the Postwar Avant Garde Period

The new music in the Soviet Union began to form at the end of the 1950s. It was created by a new generation of composers that emerged just at this time. The atmosphere in Soviet society had changed rapidly after Stalin's death: the problem of spiritual freedom gained prominence. The new attitudes are exemplified in Rodion Shchedrin's article "Creative Courage," published in the magazine *Sovyetskaya Musyka* (7, 1955). The young composer appealed to his colleagues not only to renew their own creative activity but also to extend their knowledge of modern music. By "modern music," however, Shchedrin understood the work of Debussy, Ravel, Mahler and Stravinsky, which had been inaccessible to professional Soviet composers, to say nothing of music lovers.

But the situation changed quickly. The works of many Western composers were soon heard in Soviet concert halls. Soviet musicians were able to obtain recordings and other materials from the West. Young composers could sometimes even attend festivals of modern music. The most important such event was the Warsaw Autumn Festival, which was like an open window for young Soviet composers. They could present their own avant garde work there. Compositions by more than 20 Soviet composers were played in Warsaw in the 1950s and 1960s, including, for example, Galina Ustvolskaya (1962), Alfred Schnittke (1965, 1967), Arvo Pärt (1965), and especially Edison Denisov (1964, 1966, 1968, 1969, 1970). These composers and many of their young colleagues focused their attention principally on the Western postwar avant garde. The new language was associated for them with the twelve-tone serial technique and timbre composition. These purely technological ideas were very important for the younger generation because they emphasized the rational perfection of composition above all: exact knowledge and skill, as an antidote to the pseudo-classicism and pathos of the Stalinist era, became the ideal. A similar process could be observed in Germany, where the young artistic generation felt that it had a duty to overcome the heritage of the Nazi era.

The piano cycle *Musica stricta* by Andrey Volkonsky (b. 1933), completed in 1956, was the first composition written according to the twelve-tone method. The composer was 23 years old at the time. Later works by Volkonsky were mostly compositions for voice (soprano) and different chamber ensembles: the *Suite of Mirrors* (1959), *Shchasa's Lamentations* (1960), and the *Wandering Concerto* (1967). These works were at the cutting edge of the young Soviet avant garde. Volkonsky developed Webern's refined structuralism in the direction of Boulez, but in a highly individualistic way. Volkonsky's serial method of pitch organization was not the only thing that was new for Soviet music. His delicate chamber writing was unusual in general. It marked the true introduction of a modern language in the Soviet composition.

The term "the Soviet avant garde" was coined by foreign music writers in the early 1960s. In official Soviet publications, the word had a sharply pejorative sense. But the "avant garde" movement was broad. It embraced many composers from Russia, the Ukraine, the Caucasus, and the Baltic countries. The leading lights were three Moscow composers who later came to be known as "the Moscow Troika": Edison Denisov (1929-1996), Sofia Gubaidulina (b. 1931), and Alfred Schnittke (1934-1998). Other contributors to the new style in Soviet music included Nikolai Karetnikov (1930-1994), Sergei Slonimsky (b. 1932), Roman Ledenyov (b. 1931), Boris Tishchenko (b. 1939), Valentin Silvestrov (b. 1937), Leonid Grabovsky (b. 1935) and Rodion Shchedrin (b. 1932).

The avant garde period, in the strict sense, did not last long. By the late 1960s, orthodox serial writing had been transformed and gradually disappeared as an actual technique of musical composition.

Because young composers had to catch up with western music, the distance between the mastering of the twelve-tone system and total serialism turned out to be very short. For example, Edison Denisov composed his first dodecaphonic works in 1961. A mere three years later, his *Italian Songs* featured the serial organization of rhythm and the dynamics. Denisov used numbered scales like those of Boulez; his technique developed in the same direction: towards the individualization of serial procedures in each work. In the *Italian Songs*, the serial calculation of distances between entries of parts constituted one such individual feature.

Alfred Schnittke also worked intensively with serial structures in the early 1960s. In an early composition of this type, *Music for Chamber Orchestra*

(1964), he used the technique that Boulez had used in *Structures*. However, Schnittke soon became critical of this system, and above all of the way it dealt with time. Schnittke noticed that strict adherence to Boulez's rhythmic series produced monotonous periodic structures based on the succession of equal cycles. As a solution, Schnittke offered a principle of progression based on a strict numerical sequence. Arvo Pärt and Sofia Gubaidulina had already developed similar systems of pitch and rhythmic progression.

Of course, other composers were also using the idea of progression. As a universal theory, it was developed by Karlheinz Stockhausen in his famous concept of the formant spectrum. Other principles, such as timbre composition based on micropolyphonic texture, were also in general use. The latter was discovered by György Ligeti, but his works of the early 1960s were not known to Soviet composers at the time. Therefore, the micropolyphonic texture in the works of Schnittke and Pärt emerged independently. Questions of priority are not, of course, as important in music as they are in science. Nevertheless, they must be taken into account within the context of avant garde innovation. While some new features introduced by Soviet composers may at times appear to be simple borrowings from the West, they turn out upon closer examination to be quite original.

By the late 1960s, the period of adaptation was over and Soviet composers began freely developing avant garde conceptions. Strict serialism no longer seemed irreconcilable, and elements of traditional music penetrated into new works, giving birth to stylistic mixtures or "symbiotic compositions," as Stockhausen called them. Schnittke's mature style was connected with the method which the composer himself referred to as "polystylistics." His new works, such as the first five symphonies and instrumental concertos, made Schnittke's name famous outside of Russia.

PENDERECKI AND THE AVANT GARDE IN THE CONTEXT OF CULTURE

POLISH CULTURE OF THE 1950S AND 1960S

Maria Piotrowska
Warsaw

Hope against Hope:
The European Mind in the Fifties and Sixties

The 1950s and 1960s, the decades following the most horrible of wars, did not bring the relaxation of tensions or the calm that Europe longed for. Naturally, human activity in the first years after the war was focused on recovering the substance of the old life from the rubble - in the material, social and personal dimensions.

Along with impulses towards rebirth and new growth, the powerful eternal will to survive penetrated the psychosis of suffering and irremediable loss. Yet the political contradictions that preceded the outbreak of the Second World War had been too complex to be swept away by the destructive might that removed millions of human beings from this world. Those contradictions endured and became more intense in conditions that an earlier age could not have dreamed of, the conditions formed by the nuclear annihilation of the cities of Hiroshima and Nagasaki. The annihilation of the Japanese cities occurred far from Europe and brought the military campaigns to a close. Nevertheless, it introduced to the European mentality a sense of terror that kept growing as political developments unfolded.

Publicly proclaimed and incorporated into that mentality in 1946, the existence of a "cold war" was confirmed three years later by the final division of Germany. In that same year, 1949, the Russians carried out their first nuclear test. This heightened the popular feeling that events were inevitably careening in some horrifying direction, towards an armed confrontation that, given the availability of such weapons, could only end in the total destruction of humankind. Europeans began the 1950s with a consciousness in which the memories of the recent nightmare were combined with a nightmare that was even more terrible, because it was unimaginable.

The period of eight or so years after the death of Stalin did bring a certain relaxation of tensions (felt in some countries of the Eastern bloc, especially in Poland, as political liberalization accompanied by numerous symptoms of the humanization of the system), yet the face of political life remained harsh. New military means of destruction were being discovered all the time and it was no secret that the two atomic powers were engaged in "local" armed conflicts. After a direct misunderstanding between the two powers brought the world to the brink of catastrophe in 1962, the sigh of relief brought on by the momentary recovery of reason did not last long. The second half of the 1960s passed in the shadow of the horrors of the Vietnam war, during which the often-repeated threat to use weapons of mass destruction made everyone familiar with the feeling that life could be brought to a sudden end (at the same time that conceptualism was destroying art as such by seemingly exploiting its resources to the very end). This awful certainty of the likelihood of the end tormented the European mind in the 1950s and 1960s, waxing and waning but never disappearing, regardless of whether the individual lived a middling or a desperate life, or knew extraordinary moments and acquired fame, adoration and riches. As early as the 1940s, thinkers in this century of cruel wars had begun asking: Who is to blame? Did the cataclysm of the Second World War stem only from political and economic sources, or were there other factors, deeper and more complex?

This is where people in the second half of the twentieth century learned some amazing things about themselves. They learned that the freedom acquired in bloody struggles over the course of long generations had now turned out to be an unbearable burden. They had not taken into account the fact that - limitations of freedom notwithstanding - pre-individualistic society had offered a feeling of security within its communal interdependence. As free individuals, with the ground swept from under their feet, people at the beginning of our century had been left at the mercy of their own loneliness. This in turn produced a feeling of powerlessness and of insignificance amidst the surrounding world. In the search for new "symbiotic" relations that would make it possible to break down social isolation and join in an overarching community, millions of people in the Germany of the thirties had attempted the "escape from freedom" that Erich Fromm describes. This phenomenon revealed more generalized dimensions, and could therefore be apprehended in a metaphor that applied to all forms of true totalitarianism. It is the metaphor of a fatal, contagious disease spread by a bacillus that "never dies out."

The era of bloody totalitarian compulsion is an era of plague, which can rage not only because of the madness of a tyrannical leader, but also thanks to the inborn susceptibility of people who want, in the depths of their hearts, to submit to that compulsion - since they are essentially alienated and indifferent to life and authentic values.

Authentic life and authentic values are always endangered. Writers and thinkers, whose "priestly" function became more prominent in those grim postwar decades, offer simple truths that are hard to put into practice. One truth is that in a time of plague germs and victims, one should not be on the side of the germs. Another truth is that if the absurd enters human existence, it should be recognized - not in order to submit passively to it, but rather to revolt against it by the individual, conscious act of giving one's life some sense, which in turn should not be discouraged by the fact that authentic life is in essence the labor of Sisyphus - shared but free of illusions.

This is the difficult, existential, and even heroic version of the philosophy of the absurd. The easier version proclaims despair as a result of absurdity and the "empty heaven" of freedom. Yet it was the simplified message of precisely this version of existentialism that was particularly widely accepted among young people in the slightly more benign phase of the period under discussion (in the late 1950s). Partly as a pose and an intellectual mannerism, and partly too as a slightly sentimental tone in cafe society, it left its particular mark in Poland, where the books of Camus and Sartre had begun appearing in translation in 1956.

In the early 1960s, questions also began to be asked about who the pervasive postwar sense of permanent danger and fear: Who is responsible for the specter of nuclear annihilation hanging over the world? The answer turned out to be a new one. For the first time since the moment when the Cartesian paradigm assumed supremacy in modern European thinking, the unassailable authority of science and scientists began to totter. The reasons lay in the horrifying products of applied science: besides the weapons of mass destruction, there were anti-human technologies that began to be perceived as harbingers of human regression and extinction. They had poisoned the atmosphere around cities, eliminated life from rivers, surrounded the earth with a belt of harmful radiation – yet above all they served to multiply the frightening technologies of war. Just such technologies were used by the American army in Indochina in the late 1960s.

The attribution to scientists of the blame for the threat of global annihilation coincided with the revolution in society, manners and culture that occurred in the Anglo-Saxon countries through the appearance and rapid spread of the rock music that symbolized the freedom of youthful expression. The first signs of youthful rebellion against the anti-life civilization of adults appeared in the late 1950s. Known as the counter-culture, this movement spread powerfully within a decade to every corner of Western Europe where young people discovered in various ways the dissonance between officially proclaimed values and real life. Young people protested against the involvement of science in the dangerous game known as the arms race and against the various signs of social-political domination. Young people were also openly critical of the consumer society, of the myth of benevolent technological progress, of technocratic governments and of the pursuit of material values.

The counterculture was in part a protest movement and in part an effort to bring about an "alternative lifestyle" planned in opposition to the unauthentic, alienated styles shaped on a mass scale by television programs. In countries like Poland, some alternative culture trends (such as a strong interest in Eastern religions) occurred somewhat later than in the West.

Christian personalism holds an important place in the philosophy of the time. It is without doubt an attempt at healing the terrible moral emptiness caused by the war, an attempt at establishing principles stating that all individual and social action should be carried out with a view to the good of *persons*. Seen in relation to the Divine Person, or treated as fundamentally unknowable, the human person is furnished with something that is "the most inner in its inwardness" – *caritas*, the capacity for Christian love of others. As an existentially actualized force, *caritas* is thus a guarantee of the future universal personalization of the world through the creation of living interpersonal bonds freed of alienation and the reduction of people to objects. It contains the promise of the enthronement of the human dignity that was trampled during the wartime slaughter, and of the rebirth of faith in man and of optimism –

a difficult task set against the realities of the cold war. Personalism is an attitude of *contra spem spero* – "hope against hope."

The true personalist revolution within Catholicism, however, did not take place among the Christian elites who read Maritain and Mounier. Rather, it embraced all believers without exception through the figure of John XXIII "opening wide the windows of the Church" as he inaugurated the Second Vatican Council in 1962. It carried into the Church a spirit of tolerance and dialogue towards other religions and Christian faiths (no longer "heretics," but rather "separated brothers"). It would recognize the apostolate of lay people of good will, acknowledge the "relative autonomy" of culture, and above all awaken a feeling of community and *caritas* in individual, local churches. In this way, the Church responded to the human needs of people filled with the fears of the second half of our century. Another consequence of the spirit of renewal was a striking liturgical innovation: the replacement of Latin by local languages, a bold step with a precedent in the depths of Christian antiquity when Latin replaced Greek. The positive and nourishing result of these changes was a gradual, sometimes subtle, but undeniable broadening of the light kindled by the Church three decades ago, in the gloomy decade of the 1960s, which was so uncongenial to people.

Art in the years following 1950, by contrast, offered people little that was helpful. On the contrary, art seemed intent on crushing, outraging, and confusing people, just like the technological civilization that it affirmed and welcomed into everyday life and used as a means of expression. This is the art of the Great Avant Garde, also known as anti-art, which ostentatiously negated or even ridiculed the values that people had grown used to associating with art. Its ideology and technique made it unsuitable for the therapeutic function; its hard black outgrowth denied the possibility that any sort of naive, contemporary Biedermeier could take root. Music eliminated the traditional sources of sound and the traditional performer. In those years when it was so hard to find hope, did art ever speak with a modern but deeply human voice that could help people understand and courageously accept the world they lived in? A closer look is required to find the answer.

Translated by William Brand

Andrzej Szczerski
Cracow

The Boundaries of Freedom

For Polish avant garde art, the fifties and sixties marked a radical turning point. This breakthrough was made possible by, above all, the experience that young artists gained from 1945 to 1949, between the end of the Second World War and the introduction of the official doctrine of socialist realism. The First Exhibition of Modern Art, organized in Cracow by the Young Artists' Group [Grupa Młodych Plastyków] in cooperation with artists from other centers in Poland, became a symbol of this period. Mieczysław Porębski (b. 1921) was the theoretician of the group. The participants included Marian Bogusz (1920-1980), Tadeusz Brzozowski (1918-1987), Zbigniew Dłubak (b. 1921), Fortunata Obrąpalska (b. 1909), Tadeusz Kantor (1915-1990), Janina Kraupe (b. 1921), Alfred Lenica (1899-1977), Jan Lenica (1928-2001) and Marek Włodarski (1903-1960). They showed a variety of painting and sculpture, mostly associated with surrealism and geometrical abstraction. The innovative application of photography as a means of analyzing the visual language also attracted a great deal of attention. "Unartistic" materials and objects (pipes, wire, thread) were used in a "magazine of forms" to create original spatial constructions in which a foreshadowing of future avant garde sculptural experiments may be discerned.

The organizers of the Cracow exhibition and the participating artists deliberately set about creating a mode of artistic expression that would break with traditionalism and be adequate to the new political and social reality in Poland. The artists believed that the "new Poland" offered an unprecedented opportunity for the development of modern art, and that such art was the only way of describing the changes that were underway. They wanted, therefore, to be avant garde in a double sense, in terms of both artistic and social engagement. A visible sign of this attitude was the educational program that was an integral part of the exhibition. Explanatory descriptions accompanied the works of art, and commentaries presenting the artist's intentions sounded from speakers located in the rooms.

The innovative works in the Cracow exhibition nevertheless represented "the dead-end of formalism" to the Communist authorities. In 1949, they decreed that socialist realism was the only artistic method, and that all artists would have to submit to it if they wished to participate in official cultural life. The result was a paralysis of painting, sculpture, and the various related visual, plastic and graphic arts such as had never before occurred.

The centralized state system of exhibitions and acquisitions, along with the lack of private patronage, effectively ruled out any sort of "margin of freedom." The primitive evaluative criteria that prevailed were derived from the official cultural policy of the Soviet Union, and were patterned after nineteenth-century academic conventions. Such circumstances imposed silence on the avant garde artists. An eloquent sign of opposition was the fact that the prewar communists Jonasz Stern (1904-1988) and Maria Jaremianka (1908-1958), participants in the 1948 exhibition, refused offers to cooperate with the regime.

Another avant garde painter, Andrzej Wróblewski (1927-1957), took a different position. Rejecting his earlier explorations in the domain of non-representative art, he accepted the challenge of "realism." His realism, however, did not refer to the historical models that the party acknowledged as most suitable for propaganda purposes. Wróblewski wanted to paint with the use of drastic simplification and intentional deformation. He wanted his realism to be as brutal as the surrounding world - in the artist's words, "as foul as the smell of a corpse." These principles found their fullest expression in his 1948-1949 series, *Execution by Firing Squad*. The dismembered and decomposing human bodies became one of the most disturbing and universal witnesses to the tragedy of wartime. Wróblewski's realism proved unacceptable to the regime, and his attempts at adjusting to the requirements of socialist realism turned into an artistic debacle. In 1954, he began painting new pictures in which he returned to his original achievement by creating images of everyday human life full of concentration and mysticism (*Still Waiting in Line,* 1956). Cut short by his tragic death in the Tatra Mountains in 1957, when he was still in his early thirties, Wróblewski's work was an exceptional effort at rescuing the realistic language of expression from confiscation by the communist authorities.

Bronisław Wojciech Linke (1906-1962) also made use of realistic forms, but in his paintings these forms changed into dream visions and dreadful nightmares reminiscent of the work of Bosch. Linke's 1959

The Bus, a surrealistic vision of a vehicle carrying representatives of the whole of Polish society, is regarded as a metaphor of Poland after the Second World War.

An exhibition organized at the Arsenal in Warsaw in 1955 was the symbolic end of socialist realism. The influence of the changes in the communist party structures that began after Stalin's death spread to cultural policy. The Warsaw exhibition was the first to present previously forbidden forms of expressive realism, not untinged by existential angst. The authors involved in this exhibition included Waldemar Cwenarski (1926-1953), Izaak Celnikier (b. 1923), Jan Dzięndziora (1926-1987) and Marek Oberländer (1922-1978). The latter painted the best-known picture from the exhibition, *The Branded*, which referring to Holocaust, depicted in a deformed way the figures of Jews condemned to destruction. The Arsenal show signaled the onset of the fifties "thaw," a moderate liberalization of domestic policy that the authorities skillfully exploited to create an illusion of freedom. Yet even this illusion, unknown in other countries of the Eastern bloc, made possible a new dynamism in artistic life. When a review of works from the socialist countries opened in Moscow in 1958, the Polish exhibition aroused the most interest in view of the remarkable presence of avant garde works that broke with the doctrine of socialist realism.

Modern Polish painting of the "thaw" period deliberately rejected any connection with realism. All the "moderns" of the day wanted to practice abstraction, which was the sign of freedom. In characteristic fashion, the party endeavored to control this process by admitting fifteen percent of abstract works at official exhibitions. This ruling well illustrates the sort of paradoxes of totalitarianism that artists had to grapple with. Nevertheless, various sorts of abstraction dominated painting at the time. Tadeusz Kantor's informel paintings, Maria Jarema's organic abstraction, the material-based painting of Jadwiga Maziarska (b. 1913) and Bronisław Kierzkowski (1924-1993), the allusive work of Stanisław Fijałkowski (b. 1922), Henryk Stażewski's (1894-1988) geometric and organic abstraction in the tradition of the prewar avant garde, and the exceptionally subtle colors of Stefan Gierowski (b. 1925) and Piotr Potworowski (1898-1962) garnered the most acknowledgement. Like Jan Cybis (1897-1972), Potworowski was a painter who carried on the traditions of the post-impressionist painting of the years between the wars, and who earned a dominant position in a postwar art-school faculty. Potworowski's work, however, was exceptional by any standard. Tadeusz Dominik

(b. 1928), Wacław Taranczewski (1903-1987), and the émigré Józef Czapski (1896-1993) also undertook the continuation of the colorist tradition in an original mode.

A characteristic phenomenon in the late-fifties was the formation of artistic groups and galleries engaged in propagating the new art. Group 55 arose in Warsaw, and gave birth in 1956 to the Crooked Wheel Gallery [Galeria Krzywe Koło], which showed both abstract art and metaphorical realism. Young artists and art historians in Lublin founded the Castle Group [Zamek]. The R-55 group was founded in Poznań and St-53 in Katowice. The most important and durable of them all, however, was the Cracow Group [Grupa Krakowska], founded in that city in 1957. It included most of the participants in the 1948 Cracow exhibition. The diverse artistic personalities in the Cracow Group evinced, in a very general way, attachment to the traditions of abstract art, surrealism and expressionism. In effect, each artist came up with a personal artistic program, so that Tadeusz Brzozowski could exhibit his paintings, which approached organic abstraction, alongside the work of the surrealists Kazimierz Mikulski (1918-1998) and Jerzy Skarżyński (b. 1924), and the painter (future performance-artist) Zbigniew Warpechowski (b. 1938).

Due in no small part to their charismatic leader, Tadeusz Kantor, the artists in the Cracow group rapidly staked out positions as the classics of the Polish avant garde. Kantor is one of its most important figures. His work embraces a wide range of disciplines and aesthetic conventions from painting through drawing, the art of the object, and happening, to paratheater. In the fifties, Kantor was painting informel pictures. By the end of the decade, he had created *assemblages* and was propagating his own concept of the *emballage* (packaging). He used worn-out, damaged and "poor" items to create objects with a poetics all their own. He realized his first happenings in the sixties (*The Dividing Line*, 1966, and *The Anatomy Lesson According to Rembrandt*, 1968), but his greatest achievement lay in the innovative performances of his Cricot 2 theater, with symbolic prop-objects instead of traditional sets, and without professional actors. Kantor's multi-faceted work illustrates the polyphonic artistic creativity of the sixties. Combined with expressionism and elements of the grotesque, the surrealistic tradition survived in the work of Jan Lebenstein (1930-1999), Jerzy Tchórzewski (1928-1999), and Zbigniew Makowski (b. 1930). Op-art experiments characterized the paintings of Zbigniew Gostomski (b. 1932), Jan Ziemski (b. 1920), Wojciech Fangor (b. 1922), and Jan Chwałczyk (b. 1924). The neo-Dadaist trend, with a dominant role assigned to the object, shaped Władysław Hasior's (1928-1999) expressionistic *assemblages*. Włodzimierz Borowski (b. 1930) practiced happening in his *Syncretic Shows* cycle, which undercut all artistic conventions in an ironic way. Roman Opałka (b. 1931) began a lifelong project, *1965-∞*, in the year indicated by the title; since then, he has been signing his paintings with successive numbers while recording the changes in his own face on photographic film as a way of bearing dramatic witness to time and transience. The 1960s also saw the coalescence of Jerzy Nowosielski's (b. 1923) personal formula of painting based on the tradition of the Byzantine icon. Among the sculptors, figures like Jerzy Bereś (b. 1930), with his symbolic compositions in wood, emerged; soon afterwards came Magdalena Abakanowicz (b. 1930) with her abstract textile sculpture-objects known as "abakans." The sculptor Alina Szapocznikow (1926-1973), who lived in France after 1963, achieved special status with her three-dimensional casts of her own body, intimate portraits that are also a universal description of humanity. She created a dramatic image of the disintegration of the human body in her last works, which documented the progress of her own cancer.

The subject of the human form also assumed a primary place in the work of painters associated with the "new figurative" movement, like Janusz Przybylski (1937-1998) and Teresa Pągowska (b. 1929), who were inspired to a substantial degree by Francis Bacon. Maciej Bieniasz (b. 1938), Zbylut Grzywacz (b. 1939), Leszek Sobocki (b. 1934) and Jacek Waltoś (b. 1938) of the Straight Ahead Group [Grupa Wprost], founded in 1966, offered an original vision of the figurative. Their paintings contain signs of critical commentary on the Polish realities of the late sixties.

If the fifties were a time of avant garde artistic groups, then the sixties were characterized by creative "special events" co-organized, for instance, by large industrial plants and enjoying permission from the authorities. The avant garde was attempting at this time to embark upon a political game that, on the one hand, guaranteed a degree of freedom to develop while, on the other hand, exploiting artists as an element in a propagandistic demonstration of the liberty that prevailed in Poland. Just as they had during the "thaw," the artists took advantage of this minimal scope for freedom. Among the "special events," great significance was attached to those in Zielona Góra, Osieki, and above all to the Biennale of Spatial Forms that was inaugurated in Elbląg in 1965. The streets of the city were studded with abstract sculpture of varying artistic merit, by such practitioners as Henryk Morel (1937-1968), Jerzy Jarnuszkiewicz (b. 1919), and

Adam Marczyński (1908-1985). Of far greater importance were the art galleries founded at the time, which operated within official structures but did not suffer from excessive censorship. The Foksal Gallery in Warsaw, founded in 1965 by Hanna Ptaszkowska, Wiesław Borowski and Mariusz Tchorek, and the Krzysztofory Gallery, where the Cracow Group mounted its shows, attained prominent positions.

The sixties also saw the rise of the original Polish poster school, where major emphasis was placed on the painting involved, as well as the deployment of metaphor, allusion and symbol. Poster artists like Henryk Tomaszewski (b. 1914), Jan Młodożeniec (1929-2000), Jan Lenica, Roman Cieślewicz (1930-1996) and Franciszek Starowieyski (b. 1930) garnered acclaim both within Poland and elsewhere. A similarly original idiom based on metaphor shaped such graphic artists as Józef Gielniak (1932-1972) and Jerzy Panek (1918-2001).

The Polish avant garde of the fifties and sixties was engaged in redefining the concept of art, extending its boundaries, and fighting to win freedom of artistic expression. It not only took up arms against the traditional approach to art, but also found itself obliged to play games with political censorship. The limited opportunities for joining in the international artistic life and barriers to the flow of information constituted another hindrance to free development. As a result, the originality and value of much of the work of the period, thanks to artistic individuality and in spite of the prevailing system, can be surprising. It seems that a full assessment of its achievements, especially within the international context, has not yet been arrived at.

Translated by William Brand

Michał Głowiński
Warsaw

Polish Literature after 1956

The years 1949-1955, when the authorities imposed the straitjacket of "socialistic realism," were the saddest and most hopeless period in twentieth-century Polish literature. Imported from the Soviet Union, socialist realism deprived writers of a chance that their art could serve any ends except those of propaganda. The socialist realist period was shorter in Poland than in the other countries of the Communist bloc, but it left its mark on literature. It also taught writers a lesson and stripped away any illusions about what happens to literature when it is forced into absolute submission to totalitarian power.

After the important political changes of 1956, no one wanted to write in that way again. Yet socialist realism became a negative reference point, a background against which new writing could stand in contrast as a sign of freedom and independence, or an assertion of individual artistic choices and decisions. Censorship remained as an official institution and the relevant branches of the one-party state established cultural policy; this clearly made full freedom impossible. Yet there was a significant margin of freedom, and writers operated in this margin while constantly endeavoring to widen it.

Like music and painting, Polish literature of the period was swept by waves of avant garde trends. Being "up to date" was a slogan that enjoyed esteem among both authors and readers. This meant a great deal: freedom and independence were a contradiction of all the concepts and conventions associated with socialist realism. A striking metaphor could be a mark of creative freedom, since it negated the previously obligatory ideological stereotypes.

Besides modernity, however, there was another aspiration. Writers wanted not only to make their poetry new, but also to bear witness to their time and to replace propagandistic manipulation with a true vision of current events. They wanted to show those sides of contemporary Polish reality - and not only Polish - that were being systematically falsified. This was above all the task of narrative - although here, too, there were avant garde tendencies.

Polish literature, and especially poetry, blossomed after 1956. Writers like Jarosław Iwaszkiewicz (1894-1980) and Julian Przyboś (1901-1970) established themselves as classics. As might be expected in such a situation, however, it was new writers who evoked the greatest interest. There were many of them, a whole wave of poets who were defined years later by literary historians as the "*Współczesność* generation" (after the title, meaning "Contemporaneity," of a magazine in which they published). Books by these poets are carefully studied by critics and generally well received by the public. Some of the poets who came on the scene at this time were very young, while others, like Miron Białoszewski (1922-1983) or Zbigniew Herbert (1924-1998) had been unable to publish earlier.

It was at this point that the status of the five pre-eminent Polish poets of the second half of the century was established. Two of these poets had indeed made their debuts before the Second World War: the émigré Czesław Miłosz (born 1911, Nobel Prize 1980) and the outstanding but less-known Zbigniew Bieńkowski (1913-1994), a poet who is both a metaphysical visionary and a nimble lyricist. The next two members of the leading quintet broke into print in the first decade after the war, and both had short episodes of socialist realism. Tadeusz Różewicz (b. 1921) developed a highly ascetic and severe idiom suited to describing the Nazi occupation; he gave voice to the experience of terror, concentration camps, mass murder and ruthless combat. For decades, Różewicz was the most influential and imitated of Polish poets. Wisława Szymborska (b. 1923, Nobel Prize 1996) revealed her poetic craft in the 1957 volume *Wołanie do Yeti* [Invoking the Abominable Snowman]. She proved to be a subtle ironist fascinated by universal, existential matters. I would place among this leading quintet one more poet who made his debut in 1956: Miron Białoszewski. His first books displayed a dazzling fantasy that linked allusions to ancient culture with images of everyday life. In his prose as well as his poetry, he worked wonders through a radical reliance on the casual and distorted patterns of common speech.

As has often been the case in Polish literature, poetry was the most interesting genre after 1956. There were many other noteworthy poets at work besides the five mentioned above - such as Zbigniew Herbert, already noted, as well as Tymoteusz Karpowicz (b. 1921), Stanisław Grochowiak (1934-1976) and Ernest Bryll (b. 1935). These poets favored various styles, from avant garde language games to fruitful dialogues with tradition (mainly baroque and romantic).

During the two decades beginning in 1956, narrative prose enjoyed a less favorable situation: if for no other reason, because of the fact that it is by its nature closer to the realities of society, manners, and politics – and therefore of far greater interest to the censor than poetry. In this period, the greatest prose success was the debut volume of stories, *Pierwszy krok w chmurach* [The First Step into the Clouds, 1956], by the very young Marek Hłasko (1934-1969). Discarding all ideological baggage, Hłasko turned the spotlight of everyday language on everyday events. In a different situation, this would only have been natural; at that particular time, Hłasko seemed to be giving literary expression to the attitudes of a generation of rebellious youth.

Polish prose had many other concerns as well, and was full of interesting phenomena. Ever since 1945, there had been a need to express the traumatic experiences of the war and occupation. This was not only a matter of a choice of subject, but also a question of finding the narrative form that would be capable of conveying the unique strangeness of a world in a state of destruction and agony. The greatest achievement in this field is the novel *Czarny potok* [The Black Stream] by Leopold Buczkowski (1905-1989), written immediately after the war but only published in the period under discussion. This tale of the annihilation of a small town is told in such a way that the narrator loses control of his tale; the narration collapses and sinks into a deliberate chaos, just as the world doomed to destruction had sunk into its own chaos. Adolf Rudnicki (1912-1990) described the destruction of the Jews in numerous works portraying a world that no longer existed.

Several accomplished writers of various generations produced distinguished prose after 1956: Kazimierz Brandys (1916-2000), Andrzej Kuśniewicz (1904-1993), Julian Stryjkowski (1905-1996) and, among younger writers, Włodzimierz Odojewski (b. 1930), whose outstanding novel *Zasypie wszystko, zawieje* [Everything is on the Verge of Collapse] was published after the period under discussion. This is a vision of the end of a certain historical world, namely the civilization of the former Polish eastern marches, absorbed after the war into the Soviet Union. The censor would not approve it, so the author emigrated in order to publish.

The most influential novelist, however, was Witold Gombrowicz (1904-1969), who can be named without hesitation as the finest Polish prose writer of the century. He had emigrated in 1939. His books, published in Poland in 1956-1957 but available afterwards only in editions from Paris, were read with great attention and frequently imitated. As a diarist as well as a novelist and playwright, Gombrowicz created a model of profound and innovative literary originality that was by turns metaphysical and grotesque. His "school" is a central phenomenon in the development of contemporary Polish literature.

Some of the writers associated with Gombrowicz's influence used an "Aesopian" style - an allegorical, evasive language that referred to the present-day world while avoiding conflicts with the censor. This is true, above all, of Jerzy Andrzejewski (1909-1983). However, the influence of Gombrowicz extends over the whole realm of the grotesque in the Polish narrative, poetic, and dramatic literature of the time. Sławomir Mrożek (b. 1930), author of such works as the splendid *Tango*, became the foremost exponent of the grotesque in drama. Employing absurdities, sharp contrasts and a characteristic idiom, Mrożek's grotesque is a phenomenon of great importance and is emblematic of the period. The surrealism and theatre of the absurd that arose under the influence of Gombrowicz is in itself a kind of defense against the false world of socialist realism, in service to totalitarian ideology. Surrealism and the absurd represent at times a direct and at times an indirect challenge to the compulsory system of values and the officially imposed imagination.

The present sketch is a brief and highly simplified account of the fate of Polish literature in the two decades that followed 1956. I have had to leave out the development of such important genres as the essay. However, the point that bears primary emphasis is the way in which the literature of this period represented a continual effort, using a shifting variety of forms, to find regions amenable to autonomous creation free of the shackles of a totalitarian system that aimed at controlling all aspects of human life. I am convinced that this effort, undertaken by the best Polish writers, was not in vain - and, what is more, that it yielded valuable fruits. Many of the works from this period remain vital, and some have achieved the status of classics of Polish literature.

Translated by William Brand

Leszek Polony
Cracow

Polish Controversies about the Essence of Music after the Second World War

THE TRADITION OF MUSICAL ESTHETICS IN POLAND

Reflections on the essence of music, and therefore on its relation to existence, empirical reality, the spiritual world, or human consciousness, are the domain of musical aesthetics as a division of general aesthetics. This has been called speculative aesthetics, and has been known in more recent times as the philosophy of music. Musical aesthetics thus construed is distinguished from aesthetics of musicological provenance, which is more closely associated with historical, empirical or practical knowledge of music. In practice, it is difficult to lay down a strict border: one must note the significant fluidity of the scope, methods and conceptual-methodological apparatus of musical aesthetics. Finally, aesthetic reflections on music are also of vital interest to critics and the musical public, not to mention more than a few composers. Not infrequently, these reflections become enmeshed in social, religious and political controversies. In my present considerations, therefore, I shall steer closer to the concept of aesthetic ideology, and therefore to a historical perspective on views about the subject of music.

The traditions of Polish musical-aesthetic thinking date back to the Enlightenment period and the turning point between classicism and romanticism. Two principal currents in such thinking finally emerged in the nineteenth century. First, there was the speculative-philosophical aesthetics carried out, within the post-Hegelian mode that dominated Polish philosophy, by such practitioners as Józef Kremer, Karol Libelt, Bronisław Trentowski, August Cieszkowski and Józef Maria Hoene-Wroński. This is a metaphysical-symbolic aesthetics. These philosophers regard music as an absolute art, in the emphatic-symbolic sense of the category, as a reflection of the harmony of the world, an incarnation in sound of the absolute, a delineation of the soul, an expression of human feelings that are associated with a transcendent reality and cannot be translated into words. The nature of such aesthetics is obviously more congenial to a heteronymous concept of music, although in Hoene-Wroński, for instance, we encounter a significant ambiguity. For him, music is the expression of feelings, but it is through the feelings that the "Benign Character of the World" and the "accuracy of subjective creation" make themselves manifest. In the final analysis, Hoene-Wroński defines music as the "aesthetic modification of Time, which itself constitutes *a* priori the incarnation of spirit and intelligence, forming the musical object."[1] His aesthetics thus appears like a Pythagorean mathematical-metaphysical solution, with elements of musical algebra, the concept of absolute scale, and so on.

The second current is the aesthetic thinking found in music journalism, criticism and scholarly studies. There is a marked evolution here from classical and early-romantic aesthetics, through the romantic aesthetics of undefined feelings and including such romantic aesthetic categories as infinity, the poetic, fantasy and the ideal, to an aesthetics that is literary *par excellence,* semantic, and of the nature of descriptive-programmatic hermeneutics (Zygmunt Noskowski, Stanisław Przybyszewski, Ignacy Jan Paderewski). Just as the music of Bach and the classical symphony were the most important issues in the realm of German culture at the dawn of romanticism, so in Polish aesthetic-musical thought it was the work of Chopin that was interpreted in thoroughly poetic categories and connected with the expression of the national consciousness, with romantic sentimentalism, and finally with the irrational sphere of the subconscious in the spirit of Nietzschean philosophical anthropology.

The Young Poland period at the turn of the twentieth century saw the birth of Polish musicology and the flourishing of its leading lights, Zdzisław Jachimecki and Adolf Chybiński. Both men conceived of music in a dualistic way. Chybiński writes about the necessary harmony between content and methods, and about inspiration and musical logic, while assigning pride of place to the musical forms inspired by the voice of the feelings, the spirit of poetry, and the fantasy (and which, following the example of Mieczysław Karłowicz, he referred to as "internal"). Jachimecki speaks of the dualism of the spirit and of "music itself," or sonority. He accepts the programmatic nature of music in the sense of content that is ideal, spiritual, emotional or philosophical in general, while rejecting music that is programmatic in the narrative or descriptive-

[1] Quoted by Charles Henry, *Wroński et l'estéthique musicale.* Paris 1887, p. 17.

naturalistic senses. At the same time, he advances a requirement for the "absoluteness" of music, in the sense of adherence to the laws of logic.

The period between the First and Second World Wars brought a decided turn in the direction of autonomous aesthetics, although not devoid of metaphysical justifications. Karol Szymanowski became the central figure in Polish musical life. In his writings about music he develops an ideological aesthetics that is congruent to the European avant garde of the day. Its fundamental themes are the apology for creative freedom, the idea of the synthesis of racial elements with general human values, and the instinct of musical form. His essay on the work of Chopin[2] is a fundamental text of the period; in it, Szymanowski performs a reinterpretation from the ground up of Chopin's music in the spirit of autotelic aesthetics and the idea of art of a pure form, although Szymanowski's own practices as a composer seem to be fundamentally at variance with such views. Later, in fact, Szymanowski would distance himself from his own decisively formulated theses in order to end up stating that the essence of music is found not in pure form, but in content, which conveys the mythical spirit of a race, or alternatively the emotions of man in the face of the mystery of existence.[3]

Konstanty Regamey conceives of the essence of music in a similar way at this time. The content aspect of music exists and is in fact undeniable, and yet it is also less important. The essence of music lies in the pure form of sound. Nevertheless, it is not something existing unto itself and reducible to sound alone. It is an expression of the unity of existence, of metaphysical feeling.[4]

Stefan Kisielewski formulated the most radical views in these years. Music, he proclaims, is the sum of elements of form and sound, a wholly autonomous art that exists beyond all utility.[5] The twenties and thirties also see the first formulation of theories with scientific ambitions, in the

---

[2] Karol Szymanowski, Fryderyk Chopin, *Skamander*, 1923, 28, 29/30. Reprinted in: K. Szymanowski, *Pisma* [Writings], vol. I. *Pisma muzyczne*.

[3] K. Szymanowski, "Romantyzm w dobie współczesnej. Ankieta o romantyzmie" [Romanticism in the contemporary era. A Survey on romanticism] *Muzyka*, 1928, 7/9. Reprinted in K. Szymanowski, op. cit., vol. I, pp. 229–234.

[4] Konstanty Regamey, *Treść i forma w muzyce* [Content and form in music]. Warszawa, 1933

[5] Stefan Kisielewski, "Oblicze duchowe muzyki współczesnej" [The spiritual face of contemporary music], *Muzyka Polska*, 1937, 7/8; S. Kisielewski, "O wartościach społecznych w muzyce" [On social values in music] *Muzyka Polska*, 1939, 3.

philosophical theory of Roman Ingarden (published in final form in 1958)[6] and the psychological aesthetics of Stefania Łobaczewska.[7]

Ingarden apprehends the existential status of the musical work, as of all products of human spiritual culture, in categories of the *intentional object*. This is an object that, ontologically speaking, is not autonomous in its existence. It is called into existence by creative and re-creative acts of consciousness, and furthermore has its existential foundations in certain objects and processes of the natural world, as for instance the means of musical notation, acts of performance and the psycho-physical acts of the listener. As an intersubjective aesthetic object, it is an intentional product of consciousness, given to many psychological subjects capable of reconstructing it. According to Ingarden, the musical work possesses a character that is in principle autonomous, and is a one-layered sound object with quasi-temporal structure that becomes strictly temporal in performance. At the same time, however, the sound products that make up an intentional musical object are characterized by certain properties that are objective (or, more strictly speaking, intersubjective properties that are therefore in a certain sense independent of the subjective disposition of the individual listener), emotional and aesthetic. Furthermore, there exists the possibility of program or illustrative music where so-called presentational motives (*Darstellungsmotive*) exist. In such cases, the object takes on a two-layered ontological structure.

Stefania Łobaczewska's aesthetics, on the other hand, is radically dualistic, psychological and relativistic. According to her, music is the expression in sound and sense of a special variety of feelings, and as such is grasped both physically and psychologically. The concept of musical content undergoes complete subjectivization – it is dependent on the individual listener, the culture and the epoch, although Łobaczewska remarks at a certain point that music expresses universal and timeless feelings shared by all humankind.

In Polish thinking about music, heteronomic conceptions were always stronger and dominant. In the nineteenth century, this resulted not only from the general character of the epoch (for, as Dahlhaus shows, European romantic thinking was far from unequivocal in this regard), but also from

[6] Roman Ingarden, *Zagadnienie tożsamości dzieła muzycznego* [The problem of the identity of the musical work], "Przegląd Filozoficzny". Warszawa, 1933, vol. XXXVI, p. 340 ff.; R. Ingarden, " Utwór muzyczny i sprawa jego tożsamości" [The musical work and the matter of its identity], In: R. Ingarden, *Studia z estetyki* [Studies from Aesthetics], vol. II. Warszawa, 1958.

[7] Stefania Łobaczewska, *Ogólny zarys estetyki muzycznej* [An outline of musical aesthetics]. Lwów, 1937.

national particulars and historical conditions. With the Polish state no longer in existence, literature had come to occupy the most salient position in the arts. Literature bore the brunt of the struggle to maintain national identity. By the nature of things, music, too, was subordinated to external content and programs, as is shown particularly well by the programmatic-literary interpretation of Chopin's art that Szymanowski attacked with such passion. The historical significance of the Young Poland generation, like the avant garde of the period between the First and Second World Wars, stemmed from an important shifting of emphasis: the attempt to set artistic creativity free from direct, *ad hoc* functions and tasks by pointing up its more universal calling and the significance of its existential and human content, as well as the artistic-aesthetic values of craftsmanship, technique, formal perfection, innovation and originality.

Disputes over Marxist esthetics

At the threshold of the new epoch - in which, after the cataclysm of the war, the entire Polish cultural tradition felt the impact, first, of the pressure of a communist ideology that began to weaken after an initial period of growing intensity, and second of the real need for fundamental re-evaluations that resulted from the evident crisis of "high" culture - the writer, music critic and composer Stefan Kisielewski published a famous article in the Catholic monthly *Znak* titled, "Is Music Non-Humanistic?" The title itself was striking enough, for it suggested that the humanism of music was being called into question. The cultural policy being imposed by the government of the day did indeed regard as humanistic only thematic, vocal-instrumental and above all programmatic music that had content and was emotional and expressive - that is, directly expressive of ideological-political content. Kisielewski stated firmly that "music is . . . the organization of sound, or rather the combination of a range of systems of organization carried out on various levels, from a variety of points of view." The resulting sound product was marked by "what we call the stamp of the individual work, thanks to which composers from the same epoch, using the same technique and style, nevertheless speak as individuals, with each of them saying something different."[8] Kisielewski

---

[8] See Stefan Kisielewski, *Z muzyką przez lata* [With music through the years]. Kraków 1957; *Czy muzyka jest niehumanistyczna?* [Is music non-humanistic?], p. 7 ff. Reprinted with a later (1957) commentary by the author in *Forum Musicum*, 1; *Myśl naukowa i muzyczna* [Scientific and musical thought], Kraków 1967, p. 2 ff.; *Muzyka i mózg. Eseje*[Music and the brain: essays]. Kraków 1974, p. 9 ff.

identified individual testimony to beauty and the truth of existence as the essence of artistic creativity, and defended the universal, timeless calling of art against short-term utilitarianism and opportunism. This was more of an ideological than a theoretical-philosophical controversy. Kisielewski made "Bach's fugue" the symbol of music with the highest degree of autonomy; the fugue was "perfection unto itself," "testimony to the truth and order of nature . . . like the planets spinning around the sun, or like the electron spinning around the atomic nucleus."[9] He went on to write in later essays of "heated, individual emotionalism," "profound zeal," the "ripping drama of expression," and the "intimate lyricism" in Bach's music, as well as about the wealth of emotions and moods in the music of Schubert and Schumann.[10]

The ideological contention against Marxism and socialist realism was soon settled by administrative means. At the famous composers' conference in Łagów Lubuski from August 5-8, 1949, the normative aesthetics of socialist realism in music was proclaimed. Soon afterwards, Stefan Kisielewski lost his post as professor at the Higher School of Music in Cracow. In the wake of these events came a peculiar attempt at formulating Marxist aesthetics in music. This was primarily the work of Zofia Lissa in her writings from 1950-1956. In a standard work of the period,[11] Lissa interpreted music in the spirit of the Leninist theory of reflection: as the reflection of "real reality" and an integral part of the so-called ideological superstructure, or, in other words, as an art that was *par excellence* semantic. The methodological basis of this radical thesis was supposedly the theory of the two- or three-layered representational structure in music. The former appears in illustrative music, where there is an analogy of structure (quality, form, and figure) between the arrangement of sound and the image of the external phenomenon. The latter consists in expressive motives that imitate external signs of emotion, such as gesture, mien, laughter, tears, shouts, and moans. This conception, a development of the theory of expressive movements of Bahl and Flach, could in fact trace its sources back to the late baroque and Enlightenment periods. Lissa had

---

[9] S. Kisielewski, *Muzyka i mózg...*, p. 17.

[10] S. Kisielewski, *Gwiazdozbiór muzyczny* [The musical constellation], vol. I. *Od Bacha do Strawińskiego* [From Bach to Stravinsky]. Kraków: PWM, 1958, pp. 11, 88.

[11] Zofia Lissa, "Leninowska teoria odbicia a estetyka muzyczna" [The Leninist theory of reflection and musical aesthetics], In *Materiały do studiów i dyskusji* [Material for study and discussion], 1950, special issue pp. 95 ff.

already set it out in a prewar study titled *On the Essence of the Comical in Music.*[12]

Now, it became more radical in the spirit of extreme epistemological realism: music reflects and is the mirror-image of so-called "real reality"; it is a variety of the cognitive, sensory-imagistic apprehension of this reality. The category of objective or "real" reality has many synonyms here, such as, for example, the "economic base," the "historical formation," the "ideological-material indicators," "social relations," "productive forces" and "historic time." This category is made absolute. On the other hand, obsessive themes of a doctrinal character appear, such as the discovery of the laws of Marxist dialectics in the historical development of music, the relativization of the value of the musical work (with this value being identified with changing judgments and reception), the limitation of the role of the creative individual in favor of general, goal-oriented phenomena, and the diagnosis of the crisis in contemporary music as being an outgrowth of the capitalistic system. All these theses and themes add up to advocacy of mandated socialist-realist aesthetics: extra-musical programs, a thematic approach in both the musical and extra-musical senses, the adjustment of form to imaginative-representative content (best of all, to dramatic narrative), and the use of folklore as the form of musical expression closest to life and simple people. This strongly mandated aesthetics accompanied an invasion of the territory of reflection on art by hostile political and party language, featuring such formulations as the "front-line struggle," the "situation on the musical front" and the "liquidation and mopping-up of the old base and the old classes."

Lissa's 1953 study of *Selected Aspects of the Issue or Musical Aesthetics in the Light of Joseph Stalin's Work on Linguistics*[13] is generally regarded as a glaring example of political servility. Nevertheless, it is precisely in this study that, paradoxically, Lissa relaxes and liberalizes her position, as compared to the doctrinal extremism cited earlier. Namely, she "discovers" autonomic elements in music that transcend class distinctions, and places increasingly sharp emphasis on the things that are specific to music. In her work of the same year *On the Specifics of Music,* she accentuates such moments as the undefined and objectively ambiguous significance of musical structure and the role of the composer's individuality and

[12] Z. Lissa, "O komizmie muzycznym" [On the comic in music]. In *Szkice z estetyki muzycznej* [Sketches from musical aesthetics]. Kraków: PWM, 1965, p. 9 ff.

[13] In *Studia muzykologiczne* 1953, vol. I, p. 11 ff.

subjectivism, while rejecting naturalist-illustrative program music and defending instrumental music.

From Avant Garde Formalism to Hermeneutics

The turning point of the October 1956 events in Poland, the first political "thaw" and attempt at reforming the "real socialist" system, came soon afterwards. Cultural isolation was undoubtedly broken down and the reception of Western European work accelerated. A new generation of avant garde composers came on the musical scene, led by Krzysztof Penderecki, Henryk Mikołaj Górecki and Wojciech Kilar. Bogusław Schäffer became the radical guiding light of the new direction. An uncompromising proponent of musical autonomy, innovation and artistic progress, he stood for the breaking of all conventions, and for constant searching and experimentation in the sphere of language, forms, genres; and, ultimately of the very ontological status of music.[14]

The older generation of composers and writers on music greeted the new direction with the usual doubts and polemics against the fetish of innovation and explorations of the very spheres of language and form. Zygmunt Mycielski appealed to the traditional categories of sympathetic reaction, emotion, expression, and, finally the meaning of the work of art.[15] Stefan Kisielewski stuck to his idea of the purposeful organization of sound and the logic of forms.[16]

A new generation spoke up in the mid-seventies. This debut paralleled changes in music itself. A process began of gradual withdrawal from the aesthetics of pure sound and standard sonoristic forms in favor of narrative-harmonic music that made a synthesis of a particular sort of neotonalism with the use of the full range of twelve-tone material.

These are the years of such compositions as Henryk M. Górecki's *Ad Matrem, II Symfonia "Kopernikowska"* ["Copernican"] and *III Symfonia* (*Symfonia pieśni żałosnych*) ["Symphony of Sorrowful Songs"]; Witold Lutosławski's *Livre pour orchestre, Mi-parti* and *Les espaces du sommeil,* Krzysztof Penderecki's *Przebudzenie Jakuba* [The Awaking of Jacob] and *Polskie Requiem* [The Polish Requiem], Marek Stachowski's *Poéme sonore* and Zbigniew Bujarski's *Musica domestica*. Composers who made their

[14] Schäffer's famous work *New Music: The Problems of Contemporary Compositional Technique,* appeared in 1957.

[15] Zygmunt Mycielski, *Postludia. Artykuły, felietony, eseje* [Postlude: articles, columns, and essays]. Kraków: PWM, 1977.

[16] S. Kisielewski, *Z muzycznej międzyepoki* [Between musical epochs] . Kraków: PWM, 1966.

debuts in these years included Eugeniusz Knapik, Andrzej Krzanowski, Aleksander Lasoń and Paweł Szymański. In aesthetic views, there was a return to theses about the heteronomic, expressive-symbolic or semiotic character of music. This position found expression among the older generation in the writing of Mieczysław Tomaszewski[17] and Bohdan Pociej.[18] Andrzej Chłopecki, Krzysztof Droba, Krystyna Tarnawska-Kaczorowska, Małgorzata Gąsiorowska and the author of the present piece all broke into print. A common theme is a turning away from the ideas of the musical avant garde of the late fifties and early sixties: the idea of music resulting from mathematical principles, the transposition into sound of purely intellectual constructions, and the reduction of music to the investigation of the tonal sphere alone. There were proposals for renewing romantic emotionalism, and the value of intuition, feeling, and finally of the subjectivity of composer and listener were accentuated in a new approach that was not speculative and intellectual as with the post-serial avant-garde, but rather consonant with the spirit of personalism and apologies for naturalism and spontaneity. These intellectual processes paralleled the reception of semiotics and hermeneutic thought on Polish ground, for this was the time of the first Polish translations of Levi-Strauss, Umberto Eco, Eliade, Fromm, and also of Ricoeur, Heidegger and Gadamer. The principal refrain running through the writing on music in these years sounded like this: the essence of music does not lie in arrangements, constructions and constellations of sound. It lies rather in emotional, symbolic, and philosophical significances and senses that transcend the world of sound.

Some musicologists of the older generation continued their reflections in a sociological vein. Zofia Lissa's *New Sketches in the Musical Essay* came out in 1975, and Stefan Jarociński's *Romantic Ideologies* in 1979. Lissa took up the problem of the essence of the musical work, the understanding of music, historical consciousness and its role in contemporary musical culture, and, finally, the reception of music. She melded intellectually modernized, non-dogmatic Marxism with new methodological impulses, and above all semiology. She performed a creative adaptation of the theories of aesthetic communication of Max Bense and Umberto Eco for

---

[17] Mieczysław Tomaszewski, "Wprowadzenie do teorii utworu słowno-muzycznego" [Introduction to the theory of the verbal-musical work]. In: *Spotkania muzyczne w Baranowie 1976. Muzyka w kontekście kultury* [Musical meetings in Baranów 1976: Music in the context of culture]. L. Polony (ed.), Kraków: PWM, 1978, p. 167 ff.

[18] Bohdan Pociej, *Szkice z późnego romantyzmu* [Sketches from late romanticism]. Kraków: PWM 1978.

the use of aesthetic theory or the ontology of the musical work.[19] Once again, she launched into a polemic with Ingarden's theory of the musical work. She regarded the work as a category of thought and a historically limited cultural concept. She stated that there are various phenomena of musical culture and musical existence that do not fit into these categories, such as folk music, improvisation and aleatory works.

The interpretation of music as a message in sound assumes that its significance depends on cultural context and is honed in the communicative dialogue between source and recipient. This leads to a wholly new ontology of music in which perception, reception, comprehension, receptive scheme and auditory habits all participate in creating an ontological structure of aesthetic communication while modifying its significance and interpretation. This, in turn, leads to the assignment of a special role to the concept of "cultural consciousness" or artistic consciousness, or aesthetic ideology - in a new, broader sense - as a primary ontological reality in relation to the concrete phenomena and forms of musical culture. This was the leading thesis of Jarociński's *Romantic Ideology,* which undertook a fundamental settling of accounts with German romanticism, and especially with the work of Wagner.[20] The philosophical influence of Adorno's Frankfurt school can be seen clearly here.

In our time, Władysław Stróżewski has continued and broadened the classical sort of aesthetic reflection on music in its phenomenological and Ingardenian variety.[21] Among other things, Stróżewski grapples with the problem of the temporality of music and the mode of existence of emotional qualities. Music, he states, is neither a symbol nor a sign of these qualities, but rather evokes them in their ideal purity, separate from real causes, states or events, as a specific equivalent of our experiences, and as an explication and interpretation of them in sound. One might term this a decidedly monistic and autonomous standpoint on the essence of music. At the same time, the concept of "interpretation" or "explication" clearly leans towards semiotic categories. Michał Piotrowski defined a similar position as "incarnational heteronomy," where music reveals, manifests, exemplifies, personifies, and is a mode of existence for a non-

---

[19] Z. Lissa, *Nowe szkice z estetyki Muzycznej* [New sketches from musical aesthetics]. Kraków: PWM 1975, pp. 49–50.

[20] Stefan Jarociński, *Ideologie romantyczne* [Romantic ideologies]. Kraków: PWM 1979.

[21] Władysław Stróżewski, "Czas piękna" [Beautiful time]. In: *Melos-Logos-Etos. Materiały sympozjum poświęconego twórczości Floriana Dąbrowskiego, Stefana Kisielewskiego, Zygmunta Mycielskiego* [Melos-Logos-Etos: Material from a symposium on the work of Florian Dąbrowski, Stefan Kisielewski, and Zygmunt Mycielskiego]. Warszawa 1987, p. 59 ff.

musical state of affairs.[22] Stróżewski goes on to distinguish four spheres of subjectivity to which music appeals: sensuality, emotionality, intellect, and the metaphysical. This latter is the sphere where super-aesthetic values like the sublime, the tragic, mystery, the demonic, the holy, or the ecstatic constitute themselves. This is the sphere of transcendence, Inspiration and reference to the Absolute.

In Polish aesthetic-musical reflections, the musical hermeneutic currently takes on two distinct natures: one of phenomenological provenance, for Bohdan Pociej, and another of semiotic-structuralist provenance for Mieczysław Tomaszewski[23] or Michał Bristiger.[24] I would term Tomaszewski's structuralism "generative," in view of the obvious analogies between his philosophical and methodological position, and the generative school in modern linguistics. This is a search for overarching categories of human experience that govern linguistic, musical, and, in general, the symbolic communication that makes up artistic culture. Tomaszewski captures the essence of music in "significant forms," the meaning of which is inexpressible in language, non-discursive and multisignificant. Michał Bristiger writes about music as a symbol or a form of myth in sound. Characteristically, both authors call into question the dichotomy or division of music into the heteronomic and the autonomic. There have been several significant recently contributions to musical aesthetics. Ewa Kofin[25] has indicated the possibility of interpreting music as a "language of formal significances," an explication of introverted semiosis, or a self-referring message, that is, a language devoid of internal significances (a possibility rejected as logically contradictory by Tibor Kneif and Mieczysław Tomaszewski). On the other hand, she points to the obvious examples of semioticization and codification that refer music to extra-musical reality, as in the baroque system of rhetorical figures or the Wagnerian *leitmotif* system. In a survey of the great variety of positions on the essence of music, Michał Piotrowski[26] points out the basic fact that aesthetic views on the subject are strongly marked axiologically, formulated with pretensions to universality, and normative in character.

[22] Michał Piotrowski, *Autonomiczne wartości muzyki* [Automomous musical values]. Poznań, 1984.

[23] M. Tomaszewski, *Interpretacja integralna dzieła muzycznego, Rekonesans* [Integral interpretation of the musical work: a reconnaissance]. Kraków: Akademia Muzyczna, 2000.

[24] Michał Bristiger, *Związki muzyki ze słowem* [Connections of music with words]. Kraków: PWM, 1988.

[25] Ewa Kofin, *Semiologiczny aspekt muzyki* [Semiological aspects of music]. Wrocław, 1990.

[26] M. Piotrowski, *Autonomiczne...* .

They reveal varying concepts of the values of the musical work. Maria Piotrowska investigated historical and contemporary concepts in musical hermeneutics.[27] Today, hermeneutics figures as the most serious option in the contemporary humanities. It defines itself as a theory of understanding that expresses itself in the art of interpreting texts and cultural products. Hermeneutic musicology stands in opposition to both the scientific objectivization, and the emotional subjectivization of music. It postulates the discovery of the sense and content of music in the musical material itself, in technique and form, in sound structures. Strict methods of musical analysis make sense only to the degree that they further the understanding and interpretation of the musical work. Free, subjective interpretation not grounded in the language and structure of the musical work or in the wider biographical-cultural context, as in Hermann Kretzschmar and Arnold Schering, is useless from the point of view of musical cognition.

Recently, the problem of emotional significance in music has been taken up from the perspective of analytical philosophy broadly conceived. Krzysztof Guczalski has undertaken a critical reconstruction and development of the theory of musical expression as formulated by Susanne Langer from the point of view of the contemporary theory of the sign. The symbolism of language is non-representational in nature, and "language basically shares no forms with anything that it symbolizes." Music, on the other hand, conveys the form of emotions in their *specificity*. Guczalski points out the intellectual import and relevance of the views of Aristotle, Mendelssohn, Wackenroder or Schopenhauer on music, testing them with the aid of a precise and strict analysis of terminological distinctions and conceptual classifications.[28]

What conclusions can we draw from this historical bird's eye view? They could point in two directions. First, towards historical relativism: views change, are ephemeral, reflect current states of the soul, artistic consciousness and culture. On the other hand, the fundamental permanence of certain questions and themes is striking; these include the problem of the purely sonic versus the signifying nature of music, and its reference to human existence or being on the one hand, and its role in cultural

[27] Maria Piotrowska, *Tezy o możliwości hermeneutyki muzycznej w świetle stu lat jej historii* [Theses on the possibilities of musical hermeneutics in the light of the one hundred years of its history]. Warszawa, 1990.

[28] Krzysztof Guczalski, *Znaczenie muzyki, znaczenie w muzyce* [The meaning of music, meaning in music]. Kraków: Musica Iagellonica 1999.

communication on the other. Basically, these are the questions that were posed at the beginning of European culture by Pythagoras and his pupils. Permit me to call to mind the answer: music is a reflection of the harmony of the universe, but it nevertheless remains particularly connected to the human soul, and is furthermore an ethical and emotional message of fundamental significance to the human collective. I think that it is still difficult to come up with a better answer.

Translated by William Brand

Some Aspects of the Musical Avant Garde

Zbigniew Skowron
Warsaw

Trends in European Avant Garde Music of the 1950s and 1960s

A glance at radical currents in European music during the second half of the 20th century indicates that their culminating point, just as we can observe of parallel avant garde trends in painting and literature, came in the 1950s and 1960s. The musical avant garde of that period constituted a highly dynamic and multidimensional phenomenon, which may be considered not only as mere creativity, but also from the perspective of its aesthetic or, rather, antiaesthetic program *per se*. Another revolutionary aspect of the musical avant garde may be noticed in performance and its impact on listeners. While starting from a traditional model of musical performance and communication with the audience, the avant garde initiated a particular kind of artistic manifestation, which opened up new functions of perception and changed the existing roles of listeners. These latter ceased to be only the more or less passive recipients of a creative message, coming instead to be included in the act of creation as active participants. Consequently, the aesthetic experience of the audience acquired a new dimension, often similar to the reactions of participants in ritual practices.

Although the postwar musical avant garde co-existed with other currents that maintained their ties with tradition, such as neo-classicism, it nevertheless dominated the output of the 1950s and 1960s as an expansive and influential aesthetic option. Its particular potential resulted from the combination of two tendencies. On the one hand, the avant garde exploited to the utmost the idea of breaking with tradition. As a consequence of this process, its own ideas, experiments, and explorations attained an unprecedented level of radicalism. The imperative of novelty at all costs, which became one of the main creative impulses for the avant garde, led it even to the limits of musicality, that is, beyond the accessible aural area. Among examples of such radical inventions may be cited, on the one hand, John Cage's *4'33"* with its use of silence and of pure flow of time and, on the other hand, conceptual music with its abstract sphere of soundless ideas.

What gave the postwar avant garde its particular richness and vitality was its deepened interdisciplinary relations. The Romantic idea of the correspondence des arts, which was intensified by various trends within musical expressionism such as Alexander Scriabin's vision of a synaesthetic art, became even more extended around 1950 as a wholly new sort of synthesis of the arts in the happening and the instrumental theater. What these two avant garde genres brought about was a suspension of traditional aesthetic functions of sounds and words in music in favor of a spontaneous action in full view of the public. Apart from its real, perceptible shape, including images and gestures, such an action was in fact a free play of semantic associations and an unfettered flow of events, often modeled on the poetics of dream or on surrealistic art.

In spite of their strongly marked individuality, it is hardly possible to consider the European avant garde currents of the 1950s and 1960s as isolated events, devoid of any diachronic relations. After all, these currents displayed a dualistic nature: they were both the fruit of the cultural situation *hic et nunc* - products of their own time - and also the outgrowth of what preceded them. Looked at in historical perspective, they reveal their connections with radical tendencies in music from the beginning of the 20th century. It is precisely such historical affinities that mark the beginnings of electronic and concrete music, and, on the other hand, the music of total serialism in the Darmstadt school. A full understanding of these currents and of the innovations they initiated seems impossible without considering their references to earlier endeavors of this kind, such as Varèse's project of research in electronic music from the 1930s or Webern's vision of serialism.

The first European experimental studios and centers for research into electroacoustical music after the Second World War started in Paris. The programs of such centers as the Groupe de Recherches Musicales or the Studio d'Essai were laid down by the two leading representatives of French concrete music, Pierre Schaeffer and Pierre Henry. An equally active centre was the WDR Studio für Elektronische Musik, founded in Cologne at the beginning of the 1950s, and featuring among its early collaborators such figures as Herbert Eimert and Karlheinz Stockhausen. By that time, another prominent avant-gardist from the Darmstadt circle, Luigi Nono, carried out his experiments at the Studio di Fonologia Musicale in Milan.

The electroacoustical experiments in the studios in Paris drew creative impulses from both the heritage of the Italian futurists and the pre-war projects of Varèse. Thus Pierre Schaeffer and Pierre Henry brought to realization the vision that Luigi Russolo had presented as early as in 1913, in his *Manifesto dei rumori*, calling the result "concrete music." The basic source of the sound material, considered as an object of electroacoustical transformation and montage, was for Schaeffer and Henry various sounds stemming from the surrounding world, but also some instrumental sounds and the human voice. Such works of theirs as *Étude aux chemins de fer* or *Symphonie pour un homme seul* soon became master examples of this new compositional technique. From the start, the Parisian experiments with electroacoustic music were accompanied by theoretical reflection represented, among other things, by Schaeffer's *A la recherche d'une musique concrète* of 1952 or his *Traité des objets musicaux* of 1966. The fruits of this reflection became the basic categories defining the musical status of a new sound material, its structuring, and its expressive function. One such category was the concept of the *objet sonore*, which superseded the traditional concept of sound as determined by uniform tempered tuning, the scale and timbre of available instruments, and the conventional use of the human voice.

Almost simultaneous with the Parisian centers of *musique concrète* was the foundation of the electronic music studio in Cologne, which were to determine many aspects of its future development. Among Stockhausen's first pioneering achievements were his *Elektronische Studien I* (1953) and *II* (1954), which gained a firm place in the history of 20th-century music as the first compositions ever constructed out of synthetic sound material, i.e., sinus tones and their combinations. *Elektronische Studien II* also became the first electronic work to be published as a score, which, considered in Cartesian terms of time and space rather than according to traditional ways of notating pitch and rhythm, revolutionized existing musical notation. Apart from new principles for the indication of such basic parameters as frequency, duration, and dynamics of sound, this score revealed an original graphic shape of its own, suggesting, for instance, the geometrical figures in Piet Mondrian's canvases. Gradually, along with further experiments in both Paris and Cologne, a tendency toward a synthesis of concrete and purely electronic material with the sounds of traditional instruments and the human voice emerged. The most interesting results of such explorations include Stockhausen's *Gesang der Jünglinge* of 1956, in which he combined a masterful command of electronic and vocal effects and an unprecedented spatial design in the form of multi-channel sound projection.

Another strong avant garde trend in the 1950s, i.e., total serialism, demonstrates evident connections with the heritage of the ultramodern music of the first half of the 20th century. The new vision of musical structure that was born in the Darmstadt school remained under the strong influence of the Second Viennese School and, more specifically, of its last exponent Anton Webern. Yet Stockhausen's and Boulez's attitudes towards the Viennese School reveal a significant aesthetic polarization. Their devotion to Webern's serialism goes hand-in-hand with a distancing from Schoenberg's 12-tone concept, which they accused of a lack of determination, not to say a lack of courage, in bringing to fruition all the potentials of the 12-tone method he had invented. The representatives of the post-war avant garde discovered in such mature Webern's works as the Symphony for small orchestra, Op. 21, or the Piano Variations, Op. 27, not only perfect models of serial structure, but also signposts pointing to their own further explorations, which, based on the idea of order as an all-embracing structure, led to the concept of total serialism.

It should be emphasized that the post-Webernian trend which dominated in the 1950s was created by a new generation of composers whose musical maturing took place directly after the Second World War, and who witnessed the spiritual devastation it brought about. This is what seems to explain the zeal with which the then young "angry men" – Stockhausen, Boulez, Luciano Berio, Luigi Nono, Henri Pousseur and Karel Goeyvaerts, to mention only a few – started laying the foundations of a *new* and, as they thought, *ideal* order of sound. The intentions of these post-Webernians undoubtedly revealed the traits of a group doctrine. What reinforced their sense of a common activity based on a clearly delineated aesthetic program, was the International Summer Courses in New Music in Darmstadt in the late-1940s and the early-1950s. This was, indeed, a special forum for diverse but extremely consistent endeavors, beginning with the propagation of the idea of an all-encompassing serial order along with its adequate procedures, and proceeding to actual performance of the newly created works. "The existing sound-orders," Stockhausen wrote, "are useless for the realization of a homogenous conception of music. This conception can only be associated with an appropriate ordering of material when music emerges as a total, perfect order; when one will acknowledge and accept its necessity."[1]

It was the image of a *perfect* sound structure subordinated to serial rules that became both the main premise and goal of the explorations of the young avant-gardists in the Darmstadt circle. They conceived this *idée fixe* as a guarantee to the maintenance of complete independence from the heritage of tradition, and especially from a syntax based on tonal centres and on the principles of motivic or thematic processes with their regularity and symmetry. The constant flow of musical material in multifarious, serially structured shapes became the end in itself, liberated from the traditional aesthetic function of music, i.e., from the communication of emotions and meanings. Yet although these idealistic, not to say absolutist, premises might awaken doubts as to their aural impact, the enthusiasts of serial structuralism remained fascinated by the idea of the new order, regardless of the fact that the degree of its complexity might make the aural perception of this perfect structure almost impossible.

Around 1960, the avant garde idea of musical structure with all its parameters subjected to serial ordering reached its peak in three exemplary compositions: Nono's *Varianti* for violin, woodwind, and strings (1957); Stockhausen's *Gruppen für 3 Orchester* (1958); and Boulez's *Structures II* for two pianos (1961). At this time of masterful achievements in total serialism, it was Boulez especially who started to become convinced that perfect structure *per se* cannot guarantee the aesthetic value of a work, which is measured - in addition to technical skill - on the basis of creative imagination. "Technique," Boulez stated, "is not, in fact, a dead weight to be dragged around as a guarantee of immortality. It is an exalting mirror which the imagination forges for itself, and in which its discoveries are reflected. . . . It has often been said that music is as much science as an art; how could these two entities be fired in the same crucible, except by the Imagination, that 'queen of faculties'!"[2]

---

[1]Karlheinz Stockhausen, *Texte zur elektronischen und instrumentalen Musik*. Cologne, 1963, vol. I, p. 19.

[2]Pierre Boulez, *Boulez on Music Today*, tr. Susan Bradshaw and Richard Rodney Bennett, (Cambridge: Harvard University Press, 1971), p. 143.

At the same time as the European post-Webernians started to relax the rigor of their serial structures, they became aware of John Cage's concept of indeterminacy, which he introduced at Darmstadt in 1959. From that moment on, European avant-gardists faced a diametrically opposed option based on the application of chance both during the process of composition and in the act of its performance. This particular moment seems to have initiated what may be called the avant garde's second phase, which was marked by such works as Stockhausen's *Klavierstück XI* (1962) and Boulez's Third Sonata for piano (1963). Boulez in fact developed his own aleatoric variant in such works as *Pli selon pli* (1958-1967), where chance procedures are influenced by the very nature of the poetry of Stéphane Mallarmé.

The aleatoric trend in European music has taken different shapes depending on individual approaches to the role of chance both in the compositional processes and in performance. This was also a consequence of the way particular composers understood the idea of an "open" work, and of what degree of indeterminacy they adopted. In an imposing array of aleatoric concepts, one that stood out was the coherent vision of Iannis Xenakis: he adopted a new approach to the continuity of musical process, which he conceived as a combination of various glissando lines with fluidly changing dynamics and density of texture. His orchestral work *Metastasis* (1955) is one of the best examples of this particular technique. Xenakis based his aleatory concept on the calculus of probability and on game theory, which allowed him, in works like *Stratégie* for two orchestras (1962) or *Terretektorh* for orchestra dispersed among the audience (1966), to expose new structural properties in a work, arising from its various degrees of coherence and continuity along a gamut from the state of integration to the state of chaos.

Together with the influence of Cage's concept of indeterminacy and his aesthetics, which changed previous avant garde ideas of form and process and, above all, the sense of the musical artifact, such genres as happenings and instrumental theater, as well as conceptual, graphic, and multimedia works, emerged in European music. In contrast to earlier avant garde trends, which stemmed, in fact, from the 19th-century tradition of absolute music, both aleatorism and the above-mentioned "borderline" genres were connected with other areas of avant gardeart. What influenced, for instance, the idea of a musical work as an open, spontaneously created form was action painting, abstract expressionism, the mobile, and *informel*. These "borderline" avant garde currents went far beyond the traditional model of the creation of a musical *opus* which, in turn, through its performance, was to become the object of perception and aesthetic experience. This latter model was confronted with, or even challenged by, some new genres. The first of them, defined as conceptual music, laid particular stress on potentiality, openness, and the mere sense of creative act and its immediate outcome, by limiting itself to verbal instructions, which were closely related to such modern lyric poetry as Mallarmé's *poésie pure*. It is precisely by analogy with his poetry that the essence of conceptual music can be grasped. As Hugo Friedrich wrote, "in regard to Mallarmé, however, music should not be construed merely as harmonious language. For him, music is, in addition, a vibrating of the intellectual substance of poetry and its abstract tensions, a vibrating audible more to the inner than to the outer ear."[3] Among the many examples of conceptual music, one that deserves special attention is Stockhausen's *Aus den sieben Tagen* (1968), limited to a set of short texts. These verbal messages, with their characteristic indefiniteness and openness, direct potential performers toward a sensually ineffable concept of sound, close to the idea of the ancient harmony of the cosmos.

Another avant garde current, which was developing dynamically along with conceptual music, was graphic music. It consisted basically in materializing the musical idea in the form of notation, which could become more or less precise instruction for the performer, but in most cases maintained the status of a work of graphic art. The essence of this avant garde *Augenmusik* could be reduced to the mere *suggestion* of musicality through various abstract figures and shapes. Both conceptual and graphic music involved specific action, which, although assuming an indeterminate character, was supposed to lead to their realization. Contrary to this potential, more or less suggested, action, the avant garde also exploited actual performance conceived of as the essence of a musical work. This is what developed further as so called "action music" or happening, with its spontaneous chain of actions here and now, and in direct contact with the audience. The scene of such happening practices, in which the listeners were frequently involved, was not only concert halls and modern-art galleries, but also city streets and outdoor locations.

---

[3]Hugo Friedrich, *The Structure of Modern Poetry*, tr. Joachim Neugroschel, (Evanston: Northwestern University Press, 1974), p. 103.

All these "borderline" areas of avant garde art were characterized by *collective* activity. In the broadest sense, this took the form of a worldwide movement, which was called Fluxus and brought together many representatives of various areas of art who were interested in multimedia and stood in clear opposition to the received canons of "high" art. The artistic orientation of the Fluxus movement, and especially its negative attitude toward the traditional functions of art, was clearly expressed by Georg Maciunas:

> FLUX ART - non art - amusement forgoes distinction between art and non art, forgoes artists' indispensability, exclusiveness, individuality, ambition, forgoes all pretension towards significance, variety, inspiration, skill, complexity, profundity, greatness, institutional and commodity value. It strives for nonstructural, non-theatrical, non-baroque, impersonal qualities of a simple, natural event, an object, a game, a puzzle or a gag. It is a fusion of Spike Jones, gags, games, vaudeville, and Duchamp.[4]

Collective activity in the performance of works created within the Fluxus movement was often based on improvisation, which was intended not only to reverse (or to deny) the individual sense of the composition and performance of the musical work, but also its other traditional attributes, such as content communicated in a closed form. The anarchistic tendencies of the Fluxus movement were associated with its overwhelming postulate "Art is Life and Life is Art," which was intended to rebuild the bonds between the artist and his or her potential audiences.

Although the Fluxus movement appeared in the American context as an alternative to abstract expressionism, it also had its European manifestations in the works, for instance, of Vinko Globokar and Mauricio Kagel. The latter contributed significantly to the development of an avant garde musical theater, which he conceived of as a stepping-stone for a kind of critical dialog with the whole set of aesthetic qualities (and values) that constituted the legacy of the Western musical tradition. The result of these re-evaluations was not only a radical change in the traditional status of the work as *opus perfectum* and its performance, but also the liberation of totally new relations between the sound and the action on stage or, more generally, between the aural and visual sides of the performance. In other words, Kagel's instrumental theatre not only involves auditory qualities but, more importantly, uses them as objects in

---

[4]Georg Maciunas, *Fluxus Manifesto*, quoted after Roger Sutherland, *New Perspectives in Music* (London: 1994), p. 191.

his double-dealing game of stylistic and aesthetic conventions, juxtaposing them according to the rules of Dada. This playing with separate musical elements, which are removed from their "natural" contexts, places the listener in a new situation. As Roger Sutherland has observed, "deprived of the usual signposts of musical discourse and ritual, the listener finds himself lost in a mythical darkness where every sound and gesture is invested with mystery, ambiguity, and strangeness."[5]

The idea of collective improvisation conceived as a creative act liberated from traditional rules and conventions, and especially from the romantic idea of creativity as a highly individualistic act, was taken up by several European avant garde groups. One of them was the English AMM group, founded by three musicians with backgrounds in jazz: Eddie Prévost, Lou Gare and Keith Row. They were soon joined by Cornelius Cardew, one of the leading British avant-gardists. A group that arose in its turn from the pointillist tradition was the Gruppo Nuovo Consonanza, founded in Rome in 1964, and including Franco Evangelisti, Mario Bertoncini and Ennio Morricone. The use of electronic media and technology set the direction for groups like Musica Elettronica Viva (also founded in Rome, in 1966, by Frederic Rzewski, Allen Bryant and Richard Teitel) or Gentle Fire (founded in London in 1968).[6]

A special place among European avant garde groups was occupied by the Scratch Orchestra, founded in 1969 by Cornelius Cardew, Michael Parsons and Howard Skempton. In their activity may be found elements of both graphic and conceptual music, as well as an original model of improvised music that placed more emphasis on the internal harmonizing of the players and their spontaneous interaction than on the professional level of the actual performance. All of these characteristics are embodied in Cardew's *The Great Learning* (1968), based on the texts of Confucius and divided into several "paragraphs."

Apart from aleatoric, graphic and action music, the European avant garde of the early 1960s also gave rise to other currents that made it possible to overcome the deadlock in which total serialism had then found itself. As opposed to the concept of musical indeterminacy and to the openness toward all kinds of sound-qualities in the surrounding world, these new tendencies emphasized empirical and sensual approaches to

[5]R. Sutherland, *New Perspectives…*, p. 202.

[6] Niall O'Loughlin calls this performing ensemble The Fires of London (editor).

sound material. This is what became evident particularly in the works of György Ligeti, who left Hungary in 1956 and started to collaborate with the Electronic Music Studio in Cologne. He soon decided to abandon abstract serial structures in favor of patterns whose primary goal was no longer the attainment of an ideal *order*, but rather the establishment of a broad spectrum of *sonorities*. Such a premise changed (if not reversed) the hierarchy of aesthetic qualities adopted by the serialists, since the sound effect, which in their works depended on serial ordering, now regained its foreground status as a primary parameter. What was also re-evaluated in the sonoristic current represented by Ligeti was the Cagean idea of sound material *per se*, although its principal source remained traditional instruments and the human voice.

The possibility of creating new sonorities, which would be free from an abstract and elusive order, opened for the musical avant garde a new and broad creative perspective. Such Ligeti's works as *Apparitions* for orchestra (1959), *Atmosphères* for orchestra (1961), and *Ramifications* for string orchestra (1969) testify to how attractive aural effects could be obtained through this both empirical and sensual approach to the sound material. Ligeti's ground-breaking contribution to the sonoristic tendency, however, consisted not only in his free invention of sounds, but also in his way of structuring them. Ligeti made a successful effort to return to the basic elements of a musical work, i.e., to harmony and counterpoint, endowing them with highly individual properties. As far as the harmony is concerned, in his works the equivalents of traditional chord structures are vertical constructions with varying degrees of density, depending on the number and size of the intervals used. Such chord-aggregates and tone-clusters produced their effect not only through their pitch structures, from which thirds, fourths, or fifths were practically absent, but also as "bundles" made up of other parameters, such as duration, volume, and articulation. On the analogy of his harmonic innovations, Ligeti proposed a new approach to counterpoint, which he conceived as densely layered strata moving by small intervals and thus creating an effect of micropolyphony. Significantly for his works, this new counterpoint is felt not only in a linear sense, but also, and perhaps above all, in a sonorous one. This considerable stratification of sound-layers made the tiny details of their structures indistinct and evoked the effect of fluctuation, which often takes the form of a flickering field of sounds.

In the 1950s and 1960s, that is, in the most intensive period of activity of the European musical avant garde, an unprecedented broadening of the modern musical experience, already begun in the first half of the 20th century, was taken further. The special nature of the second avant garde's explorations consisted in the fact that they were not only emerging in the works themselves, in the compositional techniques, materials, and structures, but they also involved the area of aesthetic ideas and perceptual habits. In all these areas, the avant-gardists went far beyond the borders of the conventions inherited from the romantic-classical tradition. Moreover, they replaced them with a radical, indeterminate idea of the creative process, of the musical work, and of its perception. The experiences that the European avant garde underwent at the end of the 1960s were a culminating point in its striving to broaden (or deny) inherited norms and models, often in the name of seeking *the new* at all costs. At the same time, there began to emerge an awareness of the fact that this radical imperative would inevitably be exhausted, since it led to a point from which it was impossible to see further new horizons. It was exactly at this point that two perspectives started to develop that heralded the decline of the avant garde. One of them was the radical reduction of means of expression in the minimalist trend, while the second consisted in a return to sources from the more or less distant past, which soon became the objects of post-modern games.

Krzysztof Szwajgier
Cracow

Penderecki and the Avant Garde

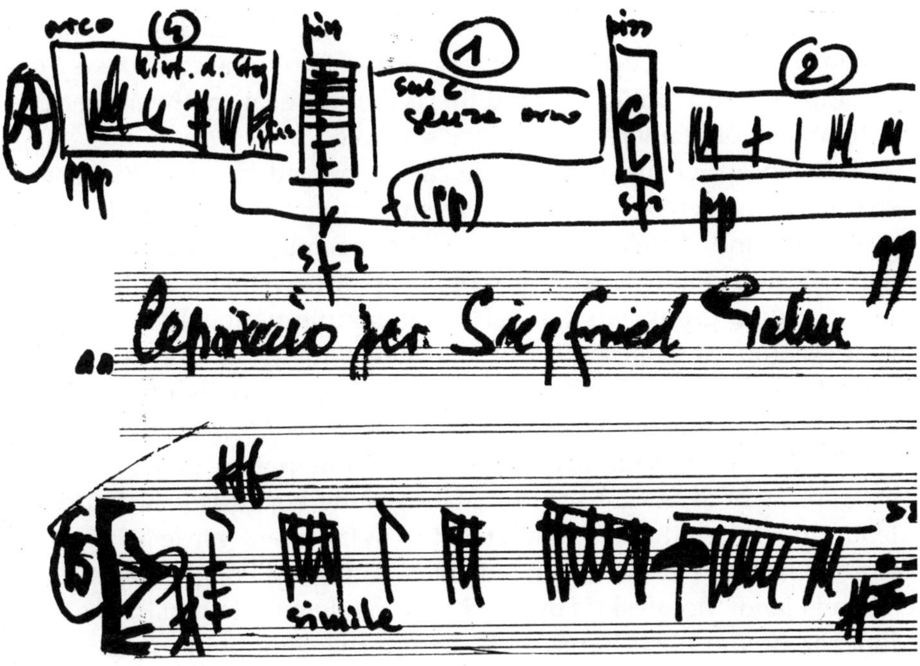

It might appear at first sight that almost everything is known about the relation between Penderecki's work and the avant garde. When placing his work in periods, a distinction is usually drawn between the first two, properly avant garde periods, which differ from the subsequent phase that is increasingly concerned with the musical past. There is the well-known accusation of "the betrayal of the avant garde" that has been leveled at Penderecki, beginning with the *Passion* (or, indeed, even from the *Stabat Mater*), and the even more damning charge of conformism or downright opportunism based on the composer's increasingly tonal musical language, his choice of texts and titles, and the occasional nature of his work. In his own statements, Penderecki tends to treat the avant garde and its practitioners with distance, while almost always enunciating the word "tradition" with esteem and in the context of the names of the great past masters. The image is completed by Penderecki's universally familiar role as the conductor of a carefully selected repertoire (Shostakovich, Mendelssohn, Beethoven, Dvorak, and Bruckner), and as a lover of old art, an exemplar of erudition, and a collector.

Today, forty years on from the avant garde breakthrough of the 1960s, we can look on this whole issue with more distance, and also in greater detail. When we do so, it turns out that judgments made in the heat of the moment to accompany the appearance of each new work by the composer might be reevaluated in terms of both the controversy over the nature of the avant garde (and this is the real heart of the matter), and the treatment of Penderecki's work as a whole.

The concept of the avant garde can be treated in a variety of ways. What we come across most often are studies that are historical (treating the genesis and development of twentieth-century avant garde movements), historiosophical (offering philosophical-aesthetic explications of the succeeding groups and classifying them into periods), or downright historicist (offering theses about the ineluctability of the avant garde element inherent in the whole history of Western art, as proved by the development of that art).

An alternative approach has been the attempt to penetrate to the very essence of avant-gardism by investigating key artistic attitudes and identifying the irreducible characteristics of the avant garde achievement (here we find the familiar, fundamental studies by Poggioli, Kostelanetz and, in Poland, Morawski, Turowski and, in reference to music, Skowron). More rarely, the issue is researched from the standpoint of semiology, sociology or psychology – yet these approaches are hardly any less valid. Who can say whether the psychological and characterological factors may not be an important element here and might be capable, in favorable external circumstances, of giving rein to the radical imperative to rebuild the whole world anew? It might well be that avant garde attitudes in themselves could constitute the starting point for the creation of radical works, genres, events, creative groups, trends, and directions, or even stylistic alignments.

Practically every artist who was active at the end of the twentieth century had, consciously or not, to take a position in relation to the avant garde as it existed at the time. In the case of the younger Polish composers who came on the scene in the mid-1950s, however, taking up this sort of fundamental reckoning coincided with the moment of their initiation into the avant garde, into that legendary and previously unknown zone of forbidden territory. They had to make up their minds quickly, at the very moment when they were bedazzled and fascinated. None of the "younger generation" of the day conceals that fascination when looking back on that period. Who knows? Perhaps the very fact that they were soaking up the Western avant garde at the exact moment when they were making the most important choices about their future artistic development could have determined the stunningly easy and spectacular rise of the so-called "Polish composers' school."

Now, in seeking the essence and origins of the twentieth-century avant garde movements, when passing over the factors of less-than-primary importance and attempting to see farther than the collective and individual self and to move beyond what is personal - and therefore, apparently, most important to each of us - and to arrive at the things that are worth devoting one's labor, fate, and at times even one's life to, we come to the domain of axiology. Things of value are precisely the sort of things that art abounds in, and indeed that it builds the sense of its existence upon. They include musical works, genres, techniques, composers, the sounds of instruments, lists of personnel, and particular skills and tastes. They also include stylistic alignments. Style, too, is, after all, a certain codification of values. Styles in European culture have, however, changed, and have ceased to be carriers of the beautiful and the good, the carriers of values, for the people actually living in a given historical period. We lose sight today of the original, pejorative meanings of terms like gothic, mannerism, baroque, romanticism, and impressionism. Regardless of whether or not we regard the avant garde as a whole as a stylistic formation, or rather as a conglomerate of styles, it nevertheless belongs to the domain of axiological choices. It has already been judged harshly and falsely, especially in the 1960s.

The eternal controversy over values remains unresolved. This is hardly a reason to completely bypass this field and to steer clear of an attempt to face the issue. Several introductory assumptions from the realm of axiology will be necessary for us before we come back to the question of the avant garde. These are the most basic assumptions that are accepted here.

1. The sphere of values can be considered in two ways: as an exemplar or an ideal (as, for instance, the beautiful, the sacrum, sublimity, honor, courage, harmony, expressiveness, and so on, and therefore as a ready value) or, alternatively, as something that we must constitute as a value

in the process of judgment (or in the creative act), and which we are often incapable of even naming at the moment of encounter. What will interest us here (leaving aside the sea of nuances in both these spheres) is the second sense, that of the created value.

2. The process of evaluation, if reduced to the most abstract mental procedures that take place in the subconscious, is a game of known and familiar characteristics perceived in the object under evaluation, and also of new characteristics that are surprising and require familiarization.
3. We call the first of them determinants, and the second indeterminants.
4. The sense of valuation arises as a result of the (inter-) subjective equation of these two spheres.[1] (To be more precise: value is a function of them).

There can be no doubt that certain more or less conscious axiological assumptions underlay basic avant garde thinking. Artists at the beginning of the twentieth century were still "bitten by Hegel." Since historical development - it was thought - is goal-directed and specific stylistic epochs in art perfected themselves through the absorption of new elements, and since musical and literary works and paintings have become increasingly complicated and integrating within themselves elements that were previously absent, and since the carrier of what is valuable is above all *difference,* then it obviously seemed that such a situation should be perpetuated as a simple recipe for obtaining valuable results. The dogma of difference, change, and otherness shined through all elements of the avant garde achievement, from the most general to the most specific. In their evaluative pronouncements, commentators upon the avant garde accepted almost without exception the elements of novelty, shock, and change as synonyms of value (this could even be a purely technical definition, such as "the variability of the material," "the unpredictability of the outcome," "the total interval series," "experimental music," "polyversionality," and so on. The game about the maximum internal differentiation of the elements of the work led to an increasingly far-reaching dehumanization of work.

Thus the post-modernist turning point was aimed, above all, at restoring contact between art and the human subject. In one of its internal

---

[1] A more precise apprehension of the nature of this process is probably impossible in view of the enormous number of elements "subsumed" in opposing sets, and also of the subconscious nature of the act of valuation.

New-Age currents, the revolution occurred through the simple replacement of characteristics proper to the avant garde by their opposites. The variability of material was replaced by invariability, atonality by (neo-) tonality, polyversionality by monoversionality, arrhythmicity by the metric pulse, and scientific experimentation by spiritual meditativeness. Generally, the principle of change was replaced by the principle of the unchanging (or more precisely, by the ideal of small changes, as in Reich's "music as a gradual process"). As long as we are talking about post modernism, we should name two more of its directions: the post-modern and so-called late modernism. The post-modern is obviously the mainstream here, and is arrogating an ever-increasing territory to itself as the years go by.

Against this background, Penderecki's profile emerges clearly. This clarity results from the impression of contrast and of not fitting in. Penderecki occupies a place of his own. If we call to mind once again the characterizations of the two schools, the avant garde and the postmodernistic (including the postmodern, New Age, and late avant garde currents), then we receive the impression that Penderecki is, of course, present there as a contemporary composer, but that he stands somewhere off to the side. And that he is often one step ahead.

During the avant garde period, he advocated a special variety of the avant garde, which proved to be a very firm basis for the nature of Polish sonorism. He was then an avant garde composer in an uncompromising way, of which the proof is a certain number of retrograde, or hesitant, and therefore *de facto* experimental works. This did not happen to other composers who were classified as experimental. Certain corrections to his works that decisively removed features that could have been construed as references to other composers (such as the removal of the "magic square" from *Dimensions of Time and Silence* or the use of the title *Threnody* rather than *8'37"*) are significant. He was one of the first shapers of the great stylistic turning-point in the 1960s. The *Stabat Mater* and the *Passion* (an example of "double encoding," according to Jencks) were heard even before the symbolic year 1968. It was noticed years later that the "betrayal of the avant garde" turned out to be an avant garde step into new regions. Finally, Penderecki's post-modern work is far removed from the universally obligatory assumptions of cold deconstructionism, from the formal entanglement of cursed dromological shortness of breath, from irony in stylization and the use of quotations, and from escapes in the direction of the "small narrative." On the contrary, the "grand narrative" is always present in Penderecki.

We are coming up to an even-more-apparent contradiction. It is now years since Penderecki was last an avant garde composer. Nevertheless, his creative posture continues to seem avant garde in the sense that it is still a transgressive, bold, outspoken posture that goes beyond the horizons of our musical imagination. Mieczysław Tomaszewski grasped these characteristics adroitly in his essay "Listening to Penderecki," where he describes them as an aspiration "towards the bottom, towards the top, towards fulfillment," noting the collision of opposites, the powerful "rhetorical gesture," the formal contours drawn with a "broad brush."[2] Reaching for grand themes, unexpected transformations of the language of sound, the introduction of new instruments, bold emotionalism - these are the "avant garde" traits that still cling to Penderecki. Let us add at once that this is a risky position (in terms, of course, of artistic risk) not often found among past composers. It is particularly uncommon at present, amidst the rather smooth, tension-free, postmodern music of our day.

To sum up: it is necessary to accept Penderecki's oft-demonstrated distance towards the avant garde in the sense of a herd instinct that is utopian and based on false axiological assumptions that regard the indeterminate as a value that is an end in itself, and not an ingredient in such a value. At the same time, the traits proper to the avant garde artist still appear in Penderecki, and are reflected in each of his new works.

Let us end by returning to the "smooth, tension-free, post modern music of our day." It is difficult just here to refrain from *fin-de-siècle* misgivings. The fact that we fail to discern significant tension in art does not mean that it is not, in fact, there. We are now in new century in which the conflict between art and mass culture looms with increasing acuteness. If we add that the art of centuries past has been petrified and dumbed down in pop-culture for the mass audience, which would mean that so-called "classical music" also belongs to pop culture, then it is contemporary art that remains as a shaky bastion of authentic creativity (and it, too, flirts with pop culture). It is clear that what is universally known as art will soon become a product of mass culture. In this situation, every form of artistic creation will necessarily turn out to be

[2] Mieczysław Tomaszewski, "Listening to Music." In *Festival of Penderecki*, Kraków 1988.

a somewhat strange activity that is "Avant garde" in some sense. All art will be avant garde – is that the next turn of the wheel of history?

Translated by William Brand

Capriccio per Siegfried Palm

KRZYSZTOF PENDERECKI (1968)

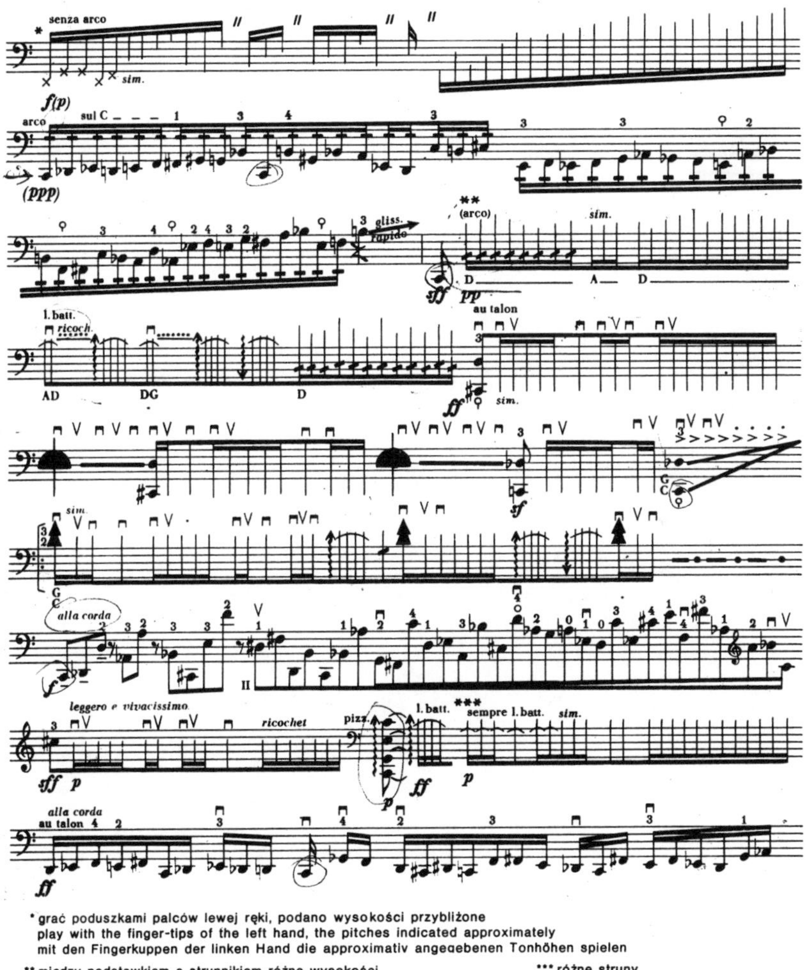

* grać poduszkami palców lewej ręki, podano wysokości przybliżone
play with the finger-tips of the left hand, the pitches indicated approximately
mit den Fingerkuppen der linken Hand die approximativ angegebenen Tonhöhen spielen

** między podstawkiem a strunnikiem różne wysokości
between bridge and tailpiece, different pitches
zwischen Steg und Saitenhalter, verschiedene Tonhöhe

*** różne struny
different strings
verschiedene Saiten

Danuta Mirka
Katowice

Penderecki's Sonorism against Serialism

In the TV interview broadcasted in 1995, Krzysztof Penderecki stated: "What I wrote in the early 1960s, was written to spite the contemporary avant garde, chiefly the Darmstadt school." Indeed, the sonoristic style inaugurated by him at that time constituted a rejoinder to the hegemony of serialism, which was so predominant in the preceding decade as to almost be considered the very measure of avant garde music. Among the commentators of twentieth century music history it has been common to scent the contrast between serialism and Penderecki's sonorism in the highly refined intellectual attitude of the former method, manifested in its strict compositional technique, and in the lack of any technical discipline, which supposedly testified to the anti-intellectualism of the latter. This common view is untenable, however, in the light of the recent studies. In my book devoted to Penderecki (Mirka, 1997) I demonstrate that his sonoristic style is based on a system of rules not less precise than those of serial composition. If one thus wants to contend, as the composer himself does, that Penderecki's sonorism was a reaction against serialism, one should seek the difference between these two styles elsewhere: in the different applications of equally strict compositional systems.

As is well known, in serial composition the systemic order rules relationships between single sounds. Every sound is here first reduced to its component parameters to be subsequently rebuilt as a combination of values chosen from them. The strictness of this method consists in that the choice of values of individual parameters is made not at random, but rather governed by series or rows. It is thus in this very procedure, where the essence of serialism lies. In turn, each row takes it that there exists a scale of values which can be thought of as a set of equidistant points imposed onto the continuous axis of a given parameter. Pitch rows, for example, are based on the semitone scale. In like manner, scales of equidistant values underlie rows governing the parameters of rhythm, dynamics and timbre.[1] From the viewpoint of the serial system, single sounds are thus to be construed as points in a multidimensional space of parametric axes. Inventory of such points makes for the morphology of this system. The syntax of the serial system requires that the succession of sounds in a given piece be conformant to the sequences of parametric values characteristic for individual rows.

The main difference of Penderecki's sonorism in relation to the serial method of composition resides in the character of sound units assumed as the axiom of the sonoristic system: not a single sound, but the sound universe in its totality – sound matter taken, so to say, *en masse.* Accordingly, the compositional operations are shifted from the level of individual sounds to that of sound masses, their textural characteristics and interrelations. Distinct states of the sound matter *en masse* are governed by binary opposition founded on the parameters of pitch, loudness and time. These oppositions constitute the basic categories of Penderecki's sonoristic system.[2] All of them are listed in the table below and correlated with their proper parameters of auditive perception.

perceptual parameters	perceptual categories		
	+		–
pitch	spatial continuity spatial mobility high register middle register	vs. vs. vs. vs.	spatial discontinuity spatial immobility low register extreme register
loudness	loud dynamics	vs.	soft dynamics
time	temporal continuity temporal mobility maximal time-span	vs. vs. vs.	temporal discontinuity temporal immobility minimal time-span

Some of the categories are self-explanatory, some others not so. Therefore, in order to avoid confusion, one is advised to keep in mind

[1] Surely, the most doubtful is the case of timbre scale. After all, how can one ascertain that the timbre relation of violin to harp is the same as, say, to trumpet? And yet, tacit assumptions of this sort lie at the base of every timbre row in serial compositions.

[2] The sonoristic system of Krzysztof Penderecki consists of two subsystems. In this article, the basic system is discussed: one that concerns pitch, time and duration whereby ruling the texture of sound masses. The other component of the sonoristic technique of composition employed by Penderecki is the timbre system.

that the opposition between spatial continuity and spatial discontinuity is meant as a relation between individually discernible pitches and bands. "Temporal continuity vs. discontinuity" is an opposition between lasting sounds and momentary impulses. Spatial mobility means a perception of pitch change, and temporal mobility is tantamount to rhythm in traditional musical terminology.

Terms of the individual oppositions are represented not by points, but by sections – intervals of given parametric values. In addition, these intervals are not precisely defined as to their breadth whereby they do not form ordinary, but fuzzy sets of points. A given set is ordinary when it is clearly delineated, that is to say, when one can univocally discern between its elements and non-elements. The situation arising here is thus "black-and-white," as shown in the following figure:

Figure 1.

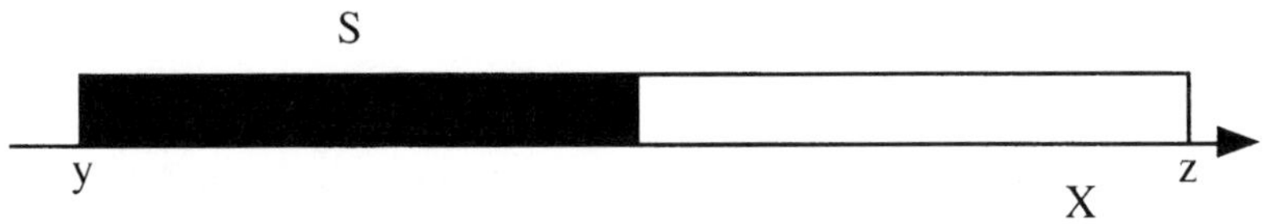

X=[y, z]

In turn, fuzzy sets are fuzzy in the sense that the discrimination between their elements and non-elements is obscured. Apart from black and white, several shades of grey are involved:

Figure 2.

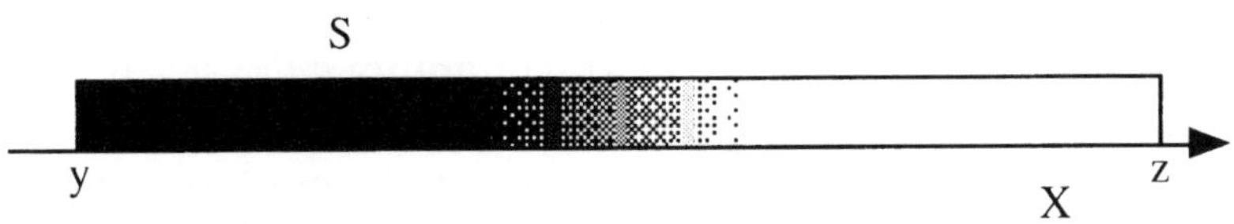

X=[y, z]

The sense of this mathematical distinction in application to Penderecki's sonorism becomes apparent when one considers, for instance, the internal structure of the opposition "low vs. high register." Clearly, there is no such a thing as a definite border of a low register. Therefore, in Penderecki's pieces, this last is represented at one time by sounds reaching from lowest possible pitches up to C_2, while at some other time up to C_4 and even higher, although otherwise C_4 represents the neutral middle register of the opposition.[3] Noticeably, such comparatively high pitches used for representing the low register occur almost exclusively in parts of high-registered instruments - like violins, flutes, oboes - whose range is not expanded enough downwards. Here rests the importance of a context provided by a given instrumental range for classifying a pitch as "low." The same can be said about the "high register." If, thus, space X represents values of audible sound frequencies, the category "low vs. high register" is to be graphically modelled as a relation of fuzzy sets S_1 and S_2 shown in the following figure:

Figure 3.

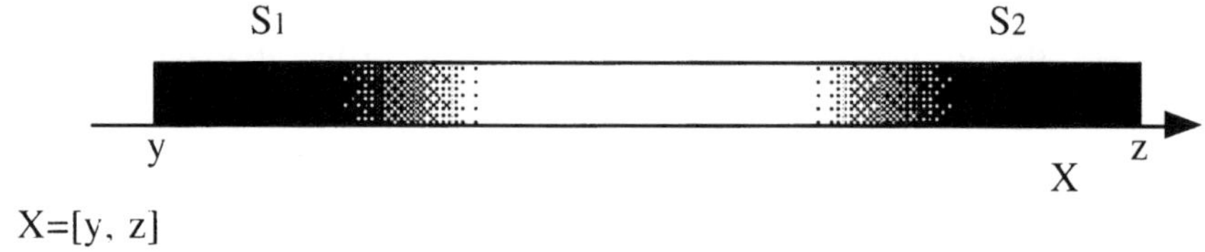

The same graphical model will also make for the opposition "soft vs. loud dynamics," provided the parameter represented by X is intensity, and for "minimal vs. maximal time-span," if the axis shows values of temporal distances between the onsets of successive sound phenomena. All these categories of the sonoristic system are tokens of contrariety as one type of logical opposition. For contrariety, what is characteristic is the existence of neutral values not included in either of the opposite terms. In Figure 3, these intermediary values are represented by the white zone which separates set S_1 from S_2.

The other type of opposition is that of contradiction. Consider the category "spatial continuity vs. discontinuity." Physically, spatial discontinuity would be represented by a single frequency value. Thus, a spatially discontinuous sound phenomenon would be an isolated pitch played by a single instrument. And yet, a pitch is perceived as a single point also when played by a number of instruments, although the resulting frequency values are never identical and, physically, form a minimal band rather than point. How thick must such a band be in order to turn in perception into a spatially continuous phenomenon? The answer cannot be univocal, as it depends on variable properties of the acoustical environment as well as on the hearing capabilities of different listeners.

[3] For instance in *Fluorescences,* when the single pitch C_4 last for more than two minutes (rehearsal numbers 68–85).

On the other hand, a spatially continuous sound phenomenon, in a strict physical sense, would be only a noise, as a band in the axis of frequencies. But an impression of spatial continuity can be also achieved by a cluster – Penderecki's favorite compositional effect which forms a ply of close yet distinct pitches. Again the question can be posed. How dense must such a ply be in order to be perceived as a homogeneous–continuous–phenomenon, and not as a conglomerate of individually recognizable pitches? And again, no univocal answer can be given. In his sonoristic pieces, Penderecki uses mostly quartertone, semitone and whole-tone clusters, but occassionally there occur also clusters whose intervals between neighbouring pitches are minor or major thirds, and even fourths, that is, intervals which otherwise, in a different context, are characteristic of discontinuous sound phenomena.[4] Clearly, the sets of continuous and discontinuous sounds are fuzzy, with a borderzone instead of a borderline between them:

Figure 4.

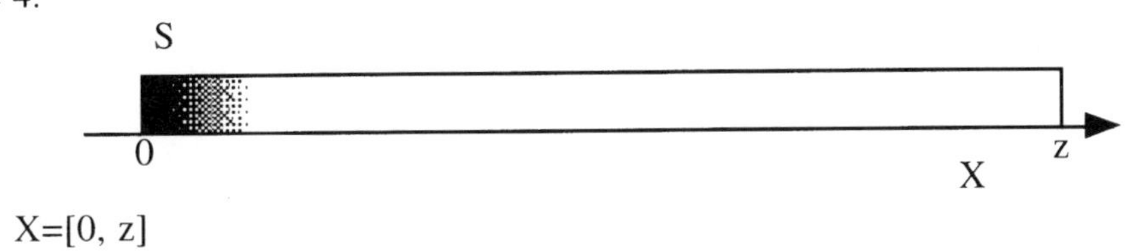

Had the parameter of space X been appropriately changed, the same model is applicable also to the oppositions "temporal continuity vs. discontinuity," "temporal mobility vs. immobility," "spatial mobility vs. immobility" as well as to "middle vs. extreme register.".

Although individual categories fixed by binary oppositions are independent of each other, they all cooperate in qualifying states of the sound matter in Penderecki's sonoristic pieces. I call such states segments, each of them constituting a set of sounds.[5] Segment can thus be defined as a combination of terms chosen from individual categories and thus as a multidimensional object. Observe, in passing, that segment as an elementary

[4] Noticeably, there is an agreement between authors that superpositions of fourths constitute not chords, but clusters. As one commentator of Penderecki's music, Tadeusz A. Zieliński, writes: "In the case of eight or twelve fourths we hear simply a very broad and saturated sound and recognize only its internal structure, i.e., the fact that there is some rather large distance kept between its individual pitches. It is thus a cluster-like type of perception" (Zieliński, 1968: 84).

[5] Even though there occasionally occur segments consisting of single sounds, they are to be treated as liminal cases of segments, in the same way as a set containing only one element forms a liminal set.

unit which accounts for the morphology of Penderecki's sonorism is equivalent to a single sound in serialism, this last resulting as well from a combinatory of values chosen from different parametric rows. A given segment can represent not only these intervals in the axes of parametric values that are characteristic of the opposite terms, but also values of the neutral term (in the case of contrariety) and of the border-zone term which arises as a result of the fuzziness (shades-of-grey zone in the case of contradiction). An example may be, respectively, a band of frequencies situated in a middle register and a slow, wide vibrato performed by a whole section of violins as an intermediary phenomenon between a single pitch and a cluster. Moreover, a segment can bear the complex or total term. While the former is a sum of the opposite terms, the latter represents the whole range of values of a given parameter. Think, for instance, of a field of pitches equally spread over the sound space as a total term of the category "low vs. high register." If the opposite terms serve to present the contradiction or contrariety characteristic of a given category, the remaining terms aim at its mediation.

In this way, the problem of syntax is arrived at. The syntax in Penderecki's sonoristic system is governed by the binary oppositions between terms of the categories. The succession of terms of a given category is allowed to assume a shape of sequences serving as either a presentation or a mediation of its binary opposition. Presentation of the opposition consists in a directly contrasting juxtaposition of its opposite terms in adjacent segments, while in the case of mediation, one or more mediative terms is inserted between the opposite. Consequently, a prohibited type of succession is a return to an initial opposite term, be it positive or negative, after a mediative term or a chain of such terms has occurred. However, changes of terms of different categories need not be simultaneous. As one categorial difference enables discrimination between two segments, a single change bringing about the slightest difference between neighboring segments suffices to change any given segment. Of course, one can also move to a following segment by changing more categories. This means that the succession of syntactical units in the chain of a given sonoristic piece may involve segments of different degrees of kinship. The lower the number of categories in which change occurs at a given moment, the higher the affinity between adjacent segments on the paradigmatic axis and the smoothness of musical narration on the syntagmatic axis. By contrast, the higher number of changing terms, the less similar the segments and less fluent the course of the narration.

Changes of terms in individual categories are touchstones of segmentation in a given piece. Since the number of changes taking place at the same moment between two adjacent segments can differ, the segmentation of Penderecki's sonoristic pieces displays a hierarchical organization. The higher the number of changing terms, the higher and hence more general the level of segmentation. Conversely, the lower number of changes, the lower and more detailed is the segmentational level in the hierarchy of a given work. It follows that the most detailed, lowest level of segmentation is that of single changes between segments. How many changes any given segment brings and, consequently, on which hierarchical level of segmentation the musical narration runs in a given section of a piece is always a matter of free compositional choices. The syntax of the sonoristic system leaves thus ample room for artistic freedom, in contradistinction to serial syntax, where the rule of non-repetition within a row results in a "flat" hierarchy of segmentation and hence in a mechanistic compositional procedure.[6]

After the comparison of the systems underlying serialism and Penderecki's sonorism has made their differences apparent, it may be interesting to note a rather ironic similarity between them: although on two different levels, both the serialism of the Darmstadt school and Penderecki's sonoristic style lead equally towards unification of all sound parameters in respect of their internal organization. Of course this aim is accomplished in opposite ways, which further sharpens the contrast between these two compositional methods. Because in serial technique all four parameters of sound perception are organized by means of discrete scales of values (which in turn form the bases for building rows), thus here discreteness (discontinuity) becomes, at least intentionally, attributed not only to pitch and duration, as the primary pattern-forming parameters, but also to dynamics and timbre (or sound color) a patterning of which is never possible because of their normally "continuous" nature (see Meyer, 1967: 247-48).[7] By contrast, the organization of pitch, time and loudness assumed by the basic system categories of Penderecki's sonorism is devoid of any concept of discontinuity. As demonstrated earlier

[6] This is not to say that in serialism any compositonal freedom is precluded. But, as soon as the rows are preformed, the freedom can be exercised either outside the syntax (e.g., by shaping motivic and harmonic relationships) or by breaking these very syntactical rules the composer has previously himself established.

[7] In terms of present-day cognitive musicology one would say that serialism requires categorization of dynamics and timbre – parameters that are not perceived categorically by listeners (see also Sloboda, 1985: 23–31).

and deducible from the geometrical models of the elementary categories, the individual terms of the categories are represented not by separate points, but by intervals which are each time indicated within the continuous axes of real numbers and, what is more, form their fuzzy subsets. In this way, the discrete scale of values is eliminated not only from dynamics, but also from pitch and duration, whereby exact relations concerning the two latter perceptual parameters - giving out, respectively, intervals and rhythm - are not structural here, even if otherwise they are akin to such a structuration, owing to natural properties of human hearing. That Penderecki was perfectly aware of this difference between his own compositional system (characterized by the tendency towards continuity) and the technical premises of serialism (founded on the discontinuous organization of sound parameters) is testified to by one of his remarks:

> As regards the Darmstadt school, in fact I have never had any tangential points with it. The difference between its representatives and me can be - in my opinion - defined in this way: that they are mainly interested in points, while I am [interested] in lines (quoted by Erhardt 1975: 13).

Here, lines should be understood as sections - intervals of values in the spaces of individual parameters proper for categories of the basic system.[8]

To say that the sonoristic style of Krzysztof Penderecki constitutes a reaction against serialism means, however, not only that these two systems of composition are opposite, but rather that, in their being opposite, the former is genetically dependent on the latter. In order to unearth this dependence, one needs to examine the evolution of the sonoristic system or, rather, its "growth." This last term is appropriate, because the system proceeds from the minimal number of segments and maximal number of redundancies between individual categories towards the multiplication of syntactical units by way of progressive liquidation of redundancies. Redundancy is meant here as a fixed assignment between terms of two different categories. For instance, in the earliest sonoristic pieces by Penderecki - *Anaklasis* (1960), *Threnody* (1960) and *Dimensions of Time and Silence* (1961) - temporal mobility is always joined to spatial mobility and, conversely, temporal immobility occurs always together with spatial immobility. In this way, these two categories form originally a more general opposition "mobility vs. immobility" from which only

[8] It may be worth observing that the solutions assumed by the founders of serialism on the one hand and by Penderecki on the other, although symmetrically opposite, are not equally good. After all, it seems more reasonable to relinguish something that is possible than to require the impossible.

later "temporal mobility vs. immobility" and "spatial mobility vs. immobility" are disentangled. In like manner, also other categories arise. This process progresses along three "branches" which concern, respectively, dynamics, registers, and all the remaining aspects of musical narration. The individual branches are independent of each other. Yet in turn, there occur several interdependencies between categories within the same branch, whereby the occurrence of a given opposition is quite often conditioned by several intermingled circumstances, these last involving (an)other opposition(s).[9] One can ascertain this fact from the "tree" chart below. If read top down, it shows the course of the system's evolution. The complete system of eight categories listed in the foregoing discussion is present in the pieces to be seen in the lowest rows.

Figure 5.

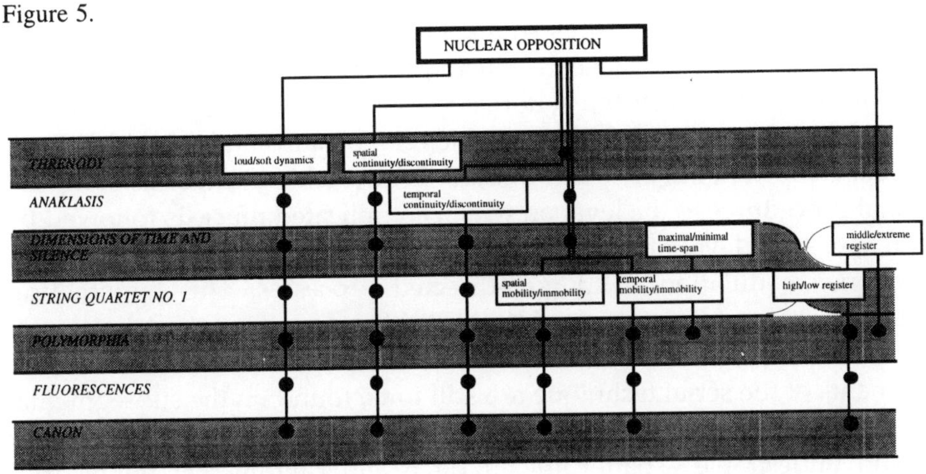

Reading the "tree" chart the other way – bottom up – one arrives instead at the beginning of the evolution: the "nuclear opposition." This opposition, from which the growth of the sonoristic system is supposed to have started, is not recorded in any concrete piece of music. Therefore it is to be treated merely as a hypothesis – a mental construct conceived by the composer at the outset of devising his sonoristic compositional technique. This hypothesis seems very plausible, however. According to it, at the beginning of the evolution lies an opposition between two polar types of musical texture: maximally heterogeneous and maximally homogeneous. Because at this original stage their contrast constitutes the sole opposition,

[9] This stems from logical interdependences between some categories. For this topic, see Mirka (1997: 50-52). The detailed discussion of the system evolution is to be found in Chapter 10 (282–292).

there are only two possible segments representing the opposite terms: pointillist texture characteristic for serial compositions and a cluster.

Of course, the serialists viewed the pointillist texture as a network of intersonic relations. Originally so did also Penderecki: for instance, when using serial technique in his youthful *Strophes* (1959). But his mature output commences only after he has shifted from the level of interrelations between individual sounds to that of the global characteristics of their masses. Indeed, it was this shift that lay at the origin of his sonoristic system. Having been applied by Penderecki to serial pieces, it transferred the focus of attention away from the complicated network of relations on their proper compositional level of individual sound phenomena (ruled by rows of dynamics, pitch, time, and touch), and onto the level of the resulting, overall pointillist texture, thereby leading him to the concept of the maximally heterogeneous sound field; this last, in turn, implied the polar, maximally homogeneous cluster, building in this way the nuclear opposition from which the sonoristic system subsequently developed.[10] By ignoring the subtleties of intersonic relationships and focusing on the global characteristics of sound masses, Penderecki adjusted his compositional procedures to the level on which complicated music is followed by listeners – the level of global sound events, their relations, crushes, mediations, modulations, and goal-directed processes. This hypothetical reconstruction of the genesis of Krzysztof Penderecki's sonoristic system is not undermined by the observation that, in pieces based on this system, elements of the serial technique are still to be found on the subsegmental level. In all likelihood, Penderecki uses them in order to neutralize possible – and undesirable – patterning of pitch and rhythm that might arise

---

[10] Of course, the same shift can be applied to any other music. Although it garbles the original compositional intentions, it requires merely a change of attitude. In this respect, Penderecki's comment, in a highly interesting interview he granted Zieliński in 1963, proves very instructive: "Try listening to some of Tchaikovsky's symphonies, putting aside its harmonic course and the concrete pitches of individual sounds, instead paying attention only to the development of the instrumental strains: their timbre, dynamics, register, duration of individual sounds, density and width within the compass of the score, types of figuration in the strings, etc. It will appear that this course is in itself very interesting, rich, and entirely consciously composed. As an artistic value of a piece, it sometimes even considerably surpasses the harmonic content – it suffices to compare it with the piano reduction alone. Naturally, in Tchaikovsky these things are still closely related to each other, and the manner of listening I have proposed to you is an artificial manipulation. Yet it allows one to realize that the habits of musical perception in terms of such global sound values have been growing for a long time, though initially basing themselves on strictly intervallic procedures. . . . For me, as a composer, this aspect of a composition, enriched with new sound values through new articulatory means, is the most essential. I can see here enough possibilities to abandon in many cases the intervallic processes" (Zieliński, 1963: 9).

between component sounds of segments. The rule of non-repetition characteristic for serialism prevents such patterns from occurring more efficiently than random procedures would.

In the light of the above remarks, the sense of the composer's utterance quoted at the outset should be clarified: that Krzysztof Penderecki's sonorism vies with serialism, it does so in bringing its own, competitively rigorous compositional system. Even though in his youth Penderecki took passing interest in the music of such composers as Boulez or Stockhausen, his own sonoristic output stands on the antipodes of theirs and constitutes a scathing critique of the "false attitude towards the very problem of artistic creation," which he found to lie at the basis of the Darmstadt style ([Discussion] 1976: 29). Seen from this perspective, the nuclear opposition between the optimally pointillist texture characteristic of serialism and the optimal sonoristic cluster at the foundation of Penderecki's sonoristic system is more than a point of departure. It assumes the proportions of a symbol.

References

[Discussion]. 1976. "Dyskusja na seminarium poświęconym twórczości Krzysztofa Pendereckiego." *Muzyka* 2(81): 29-52.

Meyer, Leonard B. 1967. *Music, the Arts and Ideas.* Chicago and London: University of Chicago Press.

Mirka, Danuta. 1997. *The Sonoristic Structuralism of Krzysztof Penderecki.* Katowice: Akademia Muzyczna.

Sloboda, John A. 1985. *The Musical Mind.* Oxford: Clarendon Press, pp. 23–31.

Zieliński, Tadeusz A. 1963. "Współczesny kompozytor a tradycja" [Contemporary composer and the tradition]. *Ruch Muzyczny*, 12: 8–9.

Zieliński, Tadeusz A. 1968. "Technika operowania instrumentami smyczkowymi w utworach Krzysztofa Pendereckiego" [String Techniques in the Works of Krzysztof Penderecki]. *Muzyka* 1(48): 74-92.

Marek Stachowski
Cracow

The Avant Garde in Poland from the Standpoint of the Composer

An artist beginning a career as a composer in Poland in 1968, the year I graduated in composition under Krzysztof Penderecki, was in a particular situation. A mere twenty years had passed since the first postwar political thaw, which had drawn back the iron curtain. That relatively brief political period and the resulting cultural liberalization sufficed for Polish artistic circles to absorb all the things that stood as symbols of modern art.

As a result of historical conditions, the tradition of avant garde movements in Poland, and especially in music, was modest. A group of progressive composers headed by Karol Szymanowski had been active in the twenty years between the First and Second World Wars;[1] they were an ideological derivative of the German neoclassical movement, and mostly of Richard Strauss, while the work of the first Polish twelve-tone composer, Józef Koffler, remained practically unknown. The doctrine of socialist realism, which cut itself off deliberately from the avant garde trends that were developing in Western Europe, had been obligatory in postwar Poland since the early 1950s. It signaled a denial of access to the works of the neo-Viennese school or the music of Arnold Schoenberg and his school, as well as the later serialists and the work of such composers as Stravinsky, Bartók, and Messiaen. During the thaw, young composers passionately mastered everything that had previously been inaccessible and forbidden. The middle generation of composers, including Tadeusz Baird, Kazimierz Serocki, and Andrzej Dobrowolski, enthusiastically accepted the new ideas and, together with Witold Lutosławski, created the new face of contemporary music in Poland. The youngest composers, Krzysztof Penderecki, Henryk Mikołaj Górecki and Wojciech Kilar, however, were the ones who became the main protagonists of the avant garde musical scene in Poland. Their highly original work made contemporary

[1] The period of independence under the Second Republic from 1918-1939.

Polish music one of the most interesting avant garde musical phenomena in Europe.

The highly distinct and original model of new music described universally as the Polish school of composition began to take shape in the sixties. The fact of having rejected tradition made it necessary to fill in the resulting void with an unprecedented imperative to experimentation. The Experimental Music School arose in Warsaw. Composers turned their attention to previously unexplored areas and enriched their compositional technique with such forms as collage, infinitive music, and open forms, and such techniques as aleatorism. Nor were the composers unfamiliar with graphical or audiovisual music, or musical events - in other words, happenings. A completely exceptional phenomenon was the short "incubation" period of twelve-tone techniques, culminating in pointillist and serial music. As opposed to many other countries where these techniques reigned in unaltered form for whole decades, and in a few cases are still cultivated, the young Polish avant gardeists treated them from the beginning as objects of modernistic procedures. The dynamics of change meant that, by the end of the sixties, Polish music represented a completely different quality from its starting point in 1956. The emancipation of sound as a result of the reevaluation of the hierarchy of the musical elements in the process of composition created the conditions for the rise of a new sonoristic technique that penetrated mostly into instrumental music, although its origins doubtless lay in electroacoustical music.

At the same time, this was the period of the first serious theoretical reflections on the condition of contemporary Polish music and its place in world music. The leading composers of the postwar avant garde manifested in their work, with increasing frequency and distinctness, the necessity of a radical reorientation as to the essence of music as art and its social function. The deepening chasm between composer and audience became an important argument for such attitudes. Krzysztof Penderecki later stated in an interview that he had never been interested in sound for its own sake or form for the sake of form. This protected him, he averred, from the sterile vacuity and ennui of abstract formal solutions. He remarked in conclusion that "the need for synthesis is characteristic of the entire modern epoch."[2]

---

[2] *Passio artis et vitae* (an interview by A. and Z. Baran with Krzysztof Penderecki. Warsaw: Presspublica, 1997).

The final two decades of the twentieth century brought an unprecedented variety of aesthetic attitudes in Polish music. Interestingly, this phenomenon applied both to the composers as a collective, and to each of them individually. Their statements and comments, usually on the first performances of their works, leave no doubt that a time of nervously seeking new perspectives in music had arrived. Krzysztof Penderecki seemed closest to the reaching the intended goal in this postmodernist race. The composer of the *Polish Requiem* spoke out loud of the need for a renewal of music in the weighty statement that "It seems to me that music written in a natural way and embodying a synthesis of all that has transpired in the last several decades has a chance of survival."[3] In other words, such a synthesis is "something like the absorption of everything that has come into existence."[4]

In conclusion, something should be said about the question, concealed in the title, about an evaluation of the Polish avant garde from the perspective of a half century. Polish music has undergone a long and complicated course of transformations, and there can be no doubt that its present form would be unthinkable without that phenomenon without precedent in our history, the avant garde that was born during the Stalinist regime's first thaw. The crisis of musical art that set in after the tempestuous period of Wagnerian ideology provoked composers, theoreticians, and musicologists to react to the disorientation and the undermining of the rules that obtained in art. The affirmation that the rules that defined the basis of the tonal system no longer afforded any further opportunities for the development of the musical language became a rallying cry for a showdown with the existing order of post-romantic music. The work of the twelve-tone classics, with Arnold Schoenberg at their head, represents a practical guide to the new philosophy of music. Everything that occurred subsequently is a simple implication from the discoveries made by the composers gathered around Schoenberg.

Translated by William Brand

[3] Penderecki interviewed for the Bulletin of the 30th Warsaw Autumn Festival, Warsaw, 1997, "Muzyki nie można zaczynać od początku."

[4] Op. cit.

K. Penderecki and M. Stachowski.

PENDERECKI'S WORKS: ANALYSES

Alicja Jarzębska
Cracow

The Aesthetic Background of Penderecki's Avant Garde Works. *Quartetto per archi* and Wordless Rhethoric

> Indeed, every doctrine of aesthetics, when put into practice, demands a particular mode of expression - in fact, a technique of its own; for, in art, such a thing as technique founded on no given basis - in short, a technique in the void - would be utterly inconceivable [...].
>
> Stravinsky, *An Autobiography*

DIFFERENCES BETWEEN THE AESTHETIC BACKGROUND OF THE DARMSTADT SCHOOL AND THAT OF PENDERECKI'S AVANT GARDE WORKS

An issue that has occupied the historian and theoretician of twentieth-century music is the question of which aesthetic-philosophical sources lie behind the compositional technique of Krzysztof Penderecki who, as a young graduate of a music-school composition department "behind the iron curtain" in the early 1960s, composed works that, on the one hand, were an explosion of non-euphonic tones that fascinated the international avant garde of the period (*Quartetto per archi, Threnody, Anaklasis, Polymorphia, Fluorescences*), and who on the other hand referred clearly to the Judeo-Christian tradition rejected by that avant garde (*Psalms of David, Stabat Mater*). The composer stated at the time (in 1973) that

> Boulez and I think in completely different ways. . . . As far as the Darmstadt school goes, I never did in fact have any points of contact with it. The difference between the representatives of that school and me could, it seems to me, be defined in this way: they are interested first of all in points, whereas I am interested above all in lines.[1]

It would seem, however, that this difference extended far deeper and was connected with both a different philosophical conception of reality

[1] Ates Orga, "Krzysztof Penderecki," *Music and Musicians* X, 22 (1973)(10), p. 39.

and a different understanding of the concept of *Klang* [sound], the creative process, musical time, and the role of music in a given society. The postwar musical avant garde, at work within the International Courses in New Music at Darmstadt, relied upon the theoretical concepts of Schoenberg and his students, as well as upon the philosophical-aesthetic views connected with the concept of the expressionist breakthrough and the "philosophy of protest" as initiated by Nietzsche and developed by Dilthey and in Bergson's *Lebensphilosophie*. The artistic doctrine of the Vienna School composers and the artists associated with them (including Vassily Kandinsky) was a symptom of the decisive transformation of the European culture that had grown out of the Greek and Judeo-Christian traditions. That transformation affected above all the *Umvertung aller bisherigen Werte* [reevaluation of all values], as Nietzsche conceived it in his concept of nihilism, in other words, as the elimination of the opposition between such categories as good and evil, beauty and ugliness, and truth and falsity - the pillars of received European culture. Theodor W. Adorno formulated an aesthetic theory according to which

> The new art of spiritualization makes it impossible to go on, as philistine culture desires, bespattering oneself with truth, beauty, and good. Art should rather introduce chaos into order than the opposite. . . . Beauty . . . becomes ugliness. . . . Ugliness is connected with the spiritualization of art. . . . That which was subjugated by expression and the formal character of beauty . . . changes into expression.[2]

According to Nietzsche, nihilism marked out new perspectives and was the foreshadowing of a new art based on the assumption that the only reality is constant change, "becoming," marked by "the curse of birth and the despair of death," but that in faithfulness to this truth, the artist ought to manifest boldly the state of metaphysical dread as well as protest and rebellion, despite discouragement and rejection by contemporary audiences.

In the ideology of progress propagated by the composers of the Vienna School and, after the Second World War, the followers of Adorno from Darmstadt, the future of music was "historically determined." The music of the future was to be dissonant and non-euphonic, and the avant garde composer therefore had to use unusual acoustic effects that were often unpleasant to the ear. The program for this "historically necessary," revolutionary rupture with tradition and the evolution of "musical material"

[2] Theodor W. Adorno, *Teoria estetyczna*, trans. Krystyna Krzemieniowa. Warszawa 1994, pp. 169 and 97.

in the direction of the "emancipation of dissonance," was combined with the nihilistic truth (combined with the authenticity of internal experience) about the senselessness of human life that lay behind such expressionistic works of art as Edward Munch's famous *The Scream*. In his *Philosophy of Modern Music*, furthermore, Adorno stated that euphonic music (the kind that gives the listener pleasure and is eagerly listened to) "conceals false bourgeois culture under the appearance of beauty and calm," and was therefore reactionary. Avant garde artists did not seek common ground with a potential wider audience for, in Schoenberg's view "art, it is not for all, and if it is for all, it is not art."[3] Avant garde artists felt more at home with an idea to which Nietzsche had given prominence: that people were divided into those endowed with the "will to power," the so-called artist-geniuses [*Über-Menschen*] cast out by society, and the remaining members of society, who were treated as "the run-of-the-mill products of nature" [*der Fabrikwaare der Natur*].

In the avant garde manifestos, the categories of tone, expression, and musical time (form) were therefore involved in a characteristic philosophical-aesthetic-sociological context. In the aesthetics of the avant garde composers who were the students or followers of the thinking of Schoenberg and the artists from the *Blaue Reiter* circle, the concept of *Klang* [tone] had a special meaning. It was connected not so much with some sort of acoustic effect as with the intellectually ineffable, defined as "spiritual" or "internal" and associated on the one hand with the "cry of terror" (heard or only imagined), and on the other with a sort of "spiritual light" made manifest by color and tone or with some sort of abstract proto-substance (*Substanzgemeinschaft, Grundgestalt*). The concept of *Klang* was therefore connected with the category of color (in such works as, for instance, Kandinsky's *Der Gelbe Klang* or *Farben* from Schoenberg's op. 16) or with a mathematical set of algebraic elements; the acoustic effect that grated on the ear was associated with the "internal necessity" of a revolutionary break with the euphonic, with liberation from convention, with the freedom of the artist who existed in a higher spiritual reality "beyond" oppositions treated in categories of beauty and ugliness, good and evil, truth and falsity.

This type of conception resulted on the one hand from an interest in theosophy and anthroposophy, and on the other from a fascination with

[3] Arnold Schoenberg, "New Music, Outmoded music (1946)." In *Style and Idea, Selected Writing of Arnold Schoenberg*, Leonard Stein (ed.). London, 1984, p. 124.

logical positivism and mathematical formalism. It was precisely within the framework of theosophy that the figure (as belonging to the external world) was demoted and the role of color and tone, as means for revealing (or even for making present) a pantheistically conceived spiritual reality, accentuated.[4] Renouncing the distinct "figure" and aesthetic pleasure, new art was treated as the concretization of the Schopenhauerian Will, the creative Absolute, and the Nietzschean "will to power." The new art was to be the "metaphysical fulfillment of life" and the conquest of death - the limit of life. This gave the new art the specific mystical-magical features that Kandinsky commented upon at length in his essay *On Spirituality in Art,* where he writes that "Schoenberg's music takes us into a totally different world, where the musical experiences are not acoustic in nature, but purely spiritual. This is where the music of the future begins."[5]

This philosophical-aesthetic basis for the non-euphonic tones that appeared in the works of the avant garde composers who saw the music of the future as being either total determinism (that is, with the subjugation of all the signs of the musical notation to the pre-compositional series treated as a mathematical set) or in indeterminism (that is, in subordination to some sort of principal of chance both in the creative process and in the performance of the work), was alien to Penderecki. He accepted neither that esoteric conception of *Klang,* nor music as a collection of brief effects determined by a pre-compositional series, nor the idea of indeterminism combined with the esoteric forces acting upon an artist-medium. He was not attracted to the idea of "pure, spiritualized art" that looked with contempt upon "material reality" (that is, direct sensory experience). Above all, however, the Nietzschean vision of a world "beyond good and evil" was alien to him.

Both Penderecki's biography and his statements indicate that his interest in the world of unusual tones arose under the influence of Franciszek Skołyszewski, the teacher who initiated him into the mysteries of the theoretical basis of music. A theoretician and musicologist as well as a "personality," Skołyszewski was fascinated by electroacoustics and the

[4] Referring to Goethe's theory of colors, the father of anthroposophy, Rudolf Steiner, defined them as *Taten des Lichtes* (works of light) and associated them with spiritual reality; in line with the idea of the synesthesia of acoustic effects, he also regarded them as the equivalent of some sort of "spiritual light" broken up into the colors of the rainbow. See Piotr Jaroszyński, *Metafizyka i sztuka.* Warszawa, 1996.

[5] [Vassily] Kandinsky, *O duchowości w sztuce,* trans. Stanisław Fijałkowski. Łódź, 1996, pp. 48–49.

tonal effects that could be achieved from generators that he constructed himself. Almost from the beginning of his independent efforts at composition, Penderecki was therefore pointed in the direction of that exotic and technological world of tones created out of long and short acoustic effects, with defined and undefined pitch, taken from the high, middle and low pitch registers as the selective or non-selective result of sound impulses, repeated over and over or "scattered" throughout the pitch scale. Penderecki shared his teacher's faith in the connection between new sound sources and the future of tone. In the 1960s, the originality of his avant garde artistic attitude consisted mainly in the fact that he treated his beloved string instruments (in his youth, he had intended to become a violin virtuoso), whose tones had been associated previously with the expressive *cantabile* melodics and with showy, virtuoso sound figures, as a medium for a plethora of tones suggesting the electro-acoustic media and, indirectly, the world of modern technology and physics. In Penderecki's concept of music, at the same time, this world of tones should be integrated with human feelings and emotions - joyous and painful - and connected with the biblical vision of the world and of man, as for instance in the character of David singing songs to praise the Lord, or with the message of the Gospel about resurrection ransomed with the voluntary forgiveness of wrongs and suffering, as in the medieval *Stabat Mater* sequence. Penderecki thus treated sound [*Klang*] as a sensory phenomenon deliberately chosen by the composer that could be associated with human feelings and with a vision of reality where a clear opposition between good and evil exists.

Penderecki's attitude also differed from that of the Darmstadt avant garde in regard to the understanding of musical time and the shaping of form. Proponents of the philosophy of new music formulated by Adorno treated the creative process as ecstasy, as a brief instance of contact between the artist-genius and the spiritual world. The fruit of this contact was an overall vision or idea of a musical work. This vision or idea was connected with the concept of "content" or the expression of the "pantheistic spirit" that, thanks to the artist-medium, was "materialized" in the work of art as "duration," as a moment that acquired "pure form," uncontaminated by imitation of what lay outside it, in the score. Such a concept of musical time and form was a categorical break with the classical metaphor of music as a beautiful architectural edifice, proportional and symmetric, and also with the metaphor of music as *l'art dramatique*. The musical work was treated as either the consequence of moments not associated with each other, or as a constant change of musical events with no clear beginning or end and not directed towards any goal.

In his avant garde musical compositions, Penderecki indeed accepted the idea of the musical work as "the emancipation of dissonance," that is, as a sequence of non-euphonic tones, but he did not break with the classical concept of musical time interpreted through the metaphor of architectural proportion and symmetry, or the drama of poetry. Even in his first avant garde works, Penderecki revealed his skill, so characteristic of his craft as a composer, at presenting a process of musical events moving towards a culmination and solution in proportionally differentiated temporality and in a way that was clear, logical, and accessible to the listener. That is why the fundamental question in the analysis of his music is not so much the "catalogue of innovative tones" as the problem of the clear prominence of the drama of contrasting sound events and the dismemberment of musical time.

QUARTETTO PER ARCHI AS AN EXAMPLE OF WORDLESS RHETHORIC AND A TRADITIONAL PRINCIPLE OF PROPOTION

The six-minute-long *Quartetto per archi* (1960) can be treated as an example of "wordless rhetoric" or, in other words, the application of the rules of *l'art dramatique* to innovative acoustic effects. The classical French theory of dramatic art laid out in *L'art poétique* by Nicolas Boileau-Despréaux (1674) divides the utterance into three parts: (1) the *exposition,* which was the presentation of the main characters; (2) the *noeud* or *intrigue,* in which the dramatic action was set up; and (3) the *dénoűment* where these complications were resolved.[6]

Penderecki adheres to these principles of the classic drama. The two major *personae dramatis* are

(A) *pitch sound-blocks,* that is, tone blocks made up of sounds of a definite pitch, long or short, repeated or making up sound figures, and

(B) *indefinite pitch sound-blocks,* that is, tone blocks made up of long or short percussion effects of indefinite pitch.

Dramatis persona (A) generally takes a triadic tonal form, and is differentiated primarily as a result of being performed (by all the players of the

[6] See Mark E. Bonds, *Wordless Rhetoric: Musical Form and the Methaphor of the Oration,* Cambridge, 1991. The attempt at codifying compositional instrumental practices at the turn of the eighteenth and nineteenth centuries by way of the categories used in the literary description of dramatic action was based on the theoretical model of Antoine-Joseph Reicha, as described in the *Traité de haute composition musicale* (1824).

string quartet) by the method of uncoordinated long sounds, or short sounds realized as the repetition of resonance or as sound figures played in a quasi-homogenous way). *Dramatis persona* (B) also appears in varied "coloristic costume"; this differentiated tone color is the result of the employment of either short percussion effects[7] long tones of an indefinite pitch.[8]

Aside from clearly differentiated segments of a definite pitch (*pitch-sound blocks*) or tones of an indefinite pitch (*indefinite pitch-sound blocks*), two other kinds of *sound blocks* can be distinguished in the *Quartetto per archi*:

(1) *transitional sound-blocks,* which highlight the "effect of evolving changes," the "effect of passage" from tones of indefinite pitch to tones of definite pitch (A→B) or vice-versa (B→A), and
(2) *polyphonic sound-blocks,* which give prominence to the effect of the simultaneous juxtaposition of tone layers of definite and indefinite pitch (AB).

Capturing this sort of musical continuum in the score requires an appropriate notation for both the innovative tone effects and their duration. Penderecki proposed new graphic signs for the notation of tone effects of an indefinite pitch, while using traditional "note and stave" notation for the sounds with definite pitch.

In order to bring out the general difference between the longer and shorter tone effects (1-3 seconds versus 6-18 seconds), Penderecki made a decisive break with the tradition of mensural notation by introducing a "time net" measured in seconds (each page of the score represented one minute of musical time) and referring to obvious audio-visual associations, that is, to the difference between the point and the line. The brief tone effects are associated with given graphical signs, while the longer and longest-duration tone effects are indicated by the lengths of the horizontal lines which follow.

In terms of duration, three types of tone effects can be distinguished in the *Quartetto per archi*:

(1) brief percussive effects (noted as graphic signs referring, in a way indicated by information in the score, to the way they are articulated)[9]

---

[7] Penederecki suggests striking the strings with the open palm of the hand (or fingers), striking the upper part of the sounding board of the violin with the nut or the finger-tips, playing between bridge and tailpiece (on one, two, three or four strings), playing the highest note of the instrument as indefinite pitch.

[8] Players have to play on the tailpiece (*arco*) or play the highest note of the instrument as indefinite pitch.

[9] See notes 8 and 9.

and brief sounds of a definite pitch (played *arco, pizzicato, spiccato,* or *legno battuto*);

(2) the longer-duration (1-, 2-, or 3-second) percussive effects or sounds of a definite pitch are noted as a combination of the corresponding graphic signs or by point-notes of the appropriate length (occupying one, two, or three fields of the "time net") on the horizontal line);

(3) long-duration (6-, 9-, 12-, or 18-second) percussive effects or sounds of a definite pitch noted as a combination of the corresponding graphic signs or by point-notes (or a wavy line indicating *tremolo*) of the appropriate length (occupying 6, 9, 12, or 18 fields of the "time net") on the horizontal line.

The varied duration of the longer and longest sound effects thus accords with the principle of simple proportion in the *numero senario* (1: 2: 3: 4: 6).

The general pause (lasting three seconds) divides the musical continuum into two almost equal parts (the first lasts 190 seconds and the second lasts 167 seconds); the first is a presentation of the main characters (A, B) and the setting up of the dramatic action. The second displays these characters in various "coloristic costumes" and is a sort of resolution of the conflict.

In the first part, the *dramatis personae* (A) and (B) appear in only two tonal versions (A, A_1, B, B_1),[10] while they appear with greater variety in the second part. In the first part, the dramatic structure of the musical events is formed in accordance with the following scheme:

$$A, B, \quad B \rightarrow A, A_1, \quad A \rightarrow B, B_1$$

In segment B→A (lasting 40 seconds) the repetition of acoustical effects of a non-defined pitch (striking the strings with the hand) increasingly gives way to sounds (and later to resonances) of a defined pitch. In segment

---

[10] **A** = this is a continuous sound-block (produced by all four players) that begins as a long-duration sound (lasting 5 seconds), followed by *glissando* changes in pitch (in a range of 1.5 octaves) at regular time intervals (3 seconds - Vc, Vl; 2 seconds. - Vn I, Vn II); in all, the segment lasts 20 seconds.

A_1 = repetition of uncoordinated eight-tones in the low and middle register: Es-G-f-c^1-e^1-fis^1-h^1-gis^2 (approx. 10 seconds), followed by a twelve-tones in the middle and upper register: d^1-es^1- f^1- g^1-b^1- h^1- c^2- e^2- fis^2-a^2-des^3-as^3 (approx. 5 seconds), ending with individual sounds and five-tones in the middle register: fis-g-a-b-h (approx. 5 seconds); in all, the segment lasts 20 seconds.

B = repetition of brief acoustic effects resulting from striking the hand on the strings (2-5 blows in one second); the segment lasts 15 seconds;

B_1 = repetition of long (2-3 seconds) acoustic effects resulting from (1) intoning the highest (undefined) pitch (Vn II and Vc) and (2) playing between the bridge and the tailpiece (Vn I and Vl); this segment lasts 20 seconds.

A→B (lasting 75 seconds, and therefore almost twice as long as B→A) in turn, the quasi-homogenous movement of sounds of a definite pitch (a variety of sound figures made up of large interval jumps played *pizzicato* and *spiccato*) is gradually replaced by acoustic effects of an undefined pitch (the highest sound on a given instrument, playing between the bridge and the tailpiece) that are initially brief and later last longer (two to three seconds). The following diagram illustrates the proportional relation of the duration of these segments:

A	B	B→A	A_1	A→B	B_1
1 :	**1** :	**2** :	**1** :	**4** :	**1**

Four variants of segment A (A_2, A_3, A_4, A_5),[11] three variants of segment B (B_2, B_3, B_4),[12] and two versions of the simultaneous juxtaposition of A and B (AB_I, AB_{II}).[13] The dramatic structure of the musical events here is shaped in accordance with the following scheme:

A_2	AB_I	A_3	A_4	B_2	A B_{II}	B_3	A_5	B_4
4 :	**3** :	**1** :	**3** :	**1** :	**6** :	**3** :	**4** :	**2**

[11] $\mathbf{A_2}$ = long pitches (lasting 6 or 3 seconds) played *senza vibrato* or *vibrato* interrupted by pauses (lasting 1, 2, or 3-5 seconds); this segment – clearly ended *glissando* – lasts approx. 25 seconds. $\mathbf{A_3}$ = repetition of an eight-tones chord (fis-g-gis-a-d^1-es^1-e^1-f^1); this segment - also ended *glissando* – lasts approximately 6 seconds $\mathbf{A_4}$ = a succession of sound-figures and longer pitches ended *glissando*; this segment lasts 18 seconds. $\mathbf{A_5}$ = long sound-block (eight-tones cluster: h-c^1-cis^1-d^1-dis^1-e^1-f^1-fis^1) played *vibrato*; this segment lasts 24 seconds.

[12] $\mathbf{B_2}$ = brief and longer acoustic effects (2-3 seconds) resulting from playing on the tailpiece; this segment lasts approximately 6 seconds $\mathbf{B_3}$ = combination of various effects of undefined pitch (brief and longer, 1 second); this segment lasts approximately 18 seconds. $\mathbf{B_4}$ = successive juxtapositions of long sound-blocks with *pianissimo* dynamics as the result of playing between the bridge and the tailpiece (Vn I, Vc) and of the highest (undefined) pitch (Vn II); this segment lasts approximately 12 seconds.

[13] $\mathbf{AB_I}$ = this is the simultaneous presentation of the *dramatis personae* of (A) – brief sounds (repetition) of a defined pitch (Vn I, Vc) and of (B) – long acoustic effects of undefined pitch (Vn II, Vl); this segment lasts approximately 18 seconds. $\mathbf{AB_{II}}$ = this is the simultaneous presentation of the *dramatis personae* of (A) – long sounds of a definite pitch (Vn I, Vc), and (B) – long effects of an undefined pitch (playing between the bridge and the tailpiece); this segment lasts approximately 36 seconds.

In the second part as well, the duration of the segments accords with the simple proportion in the *numero senario* (4: 3: 1: 3: 1: 6: 3: 4: 2).

The musical organization of time in the *Quartetto per archi* is therefore evidence that, even while offering truly new varieties of tone that often came as a shock to the both performers and audiences of his so-called avant garde works, Penderecki was carrying on the classical idea of music as a dramatic action regulated by poetics and rhetoric as well as the principle of proportion. So Penderecki's avant garde works have a radically different aesthetic background than that of Darmstadt school.

Translated by William Brand

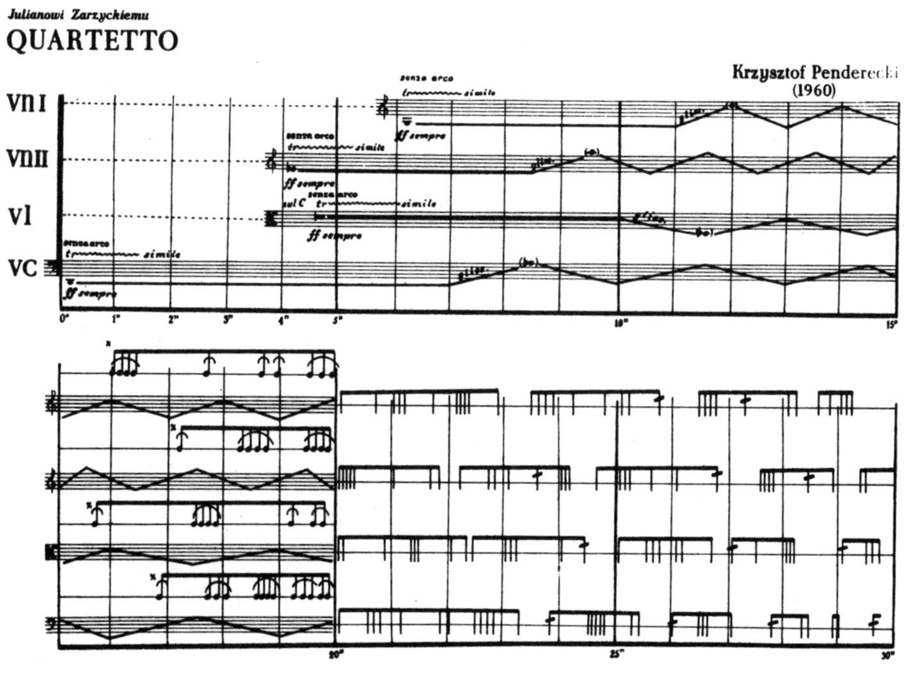

Iwona Lindstedt
Warsaw

Between Dodecaphony and Sonoristics: Post-Serial Formulas in Penderecki's Work, 1960-1962

Much has already been written about the status and significance of Penderecki's work in the history of the postwar musical avant garde. At the beginning of the 1960s, the Polish composer became the standard bearer for the most radical trend in this avant garde. Through Penderecki's mediation, attempts at broadening and enriching the sound material, the search for new techniques for organizing this material, and experimentation in notation became the trademark of the so-called "Polish School of Composition." The analysis of the phenomena that arose at the time led researchers to conclude that these phenomena marked an entirely new stage in the development of Polish music. In describing the main interests of Polish composers, Józef Michał Chomiński introduced the concept of "sonoristics," which he defined as a technique consisting in „bringing purely sonoric values to the foreground as the main means of expression and, by the same token, as the structural factor."[1] The reevaluation of the traditional hierarchy of formal factors that accompanied the sonoristic breakthrough became the subject of numerous analytical investigations, and Penderecki's music became the model for the implementation of these new qualities.[2]

---

[1] Józef Michał Chomiński, *Muzyka Polski Ludowej* [The music of the People's Republic of Poland]. Warszawa, 1968, p. 127. This researcher created an overly developed system of musical sonology in which the central category was the concept of "sonoristic regulation" (cf. Józef Michał Chomiński and Krystyna Wilkowska-Chomińska, *Małe formy instrumentalne* [Small-scale instrumental forms]. Kraków, 1983, pp. 126–152).

[2] In his search for the "philosopher's stone" of sonorism, Penderecki made use of a wide range of concepts. The most important of these were the "shape of sound" (*Klanggestalt*) (Tadeusz A. Zieliński, "Der einsame Weg des Krzysztof Penderecki," *Melos* 10 [1972], pp. 318–323) and the "sound (textural) model" meaning a sequence of sound events assigned to a single instrument part (Krzysztof Droba, "Hierarchia czynników formalnych w twórczości Pendereckiego" [The hierarchy of formal factors in the works of Penderecki], *Muzyka* 2 [1976], pp. 22-23). An unquestionable accomplishment of recent years is the research by Danuta Mirka (*The Sonoristic Structuralism of Krzysztof Penderecki*, Katowice, 1997), which describes Penderecki''s sonoristic compositional technique as a "generative grammar," a system made up of "two component subsystems of relative independence: basic system and timbre system" (p. 26). The first subsystem regulates the pitch, duration, and dynamics of sound phenomena, and the second, the generation of sound.

It would seem that the most significant result of the latest research is the observation that, despite the original credence in the particular "anti-intellectualism" of his sonoristic compositional techniques, the procedures that Penderecki used are just as refined as the serial techniques employed in the avant garde musical centers of the West. The difference between Penderecki's technique and serial composition mainly comes down to the application of those intellectualized mechanisms not to individual sounds, but to the sound material taken as a whole.[3] Both serialism and Penderecki's style lead to the unification of all sound parameters in respect of their internal organization. This observation might usefully be compared with Penderecki's own words:

> As far as the Darmstadt school goes, I never did in fact have any points of contact with it. The difference between the representatives of that school and me could, it seems to me, be defined in this way: they are interested first of all in points, whereas I am interested above all in lines.[4]

The radicalism of this statement, in which Penderecki distances his own way of thinking from the tradition marked by the works of Nono, Berio, Boulez or Stockhausen, is only superficial. Although Penderecki was aware of the differences between his own compositional system and the principles of serialism, indicated mainly by the tendency towards continuity (lines)[5] versus the discontinuous organization of musical parameters (points), he did not treat them as a rigorous contradiction. The legacy of the Darmstadt avant garde had a powerful influence on Penderecki's early work. His experiments at the time with the treatment of musical instruments and the discovery of a world of new sounds were accompanied by a meticulous probing of the boundaries of serial technique.

The main thesis of this article is therefore the assertion that the most salient element of the composer's stylistics in the 1960s is the close relationship between methods drawn from the serial tradition and sonoristics. This applies not only to the fusion of sonorism and twelve-tone means, the significance of which was identified by Danuta Mirka in what she calls the "late sonorism" phase (1963-73),[6] but also the phase that she calls

---

[3] Danuta Mirka, *The Sonoristic Structuralism*, pp. 334–335.

[4] Ates Orga, "Krzysztof Penderecki," *Music and Musicians* X, 22 (1973) (10), p. 39.

[5] Danuta Mirka argues that the "lines" from composer's statement should be interpreted "as sections – intervals in the spaces of individual parameters proper for categories of basic system". Cf. *The Sonoristic Structuralism*, p. 335 and for full explanation of "basic system" categories pp. 31–62.

[6] This is the period after the *Passion*, when the "timbre system" was excluded from Penderecki's compositional system and the constant presence of the "basic system" became the integrating factor in all the sonoristic work (cf. Mirka *The Sonoristic Structuralism*, pp. 343–344).

the "sonoristic period proper" (1960-1962), where she notes and confirms, along with other researchers, the presence of specifically rigorous procedures in the regulation of the subsegmental level of the composition.[7]

The formulation of such a thesis is possible thanks to the assumption that both the twelve-tone series and arithmetical subsegmental relations derive from a common source. Despite many differences - more of an ideological or aesthetic than a purely substantial nature - Darmstadt style was, after all, the direct continuation of the accomplishments of the Viennese avant garde in the first half of the twentieth century: Schoenberg and, even more so, Webern. The integration of serial and sonoristic techniques in Penderecki's early work, in the meantime, emerges on two levels: either in "pure" form - serial thinking in the regulation of pitch structures in cooperation with a creative imagination of sound color - or, in a sense, "inside" the system of the sonoristic organization of Penderecki's work, producing transformations of the sound structure of a serial derivation.

Confirmation of these observations is found in the analytical picture of selected phenomena that occur in a range of Penderecki's works from 1960 to 1962: *Dimensions of Time and Silence, To the Victims of Hiroshima: Threnody, Anaklasis, Quartetto per archi nr 1, Polymorphia,* and *Fluorescences.* Mirka places these works within the "sonoristic period proper" phase, while Regina Chłopicka places these works in the common domain stretching "from *Emanations* to *Fluoresences,*" which is marked by the search for an individual language and the exposition of dramatized sonorism.[8]

THE ORGANIZATION OF THE PITCH STRUCTURE

The first trace of Penderecki's connection with the European New Music was his use of the twelve-tone series. As early as *The Psalms of David* (1958), *Emanations* (1958) and *Strophes* (1959), Penderecki was exhibiting music in which serial arrangement was an important structural factor. One such passage, appearing in the instrumental accompaniment to *Psalm 143* (Example 1), has particular significance for our further investigations - it is a sort of prototype of the later chromatic-serial structures that are so characteristic of *Threnody*, String Quartet No. 1 and the *Dimensions of Time and Silence.*

[7] Mirka, *The Sonoristic Structuralism*, pp. 300–310.

[8] Regina Chłopicka, "Stylistic Phases in the Work of Krzysztof Penderecki." In *Studies in Penderecki*, vol. I, Ray Robinson (ed.), Princeton, 1998.

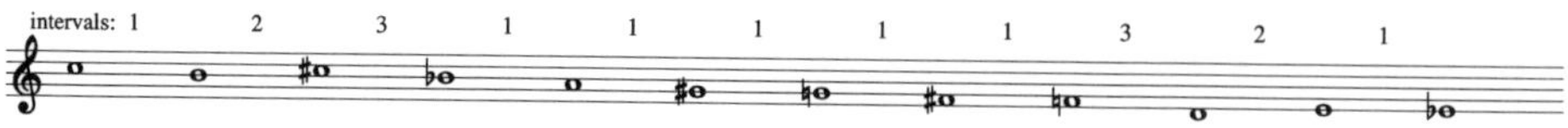

Example 1. K. Penderecki, *Psalms of David*, no. 143, twelve-tone series.
(© K. Penderecki, used by permission)

The special properties of Penderecki's twelve-tone series result from the fact that they are usually made up of four chromatic cells of three notes, the elements of which may be permuted. One of the possible ways of building a twelve-tone series from these cells is illustrated in the initial passage of the Quartet. Two series, linked by a one-element bridge, appear there.[9]

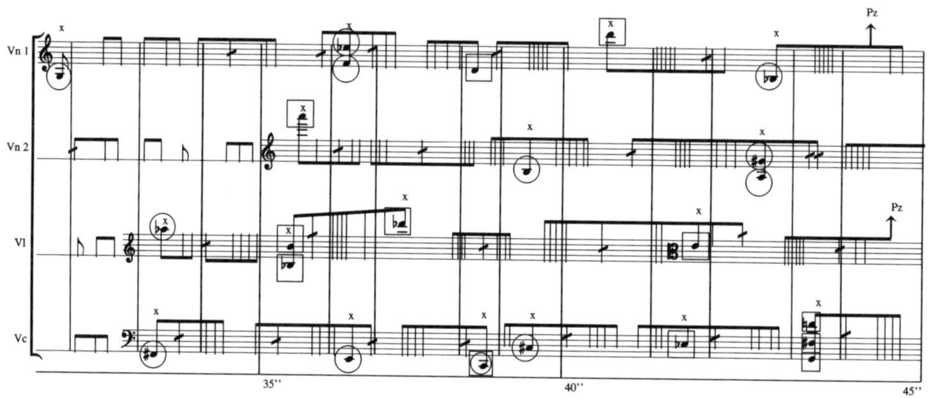

Example 2. K. Penderecki, String Quartet No. 1, part of the first minute.
(© Moeck Verlag, 1960. Used by permission)

In view of the simultaneous appearance of some notes, there are several possible versions of readings of the elements in the series. Three of them may be seen in Example 3:

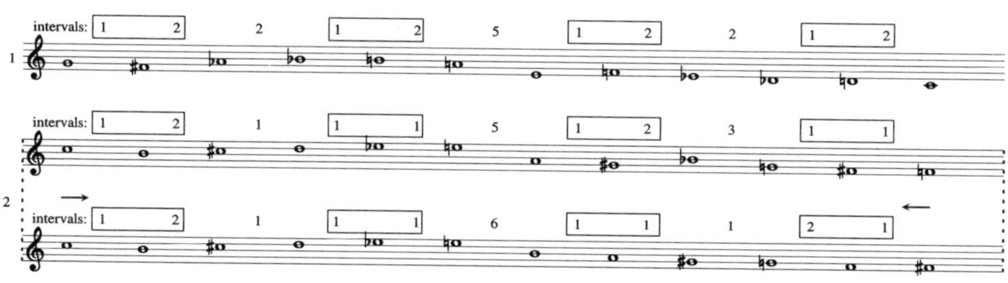

Example 3. K. Penderecki, String Quartet No. 1, part of the first minute; ordering of the series.
(© K. Penderecki, used by permission)

[9] The former is marked in Example 2 by circles, and the latter by squares.

The three-note cells of the first series are a permutation of the basic arrangement according to the chromatic scale that is stepped in units made up of semitones and whole tones – intervals progressing in opposite directions. The second series may, on the other hand, be read in such a way that the second and fourth three-note cells are protected in their original chromatic form, or, alternatively, the whole structure may also be laid out in the form of a palindrome with the tritone as an axis of symmetry, so that the order and dimension of the intervals are preserved in a simple and retrograde movement.

Series of an analogous "cellular" construction also appear in the 36-voice canon of the *Threnody*, which stretches from the 26th to the 59th measures of the score. Two series of pitches joined in a whole tone-semitone relationship appear there in the first measures of the first orchestra. Example 4 illustrates the most symmetrical option for arranging these elements, the first of which is an ideal mirror-image, and the second of which contains minor interference. Just as in the case of the Quartet, the simultaneous elements of the three-note cells of the series in *Threnody* can be arranged in another way, to create a "competing" reading.

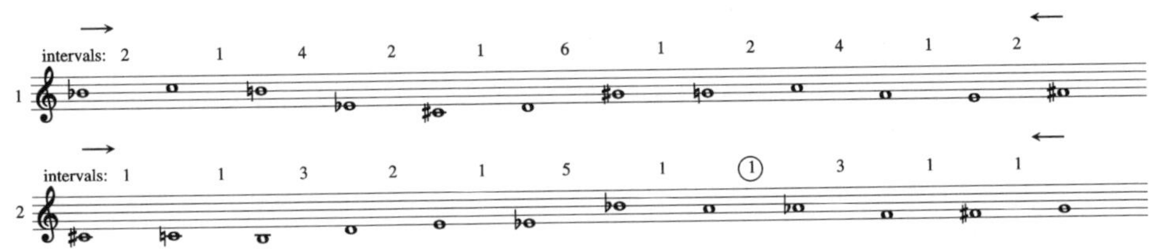

Example 4. K. Penderecki, *To the Victims of Hiroshima: Threnody*, mm. 26 –31, ordering of the series. (© K. Penderecki, used by permission)

The *Dimensions of Time and Silence* supply the next example of a series constructed of three-note cells. The 48th paragraph of the score contains twelve different notes that are symmetrically written into four trichord cells.[10] They create four possible mirror forms of semitone downwards and whole tone upwards – prime, inversion, retrograde and retrograde inversion:

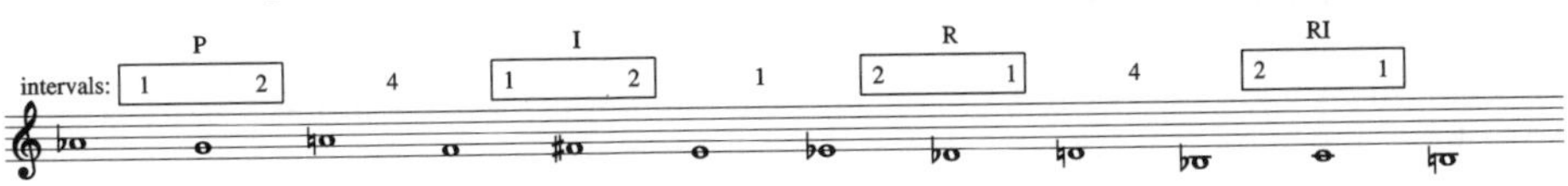

Example 5. K. Penderecki, *Dimensions of Time and Silence*, series at no. 48. (© Moeck Verlag, 1961. Used by permission)

[10] Karl-Josef Müller, "Pendereckis Musik im 'mobilen netz trigonometrischer Punkte.' Skizzierung thematischer Schwerpunkte," *Musik und Bildung* 12 (1975), pp. 622–629.

In paragraphs 10 and 72 of *Dimensions*, further interesting serial configurations appear in six instrumental voices (xylorimba, vibraphone, glockenspiel, celesta, piano, and harp). These constructions, temporally remote, are connected in a relationship of retrogradation, and each of them includes six different twelve-tone arrangements. Danuta Mirka[11] notes accurately that this is the same series, arranged with transpositions, as in paragraph 48. However, she does not explain the principle according to which the series was reshaped. Series in particular instrumental parts are made up of various interval successions and, in contrast to the rows from paragraph 48, they do not make up palindromes. Only the retrograde of the harp part is situated in a model that is close to being symmetrical. Other trichordal segments also appear alongside the whole tone-semitone ones. The most frequently exhibited cells are 5-1 and 1-5, as well as 1-6; 1-4, 3-3, 2-5, and 5-2, as well as 3-2 and 2-3 interval arrangements also manifest themselves. If there is any way of explaining the connection of these series with the symmetrical arrangement that is characteristic of Penderecki's work, or, in general, with the composer's beloved "chromatic series" built of cells, then it is only through the procedure of permutation.

The principle for the rearrangement of the elements is illustrated in Example 6, in which each actual serial succession is contrasted with its chromatic source series. The trichord cells of the source series are permuted. In each case, the derivative series contain at least one element that has not been transformed (most frequently, this is the final trichord of the source form, and the remaining elements are grouped according to the 2+1 and 1+2 pattern in locations fairly remote from each other within the series. The model of grouping from the xylorimba part is repeated in the glockenspiel part, and the model from the vibraphone part in the celesta part. The most irregular form of permutation occurs in the piano and harp parts. The attempt at graphical interpretation is justified by what Penderecki himself had to say about the process by which he composed the work:

> First, in fact, I sketch the work. I put it together out of graphic elements that work for me in music. I have applied this principle from the beginning, and not only in works like the *Threnody*, which can be sketched on a small sheet of paper. The graphical logic checks out in the logic of the sound. It constitutes a sort of shortcut that makes it possible to envision the work.[12]

[11] Mirka, *The Sonoristic Structuralism*, pp. 302–303.

[12] Krzysztof Penderecki, statement at a seminar on his work, Cracow, January, 1975. Cf. *Muzyka* 2 (1976) p. 30.

I therefore feel that it is possible to carry over onto the micro-level the mechanism used in the production of the macrostructure, as revealed by the composer, and adopt it in constructing a twelve-tone series, as in Example 6:

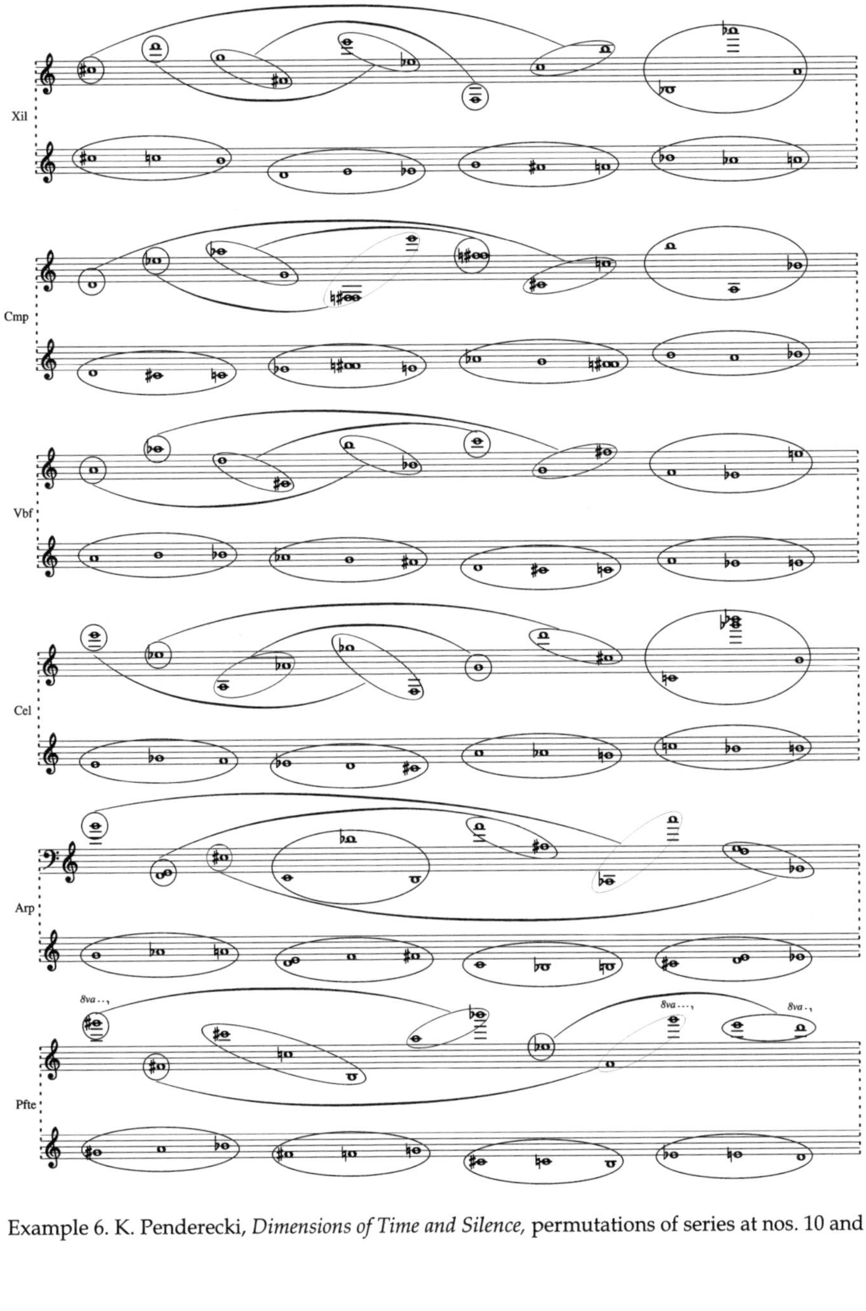

Example 6. K. Penderecki, *Dimensions of Time and Silence,* permutations of series at nos. 10 and 72.

There can be no doubt that Penderecki is questioning the rigor of the twelve-tone idea here, playing at deconstructing it, and leading analysis astray by seducing it with the hope for the discovery of an ideal order. For it is not the series to which the primary formal-structural importance attaches in this work. It attaches rather to the geometrical-spatial thinking. The serial principle is only a starting point for the process of constructing and disassembling the various arrangements of sound phenomena. They are the most important issues.

THE ORGANIZATION OF THE SOUND STRUCTURE

The main extra-musical unifying idea in Penderecki's *Dimensions* is the "magic square" (matrix) model. In view of the origins of the work, this is one of the most fascinating options for interpretation.[13] Hints of the idea that unifies all the dimensions of the musical space can be found on various levels of the composition, from details such as the symmetrical construction of the twelve-tone series in paragraph 48, to general aspects such as the construction of form.[14] Above all, however, Penderecki uses this idea to link different directions of movement in presenting the sound structure, and combining it with permutations taken from the catalogue of serial transformation techniques. The functioning of this idea at the level of sound segments is most fully explained through an analysis of the sequences of consonants in the choral parts in paragraph 47.

Series of six consonants generated from the sequence GTKBDPKD, which appears in the soprano and tenor parts at the previous paragraph, occur here. Karl-Josef Müller[15] has noted that, after the removal of the repeated consonants in paragraph 47, the following orders remain: DKBTPG in the sopranos, GBPKTD in the altos, TPGBKD in the tenors, and DTKPBG in the basses. If the series that appears in the sopranos is taken as the prime form, 1-2-3-4-5-6, then the alto will be a transformation of this order in which elements from the first half are combined with

[13] There was an original version of the *Dimensions* in which Penderecki used an *a cappella* choral passage based on the text of the Latin stanza SATOR/AREPO/TENET/OPERA/ROTAS, mentioned by Pliny, which Webern used in his 1932 lectures as an example elucidating the principle of the total integrity of the twelve-tone series. Penderecki ultimately opted to forego the inclusion of a choral setting of the motto.

[14] Its basis is the contrast of the first phase with the succession of the four segments ABCD in the second phase, as a result of which it appears in retrograde movement with the exception of the final segment, which is modified and abridged. The work concludes with a third phase that indicates its synthetic nature.

[15] Müller, "Pendereckis Musik," p. 625.

the corresponding elements from the second half (a retrograde of the "every third element" permutation) – 6-3-5-2-4-1. The tenor permutation consists in the second and first halves of the original changing places, with the second, in addition, being presented in retrogradation: 4-5-6-3-2-1 (the halves of the series are centered). The bass, on the other hand, displays the retrograde of the alto part: 1-4-2-5-3-6. The German researcher did not interpret the entirety of paragraph 47, which in fact contains eight, and not four, series of consonants. Let us take a closer look at the remaining four.

The first tenor series (KTDPBG) displays a permutation of the prime form: 2-4-1-5-3-6, or a retrograde of the first half of the second series of the bass part (DTKPBG) combined with the unchanged order of the second half. The first series in the bass part (BTKPDG), on the other hand, is an arrangement of the basic pattern in the order 3-4-2-5-1-6 – in other words, a "centrifugal" reading of it. The second alto series (GPTBKD) is a retrograde of the prime form, and the second soprano series repeats the arrangement of the elements that appear earlier in the alto. And here is the "magic square" (see Example 7) configuration that synchronizes the choral voices for the entirety of the structure under discussion, constructed according to relationships to the prime form as identified by Müller (soprano row):

S	DKBTPG 1-2-3-4-5-6		GBPKTD 6-3-5-2-4-1	
A		GBPKTD 6-3-5-2-4-1		GPTBKD 6-5-4-3-2-1
T	KTDPBG 2-4-1-5-3-6		TPGBKD 4-5-6-3-2-1	
B		BTKPDG 3-4-2-5-1-6		DTKPBG 1-4-2-5-3-6

Example 7. K. Penderecki, *Dimensions of Time and Silence*, no. 47, "magic square" 1.

The actual order of appearance of the canonical sequences of consonants at paragraph 47 of *Dimensions* provokes a "competitive" reading of the permutation arrangements. The prime form for them will be the KTDPBG succession that appears first in the tenor. Thus interpreted, and this time vertically synchronized, the "magic square" looks like this:

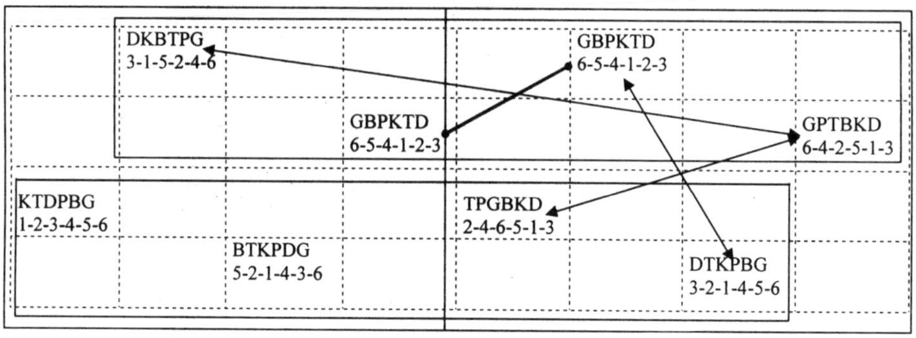

Example 8. K. Penderecki, *Dimensions of Time and Silence*, no. 47, "magic square" 2.

The basic permutations of the original model can be divided into three categories. The first of these is the choice of succeeding even and odd elements, or the converse, and the possible recurring permutation of this structure, as in the arrangements 3-1-5-2-4-6, 2-4-6-5-1-3 and 6-4-2-5-1-3. The second is the division of the series into halves and the changing of the order of their occurrence, as in the order 6-5-4-1-2-3, or 3-2-1-4-5-6, which appears here twice. The third option, characteristic for the first series in the bass part, is the selection of "every third element" and its further permutation to the order 5-2-1-4-3-6. Furthermore, the rows may be a related by retrograde, as in the case of 3-1-5-2-4-6 and 6-4-2-5-1-3. It is worth noting that new possibilities for the interpretation of the series arise after each change of the point of reference. For example, the series 3-1-5-2-4-6 could arise through the selection of "every second" ("odd elements – even elements") element of the series 3-2-1-4-5-6.

Nor is the diagonal dimension of the square devoid of significance. The temporal differences in the presentation of the several series of consonants mean that the patterns given above can, in fact, be discerned twice in each of two magic squares: the first will cover the repeated succession of voices – tenor-soprano-bass-alto – while the second will consist of series included in the soprano and alto and the tenor and bass parts.

In the second square of the arrangement read in order, we note a strict diagonal relationship: a symmetrical relation between the series GBPKTD in the soprano and its retrograde in the bass (DTKPBG), and the connection between the series GPTBKD and the series TPGBKD, which consists of the reversal of the direction of the presentation of the first half. The upper one of the squares that arises as a result of the division of the voices into two layers also exhibits an interesting diagonal property. The sequence GBPKTD appears in both the alto and the soprano, while the two remaining elements of the structure, GPTBKD and DKBTPG, are connected by retrogradation. The essence of an analytical examination of paragraph 47 is thus a multiplicity of equally entitled readings. The arrangements seem to be equally logical in various interpretative lights, with changes in the direction and order of the reading of individual segments.

The idea of the "magic square" also illuminates the organization of the sound structure in Penderecki's First String Quartet and in his *Threnody*. In these works, it has to do with the means of the spatial composition of multi-element series of sound events. The internal construction of these series, on the other hand, is the result of the application of mathematical procedures.

Numerical series are used to order the so-called ligatures - groups of notes joined by a single full beam in the initial fragment (to approximately the 60-second mark) of the Quartet. Krzysztof Bilica elucidated the principle governing the distribution of elements in the ligatures.[16] Namely, there are four formulas for arithmetical organization here:

(A) a series of odd numbers: 1-3-5-7-9
(B) a series of natural numbers: 1-2-3-4-5-6-7-8-9
(C) a series of pairs of alternately odd and even numbers: 1-3-2-4-5-7-6-8
(D) a Fibonacci series of numbers: 2-3-5-8-13 or numbers with an increasing difference between the successive elements: 2 -(+1)-3 -(+2)-5-(+3)-8-(+4)-12

[16] Krzysztof Bilica, "Pozaekspresyjne porządki w Kwartecie smyczkowym (nr 1)" [Beyond-expressive orders in String Quartet No.1]. In *Współczesność i tradycja w muzyce Krzysztofa Pendereckiego* (selected conference materials), Regina Chłopicka and Krzysztof Szwajgier (eds.). Kraków, 1983, p. 75.

Each of the series is used as in its original form, or is retrograded. Their distribution over the four voices therefore results in a series of skillful higher-level structures, which can be ordered by the "magic square" principle, as in the configuration below (see also Example 2):

RA (vn1)	11-9-7-5-3-2(1)	**B (vn1)**	1-2-3-4-5-5(6)-7-8-9	**RC (vn1)**	8-5(6)-7-5-4-2-3-1	**D (vn1)**	2-3-5-8-13(13)
RB (vn2)	8(9)-8-7-6-5-4-3-2-1	**A (vn2)**	1-3-5-7-9-11	**RD (vn2)**	12(13)-8-5-3-2	**C (vn2)**	1-3-2-5(4)-5-7-6-8
RC (vl)	8-6-7-5-4-2-3-1	**D (vl)**	2-3-5-8-8(13)	**RA (vl)**	10(11)-9-7-5-3-1	**B (vl)**	1-2-3-4-5-6-6(7)-8-9
RD (vc)	12(13)-8-5-3-2-1	**C (vc)**	1-3-2-4-5-7-6-8	**RB (vc)**	9-8-7-6-5-4-3-2-1	**A (vc)**	1-3(2)-4(5)-7-9-11

Example 9. K. Penderecki, String Quartet No.1, "magic square" of ligatures.

The horizontal arrangements (the sequence of ligatures that occur one after another in each of the four voices) are here a specific permutation of the vertical configuration, made up of alternating retrogrades and prime forms of elementary numerical series. It is, additionally, worth noting that the first vertical arrangement is a retrograde of the ligatures of the fourth column, and the third and second arrangements have an analogous relation to each other. The pairs of sequences of retrograde and prime forms arranged in the vertical columns of the „magic square" are, additionally, connected through the rotation of the elements – RA-RB-RC-RD with RC-RD-RA-RB and B-A-D-C with D-C-B-A.

An arrangement inspired by the idea of the "magic square" can also be found in the canon of the sound (textural) model included in measures 6-9 of the score of *Threnody*. The four models appearing canonically in the part of the ten cellos, which the composer recommends that the performers select as they prefer and perform in a designated time period (15 seconds) "as fast as possible,"[17] creates a special pattern, "stretched over time," for the "magic square."[18] The basic model (A) is made up of seven various articulations that can be designated as series of the successive natural numbers 1-2-3-4-5-6-7. The three subsequent groupings are a model of its transformation:

---

[17] This composer's note introduces an element of indeterminacy, and thus these complicated interrelations are discernible only during the examination of the score and cannot be perceived by ear. The same remark should be applied to the other examples of complex subsegmental regulations presented in this article where a common beat is missing and temporal relationships are not precise.

[18] See also Wilfried Gruhn, "Strukturen und Klangmodelle in Pendereckis *Threnody*" [Structures and Sound Models in Penderecki's *Threnody*], *Melos* 10 (1971), p. 10.

(B) retrograde: 7-6-5-4-3-2-1
(C) decreasing series of even and odd elements: 6-4-2-7-5-3-1
(D) an increasing series of even and odd elements: 2-4-6-1-3-5-7

They appear in successive measures in the viola, violin, and double bass parts in the segment under discussion. The following pairs of sequences of the model, joined by retrogradation – A-C-B-D in the cellos and D-B-C-A in the violas, C-D-A-B in the violins, and B-A-D-C in the double basses, appear in succession. The synchronization of the canonical voices makes it possible to construct a "magical square" for this passage, in which four different arrangements of the sound model described here appear in both the horizontal and the vertical dimensions. The vertical arrangements here are a specific, "centripetal" permutation (the original order of the elements, 1-2-3-4, changes to 1-4-2-3) of the horizontal arrangements, as in the example below:

A	1-2-3-4-5-6-7	**C**	6-4-2-7-5-3-1	**B**	7-6-5-4-3-2-1	**D**	2-4-6-1-3-5-7
D	2-4-6-1-3-5-7	**B**	7-6-5-4-3-2-1	**C**	6-4-2-7-5-3-1	**A**	1-2-3-4-5-6-7
C	6-4-2-7-5-3-1	**D**	2-4-6-1-3-5-7	**A**	1-2-3-4-5-6-7	**B**	7-6-5-4-3-2-1
B	7-6-5-4-3-2-1	**A**	1-2-3-4-5-6-7	**D**	2-4-6-1-3-5-7	**C**	6-4-2-7-5-3-1

Example 10. K. Penderecki, *To the Victims of Hiroshima: Threnody,* mm. 6-9, "magic square" of sound models.

The "magic square" is therefore the fullest concrete realization of the idea of spatial symmetry in the works of Penderecki. Thanks to integration into its structure of permutational and mirror arrangements, it is also a lasting element in the heritage of the serial epoch, with which the composer was grappling in the initial period of his career as a composer.

The most frequent and, by the same token, the simplest form of subsegmental regulation in Penderecki is, however, simple mirror symmetry as embodied in structures of the "original-retrograde" type of configuration. Its power is frequently comprehended in presentations of shorter and longer sound models, similar to the seven-element articulative series in *Threnody*, as described above.

Five basic sound models, contrasted with their variants, can be distinguished in the section included between paragraphs 38 and 45 of *Polymorphia.* The basic means for the transformation of the first three structures is retrogradation. Especially at paragraphs 42 and 43, there are agglomerations in prime and retrograde form of four variants of a single model. The first three models with their transformations are specified in Example 11:

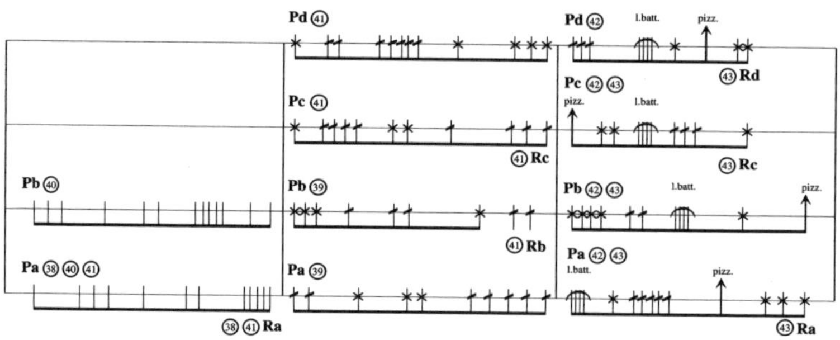

Example 11. K.Penderecki *Polymorphia,* nos. 38-42, juxtaposition of sound models. (© Moeck Verlag, 1961. Used by permission)

The score of *Fluorescences* also contains a fairly developed section of full symmetrical relations between the basic models and their mirror-images. In the fragment included between paragraphs 45 and 54, each sound model is juxtaposed simultaneously with its retrograde, as in the example below:[19]

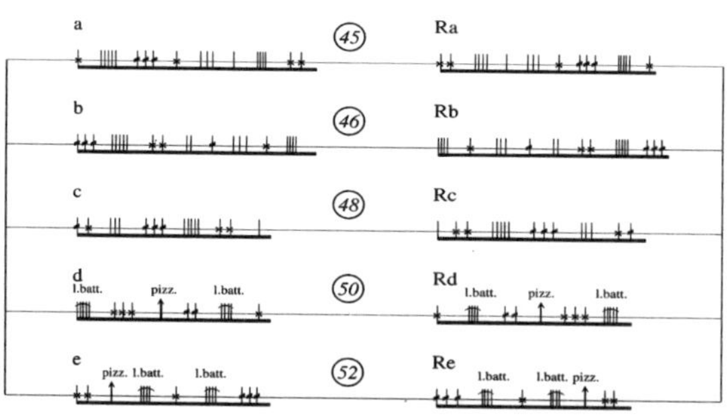

Example 12. K. Penderecki *Fluorescences,* nos. 45-54, juxtaposition of sound models. (© Moeck Verlag, 1962. Used by permission)

[19] The sequence presented in the viola 5-8 parts at paragraph 45 is a retrograde of the sequence played by violas 1-4. At paragraph 46, cello parts 1-4 and double bass parts 1-3 are in an analogous relationship, reflected symmetrically in the cello 5-8 and double bass 4-6 parts. Paragraph 48 is filled with the next model and mirror-image of the violin 1-12 and 13-24 parts. The two last models that proceed simultaneously in original and retrograde forms appear in paragraphs 50 (cellos and double basses) and 52 (violins and violas).

Arrangements of the "original-retrograde" type are also characteristic of the rhythmical progression of *Anaklasis*. Alfred Huber has noted that, in the section including measures 22-37 and written for six groups of percussion instruments, there is a particular arithmetical type of the regulation of rhythm.[20] From three various divisions of quarter notes, the composer created three basic rhythmical forms here: a group of four sixteenth notes, a quintuplet, and a sextuplet presented as individual values surrounded by pauses. The internal order of these units is variable, since the notes can change places with the pauses. The regular division into four sixteenths is subordinated to the fourth and sixth groups of instruments, the quintuplets to the first and the third, and the sextuplets to the second and fifth. The rhythmical models always appear in one half of the measure, while the second half is taken up by a quarter-note pause.

Example 13. K. Penderecki *Anaklasis*, mm. 28-31, symmetrical relations.

20 Alfred Huber, "Pendereckis *Anaklasis* für Streicher und Schlagzeuggruppen" [Penderecki's *Anaklasis* for Strings and Percussion], *Melos* 3 (1971), pp. 87–91.

The essence of the symmetry here is the fact that these „basic rhythms" are connected in pairs of instruments belonging to one group according to the principle of retrogradation, both within the individual measure, and also across the measure-line. In the fifth group of instruments, which appears to be a deviation from the pattern of rhythmical structuring that has been adopted, the principle of retrogradation extends not only to the halves of the measures, but also to the entire rhythmical course of the section. The „basic rhythms" thus correspond with themselves over the central axis of symmetry that is located between measures 30 and 31. A similar phenomenon applies to the bongos part in the section that includes measures 54-75, and the axis of symmetry lies between measures 70 and 71.[21]

Among many other examples, a relation of the "original-retrograde" type also appears, in an interesting way, in paragraphs 175-187 of *Dimensions of Time and Silence*. Here, it applies to the quasi-canonical rhythmic progression performed by the choir in sequences of consonants. The four basic sound models included in the sopranos and alto parts are juxtaposed with retrograde versions of themselves in the tenor and bass parts (see Example 14):

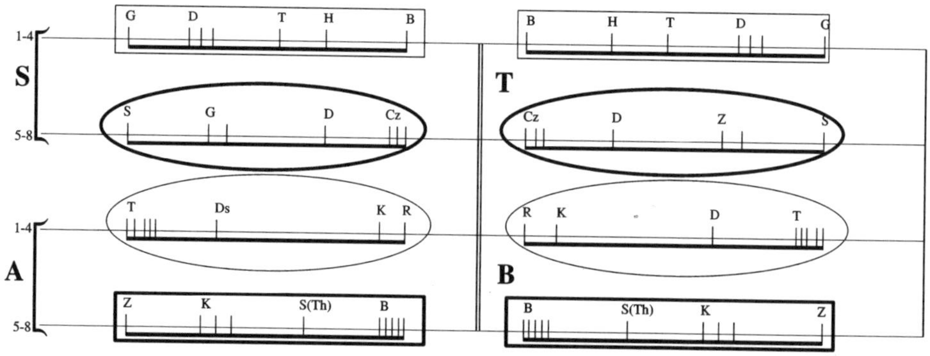

Example 14. K. Penderecki *Dimensions of Time and Silence,* choral part, mm. 175-187, symmetry of consonant series.

* * *

The innovativeness, precision and verve with which Penderecki shapes the internal sound structures in his early works is eloquent proof of his mastery of the composer's craft. The symbiosis of these intellectually refined methods with the twelve-tone organization of pitches and an

[21] See also Mirka, *The Sonoristic Structuralism*, p. 302.

overall sonoristic organizational system adds up to a unique stylistic idiom without precedent in the history of the "new music." All things considered, it must be acknowledged that Danuta Mirka is correct in asserting that the subsegmental regulation in Penderecki's music is generally a factor subordinated to a superior category – the sonoristic system.[22] Nevertheless, it must be acknowledged that this regulation has more than a marginal significance. The post-serial procedures that the Polish composer employs in the *Dimensions of Time and Silence*, the *Threnody*, and the String Quartet are proof of the exceptional vitality and endurance of the tradition of Webern and Boulez in Penderecki's work. This tradition, however, is creatively transformed and woven into entirely new contexts.[23] Penderecki's aesthetic consciousness indeed centered primarily on the empirical aspects of sonoristics, his general treatment of sound material implied no aversion to the catalogue of serial transformations. In this particular way, Penderecki seems to second Stockhausen's dictum that "serial thinking is something that has come into our consciousness and will remain there forever."[24] Penderecki himself supplied the point to this tale in a formulation from a 1963 interview with Tadeusz Zieliński:

> Is it possible in practical terms to cut oneself off from the whole history of music and create a system of entirely new laws without making use of the accomplishments of earlier periods? . . . Each generation of composers, beginning with the romantics, may have dreamed of doing so. Afterwards, it always turns out that the revolution was only partial; after all, we are too heavily burdened with the enormous ballast of habits that make themselves apparent even in the boldest explorations. . . . Can anyone imagine the style of Boulez without the positive accomplishments of Webern and Messiaen? And the origins of those composers are known. Contemporary music is a result of a long evolution, and its roots grow not only out of the innovative accomplishments of the previous generation, but reach deep into the past, and we do not always realize this.[25]

---

[22] Mirka, *The Sonoristic Structuralism*, p. 310.

[23] This mechanism of reevaluating traditional qualities is characteristic as well of the greater part of the reception of dodecaphony and serialism in all Polish composing of the 1960s. The serial formulae are intertwined there not only with the sonoristic elements most characteristic of the "Polish School," but also with techniques of indeterminacy (e.g. in H. M. Górecki, A. Walaciński and B. Schaeffer). Processes of transformational reception manifest themselves also in attempts at using series to control the various aspects of musical space, independent of the tradition of Schoenberg and the Darmstadt circle (e.g. W. Lutosławski, Z. Mycielski, A. Prosnak).

[24] Johann Cott, *Stockhausen: Conversations with the Composer*. New York, 1973, p. 101.

[25] Tadeusz Zieliński, "Współczesny kompozytor a tradycja. Rozmowa z Krzysztofem Pendereckim" [The Contemporary Composer and Tradition. Conversation with Krzysztof Penderecki], *Ruch Muzyczny* 12 (1963), p. 8.

Józef Rychlik
Cracow

Krzysztof Penderecki's *Psalmus*

Psalmus is Penderecki's only autonomous electronic work. It was completed on Good Friday in 1961 in the Polish Radio Experimental Studio (founded in Warsaw by Józef Patkowski in 1957) and had its world première shortly afterwards, on April 10, at the Fylklingen Studio in Stockholm. It was produced by Eugeniusz Rudnik, who cooperated with Penderecki in all the latter's studio work (film music and the opening anthem for the 1972 Munich Olympics). The interest in the electronic studio in the 1950s and 1960s was connected with the lively universal fascination at the time with new technology and its promise of freedom to create unprecedented structures and expression. This was a time when the avant-garde was becoming the aesthetic standard, and the studio seemed to meet the expectations of composers in at least two regards: the precision of the serial editing of aural phenomena, and experimentation with sounds (creating new phenomena from scratch and transforming sound-color).

Psalmus appeared at a time when Penderecki was greatly interested in studio technology. This was also a time of intense searching for new means of musical language in the instrumental and vocal areas. In the period from *Strophes* and *Emanations* through *Threnody* and *The Dimensions of Time and Silence* to *Fluorescences, Psalmus* can be seen as an important stage, in the composer development despite the fact that it is different in genre.

Among the critics who described *Psalmus* at the time, we find the opinion that it does not sound like an experimental work (Erhardt).[1] This is a highly significant observation in reference to an electronic composition, and indicates that Penderecki had facilitated aesthetic contact with the listener. This contact was surely based on skill at the appropriate choice and construction of elements of the musical language after beginning with raw, recorded aural material, and the achievement of a clear form and the effect of musical drama.

[1] Cf. Ludwik Erhardt, *Spotkania z Krzysztofem Pendereckim* [Meetings with Krzysztof Penderecki]. Kraków: PWM, 1975.

At the time, form as a category that was closed in terms of process was not a standard to be taken for granted by an avant-garde composer. The model of aleatoric form, found in instrumental, vocal, and so-called "live electronic" music, constituted a parallel alternative that was also possible in taped electronic music, although the tape is the ultimate physical determinant of the overall course of the work, and interpretation ends precisely at the moment when the recording of the work in the studio is finished.

Regardless of the intensity with which he was developing his avant-garde language, Penderecki always paid attention to the formal shape. He succeeded in achieving coherent structure in his compositions either by using a linear-counterpoint technique or through the appropriate shaping of the energy context for a given fragment of the composition (whether this was sonoristic or punctual, with that amorphousness that, paradoxically, is always risky). *Psalmus* expresses similar thinking. Its simple, discontinuous form consists of five segments, with the culmination occurring in the fourth. It demonstrates a variable intensity of tension and expression.

The source of the basic expressive categories of the composition doubtless lies in its vocal origins. After all, the original material is made up principally of six spoken syllables: t, b, d, th, h, and r, as well as of two sung sounds. The performer (of the speech and the singing) is the soprano Halina Łukomska. The transformation of the material creates the impression that the sources of the sound are highly differentiated. The colors and registers thus obtained can even be arranged in the following scale of color categories: the timbre of the voice of Halina Łukomska, the colors of female, male, and human voices, and the color of unspecified sound.

The initial material became the basis for the creation of two sorts of elementary structures; impulse and continuous. The impulses come directly from individually pronounced syllables. The continuity and linearity are either composed of sung sounds, which lends the progressions in question a natural, "vocal" character, or are also made up of the syllables mentioned above, repeated rapidly and regularly to create series that are markedly percussive in nature. The contrast derives from these two different types of structure. The source, be it speech or singing, is almost always recognizable, and therefore structural contrast is interwoven with contrast expressed through sounds coming from the same source.

The punctual and banded organization of texture is a highly salient characteristic of *Psalmus*. This is a sign of the times in which it was composed. There can be no doubt that the initial recording of the raw elements was planned in advance as material for shaping a definite textural model, with the syllables as the punctual ingredient and the sung sounds as the banded ingredient. This is frequently associated with para-serial rhythmic structuring and the expressive use of the scattering of sounds (enriched by reverberation) throughout the register space.

The sung sound is inseparably associated with a definite pitch, and the progression of these sounds with a scale. Here, Penderecki is just as consistent as he is in the relation of the nature of the raw material to the textural model. With the aid of changes in the speed at which the tape is played, he obtains a collection of sounds of various pitches from the original sung sound. As we know, this technique allows the material to be scaled at any value, even a microtonic one (with the only limitation being the precision of the equipment itself). Penderecki creates a network of pitch references in the nature of a tempered scale. In *Psalmus*, a given sonic pitch becomes an extremely important expressive and structural value. Its influence is felt even where it becomes hard to recognize as a result of the addition of a high-reverberation effect.

Obviously, the mixed sounds fall into resonance with the distinct expressive domination of specific intervals. Small and large seconds dominate in various register constellations; tercet and resonance resonances also occur. The enriching techniques of glissando, retardation, detachment, and the evocation of sounds result in an effect of bands of varying harmonic-coloration structure.

It seems at first that the diversity of colors and shades obtained from the original material in *Psalmus* derives mainly from the application of filtering, reverberation or mixing. This is surely an accurate observation to a significant degree. Nonetheless, the basis here is in fact the idea of obtaining material that is diverse in terms of pitch (this is true of both the spoken and the sung material). As we know, the classical technique of changing the speed of the tape, as used at the time for this purpose, introduces profound changes in the spectrum of the sound. The external symptoms of this are changes in the scale of brightness, recognizability, and – no trivial problem – semantics (it suffices to recall the experiences of Pierre Schaeffer). The continual dependence of color on changes in pitch is not hidden in *Psalmus*. For instance, we encounter the forthrightly deliberate use of these acoustic properties in, for instance, the initial segment of the work. The vibrating sound is transposed upwards. The density of vibration is proportional to the changes in pitch. At a certain moment, it becomes mechanical and sounds alien in the context of the still-recognizable color of the human voice. This reveals the necessity for the further differentiation of the category of vocal material; that is, there is a need to take into account, beyond speech and song, the distinction between the natural human voice and the artificial human voice.

Understood as transcending the "naturalness" of the instrument, the range of means of articulating the artificial voice resembles the transcending of the classical ("natural") borders of articulation in, for instance, the string instruments - although, of course, it is done differently. To put it another way, Penderecki uses new sound generators in both cases. In this regard, *Psalmus* reveals deeper connections with other works on levels beyond that of technical compositional means. The experimental sonoric thinking that appears so blatantly in, for instance *Fluorescences* (such as the use of typewriters or wood saws as sound generators) has roots in *Psalmus,* among other places. This particular "futuristic" tendency in the music is a sort of particular sign of that period in the history of music.

In summary, it can be said that *Psalmus* is an electronic psalm without words. Despite its distinctiveness, it blends into the family of vocal-instrumental works. Even though it is not "experimental" within the framework of electronic music, it became - through its distinctiveness - a particular sort of "experiment" within the framework of its composer's work. Bearing in mind its date, it stands together with *Threnody* as the beginning of the experimental sonoric stage.

To a significant degree and without even mentioning the time involved in such work, the classic means of studio technology, including multiple overlays, loops, and painstaking editing through cutting and gluing tape, limited the possibilities for freely shaping the various sound cells and structures. It is tempting to think that, in *Pslamus,* Penderecki might have intuitively anticipated realization today with the use of digital techniques, and especially sampling. In such a case, Penderecki may well have created some sort of virtual vocal group on which to "play" *Psalmus.*

Ray Robinson
West Palm Beach

The Evolution of Penderecki's Orchestra from *Threnody* to *Fluorescences*

> What the New Music movement of the 1950s and 1960s (Boulez, Stockhausen, Berio, Ligeti) shared with the spirit of early modernism (Schoenberg, Berg, Webern) was the commitment to a specialized, progressive and "authentic" art and to a "rhetoric" of endless innovation.[1]

Penderecki's search for new instrumental sonorities reached its climax on October 21, 1962, with the première of the orchestral work *Fluorescences* at the Donaueschingen Festival in Germany's Black Forest. In a four-year period (1958-62), through experiments with instrumental sounds that were part of a search for a personal musical language, the twenty-nine-year-old Polish composer revolutionized the way traditional orchestral instruments were played, created a notational system to make the symbols he placed in the score more accessible to performers, and introduced a series of new "instruments" into the modern symphony orchestra. In doing so he met a basic requirement of the New Music:[2] to cause a radical departure from tradition by making a commitment to a specialized rhetoric of endless innovation.

Emanations (1958), a work for string orchestra, gave the first hint of the direction Penderecki was taking in his experiments with orchestral sonorities. By dividing the ensemble into two equally-sized orchestras and tuning the second a semi-tone higher than the first, he was paving the way for the graphic notation and sonoric innovation that would follow in *Anaklasis* (1959), *Threnody to the Victims of Hiroshima* (1960),

---

[1] Jim Samson, "Avant garde." In: Stanley Sadie, ed., *The New Grove Dictionary of Music and Musicians*, Second edition, Vol.2 (London: Macmillan Publishers Limited, 2001), p. 247.

[2] Some writers make a clear distinction between the spirit of the early 20th-century avant garde movement (Schoenberg, Berg, Webern) and the New Music of the 1950s and 1960s (Boulez, Stockhausen, Berio, Ligeti, Penderecki). The term New Music as it is used in this article refers to avant garde efforts in the mid-20th century.

Fonogrammi (1961) and *Polymorphia* (1961).[3] The significance of *Fluorescences* lies in the fact that it brings the results of these experiments together into one monumental summary statement. Above all else, *Fluorescences* is a study in sonority. It is a work in which the musical element of "sound colorism" functions as the primary factor in its construction. While many of these new techniques of orchestral writing were developed specifically for Penderecki's early experimental instrumental compositions, the original musical language that resulted not only served the cause of the New Music but has remained an integral part of the composer's musical language even into the fifth decade of his compositional career. Fascination with the Penderecki orchestra has continued as his list of works has expanded to include 4 operas, 6 symphonies, 14 other orchestral works, 11 concertos and concerto-like works, and 20 compositions for chorus and orchestra.

PENDERECKI'S ORCHESTRA 1958-1962

The evolution of Penderecki's experimental orchestra occurred over a period of four years (Table 1). It is quite well-known that his earliest instrumental works explored new directions in string sonorities, but it is not as clearly recognized that he did not write his initial work for full orchestra until 1962 and his first symphony until eleven years later (1973). But the early Penderecki orchestra did not stop with traditional instruments: the forces of the orchestra were expanded to include a number of new percussion instruments - typewriter, hacksaw, siren, etc.[4] - that advanced the concept of orchestral sound far beyond the traditional ideas of Berlioz, Widor and Rimsky-Korsakov.[5] For example, in *Anaklasis* and specially in *Fluorescences*, the percussion section is expanded. (Table 2)

---

[3] Cf. Danuta Mirka, *The Sonoristic Structuralism of Krzysztof Penderecki*. Katowice: Academy of Music, 1997.

[4] The alarm siren was previously used by Varèse in *Hypertension* (1922-23).

[5] Three works on the theory and practice of orchestration appeared in the mid-19th and early 20th century. Berlioz' *Grande traite d'instrumentation* (1843) brought to the student's attention admired passages from the works of Beethoven and Gluck, but it was designed to guide the reader to the practicalities inherent in the contemporary orchestra. Widor's *Technique de l'orchestre moderne* (1904) was, for all intents and purposes, an extensive supplement to it. And Rimsky-Korsakov's *Principles of Orchestration* (1913) drew upon the author's brilliant practical gifts as a composer.

Table 1. The evolution of Penderecki's orchestra (1958-62). [6]

	Emanations (Two string orchestras) (1958)		*Anaklasis* (1959)	*Threnody* (1960)	*Polymorphia* (1961)	*Canon* (1962)	*Fluorescences* (1962)
Flute/Piccolo							4 *
Oboe							4
Clarinet in B-flat							4
Bassoon							4
Horns in F							4
Trumpets in B-flat							4
Trombone							3
Tuba							2
Percussion			6 **				6 **
Harp			1				
Celesta			1				
Piano			1 (pft/claves)				1
	I	**II**					
Violin	20	20	20	24	24	24	24
Viola	8	8	8	10	8	8	8
Cello	8	8	8	10	8	8	8
D. Bass	6	6	6	8	8	6	6
						+ 2 tape recorders	

* The numbers in parenthesis refer to doubling. If an instrument is listed in parenthesis it means that a player in the flute, oboe, clarinet, bassoon or brass section would "double" on piccolo, English horn, bass clarinet, bass trombone, etc.

** The percussion batteries in *Anaklasis* and *Fluorescences*: see Table 2.

Even Richard Strauss' use of "everything but the kitchen sink" in his opera *Elektra* does not dwarf the size of the percussion section in *Fluorescences*. The percussion battery becomes such a distinctive element of orchestral sound in Penderecki's works in the 1960's that it is often considered a "Penderecki Signature." But this near obsession with percussion instruments comes to an abrupt end with the landmark orchestral

[6] The abbreviations in Table 1 refer to the orchestral works: *Emanations, Anaklasis, Threnody, Polymorphia, Canon* and *Fluorescences, De natura sonoris No. 1, De natura sonoris No. 2* and Symphony No. 1.

work, *The Awakening of Jacob* (1974). The percussion section never again reaches the sheer size or designed diversity in later works.

Table 2. The percussion battery in *Anaklasis* and *Fluorescences.*

Anaklasis (1959)		*Fluorescences* (1962)	
Battery I	***Battery II***	***Battery I***	***Battery II***
Xylorimba	Vibraphone	Soprano cymbal	Alto cymbal
2 Congas	2 Bongos	Metal plate	Gong
3 Casse di legno	3 Bells	Triangle	Vibraphone
		4 Wood blocks	A piece of glass
		Bongos	Bongos
		Whistle	Whistle
Battery III	***Battery IV***	***Battery III***	***Battery IV***
2 Cymbals (1, 2)	2 Cymbals (3, 4)	Javanese gong	Tam-tam
Little bells	3 Tom-toms	Gourd	Claves
	Bell	Bell	Rattle
	Triangle	Flexatone	2 Cowbells
		3 Tom-toms (S.A.T)	Bass Tam-tam
		Whistle	2 Military drums
			Whistle
Battery V	***Battery VI***	***Battery V***	***Battery VI***
2 Cymbals (5, 6)	Gong	Triangle	Electric Bell
3 Tom-toms	Tam-tam	Tam-tam	A piece of wood
	4 Timpani	Claves	Saw
		Un pezzo di ferro	Typewriter
		4 Timpani	Siren
		Whistle	Whistle

PENDERECKI'S SOUND EFFECTS

Our identification of the instrumentation in Penderecki's "sonoristic" orchestra might well lead the reader to ask: "We now know the makeup of the composer's avant garde orchestra, but what is it that makes this orchestra sound so distinctive?" The answer is relatively simple: it is the way he writes for these instruments, especially strings. As a violinist himself, Penderecki knows the string idiom thoroughly and is able to build on the innovations he inherited from the composers of the 19th and early-20th centuries. These scores use both traditional string effects [such as those listed below in (Table 3)] and new ones "invented" by the composer in the period 1958-62. (Table 4)

Table 3. Traditional string effects inherited from the past.

ordinario	
s. t. (*sul tasto*)	play near the finger board
s. p. (*sul ponticello*)	play near the bridge
c. l. (*col legno*)	striking the string with the wood of the bow
l. batt. (*legno battuto*)	strike the wood of the instrument

Table 4. Innovations for string players developed by Penderecki in the works written between 1958-1962.

 - several irregular changes of bow in succession

 - play between bridge and tailpiece (one or two strings)

 - play between bridge and tailpiece (*arpeggio* on four strings)

 - play on the tailpiece

 - played on the bridge rectangular to its right-hand edge

 - strike the strings with the open hand or with the fingers

 - tap on the fingerboard with the heel of the bow or fingertip

 - tap the music stand with the bow

There are also special instructions given by the composer to assist performers to achieve the desired effects in a given work. For example, in the section called "Abbreviations and symbols," at the beginning of each printed score, Penderecki explains the meaning of the notation in that particular composition. Table 5 reveals the meaning of the instructions in *Fluorescences*.

Table 5. The explanation of general abbreviations and symbols in a given work.

 - play the highest note on the instrument (no definite pitch)

 - play the lowest note on the instrument (no definite pitch)

 - play a wide vibrato

 - play a very slow vibrato with ¼ tone frequency difference

 - play a very rapid non-rhythmical tremolo

 - repeat the tone as rapidly as possible

 - repeat the indicated group of tones as rapidly as possible

Below are listed some special instructions in *Fluorescences* for wind players. (Table 6)

Table 6. Instructions for wind players in Pendercki's avant garde orchestra.

 - play on the reed or mouthpiece only

\+ - strike the keys only

 - *frullato*

Then there are the innovations that have to do with pitch. These effects create the impressive density of sound that is heard in works like *Threnody, Polymorphia* and *Fluorescences.* In addition to the standard micro-tonal adjustments to raise and lower a pitch by a quarter-tone (Table 7), Penderecki employs four different kinds of clusters in Fluorescences: *stationary, rotating, glissando and expanding-contracting*. (Table 8)

Table 7. Pitch abbreviations in the avant garde works of Penderecki.

 - raise the note by ¼ tone

 - raise the note by ¾ tone

Table 8. Pitch clusters used in *Fluorescences.*

Rehearsal 26: *stationary* cluster in the woodwinds and strings
Rehearsal 28: *rotating* cluster in violins
Rehearsal 60: *glissando* cluster
Rehearsal 85: *expanding–contracting* cluster

In addition there are the instructions for the percussion section. Not only is the percussion battery exceptionally large in these works, but the composer creates certain effects that give the section a distinctive sound. (Table 9)

Table 9. Instructions for percussion players in *Fluorescences.*

 - play with the triangle rod

 - play with the drumstick

 - play with the timpani stick (with a soft head, i.e. vibraphone)

 - play with a mallet

 - play with jazz brushes

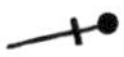 - with one drumstick strike the other drumstick, after having laid it on the striking surface of the instrument

 - strike the striking surface and the edge of the instrument with the same drumstick simultaneously

 - strike the edge of the instrument

As a means of making his intentions absolutely clear in the score of *Fluorescences,* Penderecki includes 29 specific instructions to performers. These appear at the bottom of the score pages and are keyed by the icon (i.e. *, **). A few of these are listed below, followed by the rehearsal number (in parenthesis) of the specific event for which the instructions are given. (Table 10)

Table 10. Specific instructions for the performers of *Fluorescences.*

1. "Vigorously rub the lowest string of the piano with a triangle rod." (1)
2. "Saw a piece of wood (or iron) with a hand saw." (2)
3. "Vigorously rub with a file." (3)
4. "Take whistles with a high, sharp sound [and blow them]."(6)
5. "*Glissando* [in the cellos] – speed at choice – between the indicated highest and lowest note; each player starts from the tone allotted to his instrument." (8)
6. "[French horn clusters]. Each instrumentalist plays the note allotted to his instrument." (9)
7. "At the heel [of the bow] with great pressure so that's to hear a violent creaking [*sul ponticello* clusters]." (12)
8. "Rub the lowest string [of the piano] with one of the cymbals." (12)
9. "Repeat *pizzacato* tone [of the violin] as rapidly as possible." (17)
10. "Strike various keys [of the typewriter]." (19), etc.

It was this attention to detail that made it possible for performers to realize composer's attentions as fully as possible in works like *Fluorescences.*

At its première, *Fluorescences* evoked both wild protest and enthusiastic support from the audience. It is not surprising that Hans Oesch, in his review for the *Nationale Zeitung-Basel* [reprinted in *Melos*], wrote at the conclusion of the first performance:

> All that was left was sawdust. . . . [7]

It was also apparent to Penderecki that his experiments with sound colorism and sound had gone far enough. Further commitment to a "rhetoric of continuous innovation" was only sensible as long as an unknown frontier still remained to be pursued. The experiments of these years (1958-1962) had served their purpose. By the composer's own admission, the direction of the avant garde was a dead-end street:

> I realized that there was more of destruction than of building anew in the innovation that boiled down mainly to formal experiments and speculation; the Promethian tone of those days was a utopia. The escape from the avant garde trap of formalism enabled me to turn back towards tradition.[8]

The clear style of *Stabat Mater* and the eclectic language of the *St Luke Passion* were the outgrowth of this kind of introspective thinking. Penderecki would now pursue his own musical agenda, not that of the avant garde.

In spite of its "experimental" qualities, the Polish writer Tadeusz A. Zielinski suggested in 1964 that "the music historians of our era should mark the dates of its composition in red letters."[9] *Fluorescences* had indeed captured the spirit of the New Music.

---

[7] Hans Oesch, *Nationale Zeitung-Basel* [reprinted in *Melos*], October 22, 1962.

[8] Krzysztof Penderecki, *Labyrinth of Time* (Chapel Hill: Hinshaw Music, Inc., 1998), p. 16.

[9] Tadeusz A. Zieliński, "*Fluorescencje* Krzysztofa Pendereckiego" [Krzysztof Penderecki's *Fluorescences*]. *Ruch Muzyczny* 7:2 (1964), p. 6.

Regina Chłopicka
Cracow

Extra-Musical Inspirations in the Early Works of Krzysztof Penderecki[1]

INTRODUCTION

The notion of inspiration is often resorted to in reflection on art, although its use is far from precise. An insightful analysis of the concept has been conducted by the Polish philosopher Władysław Stróżewski, who postulated the following definition:

> I understand inspiration as a particular stimulation of our cognitive powers and creative dispositions by something contentually definite, which is experienced as external, not coming from ourselves, but which induces or even forces us to a creative response to it (Stróżewski, 1993: 141).

Stróżewski distinguishes elements which jointly define the context of inspiration, indicate various types and modes of inspiration, specify and emphasize the significance of creative process, which entails the active response of the inspired subject:

> True inspiration motivates genuine, innovative action. It moves one to achieve something new, and the more innovative is the artifact generated thanks to it, the greater is its value. Indeed, evoking the subject's creative powers is equally significant as conveying a particular content (Stróżewski, 1993: 141).

In the early works of Krzysztof Penderecki, the composer's artistic tendencies were connected with his desire to create an individual musical language and find new formal solutions for his music. Penderecki sought inspiration in various fields, which made him transfer into music certain extra-musical conceptions and experiences. This had a crucial importance for shaping various elements of the works: their sound material, organization techniques, texture and form, as well as principles of internal integration. An important source of extra-musical inspiration for many works created at the time was the selection of titles which would refer to

---

[1] The previous version of the article was published in *Krzysztof Penderecki: Musica Sacra – Musica Profana. A Study of Vocal-Instrumental Works.* Warsaw: IAM, 2003.

a given general idea, whose musical, internally coherent instantiation was the work.

In other works, there were certain arrangements at the level of musical language which were inspired by numerical sequences drawn from mathematics (they were mainly applied to grouping sounds and rhythmical patterns, sequences of ascending or descending order of varying divergence, Fibonacci's sequence, etc). In still others, the inspiration came from the plastic arts.

The work in which the inspirations coming from various fields are particularly strong is the vocal-instrumental work for mixed chorus, strings and percussion written in 1960 and entitled *Dimensions of Time and Silence*. Indeed, the work has a meaningful title, in which we find the original application of structural principles of the magic square; it is also an attempt to transfer to music the artistic conceptions derived from plastic arts (Paul Klee, Yves Klein).

THE TITLE AS SOURCE OF INSPIRATION IN EARLY INSTRUMENTAL WORKS

In the works written in 1958-62 we can distinguish between two categories of titles given to musical pieces. The first is linked to music and concerns the composition technique employed (*Canon*), the typical features of sound notation (*Fonogrammi*), the definition of the forces and the genre attribution (String Quartet no 1), or the type of expression (*Threnody 'To the Victims of Hiroshima'*).[2]

The second category of titles comprises the works where the title draws attention to a general extra-musical idea, which significantly influences the shape of the piece and frequently forms the basis of its internal coherence.[3] This category is especially important for further development of Penderecki's thinking about composition, as it anticipates his tackling of great themes present in European culture for centuries and creating their contemporary, original interpretations (such as *Passion According to St. Luke, Paradise Lost* or *Polish Requiem*). Among the instrumental works labelled with titles from this category, we have e.g. *Emanations, Anaklasis, Polymorphia,* and *Fluorescences,* and among vocal-instrumental

[2] The title was given to the work only on its completion.

[3] The concept of the idea is used here in accordance with the understanding of the term in literary theory: "Idea (z gr. kształt, gatunek) to centralny element zawartości ideowej utworu, jego myśl przewodnia, główna prawda. . . . Idea sprzęga wewnętrznie materiał dzieła" [The idea (from Greek "shape," "species") is the central element of the conceptual content of the work, its leading thought, principal truth. . . . The idea makes the material of the work internally coherent] (Sławiński, 2000).

works - *Dimensions of Time and Silence,* although the title of this latter piece functions in a peculiar way.

Emanations is a work for two string orchestras written in 1958. The title brings to mind the image of light or heat, radiating or spreading around the object it emanates from (Lat. *emanatio* - flow out, spread out). This general idea of a certain movement in space becomes the inspiration both for the characteristic, strikingly symmetrical layout of orchestral formations and for the spatial modeling of sound material. It is worth noting that the pitch of one of the orchestras is half-tone higher than that of the other, which makes the two formations distinct with regard to tone-color and allows the audience to follow sound patterns more closely.

Anaklasis was written in 1960 for unusual forces: 42 string voices and 6 percussion groups. The word *anaklasis* is Greek: it was used by Aristotle to signify a reflection of light or sound, by Hippocrates to signify a curve or bending, and by Polybius to signify the diversion or straying from the course. In the musical analyses of the work, the title is usually translated as transformation or refraction. The general idea is exemplified in the work by means of a characteristic cluster technique: the clusters are frequently transformed, e.g. in their width, direction of movement or the way in which sound layers overlap.

Polymorphia for 48 string instruments was composed in 1961. The Greek *poli–morphe* meant "having multiple shapes." In biology the word *polymorphic* refers to organisms of the same species occurring in different forms or stages. In linguistics it is the property of word-formation which consists in the lack of one-to-one correspondence between the basic meaning and the form of the word: the word with the same meaning is used in many different forms. This idea of multiple shapes being compatible with the recognizable unity of sound patterns finds its illustration in the operation of models in the work which create particular sonorities, their variants and the whole families of models which, in turn, become the structural basis of the segments of a given texture, out of which the entire work is constructed.[4]

Fluorescences for large symphony orchestra, is a work written in 1962, the year which concludes the early phase of the composer's career. It is another work whose title deals with light. In Latin *fluor* meant "flowing"

[4] Krzysztof Droba discusses the way the form is constructed in the early works of Penderecki, taking *Polymorphia* as an example (Droba, 1976). See also Mirka (1997).

or "current." Fluorescence in physics is the self-induced emission of visible light by certain bodies immediately after the absorption of radiation. The light disappears as soon as the stimulating factor ceases to operate. What we deal with here is then a certain kind of "de-materializing," a certain eeriness, which also connotes richness of shades, flickering and glittering. Thus it seems that the main idea of the work, determining its musical shape and internal structure, should be understood roughly in that way. The characteristic rich sound effects in brass instruments, the highly varied and colorful percussion expanded to six groups, the unconventional means of sound articulation in the strings, new tone-colors and sonorities created by making use of new sources of sound in combination produce perhaps the richest repertoire of colorings among the composer's works.

Dimensions of Time and Silence – the title of the work has a function similar to the titles of works discussed above, although it concerns a different semantic field, drawn from artistic conceptions of painters. It will be discussed in detail below.

DIMENSIONS OF TIME AND SILENCE: INSPIRATION WITH THE MAGIC SQUARE

Dimensions of Time and Silence, a work for 40-voice mixed chorus, percussion and strings, was dedicated to Józef Patkowski, the Head of the Experimental Studio of the Polish Radio in Warsaw. Its first performance, conducted by Andrzej Markowski, took place in Kraków in 1960, and the work was soon performed again in Warsaw during the 4th Warsaw Autumn Contemporary Music Festival. The performance of the second and final version of the work was organized in Vienna in June 1961 during the 35th SIMC Festival, where the piece was conducted by Friedrich Cerha.

Dimensions of Time and Silence constitutes an attempt to apply to music the unique structural principles of the magic square. Its structure became an inspiration both in the way the elements of language were selected and in the way the work's form was organized.

The magic square is a symmetrical pattern which is unusually internally coherent. Its well known instantiation is the text of a 12-syllable Latin pentastich, whose words could be read in many directions:

S	A	T	O	R
A	R	E	P	O
T	E	N	E	T
O	P	E	R	A
R	O	T	A	S

Example 1. The Magic Square.

The square (which was mentioned already by Plinius) was previously interpreted in a range of ways: from the view that it symbolizes the cosmic wedding of fire and water to attempts to derive the word *arepo* from Celtic tradition to the Christian interpretation in which it represents the cross holding the world (from the way the word *tenet* appears in the middle of the square). The magic square, through its symmetrical pattern, could also symbolically represent the idea of order and harmony of the world. Penderecki, who had searched for new principles of arranging musical matter, could indeed be fascinated with this highly coherent structure.[5]

The inspiration of *Dimensions of Time and Silence,* with the structure of the magic square, is noticeable in more ways than one. In the first version of the work, side by side with sequences of vowels and consonants the full Latin text of the magic square appeared in the chorus part. Nevertheless, the fascination with certain regular arrangements of elements did not suppress the composer's sense of distinctiveness of musical dramaturgy, and after the first performance he prepared the second version of the work, disposing of the text of the pentastich (among other changes). The change did not deprive the work of its link with the structure of the magic square, however, where different directions of movement (forward, backward, upward or downward) lead to the unraveling of identical words. The idea has obviously been known in music since the Renaissance as generating means to arrive at polyphonic composition, such as retrograde, inversion or retrograde inversion of musical motives or themes.

5 We also find traces of this fascination in String Quartet no 1; cf. Bilica (1983: 76).

In *Dimensions of Time and Silence* the idea of taking advantage of various directions of movement in order to present certain sound structures comes strong on various levels of the work, from the characteristic construction of the series to the general construction of the form. The twelve-tone series in the work is the basis of the organization of pitch material. It assumes a typical arrangement of intervals, which like in the magic square, yields the same reading (sequence of intervals) both in the straight and the inverted sequence. Characteristic relations occur also when the series undergoes division into four three-tone cells. If the first three-tone cell is taken to be the original sequence, the second is its inversion, transposed down a third, the third, in turn, is its retrograde transposed by a tritone, and the fourth is the retrograde inversion.

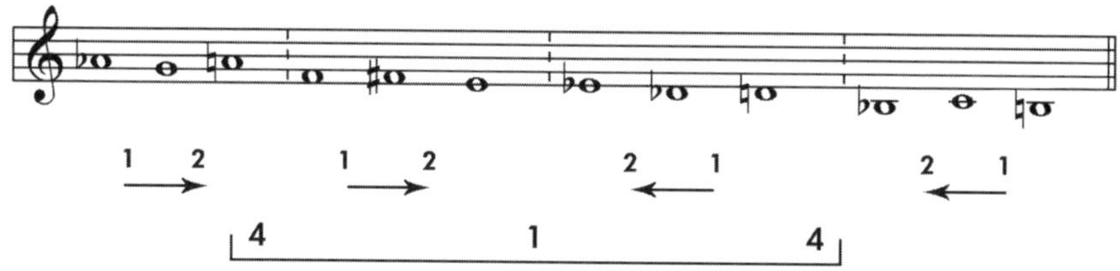

Example 2. K. Penderecki, *Dimensions of Time and Silence,* the twelve-tone series.

The series thus constructed could overlap with other regular sequences of elements based on the same principle. For instance, in No. 46 of the score, the consecutive tones of the series coincide with a series of vowels in different parts, the vowels following their own strict sequence. Also the sequence of consonants which occur in choral parts at an uncertain pitch are subject to imitation, either in the their original form or in retrograde, with the number of consonants being simultaneously reduced in consecutive groups - 9, 7, 6, 6, 3 (Ex. 3). There are many similar examples of the use of orderings at the level of organization of material which are inspired with the regularities present in the magic square.

The composer, however, does not limit himself to applying the magic square idea at this level. It has its musical equivalent at two levels of formal internal organization of the work as well. What is the basis of the formal construction of the work is the contrasting of its first phase, which contains the simple succession of four formal sections, A, B, C, D, with the second phase, in which they reappear in retrograde, with the exception of the last section, which - modified and shortened - appears also at the end of the phase. At the same time, each formal section (A, B, C, D) in the second phase occurs in retrograde.

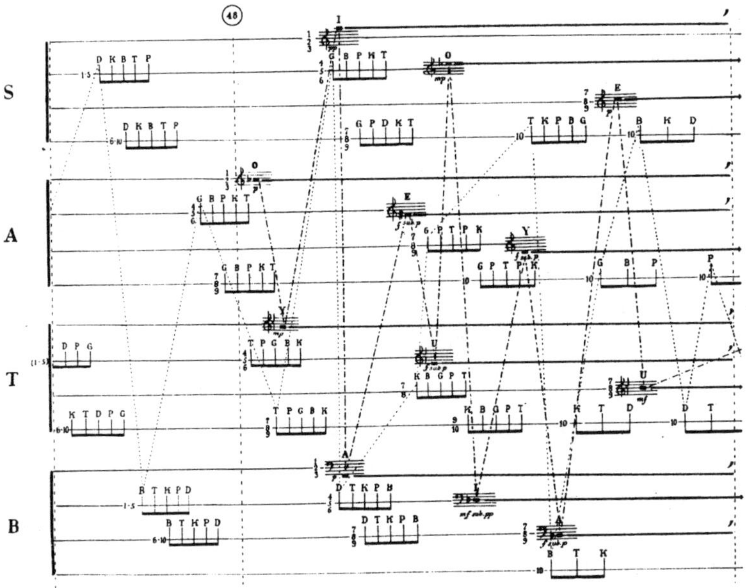

Example 3. K. Penderecki, *Dimensions of Time and Silence,* p. 12.

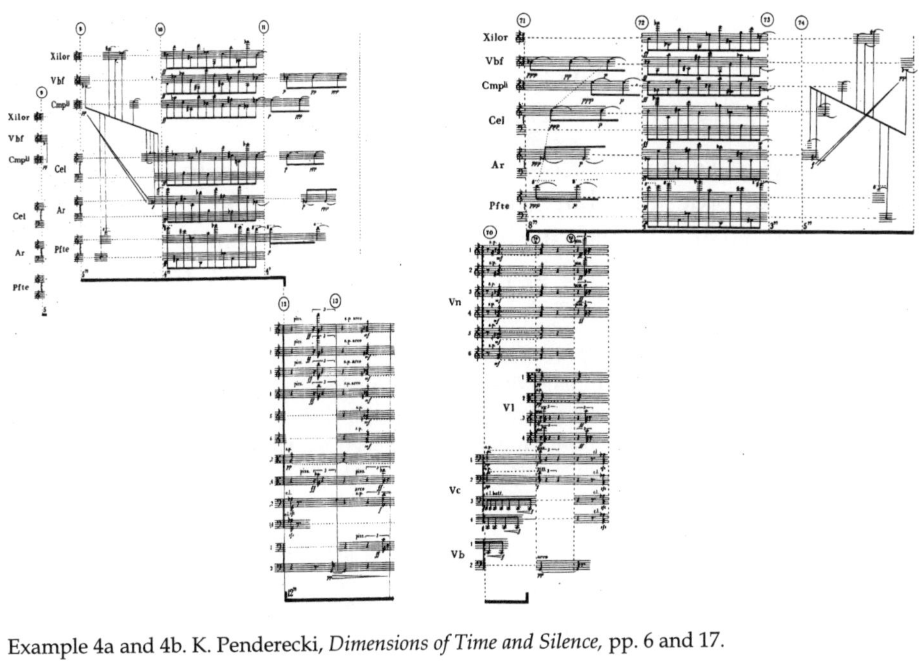

Example 4a and 4b. K. Penderecki, *Dimensions of Time and Silence,* pp. 6 and 17.

After this formation has been presented (this takes about two thirds of the work), the third phase arrives, which has been dubbed "synthetic" by Schwinger (1979: 195-7). The description might be misleading since a number of new elements are brought in there. The presence of this phase seems to be quite typical of Penderecki: the constructive, combinatorial thinking never quite dominates his artistic thinking. The third phase, fairly free in construction, is required for the dramaturgy of the work to reach completion. First the culmination arrives, followed by the relieving of tension and gradual dying down of sound until the closing *ppp* section.

Dimensions of Time and Silence

I	phase	-	A	B	C	-	D
II	phase	-	r C	r B	r A	-	D1
III	phase	- free sequence leading to culmination and ending					

It is worth noticing that the A and A-flat notes, although unconnected with the magic square model, play an important structural role in the work. These short sections keep returning in unison and, iterated in a macro-rhythm, they constitute characteristic vantage points in the formal course of the work. This composition technique was employed by Penderecki not only in *Dimensions of Time and Silence*, but in many other works of the time. The clear harmonies at a definite pitch returning at particular junctures of the work emphasize the general harmonic plan of the sonoristic course, and thus constitute a formal integrating factor.

DIMENSIONS OF TIME AND SILENCE: INSPIRATION WITH ARTISTIC CONCEPTIONS OF PAINTERS

Dimensions of Time and Silence is a work inspired not only by the magic square type of orderings, but also by painting. It is one of the very few works of Penderecki to which the author's commentary has been published, indicating the source of its inspiration. The composer thus writes of *Dimensions of Time and Silence*:

> This composition is an attempt to transplant certain technical assumptions of Paul Klee and Ives Klein to the language of sound. The analogies are made distinct in the use of sections of different color and structure, combined so as to "penetrate" one another (Klee), and in the employment of static sections which operate with the vibrating "sound space" or only with its resonance (Klein).[6]

[6] The commentary of K. Penderecki on *Dimensions of Time and Silence*(1960). It is worth noting that in the 1950's and 1960's artistic ideas and works of Paul Klee inspired several dozen musical works, including G. Klebe, *La machine gazouillante, metamorphose sur la peinture du même nom de P. Klee*; S. Veress, *Hommage à Klee*; H. Heis, *Configurations pour orchestre d'après des titres de P.Klee*; G. Schuller, *Seven Studies on Themes of P. Klee*. This is discussed in detail by W. Salmen (1985/6).

In the 1950's and 60's, the composers who searched for inspiration among artistic conceptions derived from plastic arts were by no means isolated individuals. The much earlier artistic ideas and paintings of Paul Klee exerted a particularly strong resonance in music. What could partly be the reason was the fact that Klee was an educated musician himself and musical inspirations played a significant role in his works. Indeed the titles of many of his paintings referred to forms, techniques, sound patterns or musical instruments.[7]

The majority of musical works inspired by the paintings of Paul Klee, however, were composed not in his lifetime, but after 1950. It was the period in music dominated by avant-garde trends, which rejected the traditional hierarchy of musical elements and methods of shaping form, and new esthetic principles, new material and new forms were searched for. Artistic conceptions of Paul Klee, who approached elements of painting (line, value, color) in a new way and found an original approach to the form of the painting, inspired many composers. Several dozen works were written, whose authors openly declared the links of their music to Klee's painting, although the inspirations were of highly different types. In one of the two works of Herman Heis, for instance, which had a link to Klee, the source of the inspiration - as the composer put it himself - were only the titles of the paintings, without resort to their artistic interpretation.[8] Giselher Klebe, on the other hand, described his work *Die Zwitschermaschine* as a "metamorphosis" of Klee's painting of the same title, specifying in detail the principles of his musical interpretation of the work.[9]

---

[7] Musical inspirations in the drawings and painting of Klee are connected e.g. with performances of musicians, opera characters, instruments or performance situations, e.g. in *Concert of the Branch, Somnabulant Dance, Timbalist, Stage Rehearsal;* with visualisations of characteristic musical textures, such as e.g. polyphony *Fugue in Red;* with transferring into painting of the composition technique of developing and transforming themes; with common categories of expression: *Ecstatic Priestess, Constructive-Impressive;* as well as with the equivalent in painting of sounds of particular tone-color, harmony etc.

[8] *Configurations pour orchestre d'après des titres de Paul Klee* – the work commissioned by Radio Hesse. The composer, in his letter of 1957, indicates that it was only the titles that were the inspiration. See W. Salmen (1985/6).

[9] The transformation of the static, formal shape of the painting into a temporal sequence (four movements of the work refer to four heads of birds from the painting), of profound color effects in the painting into the sound volume of great orchestra, or of associations derived from the title into sound motives which are present throughout the work in numerous variants (such as rotational sound figures, ostinato oscillating between two notes, or ascending and descending chromatic melodic progressions); see Clemens Kuhn (1985/6).

Another type of inspiration could be found in the output of Sandor Veress, Gunther Schuller, or Peter Maxwell Davies, where selected pictures of Klee inspired cycles of works.[10] Consecutive movements which preserve the titles of paintings form the framework of the cycle patterns. In such works, inspirations with paintings may concern musical elements or structures in various layers of consecutive parts; what comes into the foreground, however, is the creation of formal unity by differentiating the types of expression of particular movements stemming from the distinct character of the paintings being referred to.

Robert Nessler's *Quatre etude pour flute et violoncelle* is an example of still another type of influence, the starting point for which was Klee's painting *Les poissons magiques*.[11] The titles of consecutive parts of the work combine to create an original story of various events which happen to fish (the meditating fish which is made to flee, the fish caught and devoured by a larger one, the sad fish, and finally, the fish which discovers its fate). The work becomes a kind of musical parable which contains a disguised reflection on the fate of man in the world. On the whole, the works of Klee became inspiring for many musical pieces, although the composers referred to various elements or features of his painting.

Krzysztof Penderecki, when writing on Klee, did not focus on particular paintings, but rather on his general artistic conceptions, mainly on the postulated hierarchy of formal elements in painting. Indeed, Paul Klee, discussing typical dimensions of artistic work, distinguished three principal formal elements in painting: the line, the value (chiaroscuro), and the color, and then established their hierarchy:

> The **line** is the most limited element of all: it relates only to measurement. . . . **Tone value** or chiaroscuro, as it is also called – the numerous gradations between black and white – is somewhat different. In the latter case we are dealing with weight. . . . I would like to regard **colors** as qualities. . . . We thus have formal means: measurement, weight and quality, which . . . have certain mutual relations. . . . Color is primarily quality, secondly weight . . . and thirdly dimension. . . .

---

[10] S. Veress, *Hommage à Klee - fantasie per due pianoforti e orchestra d'archi* (*Signes en jaune, Vent de feu, Sonorité ancienne, Haut et bas, Collection de pierres, Vert dans le vert, Diabblotin bleu*) 1951; G. Schuller, *Seven Studies on Theme of Paul Klee* (*Harmonies antiques, Trio abstrait, Diablotin bleu, Machine gazouillante, Ville arabe, Un moment angoissant, Pastorale*) 1959; P.M. Davies, *Five Klee Pictures* (*A Crusader, Oriental Garden, The Twittering Machine, Stained-Glass Saint, Ad Parnassum*) 1961, rescored 1976; see. O. Knussen (1978); S. Bruhn (2000).

[11] I. *Le poisson medite mais quelque chose toujour le fait fuir;* II. *Le petit poisson est chasse et attrape par un plus grand (quasi scherzino avec coda);* III. *Le poisson se montre elegiaque (lamento);* IV. *Le poisson se dechaine et comprend, epuise, la vanité de son agitation (rondo grotesque avec coda).*

> Tone value is first and foremost weight, but it is also dimensional in its extension and limitation. The line is purely dimensional (Klee, 1977c: 294-295).

The transfer into music of the thinking in terms of tone-color quality, density, and weight, as well as the point, the line and the plane, combined with establishing their different hierarchy, seem to have opened new possibilities of shaping sound material for Penderecki. He built musical narration by operating with segments of a specific tone quality (the equivalent of color), which had their own density (the equivalent of chiaroscuro) and temporal dimension (the equivalent of measurement). What was of use for constructing colorful segments and sonoristic treatment of sound material were numerous conventional and unconventional means (unique selection of sound sources, a number of new types of articulation and sound effects, varying types of texture, etc.). Thus the inspiration with Klee's conceptions in the early phase of Penderecki's career became the starting point for the composer to seek his own individual musical language and principles of construction.

The ideas derived from painting became an inspiration for the title of the piece, too: *Dimensions of Time and Silence.* The first part of the title, "dimensions of time" brings to mind both the notion of line as measurement as described by Klee (the line and the plane being created from the point through motion in time) and that of the value and color, with their own measures of time.

The second part of the work's title is simpler and seemingly unrelated to plastic arts: the expression "dimensions of silence" could simply refer to those moments in the course of the work where there is no sound (the pauses), so that their varying duration could be emphasized. Penderecki, however, indicates in his commentary a possibility of a different understanding of this part of the title. Writing of the static and vibrating "sound spaces," he also mentioned their resonance, pointing out his inspiration with the artistic ideas of Klein. The phrase "vibrating sound spaces" is probably a reference to static, monochromatic paintings of Klein, who

> . . . searched for color in itself, a living, tangible color matter. He treated it as thoroughly human. . . . He influenced the human emotional activity with it. [He believed, however, that] all that is material can vanish at any moment. It is only the things imagined and the things felt that will remain (Kowalska, 1989: 113).

The separation of color from the material sphere was facilitated by an artistic experiment described by the same scholar:

> He painted the interior of the gallery white and emptied it completely. The sky-blue color, which, in accordance with the eternal symbolism of colors, signifies the spiritual element, the distance, the infinite, was left by him outside, on the curtain of the entrance door, on the window panes painted from the side of the street, and on the obelisk set up in front of the gallery. The viewers, entering the monochromatically white space of the interior, brought the blue inside in their eyes. So, although absent, it triumphed as "blue sensitivity," the invisible, the immaterial (Kowalska, 1989: 114).

"Dimensions of silence" – the second part of Penderecki's title – seems to be a reference to an experience of a similar kind, transferred to musical territory. For in the course of the work there are numerous pauses, lasting silences, which are clearly marked with this immaterial resonance of the preceding tone-colors. Thus the rhythm of colors which actually appear rings its own unique echo in those colorful dimensions of silence.

Dimensions of Time and Silence is a work where traces of many extra-musical influences may be found, from the structure and construction principles of the magic square to references to ideas borrowed from painting and Klee's new hierarchy of elements to artistic conceptions of Klein. They are an example of inspirations which stimulated the creative activity of the composer, allowing him to discover new areas of experience and new artistic ideas. They affected the development of his musical language and style, as well as his way of thinking about the form. As stressed by Penderecki himself, the way the form of the work is constructed in this period from segments of varying texture and tone-color is largely inspired by the artistic ideas of Paul Klee, whose paintings (in the central phase of his life and work – the time of squares) are formed mainly by the characteristic arrangements of colorful segments. The play of colors, strengthened by chiaroscuro effects, creates certain equilibrium of tension in the painting. In his musical works, Penderecki operates with consecutive or overlapping segments of varying texture and color in a similar way.

Nevertheless, the dramaturgy is different in Penderecki's compositions. This is the result not only of the difference in the medium, but also of the personality difference between the artists. Paul Klee (often called a lyrical abstractionist), even though he evoked certain tensions in the painting, aimed at reaching a state of equilibrium, at creating a certain distance.

> Every energy requires complementation so that a state of internal peace may be achieved, and a certain distance over the power struggle may be achieved (Klee, 1977b: 290).

Penderecki, on the other hand, seems to be directly involved in the play of opposing forces taking place in his works; he takes an active part in the events. His dramaturgy is typically contrastive: static sequences are overwhelmed by dynamic sequences which develop towards the culmination and resolution. These contrasts and tensions in *Dimensions of Time and Silence* are indeed considerably restrained, although the principle of the dramaturgy of musical events, taking place within the closed form, remains the same.

In spite of those differences, both artists meet again at the level of the general idea of the form of their works and take a similar position on art, its function and sense in the contemporary world:

Klee:

> We examine the form in order to learn how to express ourselves and how to deepen the knowledge of human soul. Apparently, philosophy seems to have the inclination towards art: at first I was astonished at what they were able to find. I thought only of the form and the rest took care of itself. The more elaborate awareness of the rest helped me very much, however. . . . When I managed to move successfully through formal matters, I was even ready to become an illustrator of ideas again. And then the abstract art was no longer there for me. What remained was only abstracting from that which is temporary. The subject was the world but not the visible world.[12]

Penderecki:

> I have never been interested in the sound for the sound's sake, which saved me from the illness of avant-gardism, the barren emptiness and boredom of formal solutions. The need for synthesis characterizes the whole modern epoch. This is the answer to the poignant feeling of our world's decline. The synthesis cannot consist in the mechanical combination of elements, but it must stem from the uniting experience.[13]

Klee:

> To liberate the elements, to unite them in complex groups, to dismember them and built new wholes from various sides at the same time, to attain artistic polyphony . . . these are all great formal problems . . . but this is not yet art of the grandest dimension. The grandest dimension contains the ultimate mystery, clouded in ambiguity: here the light of intellect helplessly turns off. . . . Everything that passes is just a metaphor. What we see is a proposal, a possibility, a hypothesis. . . . The foundation is the actual truth, initially imperceptible. . . . The form must fall in with the outlook on the world.[14]

[12] Klee (1977a: 286).

[13] Penderecki (1997: 66).

[14] Klee (1977b: 292) and (1977 a: 285).

Penderecki:

> I would like my music to be a confession. I have looked for an authentic, modern expression for eternal themes.[15]

Klee:

> Art is always a metaphor of outer space. . . . From abstract formal elements . . . the universe of form comes into being, which exhibits such a great affinity to Creation that it is enough to breathe and the expression of religious experience . . . becomes reality.[16]

Penderecki:

> My art . . . aims at rebuilding the metaphysical space of the human being, shattered by the cataclysms of the 20th century. The restoring of the sacred dimension of reality is the only method of saving man. Art should be a source of difficult hope.[17]

REFERENCES

Bilica, Krzysztof. 1976. "Pozaekspresyjne porządki w *Kwartecie smyczkowym* (nr 1)" [Non-expressive systems in String Quartet No.1]. In *Współczesność i tradycja w muzyce Krzysztofa Pendereckiego,* Kraków: Akademia Muzyczna.

Bruhn, Siglind. 2000. *Musical Composers Responding to Poetry and Painting.* Hillsdale, New York: Pendragon.

Droba, Krzysztof. 1976. "Hierarchia czynników formalnych w twórczości Krzysztofa Pendereckiego" [The hierarchy of formal factors in the compositions of Krzysztof Penderecki]. In *Muzyka* 2.

Klee, Paul. 1977a. "Z Dzienników VII" [From the diaries]. In *Artyści o sztuce,* E. Grabska, H. Morawska (eds.), Warszawa: PWN.

Klee, Paul. 1977b. "Wyznania twórcy" [Confessions of an artist]. In *Artyści o sztuce,* E. Grabska, H. Morawska (eds.), Warszawa: PWN.

Klee, Paul. 1977c. "O sztuce nowoczesnej" [On modern art]. In *Artyści o sztuce,* E. Grabska, H. Morawska (eds.), Warszawa: PWN.

Knussen, Oliver. 1978. "P.M. Davies's *Five Klee Pictures." Tempo* no. 124.

Kowalska, Bożena. 1989. *Od impresjonizmu do konceptualizmu* [From impressionism to conceptualism]. Warszawa: Arkady.

Kuhn, Clemens. 1985/6. "G. Klebe." In *Klee et la musique,* Musee National d'Art Moderne, Centre G. Pompidou.

Mirka, Danuta. 1997. *The Sonoristic Structuralism of Krzysztof Penderecki,* Katowice: Akademia Muzyczna.

Penderecki, Krzysztof. 1960. *Wymiary czasu i ciszy* [Dimensions of Time and Silence], the composer's commentary on the work. In *The Programme of 4th Festival 'Warsaw Autumn.'* Warszawa, p. 32.

---

15 Penderecki (1988: 3).

16 Klee (1977b: 292).

17 Penderecki (1988: 3).

Penderecki, Krzysztof. 1988. "Kulturotwórcza moc chrześcijaństwa" [Culture-generating power of Christianity]. *Tygodnik Powszechny* no 1.

Penderecki, Krzysztof. 1997. "Passio artis et vitae" [conversation of A. and Z. Baran with K. Penderecki]. In *Labirynt czasu. Pięć wykładów na koniec wieku,* Warszawa: Presspublica.

Salmen, Walter. 1985/6. "Oeuvres orchestrales et musique de chambre inspirees par des tableaux de Paul Klee." In *Klee et la musique,* Musee National d'Art Moderne, Centre Pompidou.

Schwinger, Wolfram. 1979. *Penderecki. Begebnungen, Lebensdaten, Werkkommentare,* Stuttgart: Deutsche Verlag-Anstalt. (English edition: 1989. *Krzysztof Penderecki. His Life and Work. Encounters, Biography and Musical Commentary,* London: Schott, p. 195–197).

Sławiński, Janusz. 2000. Entry "Idea." In *Słownik terminów literackich,* Wrocław: Ossolineum.

Stróżewski, Władysław. 1993. "O pojęciu inspiracji" [On the notion of inspiration]. In *Inspiracje w muzyce XX wieku,* Warszawa: ZKP.

Translated by Władysław Chłopicki

Robert S. Hatten
Bloomington

Structure and Spiritual Expression in Penderecki's *Psalms of David*

Penderecki's *Psalms of David* was written for mixed choir (divisi), percussion (including 2 pianos, celesta, and harp) and 4 string basses. It is in four movements, each based on the opening verse or verses from one of the Psalms. The work offers an engaging hybrid of historical and recent styles available in 1958, the year of its composition. One finds echoes primarily of Stravinsky (thematically, *Symphony of Psalms* and *Canticum sacrum*, but also texturally, the use of percussion in *Histoire du soldat* and *Les noces*) and Schoenberg (thematic serialism, *Sprechstimme*), with a touch of Webern (pointillist textures, octave-displaced chromatic gestures).

Penderecki's *Strophes*, for soprano, reciter, and a chamber group of ten instruments, was written the following year. This more avant-garde work draws heavily from the post-Webern sound world of Boulez, with a correspondingly greater sensitivity to individual timbral effects and a rhythmic complexity in the solo voice that would not be possible in a choral setting. Although some of the "strophes" are also drawn from the Old Testament, the work has a more secular flavor, with philosophical and gnomic perspectives on morality, suffering, evil, and death.

Whereas *Psalms of David* dramatizes its prayers to God as desperate or insistent pleas for justice and protection from evil, *Strophes* presents a more contemplative and mystical reflection on the human condition. Its texts and languages (Greek, Hebrew, Persian) are intentionally remote and incomprehensible for most listeners, and the focus is shifted to the musical interaction of instrumental and vocal timbres. Of these two striking vocal works from the beginning of Penderecki's career, the *Psalms of David* is thus more amenable to expressive interpretation - specifically, the ways in which Penderecki's choice of modernist techniques, and their integration, offer a distinctive interpretation of the interrelated themes in four Psalms.

For the origin version, the Psalm verses are in Polish, from a 16th-century translation by Mikołaj Gomółka, found in a psaltery, "Melodie na Psałterz Polski."[1] The English translation of the Polish yields a result that is markedly different from the English of the King James Version; thus, I will provide both transliteration and translation of the Polish, followed by the King James Version, for comparison.[2]

I. Psalm 28, verse 1 (first half)

King heavenly health soul my Królu niebieski zdrowie duszy mojej	O Heavenly King, health of my soul,
To You I cry Do Ciebie wołam	To You I cry.
And You face your don't hide from me A Ty twarzy Swojej nie kryj przede mną	And You, do not hide Your face from me.

King James Version: "Unto thee will I cry, O Lord my rock; be not silent to me:"

The first of the four Psalm movements presents the greatest synthesis of compositional influences; it is also the most forward-looking in its timbral and textural explorations. Intercutting and stratification among timbral groups recall Stravinsky's formal processes; the atonal cells and use of *Sprechstimme* recall Schoenberg's pioneering use of these techniques, and the timbral pointillism and prominent minor-ninth melodic gestures recall Webern's style. The minor ninth is clearly referential in this movement, embodying the gestural "cry" of the Psalm in three ways: pointillistically in the instrumental voices (Piano I, mm. 6-12), vertically as a static plaint in the choral voices (mm. 6-8 and 11-15), and melodically as an expressionistic "sigh figure" in the sopranos (mm. 65-70). The Psalm verse focuses on this cry to God for help: "Do Ciebie wołam."

The movement only gradually unfolds a complete 12-tone sequence. In mm. 44ff., the twelve pitches from F form nearly a complete chromatic ascent, and in mm. 51ff. there is a complete chromatic descent from Eb. But the movement is far from consistently serial; rather, the focus appears to be on three- and four-note chromatic cells and segments (012, 0123). These cells are used to form significant choral sonorities. Measures 11-14 presents 0123 as two minor ninths; mm. 24-27 features interlocking 012s forming a 012567 hexachord (but stacked as two 016 Viennese trichords);

[1] As the composer intended, there are both Polish and Latin versions of this work.

[2] I am grateful to Danuta Mirka for information about the Polish translation, and for the transliteration and translation into English.

and m. 54 offers divided choirs alternating between two five-note subsets of that hexachord, 01267 and 01256). The cells reflect Penderecki's penchant throughout his career for chromatic segments – here used atonally, later adapted to a late-Romantic expressive context.

A timbral map of the movement would display alternations (intercutting) and overlaps (stratification) of four contrasting types. Among the percussion, the shimmering of suspended cymbals, gong, and tam-tam, with low second piano trill, forms the first timbral group. Pointillist accents in the first piano comprise a second group, joined by tympani and tom-toms. The chorus offers two further contrasting timbral types: (1) sung sonorities prolonged by fortissimo repeated notes (mm. 6-8, 11-15, and 24-27); and (2) more recitative-like or Sprechstimme settings in soft, more articulated fragments of repeated notes (mm. 18-23). From mm. 28-45 the choir is divided, with one group alternating sustained and staccato treatment of fragmented syllables, and the other chanting in whispered fragments (*sussurando*). This timbral and textural developmental strategy foreshadows Penderecki's sonoristic experiments in the next few years, culminating in works such as *Threnody* (1960). Here, the subtle changes in timbre are a logical working out of the contrasts established in the first part of the movement.

After the *a cappella* development of choral timbres and textures, the piano and timpani mark a transition back to a highly varied return. The low C# in the piano recalls its framing role in mm. 6 and 11-12, but the timpani moves the "shimmering" timbral component down to the lower register with its series of glissandi. The pointillist instrumental group is now comprised of xylorimba, harp, and contrabass, with timpani punctuation. When the choirs return at mm. 54-55, they are again divided, but integrated timbrally (pianissimo repeated chords) and sonoristically (nearly equivalent set types: the 01267 and 01256 mentioned above). Nevertheless, the two groups are stratified texturally, by a near-hocket alternation of text, and rhythmically, since the repeated eighths in choir I undergo augmentation in choir II. At m. 65, the sopranos' minor ninth cry is leitmotivic above the harrowing, chant-like repetitions in the remaining voices. The two choirs are then unified with augmented rhythmic repetitions, excepting the altos, who shift to Sprechstimme for a closing counterpoint of timbres (sung, declamatory, and spoken softly). Sparse, pointillist accompaniment in the pitched instruments gives way, at the very end, to a recall of two of the timbral groups from the beginning: the shimmering cymbals and tam-tam, and the dry rhythmic tom-toms, as this movement fades away into silence. The cry, though insistent, apparently goes unanswered.

II. Psalm 30, verse 1

I will you praise Lord Będę Cię wielbił Panie	I will praise you, O Lord
As long as I in the world stay Póki mię na świecie stanie	As long as I am (alive) in this world
Because me in oppression saved Boś mię w przygodzie ratował	Because you saved me from oppression
And derision people's protected i śmiechów ludzkich uchował	And protected me from people's derision.

King James Version: "I will extol thee, O Lord; for thou hast lifted me up, and hast not made my foes to rejoice over me"

The second movement, for *a cappella* choir, is the shortest and most straightforward to analyze. It is serial, but uses only four row forms: the prime and inversion, in their original forms and transposed a perfect fifth, recalling Schoenberg's play with fifth relationships between row forms as vestiges of their structural role in tonality. The row itself is conspicuously atonal. Its four trichords are 012, 014, 013, and 016 - a virtual inventory of 3-note atonal sets - and its two hexachords are each nearly chromatic: 012347 and its complementary Z-related set, 012356. But the melodic disposition of the row features intervals more suited to the chant-based melodic lines of late Medieval and early Renaissance polyphony, and the synthesis of old and new is analogous to Stravinsky's appropriation of serialism in *Canticum sacrum*. Taking intervals by pairs yields a set of two M2s followed by a pair of minor thirds (sequenced by M2), then another M2. This emphasis on melodic steps (there are also three m2s) not only gives the theme its chant-like character, but is used to create a gradual melismatic ascent on the word "praise." The initial effect is one of (Romantic) yearning, but it is melodically reversed by a precipitous drop in the final three notes, melismatically setting the word "Lord" by means an arpeggiated Viennese trichord (set type 016).

The monophonic alto presentation of P0 is completed before being answered in the bass with I0, and the subsequent soprano and tenor entries occur simultaneously on P7 and I7 respectively, creating a literal mirror inversion for one bar, until the rhythms change. The text is set both syllabically and melismatically, but pitch repetition occurs only at the beginning and end of row statements, thereby signalling the opening and close of each phrase. All four voices finally join together in m. 11, where the repeated-note cadential marker is expanded, and a tight imitation of repeated notes in each voice creates a medial "cadence" on a "D major chord with added #4," a relatively consonant moment in the atonal environment.

Up to this point, row forms have been used exclusively melodically, one per choral line. The second half of the short movement begins to trade row material between tenor and bass, and alto and soprano share the last seven notes of P0. All four parts join together only at the final cadential sonority, which verticalizes the last three pitches of P0 with the last pitch of I7 in the basses. That sonority, 0127, integrates the first and last trichords of the row - 012 and 016 are prominent subsets - and echoes the D in the bass at the first "cadence" in m. 11-12.

The text of this soft, slow movement is given stylistic expression by means of an antique polyphonic allusion, perhaps suggesting, as in Beethoven's Renaissance-flavored hymn of thanksgiving in the String Quartet in A minor, Op. 132, a reservoir of primal faith. But the slow tempo and devout style are nonetheless charged with a Romantic fervor. Though framed by stasis (repeated notes), the melodic lines are expressively contoured along Romantic lines, and Romantic yearning is easily interpretable as spiritual longing. The plaintive faith expressed in this verse setting will be rhetorically reversed in the next movement, which expresses an angry questioning in the face of the Lord's presumed rejection ("why do You push me away from your sight?").

III. Psalm 43, drawn from verses 1-2

Innocence Lord my Niewinność Panie moją	O Lord, take my innocence
Receive in protection Your protection Przyjmij w obronę Swoją obronę	under your protection
Lord in whom defense my is laid down Panie w którym obrona moja jest położona	O Lord, in whom my defense resides

Why	me	careful	push	away from	visage	your
Czemu	mię	troskliwego	pchasz	od	oblicza	Swego

Why do you push me (careful, i.e., when I have taken pains to be righteous) away from your sight?

King James Version: (1) "Judge me, O God, and plead my cause against an ungodly nation: O deliver me from the deceitful and unjust man. (2) or thou are the God of my strength; why doth thou cast me off? Why go I mourning because of the oppression of the enemy?"

Penderecki creates his greatest musical contrast between these two movements, injecting a driving scherzo with rhythmic counterpoint (6/8 vs. 3/4 with triplets) in the percussion. An ostinato in the piano features paired M2s a half-step apart, punctuated dissonantly by pizzicato double basses. When the choral basses enter with a repeated-note motive, the allusion to Stravinsky's "Laudate Dominum" from the third movement of the *Symphony of Psalms* (mm. 114-49) is complete. But the expressive sense is different here. Penderecki is creating a similar sense of power, but instead of being directed in praise of God, the power suggests a threat from the outside, from the "oppressor" that the believer fears will overcome him. It expresses a heated insistence that the prayer be answered. The mechanistic ostinati in the percussion and basses, and the vocal lines reduced to repeated drones, together portray the character of that threat (of authoritarian regimentation?) and the urgency of response. At mm. 24 and 28ff. the pitched percussion (xylophone, xylorimba, 2 pianos, harp) and string basses underline and reinforce the repeated chords in the choral parts, producing sonorities featuring quartal, quintal, and added-note formations. The entire movement sustains a frantic intensity, and the closing gesture in the choir is a unison glissando down a minor ninth from Bb to A – a negative cadence of despair or dejection.

Is the anger directed against God, or is it anger against the reality of oppression (in whatever form, external or internal)? The Psalms are filled with the working through of doubt, frustration, and fear, but the constant is prayer – insistent, turbulent, and yet constant in its directed plea to a Divine Presence. By choosing to set these texts with such extremes of dissonance (variously implying suffering, anger, or despair), Penderecki is not choosing an existentialist posture but conveying a realistic struggle from within the context of an active faith.

These are heightened prayers that embody the depths of human suffering. In that they are collectively expressed by choral as opposed to solo setting, they inevitably suggest an association with contemporaneous and turbulent political events within Poland – but the precise "extramusical" dimension of these associations is not retrievable from the score alone. Instead, my hermeneutic interpretation is geared toward reconstructing types of expressed feeling and, to a speculative degree, the presumed agency of musically embodied expressions.

IV. Psalm 143, drawn from verses 1 and 11

Hear eternal God prayers my Wysłuchaj wieczny Boże prośby moje	Hear, O Eternal God, my prayers
And incline toward me holy ears your A nakłoń ku mnie święte uszy Swoje	And incline your holy ears toward me
According to your truth, according to your pity be so kind as to me Według swej prawdy, według swej litości racz mię	
	According to your truth and mercy, be so kind as to
Save in my oppression Ratować w mej dolegliwości	Save me in my oppression.
Wysłuchaj wieczny, Wysłuchaj Boże prośby moje A nakłoń ku mnie święte uszy Swoje	Hear, O Eternal God, my prayers And incline your holy ears toward me

King James Version: (1) "Hear my prayer, O Lord, give ear to my supplications: in thy faithfulness answer me, and in thy righteousness." And (11) "Quicken me, O Lord, for thy name's sake: for thy righteousness' sake bring my soul out of trouble" [=save me in my oppression]

The fourth and final movement returns to a 12-tone, if not rigorously serial compositional technique. It opens with a Webernesque texture that progressively adds instruments on sequential pitches or pairs of pitches from the row, building up to a sustained and climactic 12-tone chord. The altos then state the complete row (m. 7), *recitando ad libitum,* in a chant-like reminiscence of the second movement. This row is atonal by virtue of its completely chromatic construction: four chromatic trichords (012) creating two chromatic hexachords (012345). The row is generated around C by an approximate chromatic wedge, perhaps alluding to

Berg's symmetrical wedge derivation of an all-interval row. But Penderecki's row is asymmetrical, in that the descending chromatic line is given more pitches than the ascending one, and the effect is telling – the near-chromatic descent alludes to the tragic lament figure, with a brief ascent providing relief at the end.

The verse is an anguished plea for answer to prayer, and the chromatic supplication suggests a voice calling out from the depths: "Hear my prayer, O Lord." Once again, repeated notes in the vocal lines are used to mark beginnings and endings of phrases, and the movement climaxes with an enormous crescendo on a series of repeated quarter-note E's in the sopranos and basses, surrounding repeated notes and dyads in the faster inner voices. Instead of a cadence, Penderecki again builds to a twelve-tone chord (only 11 pitches are actually sounding, but the 12th was part of an oscillation in the alto I), as individual pitched percussion instruments enter one by one. It is a dissonant climax, colored by the irrational overtones of tam-tam and gong in the last measure (compare the dramatic effect of this device with the expressionistic cry on a 12-note chord in the third act orchestral interlude of Berg's *Wozzeck*). Penderecki's dissonant ending might be interpreted as an insistent cry from the throes of suffering, insistent in its repeated-note, obsessive march to an unremittingly tragic and climactic close. Whatever God's answer, it is not to be found in this setting of prayerful pleas, and yet the possibility of an answer is what inspires the overwhelmingly powerful outcry in the face of suffering and despair.

Penderecki's "symphony of psalms" goes beyond Stravinsky's in its skillful timbral treatment of the formal principles of stratification and intercutting in the first movement. The inner movements suggest the traditional slow and scherzo movements, but the Classical analogy breaks down in that the "scherzo" is here the weightiest and most insistent of all the movements. The pointillistic finale emerges from the aftermath of the scherzo, and only gradually converges on a dissonant point of focus at the end. In that climax, the combined choirs implacably insist that their prayer be answered – even in a context that is far from resolved.

The four movements of *Psalms of David* are perhaps best understood as a modernist reinterpretation of faith, where prayers are cries that echo an underlying, tragic condition, and where an Old Testament God may seem as remote from human suffering as He is present as the focus of determined prayer. Whether the work references a world threatened inwardly by spiritual nihilism or outwardly by physical annihilation, we can clearly interpret Penderecki's work as an unflinching portrayal of human suffering crying out to God. In turn, God's responses would be explored in Penderecki's later sacred works.

K. Penedercki, *Psalms of David,* PWM, p. 6.

Niall O'Loughlin
Loughborough

Threnody and Performance

> I had to invent a special kind of notation which allowed me to write a piece for 52 instruments like *Threnody* on one small piece of paper.[1]

INTRODUCTION

This simple expedient allowed Krzysztof Penderecki to compose the music he wanted on a small table in a Kraków coffee shop. The resulting notation was a revelation. "When I wrote *Threnody*, I needed a harsh, brutal noise. Then I heard the squeal of a tram and transposed the sound to the strings."[2] This process described here opened a sound world that at that time had hardly begun to be explored.

These two statements by Penderecki give some idea of the background to and rationale of one of his most famous works. We can be forgiven for forgetting how strange and surprising *Threnody to the Victims of Hiroshima* (1959-60) sounded at its first performances in the early 1960s. Some similar sounds had been produced electronically in a number of works that had appeared in the late 1950s. However, hearing these sounds played live by a traditional string orchestra invited incredulity from ordinary concertgoers.

For the performers there was the problem of reading the notation and, once that was deciphered, there were the technical difficulties in actually producing the sounds, to say nothing of the potential antagonism to these sounds themselves. There have been numerous occasions when orchestras have virtually refused to play music which made such demands on the techniques of the players and seemed, at least on the surface, to counter all the aims of the instrumental techniques which they had spent many years developing up to that moment.

---

[1] Krzysztof Penderecki in the video documentary by Andreas Missler-Morell called *Krzysztof Penderecki* included in the DVD recording of *The Seven Gates of Jerusalem* (Arthaus 100 008), Chapter 4.

[2] Ibid, Chapter 4.

The consequence of this problem with decoding the notation is that it is quite possible that there would be a wide variation in the end results of a number of different performances. The first performers needed to work out their techniques from first principles, as there was no tradition of performance to follow. In over forty years since *Threnody* first appeared, we might expect a wide variety of interpretations, a possibility which this study investigates.

THE GROUND PLAN

In order to provide the basis for comparing three representative recordings of *Threnody*, it will be useful to examine its ground plan and determine the important aspects of each part of the work. Even one hearing makes clear to the listener that it depends on a number of fundamental features, the most notable the use of contrasting sonorities. The wide variety of string techniques, especially how and where (if at all) one uses the bow, determines the character of these different sounds. As we will see, these techniques can be used singly or in combination.

The sections marked out by these techniques are mostly discrete and separate from each other in the first half of the work, although there are some small overlaps. In the second half (from fig. 26 to the end), however, there is considerably more overlapping of sections; in fact, in this last part of *Threnody* the sectional approach is abandoned for a more developmental method. There is a very good reason for this: the first part presents the different techniques separately so that the listener can absorb them without confusion, but once they have been heard and understood then the composer felt free to combine them in a way that can readily be appreciated by the listener.

Threnody can be divided into a number of sections, here called "Materials," as shown in Table 1. Material 1 (fig. 1-7) is played on the "highest note of the instrument (no definite pitch)." This example of deliberate ambiguity produces a very variable cluster of microtonal pitches in the highest range of the instrument. In theory, there could be a unison within each group of the four, five or six instruments specified by the composer for each entry, but in practice, however, the resulting sound consists of a group of pitches very close together, producing a strongly discordant cluster. As these are marked *ff* there is no mistaking the intention of creating loud and discordant sounds. The volume is then scaled down, first to *f* and then to *ppp* and overlapping with the entry of Material 2 (fig. 6-10). Here the players in various sizes of groups work through a group of seven techniques of sound production; the score does not make this clear, but the intention is to produce a random order.[3] Each group of instruments enters in turn, and within each the subgroups of each string section enter in a form of canon. Surprisingly, the score does not specify a dynamic level. This music stops suddenly to reveal Material 3 (fig. 10-17) which involves microtonal clusters, moving from and/or to a specified unison, staying constant or moving all the notes together in parallel *glissando* to a cluster of different pitches. There is no overlap with the next section but no pause is indicated either. Material 4 (fig. 18-25) builds up clusters note by note from a central pitch, one group of instruments at a time, sustaining them, before using the group glissando in the cellos and basses and ending on a single pitch, followed by a five-second silence. Material 5 (fig. 26-59) is the most complex in the work. Its pointillist textures use a wide variety of string articulation and sound modification techniques; included are *arco, pizzicato, con sordino, col legno, tremolando, sul ponticello,* and the use of specified strings for sound effect. The string orchestra, reduced to 36, is divided into three groups of 4. 3. 3. 2. A sub-section, called here Material 6 (fig. 56-63), introduces mostly short sounds synchronised across the whole of each of the three groups. Before this music finishes, there is the entry at fig 62 of two new elements: Material 7 (fig. 62-65) which consists mostly of clusters but also includes the cellos and basses entering *fortissimo* playing at an angle of 90° on the tailpiece or bowing the bridge at a right angle. Also at fig 62 is the re-entry of the remaining players for the final Material 8 (fig. 62-70) consisting of steady microtonal clusters. The concluding 52-note cluster moves from *fff sul ponticello* through normal bowing position with a *diminuendo* to *pppp sul tasto.*

Table 1
Penderecki: *Threnody* - Sections with features, including overlaps.

Material	Figures	Pages	Duration	Features
1	1-7	5	1′ 19″	Highest notes on different groups of strings in turn, first *fortissimo*, then *subito forte*, then *subito ppp*
2	6-10	6-7	1′ 0″ ca	Mixture in rapid succession of different techniques in random order, including *arco, pizzicato, col legno, arpeggio* behind the bridge. Dynamics not specified.

[3] Wolfram Schwinger, *Krzysztof Penderecki: his life and work*. London, 1989, p. 125.

3	10-17	8-10	2′ 23″	Unison to microtonal clusters and/or vice versa, then sustained clusters moving by parallel *glissando* and fading away.
4	18-25	11-12	1′ 19″	Unison to clusters by step, by each sting group in turn (cellos, 2nd violins, violas, double basses, 1st violins) *crescendo* to *fortissimo* on reaching complete cluster. Sustained clusters (cellos and basses) gradually fading away.
5	26-59	13-17	1′ 25″ ca	Held notes and pointillist textures. Wide range of attacks and sound qualities. Strings divided into three groups.
6	56-63	17-18	0′ 20″ ca	Synchronized "chords" and short sharp sounds from three groups in turn. Varied attacks and techniques. No specified pitches.
7	62-65	18-19	0′ 22″	Cellos and basses bowing at right angles on tailpiece and bridge *fortissimo* with varied entries.
8	62-70	18-20	1′ 30″	Steady clusters at different volumes, followed by final *tutti* cluster, *fff* to *pppp*, changing *sul ponticello* to *ordinario* to *sul tasto* over duration of 30″.

THREE RECORDINGS COMPARED

The appearance of Krzysztof Penderecki's *Threnody* in the early 1960s was a revelation. It provided a new way of thinking about composition and demanded new techniques of performance. In the first instance, the performers needed to establish a method for playing, as there was no "performing tradition." As the required techniques became more familiar some liberties could be taken with certain details in order to obtain the maximum impact. By the late 20th century, *Threnody* had gained something of a classic status, even if its impact in sonic terms was the same. This involved taking a fresh look at the details of the score and perhaps taking an "authentic" view of the work. In order to chart these developments we take three representative recordings to show how the approach has changed. For the early performances the 1963 recording by the Warsaw National Philharmonic Orchestra conducted by Witold Rowicki[4] is a good example, the mature and considered performance that was recorded in 1975 by the Polish Radio National Symphony Orchestra in Katowice under Penderecki himself[5] represents later thoughts and finally

[4] Reissued on compact disc in 1989 by Polskie Nagrania on PNCD 017 B.

[5] Originally issued by EMI on LP in 1976 on EMD 5529 and reissued on compact disc in 1994 on CDM 5 65077 2 and again in 2000 on CZS 5 74302 2.

the recording by the same orchestra in 1998 conducted by Antoni Wit[6] shows us the latest approach.

The most immediate difference between the performances is the duration. While Rowicki in his pioneering recording and Wit in his recent one take a few seconds more or less than nine minutes, the composer takes nearly ten minutes. While the recordings by Rowicki and Wit are only a little longer than that indicated in the score, that by Penderecki is considerably longer. Taking a piece with such a carefully calculated time-scale, this should be an important point. The work itself was originally going to be called 8′ 37″ according to its duration[7] and later 8′ 26″ which is the actual duration given in the printed score.[8] It is interesting to find out where he departs from the score's timings.

The opening sections are very revealing. The duration of the first three Materials is indicated as 4′ 12″ in the score. Wit takes 4′ 07″, Rowicki 4′ 38″ and Penderecki 5′ 20″. Most of the difference is in the first page. Wit reads the score very literally and reduces the volume to *subito f* after 14 seconds (the score gives 11 seconds). Rowicki takes much longer over the initial entries, letting the sound make its full impact, without cutting it off prematurely and reaches the *subito f* at 24 seconds. Penderecki is even more emphatic as he makes the presence of the string sounds overwhelming by sustaining the *fortissimo* for 47 seconds (36 seconds longer than he indicated in the score) before letting his dynamic level drop. The string players also add to the tension by producing a wider range of "highest" notes to enhance the discordant nature of the opening. The continuation provides similar contrasts. In the composer's version, Material 2 starts 35 seconds later than marked in the score.[9] As noted earlier, he did not give Material 2 a dynamic marking in the score, a fact that leads to some strikingly differing interpretations. Wit seems to aim to blend the new collection of string techniques into the *ppp* of the highest notes at the end of the first page and then introduce a modest *crescendo* as the other players enter. Rowicki, however, ensures that the entry of Material 2 is not played too quietly with the entry being moderately loud, but it is the composer's version which makes the strongest impression.

---

[6] Issued on compact disc in 2000 by Naxos on 8.554491.

[7] W. Schwinger, *Krzysztof Penderecki. . . .* p. 124.

[8] Published originally by PWM, later reprinted by Schott in their Edition Eulenburg, Musik des 20. Jahrhunderts, and now published by EMI Music Publishing.

[9] Schwinger, *Krzysztof Penderecki. . . .* p. 125, notes that Penderecki brings in section 2 after 100 seconds though the figure is in fact approximately 85.

After the continuous bowing of Material 1, the mixture of short attacks is violent in its immediacy, with the contrast being really effective. All three conductors have a similar approach to the return to the sustained notes of Material 3, with a carefully graded approach to the glissandos and strict observance of the dynamic markings. As before, Penderecki lingers on the microtonal clusters, savoring their every nuance. Unlike Rowicki and Wit, he also allowed himself a long pause for clear dramatic effect before Material 5 which builds up microtonal clusters, not by *glissando* as in the previous section, but by step. All three recordings treat this in a similar way with not many major differences. Material 5 is in many ways the most complex in the work and brings some interesting differences. Rowicki steers his players through the complex textures with great assurance in approximately one minute before the first entry of the synchronized attacks from the first string group (Material 6). Wit approaches the notes very carefully and takes close to the one minute and a quarter indicated in the score. Penderecki throws caution to the winds and races through this section in less than a minute but without losing the full significance of any of the notes in the most virtuosic and accomplished version by far. The way the music rushes headlong into the synchronized attack section and the huge climax between figures 62 and 66 with the various Materials competing for supremacy is quite breathtaking. As in the rest of this recording the effect is stunning.

Conclusion

All three recordings represent *Threnody* as an important and forceful work, and none is unsatisfying. Inevitably even with such a carefully notated score, there will be differences in these recordings. Antoni Wit seems determined to make the work as effective as possible by following the score as closely as he can. His timings correspond with those given and at all stages he follows the details meticulously. Rowicki's version makes some deviations from the score without taking a large number of liberties, all of which are achieved for their musical effect. His players play with a freshness that makes the work sound as if it had just been composed. The composer's divergences from the score are important as they show us what can now be seen as considered second thoughts on how to perform the work. In his hands the opening section no longer sounds like a short shock to the ears that should not be prolonged for fear of offending the audience, but one in which the searing discords can be savored. This must be the result of the altered emphasis by the composer indicated to us by his changing the title from a prosaic duration, 8′ 26″ or 8′ 37″, to that of one of the most memorable titles in all of 20th-century string orchestral music, *Threnody to the Victims of Hiroshima for 52 strings.* This raises a question about the published score. Is it now time that this is reissued in a revised version which takes account of the composer's newest thoughts about how *Threnody* should be performed? It would certainly allow all performers to present the work with the full emotional impact that the composer intends it to project.

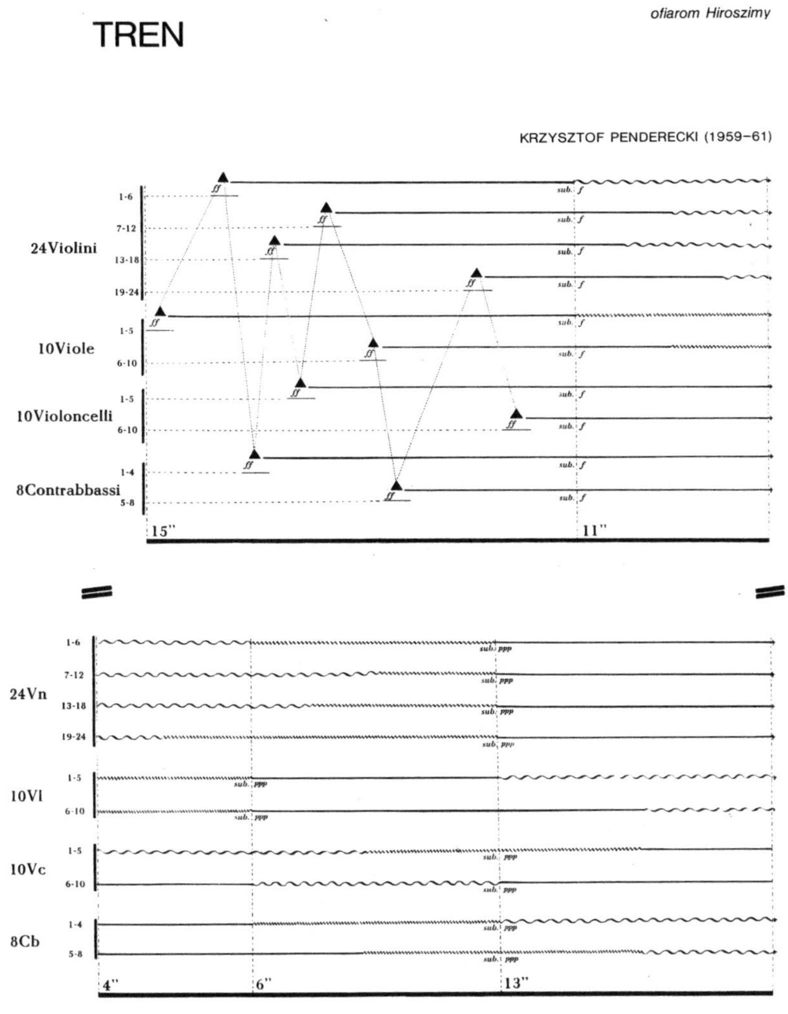

K. Penderecki, *Threnody to the Victims of Hiroshima*, PWM, p. 7.

REVIEWS

BOOKS

Leszek Polony
Cracow

Apocalypse or Hope?
Remarks on the Lectures for the End of the Century

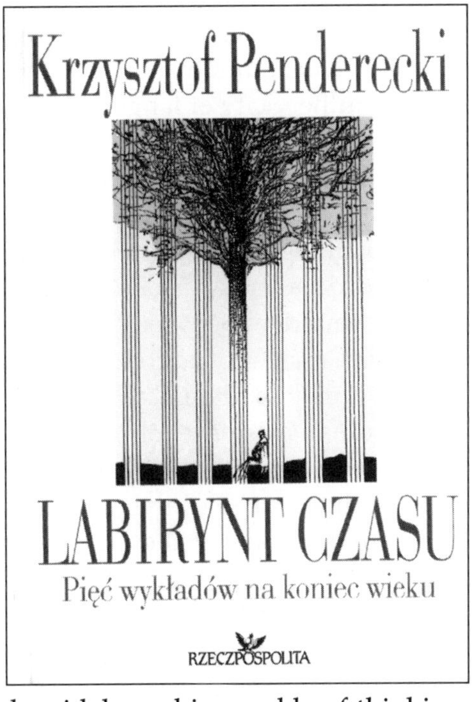

Labirynt czasu: Pięć wykładów na koniec wieku [Labyrinth of Time: Five Lectures for the End of the Century] is a striking read. Penderecki's essays were delivered when he received honorary doctorates from various universities between 1994 and 1996. Arranged in chronological order, they form a coherent whole. They form a compact system of views characterized by logical explication, original thinking and penetrating discrimination. One would also add that they testify to the author's extensive erudition – were it not for the fact that this assertion has been repeated *ad nauseum* by previous reviewers, apparently out of amazement that a composer – a tunesmith – reads widely and is capable of thinking, to boot.

"Symbols give us something to think about." I would like to make that memorable motto of Paul Ricoeur's the starting point for my attempt at a reading of Krzysztof Penderecki's reflections. "In Lusławice," the composer remarks in one of his essays, "I have surrounded my property, my garden, with a high wall in the belief that – in accordance with symbolic thinking – the wall strengthens the internal powers that arise there."

Three symbols dominate these lectures: the Labyrinth, the Tree, and the Ark.

In the composer's thought, the symbol of the **Labyrinth** has an ambivalent significance, both negative and positive. In the first place, it serves as a diagnosis of the situation of contemporary culture, of the spirituality of the end of our century. This is a highly critical diagnosis, resounding with catastrophic tones. Penderecki shares the assessments that were once formulated by Oswald Spengler, and more recently by such figures as Italo Calvino, the British sociologist Dwight Macdonald, or the American critic William A. Henry III. Our times appear as a confusion of tangled paths. They are characterized by the complete destruction of the hierarchy of values. The levels of culture are mixed up. The chaos of information and the kaleidoscope of images on television create an illusion of universal understanding, while in fact destroying the imagination and the authenticity of language. Penderecki sees the greatest threat in the disease of populism. Mass culture leads to the homogenization of ideas and the vulgarization of life. It destroys barriers and human distinctiveness. The reaction by intellectual and artistic circles only makes the situation more appalling. These circles have been overwhelmed by a feeling of decline and decadence, exhaustion, ossification and artificiality. Contemporary art flounders between a collective system and a vision of the apocalypse, with images of aggression, decay and death.

Nevertheless, the Labyrinth also has a positive meaning. It is a symbol of human existence, of our fate and destiny. It signifies the search for one's own way, with the inevitable hesitations and missteps, but also with the hope of reaching the goal, of final fulfillment. This is true, to a particular decree, of the artist. Penderecki believes in the artist's creative powers, in expressions of fundamental significance. He does not share the post modernist "philosophy of powerlessness." Nor does he believe in the death of the author, or in the demise of all form. He attaches a particular and distinguished significance to the concept of artistic form. This concept is, of course, the crystallization of spiritual meanings, and especially of those which meet the criteria of vitality and originality. It is a testimony to the creative individuality, the constructive imagination of the artist. At the same time, it is capable of awakening a resonance in the beholder.

The **Tree** is a symbol of creation, of the organic unity of the world, and of the way that nature is under threat from civilization." An Elegy on the Death of a Forest," the fourth of the lectures, is a shocking warning against cutting out the roots of one's own being. It has to do with more than mere pro-ecological slogans. Penderecki is sounding the alarm, pointing out the deep-seated reasons for, and consequences of, the crisis of contemporary civilization. The technological consciousness leads to the loss of unity with nature, to the loss of connection with the world as a source of existence. This is not a purely biological problem. Penderecki associates it with the "Faustian passion for destruction," a degree of anthropocentrism that leads to the desacralization of nature and culture. It is accompanied by the inevitable decay of human spirituality. Spiritualistic substitutes are offered instead.

The Tree, after all, is also a symbol of man himself, of his integrity and the power of his spirit. Penderecki cites the beautiful words of Rainer Maria Rilke, and above all of the Psalms, which he used in his own youthful avant-garde compositions. The devout man, the *homo religiosus*, "will be like a tree planted over the brook, which gives forth its fruit in the proper time, and whose leaves do not wither." "The internal tree" is the personal search for the essence of one's own life and calling, an attempt to reach the mysterious *materia prima* that is the stuff of the work of art, and perhaps the harbinger of a future synthesis, the Opus Magnum. Composing one's own garden, "making mathematics of nature," is identical, in Penderecki's mind, with composing music. He asks himself: Is this an escape into my own tiny world, into a private Arcadia? In the essay "The Internal Tree," he admits that he feels increasingly inclined to express himself in the quiet, condensed language of chamber music. Two pages on, or less than a year later, he refutes the arguments of post modernism by expressing his faith in the great forms, and also in the prospects for the regeneration of art, and for the significance of art as a "message from the ideal world." Chamber music, it appears, is, in essence, to be the way to a new synthesis, a new universal language of art, big enough to meet the challenges of the new times.

The **Ark** is a symbol of rescue and hope. Once again, Penderecki evokes a vision of the Apocalypse. The world is threatened by a catastrophe on the model of the Biblical flood. The confusion of ideas and "communicative liquidity," are reaching their culmination at the close of the second millennium. We have rejected the totalitarian utopia, but we have replaced it by a naive belief in almighty technology, a universal communion that takes place with the help of the mass media, a millenarian concept of the end of history in the shape of "the telematic world." In effect, our times are marked by the collapse of unity and equilibrium, by the undermining of all norms and values.

Is it possible to rescue ourselves through art? – asks the contemporary Savonarola. Could art be the Ark that would save a community of the chosen, as the basis of a future life? Kandinsky once believed in such salvation. He saw the strength of art in form, as an expression of the spiritual element. Construction and balance, as an antidote to "revolutionary" chaos, were also the ideals of Stravinsky. Italo Calvino also believed in the future of verbal art, as an Ark that would enable humanity to ride out the deluge of the televised culture of images. He recommended a literature of "Lightness, Celerity, Precision, Transparency, Variety," and finally, "Conciseness."

An affirmative answer to the questions posed above would testify, of course, to a naive optimism. In the interview published with the lectures, and conducted by Anna and Zbigniew Baran (in the Polish edition), Penderecki confirms that he lost his youthful, avant-garde faith in the mission of art long ago, his faith in art's role in the improving the world.

And yet, an analogy can be drawn to the situation 100 years ago. Then, the works of Gustav Mahler, who only today is properly appreciated, represented an attempt at a synthesis in times of dramatic dissolution, disintegration and crisis. This analogy suggests that we should go on believing in the heroic effort of "constructing the world." In this spirit of the Greek *Storge*, which was addressed by Oskar Miłosz, that is, "the love of future generations" and the hope in the different world, Penderecki points out his own, purely personal path. The path of individual salvation: "Long ago, I overcame the temptation of saving the world. I am, however, concerned with saving what is most important to me, in the artistic and human dimensions."

One might say in conclusion: only so much, and yet so much. The salvation of one's own soul should not be reduced to the egoistic idea of saving one's own skin. One should come right out and say it: Oskar Miłosz's message, as cited by Penderecki, is far from obvious. Nor should this surprise us. Miłosz was a poet and not, let us say, the Bishop of Lublin. It is therefore not clear whether the all-embracing love and mythical projection of the paradise of childhood into the future signifies a Christian vision of salvation or only a non-specific mystical hope. It is, in any case, "a fertile ambiguity," thanks to which that message can speak to people of various faiths and views. The artist, like everyone, will be tortured to the end of his days by questions about the objective value of his work and the sense of his whole life. In the final analysis, the most important thing, perhaps, will be his ambitions and intentions, the ethical value of life directed towards the good, the true and the beautiful, even if the results are judged to be, in the spirit of Milan Kundera's ironical description of Mahler, a "cathedral of uselessness."

Today, however, we can state one thing with a large dose of certainty. Penderecki's thinking is one of the most interesting intellectual reflections of the last decade of our century. It poses crucial questions and problems on the condition of man, the contemporary world, and the future of culture. It is a significant sign of the times. It restores our faith in the sense of such reflections on the world, which are held in so little esteem today. Penderecki's *Black Mask* was an artistic discourse on a troubled, divided world full of aggressive evil, plunging into a mad dance of death towards destruction. The composer treats his role as an intellectual with the highest seriousness. He contrasts it to the minimalization of art and the treatment of art in opportunistic terms, to the subjugation of art to the needs of the moment and commercial interests. Adherents of the philosophy of post modernism will surely say that Penderecki has fallen into the trap of elitism, that he has pronounced aesthetic laws where he has no right to pronounce, and elevated himself above the taste of "the common man." As to myself, I can see worse dangers: the control of the collective imagination by new, false prophets, the enthusiasts of simple rules and principles according to which the "global village" is to be ruled. Between the lines of his penetrating, sharp vision of the crisis of the contemporary world, Penderecki seems to warn us against just such a danger.

Krzysztof Penderecki, *Labyrint czasu. Pięć wykładów na koniec wieku* [Labyrinth of Time: Five Lectures for the End of the Century], with *Passio artis et vitae,* an interview with Krzysztof Penderecki by Anna and Zbigniew Baran. Warszawa: Presspublica, 1997.

English version: *Labyrinth of Time: Five Addresses for the End of the Millenium* with an interview with Krzysztof Penderecki by Ray Robinson. Princeton: Prestige Publications, 1998.

Translated by William Brand

Zofia Helman
Warsaw

Review of Regina Chłopicka, *Krzysztof Penderecki między sacrum i profanum. Studia nad twórczością wokalno-instrumentalną* (Kraków: Akademia Muzyczna [Academy of Music], 2000, pp. 250)[1]

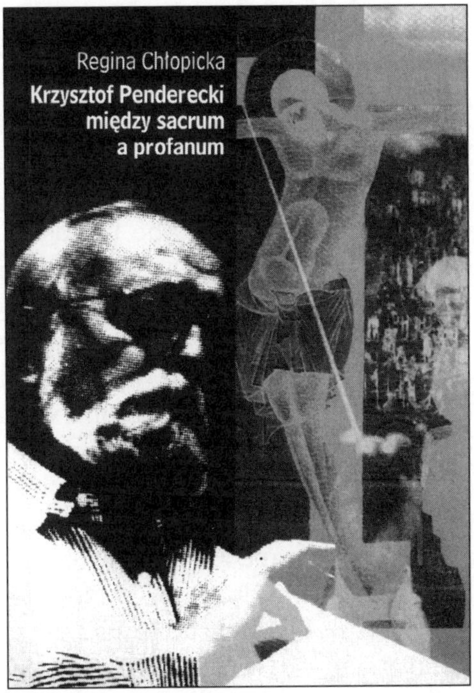

Regina Chłopicka's book about Krzysztof Penderecki's operatic and cantata-oratorio works occupies an important position in research on Polish contemporary music. This is due not only to the choice, as subject, of a composer whose work has awakened broad interest around the world, but also to her original approach which places Penderecki's work within the contexts of both the European artistic tradition and the contemporary cultural situation. Her use of two different research perspectives also reflects the breadth of her approach. In the section titled "Interpretation," she employs an analytical-interpretive technique, while, in the section titled "The Style and the Way It Changes," she concentrates on transformations of the composer's stylistic idiom. Additionally, there is a documentation that includes a bibliography and a discography in addition to a list of Penderecki's vocal-instrumental works.

1 [Krzysztof Penderecki Between the Sacred and the Profane: A Study in His Vocal-Instrumental Art]; English expanded edition: *Krzysztof Penderecki: Musica Sacra – Musica Profana. A Study of Vocal-Instrumental Works*. Warsaw: IAM, 2003, pp. 352.

In her introduction, Chłopicka sets up the principles and criteria according to which she divides the work into two groups, one associated with the sphere of the *sacrum*, and the other with that of the *profanum*. Within the sacred music, in turn, we find three subgroups: (a) works with religious themes based on Biblical and liturgical (both Roman Catholic and Eastern Orthodox) texts; (b) works with religious themes based on texts that are literary and non-liturgical, but which nevertheless have the character of a mystery (*Paradise Lost*); and (c) works on secular themes based on literary texts that refer to the sphere of the *sacrum* (such as *The Devils of Loudon*). Within the section on secular music (the *profanum*), she also distinguishes three groups: (a) works that are based on literary texts and emphasize humanistic and super-aesthetic values (such as *Cosmogony* and *Dies Irae*); (b) works that are based on literary texts and that call into question or even deny these values (such as *The Black Mask* and *King Ubu*); and (c) works that do not refer to the sphere of values (such as *Dimensions of Time and Silence*).

Keeping to this division, Chłopicka discusses selected, highly significant works by Penderecki. She builds her reflections on both the texts that serve as inspiration for the compositions and the musical form, while placing special emphasis precisely on the verbal-musical connections at various levels of the structures and symbolic associations of the works. She presents each of the works she discusses in a slightly different way, depending on the cultural context that defines it. One might say that, in each case, the musical work itself suggests a characteristic range of issues with its own hierarchy of importance, as well as the way that those issues should be studied. Chłopicka herself refrains from imposing a system of analysis from above. Aware of the potential of various interpretative approaches, she does not try to resolve every technical-formal question. She chooses the stylistic traits that she regards as most salient and most idiomatic in a given work, as well as those that point to an extra-musical context. In the *St Luke Passion*, therefore, the crucial elements are those linked with the tradition of the genre and, in very general terms, with the tradition of Christian sacred music. A concise outline of the history of the passion, from Gregorian chant through polyphonic works from the Renaissance to the passions of Schütz and Bach, shows how Penderecki provides a fresh perspective on the genre. Chłopicka devotes less space to connections with the earlier compositional techniques and formal principles of construction that have usually been discussed in the musicological literature, while placing her main accent on the way the text is dealt with and the dramatic treatment of the form and the musical symbolism. She reveals the complicated interaction of the textual and musical elements and the impact of various stylistic levels and varieties of expression that make up this great synthesis of tradition and the contemporary.

Chłopicka also brings up the connections with church music and liturgy in her chapters on *Matins* (Orthodox liturgy), *The Magnificat* (biblical tradition), *Polish Requiem* ("oratory theater"), and a pair of works from the second half of the 1990s, *The Seven Gates of Jerusalem* and the *Credo*, which are defined as a synthesis of Penderecki's experiments "in musical language and the technique of shaping narration . . . architectural construction, and the drama of the great symphonic, cantata-oratorio, and operatic forms" (p. 109).

The issues of Krzysztof Penderecki's stage works is unusually varied. In discussing *The Devils of Loudun*, Chłopicka concentrates on the synthesis of musical-theatrical forms (opera, musical drama, the passion, oratorio, and the mystery play) while highlighting the interplay of elements of expressionistic theatre, both in the dramatic structure and in the way that the subject is treated. A comparison of Aldous Huxley's *The Devils of Loudun* with John Whiting's play *The Devils* allows her to indicate Penderecki's individual concept of the story of Father Grandier and Mother Joanna, which has been taken up many times in literature, the theatre and film. What Penderecki accentuates above all is the internal experience of the characters, laying bear their moral quandaries and motivations and, ultimately, the spiritual transformations that allow them to start on the way towards truth and goodness. In this way, the events take on a sacred dimension.

Paradise Lost, based on Milton's epic, is one of Penderecki's most significant—and also one of his most large-scale works, and it could serve as the theme for a study all its own. Regina Chłopicka therefore picks out the crucial issues: the way in which Milton's text is transformed in Christopher Fry's libretto, and the musical conception of the work. The enormous abridgement of the text in comparison to Milton's original leads not only to a condensation of the subject matter, but also to a different placing of dramatic accents. Milton's antinomy between God and Satan may indeed be preserved in Penderecki's work, yet the central position nevertheless belongs to man, and the history of his fall and gradual internal transformation. In terms of musical form, Penderecki's monumental work, subtitled a *sacra rappresentatione*, constitutes a fusion of the opera and oratorio traditions with elements of religious ritual. It also makes use of all the possibilities afforded by contemporary theater. An extraordinary wealth of means of musical characterization serves the presentation of the three worlds of God, Man and Satan. Among other things, Chłopicka enumerates the hierarchy of intervals, chord-symbols (for instance, the world of evil as a chord made up of tritons, and the world of man as a triad with major and minor trios), vocal register and color, and types of melodies and instruments (solo or in groups).

According to Chłopicka's classification, Penderecki's next two stage works belong to the sphere of the "profane." *The Black Mask*, based on the play by Gerhart Hauptmann, is an example of expressionistic musical theater. Here, Chłopicka concentrates on the dramatic construction of the work, pointing out the dominance of the principle of contrast on various levels of organization. This is true of the heterogenous musical material woven into the opera (such as the protestant chorale, baroque dance music and self-quotations) and also of the vocal means, the methods of organizing musical time, space and expression, and the musical symbolism and structure. As the author notes, the closed musical form does indeed lead to a modification of the open-ended finale of Hauptmann's play; nevertheless, it fully preserves and even enhances all the themes and internal conflicts. "*The Black Mask*," we read in the conclusion to the chapter, "is a symbolic presentation of the complexity of the world and a representation of the universe. By means of contrasts that magnify and intensify feelings and emotions, the composer takes up the universal problems of tolerance and intolerance, guilt and punishment, the avenger and his victim, love and hate, and above all suffering and death" (p. 149).

Penderecki's last opera, *King Ubu*, represents a thorough-going contrast to the preceding, monumental operatic and oratorical forms that summon up the great universal themes of Euopean culture. In this case, we are dealing with a musical theater of the grotesque and the absurd, and the composer's playing with various stylistic conventions of text, music and theater that are piled on top of each other and intersect with modern compositional techniques. Chłopicka points up the differences between Alfred Jarry's play *Ubu roi* and Penderecki's opera. Each work makes its own sort of protest gesture against a world that permits the negation of ethical values. The opera, however, is less aggressive and provocative. There is more ironic distance in it, and the dialogue with various stylistic conventions even extends to Jarry's original work. Yet *King Ubu* is also a warning against a world in which all values have become relative.

The realm of tradition – religious, literary, theatrical, historical and musical – is, after all, summoned up in order to reveal the perspective of our times and to illustrate the existential situation of contemporary man. The Biblical and liturgical texts in the great cantata-oratory forms (*The St Luke Passion*, *Matins*, *The Magnificat*, the *Credo*, and *The Seven Gates of Jerusalem*) make us aware of the Judeo-Christian roots of European culture, including Polish culture. This is of particular significance at a time when there is an attempt to deny these roots. The reference to the sphere of the *sacrum* invokes the eternal questions "about the sense of life and death, about good and evil" (p. 66). *The Devils of Loudun* remind us that the world of evil, intolerance, hypocrisy and hatred is, in a way part of the "cosmic dimension," and is not confined only to historical events. *Paradise Lost* is a bridge spanning mythical time, the historical events of the past, and an apocalyptic vision of the future. The accent falls, everywhere, "on the goal towards which man aspires. Man's difficult path towards God is steeped in the hope of achieving a mysterious harmony" (p. 89).

All of Penderecki's work is united by the theme of death, shown in various aspects. Mulling over this problem in Chapter 3, Chłopicka states that a perspective of eternity opens in the works on the religious theme of death, revealing a metaphysical dimension. In the works with secular themes, on the other hand, the introduction of the subject of death leads to a confrontation between good and evil, "which brings in, as a result, a feeling of the sense and order of the world" (p. 175).

If the section titled "Interpretations" is dominated by a synchronic outlook, then Chłopicka offers the diachronic viewpoint in the following part of the book, "Style and its Transformation." When considering the problem of the stylistic periods in Penderecki's work, she takes as her bases, on the one hand aesthetic categories (such as universal values, national identity and classical beauty) and, on the other, the subordination of them to the characteristics of musical language and style (sonorism, the new romanticism and postmodernism). Chłopicka identifies eight stylistic phases in Penderecki's music. This is a new solution to the question of periods in Penderecki's work, and can be contrasted with the six phases discerned by Mieczysław Tomaszewski, or the three phases enumerated by Ray Robinson. Chłopicka's conclusions as to the constant characteristics in Penderecki's music, which remain in place regardless of the transformation of the composer's musical language and aesthetic assumptions, are unusually important. Among such constant elements, Chłopicka enumerates Penderecki's approach to the problems of drama and form in music and the way they influence his characteristic sort of narration, and even the "rhetoricization" of the musical process.

Chłopicka devotes her last chapter to Penderecki's aesthetic thinking, as formulated in the lectures published in the *Labyrinth of Time* collection. Here, the composer offers an explicit statement of the artistic credo that he realizes in his music. This credo can be most precisely encapsulated in two symbols: the "labyrinth" of the title and the "ark." The labyrinth defines human existence with all its straying from and seeking of the path. The ark, the "symbol of rescue and hope," shows how art, the domain of order and harmony, can bring salvation in a world of chaos.

Regina Chłopicka's book adds an important sort of depth to our knowledge of Krzysztof Penderecki's music and illustrates its multidimensional nature. The author penetrates into the stylistic and aesthetic strata of the works she discusses and, what is more, brings out those aspects of the works that are "supra-aesthetic" and that come most distinctly to the fore in the sphere of the *sacrum*. In her interpretation, she endeavors to pitch her text to the high tones of Penderecki's music, and ventures on occasion beyond the borders of traditional musicological discourse. The themes she deals with are resistant to unequivocal explication, yet the interpretations that Chłopicka presents are suggestive and convincing, and testify not only to her highly-developed erudition, but also to her great artistic sensitivity.

Translated by William Brand

Zbigniew Skowron
Warsaw

Danuta Mirka, *The Sonoristic Structuralism of Krzysztof Penderecki*

(Katowice: Akademia Muzyczna [Academy of Music], 1997, pp. 363)

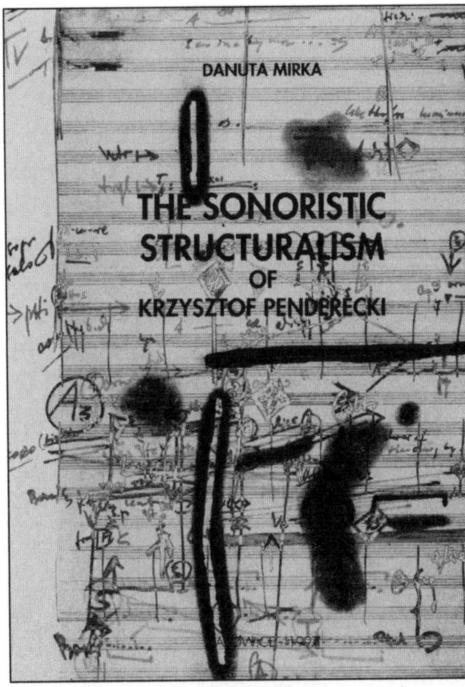

A series of Krzysztof Penderecki's works composed after his début at the "Warsaw Autumn" Festival in 1959[1] displayed a range of radical innovations which were unparalleled in both European and American music at that time. Such works as *Anaklasis, Threnody to the Victims of Hiroshima, Polymorphia* or *Fluorescences* became not only a hallmark of Penderecki's individual *métier*, style and aesthetic, but also a part of the most important achievements of the musical avant garde of the 1960s. The reception of these works in Poland, especially the attempts at their analysis and interpretation, leaves no room for doubt that the main issue of Penderecki's creative explorations was immediately associated with the realm of sound-material. One of the interpretative keys in this connection was the term "sonorism" proposed by the distinguished Polish musicologist Józef Chomiński in the first volume of his *Formy muzyczne* [Musical Forms].[2] Yet paradoxically enough, this somewhat automatic classification of Penderecki's

[1] At this festival Penderecki's *Strophes* for soprano, speaker and 10 instruments to the original texts of Menander, Sophocles, Isaiah, Jeremiah, and Omar Kháyyám, were performed.

[2] See Józef M. Chomiński: *Teoria formy. Małe formy instrumentalne* [Theory of Form. Small Instrumental Forms]. Kraków 1983, especially the chapter *Podstawy sonologii muzycznej* [Foundations of Musical Sonology, p. 126-153], where the author writes that "sonoristic regulation consists in an exploration of the pure sound properties of the sound-material" (p. 126).

early output as sonorism, as in the case of the early works of Henryk Mikołaj Górecki and Wojciech Kilar (Penderecki's contemporaries), has been made first and foremost through the listening experience. Moreover, this empirical approach became for quite a long time the only point of departure for the analysis of Penderecki's works. Such an approach aimed at a description and classification of the sound materials, timbres, articulations and textures of his compositions, in short – all the wealth of these new sonorous qualities. What was long neglected in this kind of classification approach was the issue of the internal structuring of Penderecki's avant garde works. The multitude, variety and radical character of their sonorous appearances, seemed to exclude *a priori* the presence of any structured rules of a systematic nature. No wonder that in the existing studies of Penderecki's sonorism, which focused on the empirical and sensual side of his innovations, little space has been dedicated to structural aspects. This approach is the main subject of a pioneering study by Danuta Mirka, *The Sonoristic Structuralism of Krzysztof Penderecki*, published in Poland in 1997 by the Academy of Music in Katowice.

This book, which is a PhD dissertation, written at the Institute of Musicology at the University of Helsinki under the guidance of Eero Tarasti, originated from the author's intuitive conviction, confirmed by Penderecki himself, that his early works, which apparently seemed to be a musical type of chaos, were in fact governed by internal, systematic rules. The main aim of the author is, as she writes, "to reveal that the technique in question is not a loose assembly of compositional devices, occurring here and there, and only organising individual parts or sections of a few works. Rather, it will be shown that Penderecki's compositional method constitutes a rigorous system of interrelated rules that display highly logical precision and rigidity which thoroughly govern the entirety of the composer's sonoristic output" (p. 26). The search for these rules is mirrored in the arrangement of this book, the main body of which – apart from *Introduction* and *Conclusions* – consists of *Part One: The System ('Langue')* and *Part Two: The System at Work ('Parole')*, indicating the connection of the author's method with the foundations of structural linguistics. Thus she distinguishes two intrinsically connected analytical levels: firstly – the area of systematic elements (the norms of structuring the musical material) in the sense of a "language," and secondly – the area of the actual, concrete qualities in the sense of "speech." This structural approach stemming from linguistics is an original point of view and a useful methodological tool. It fully allows the author to verify her hypothesis on the *structural* character of Penderecki's sonorism both in its purely compositional dimension and in its wider aesthetic context.

The first part of the book contains three sub-sections: *Basic System, Timbre System* (they both have the same plan: *Elementary Structures, Morphology, Syntax*), and *Articulation* (*Articulation of the Timbre System, Articulation of the Basic System, Orchestration and Instrumental Techniques in Penderecki's Sonoristic Works*). In this part, which presents – as the author states – "a temporal, synchronic set of abstract invariants comparable to 'language'. . . in the terminology of . . . Ferdinand de Saussure" (p. 26), the basic structures are discussed within the range of three parameters; pitch, dynamics and durations. Each of these parameters includes particular perceptional categories put into rows of binary oppositions, such as spatial continuity vs. spatial discontinuity, spatial mobility vs. spatial immobility, high register vs. low register, middle register vs. extreme register; loud dynamics vs. soft dynamics; temporal continuity vs. temporal discontinuity, temporal mobility vs. temporal immobility, maximal time-span vs. minimal time-span. Similarly the basic structures concerning the timbre system and the issue of articulation are also presented. All these systematic criteria allow the author to recognize Penderecki's sonorism not only as a sensual, complex sound-world, but also as a structurally cohesive phenomenon, which is integrated on both morphological and syntactical levels.

The complementary, second part of the book, entitled *The System at Work (Parole)*, consists of six chapters: *Expressive and Redundant Features, Analyses of Musical Texts, Evolution of Expressive Features, Evolution of the System, Evolution of Articulation, and Sub-segmental Regulations.* In this part, which includes analyses of the most representative of Penderecki's avant garde works,[3] the author applies the elements of the previously discussed system to Penderecki's compositional practice. Each of these detailed analyses is accompanied by a series of meticulously elaborated diagrams showing the structural arrangements within particular binary oppositions of a "basic system," and – on the other hand – the entire structure of a given work. However, it is to be regretted that the author left her "summarizing" diagrams with no comments on the overall structural

[3] The analysed works are successively: *Anaklasis* for percussion ensemble and string orchestra (1959-60), *Dimensions of Time and Silence* for mixed choir and a chamber ensemble (1960-61), *Threnody to the Victims of Hiroshima* for 52 string instruments (1960), *Quartetto per archi I* (1960), *Polymorphia* for 48 string instruments (1960), *Fluórescences* for orchestra (1962) and *Canon* for 52 string instruments and 2 tapes (1962).

peculiarities of the analyzed works, especially as far as the nature of their unfolding (or their internal dramaturgy) is concerned. The fact that each of these works displays a different "dramatic" trajectory (with its different ways of growing, culminating and fading away), certainly gives an opportunity to pinpoint the expressive effects of a given structural scheme. This kind of approach, i.e. an attempt to discuss expressive qualities of Penderecki's works, but still without reference to their overall form, is to be noted in one of the closing chapters of the analytical section (*Evolution of Expressive Features*). Here the author presents a systematic overview of, as she states, "optional expressive features" as opposed to "regular expressive features." Among the former ones, which have an extra-systemic character, and – to quote the author – "are always intended to bring dynamic processes into relief . . . , to make it more salient" (p. 272) are such features as *glissandi* (with their sophisticated form of sinusoidal *glissandi*), trills, *tremoli* and *vibrati*. They are often combined, and one of them is even identified as a "gesture of decay," as its concluding function. The author notes: "Because most of the regular as well as optional expressive features enhance soft dynamics, their combination also appears to be directed mostly towards low volume, or amplitude levels. From among such groupings . . . one is particularly significant, since it is used several times in similar contexts. This is a combination of *glissando* with a varying set of other features – *tremolo*, harmonics, mutes, *sul ponticello*, and the like – which enhance a *diminuendo*. The expressive content of this grouping allows one to speak here of a 'gesture of decay' – an 'unravelling' of the musical thread. Accordingly, it usually occurs at the conclusion of long passages or of entire pieces" (p. 279).

In the *Conclusions*, which consist of five condensed chapters (*The System in Penderecki's sonorism, Penderecki's Sonorism in the Landscape of Contemporary Music, Periodisation of Penderecki's Output, Penderecki and Structuralism, Postscript: A Semiotic View*) the author discusses the broader aspects of the composer's sonorism, especially its formal and aesthetic implications. She also makes an interesting comparison between his and other avant-gardists' approach to the sound-material as the main object of innovative creativity and as a vehicle of individual style. One of the most important topics discussed in this part of the book is the issue of the development of Penderecki's system. The author points to the fact that his "basic system" underwent a kind of evolution, analogous to the process of learning the phonological system of a given language.[4] This growth of the "basic system," which may be observed particularly in the area of texture, started – as she convincingly argues – with an opposition between two kinds of texture: a heterogeneous pointillist texture and a homogenous cluster. And it was this "nuclear opposition" which further developed into various intermediate stages between homogeneity and heterogeneity, and took the shape of multifarious textures in his successive works. Another important factor in this context was also the opposition of registers, which was fully used in *Polymorphia*. This is how the author summarizes the entire process under discussion: "The evolution of the basis system of Penderecki's sonoristic style can be aptly called 'growth.' This last term is appropriate, because the system proceeds from the minimal number of segments and a maximal number of redundancies – a state characteristic of the 'nuclear opposition' – towards the multiplication of syntactical units by way of progressive liquidation of redundancies between individual elementary categories. This process progresses along three 'branches' which concern, respectively, dynamics, registers, and all the remaining aspects of musical narration" (p. 289).

A full understanding of the way in which Penderecki's "basic system" developed would be impossible without considering such fundamental aspects as the timbre system and articulation. With regard to them, the author emphasizes the fact that they not only evolved quantitatively along with the "growth" of the "basic system," but that this evolution had a dialectical character and, as such, it caused both areas to be mutually connected. "The evolution of the system," writes Danuta Mirka, "stimulated the evolution of articulatory phenomena. But on the other hand, the stages of the evolution of the system . . . were vitally contingent upon the articulatory resources at the composer's disposal when he was writing individual pieces" (p. 295).

What is worthy of notice in the *Conclusions* is part of the chapter *The System in Penderecki's sonorism*, which examines the formal aspects of his avant garde works. Although the author declares that "a study of forms making for the idiolects of individual musical texts, and hence accounting for their mutual differences, lies outside the main scope of the investigation" (p. 328) – and this most likely explains the previously mentioned

[4] It is a process in which, according to Danuta Mirka, "the oppositions embodied directly into the optimal consonant and optimal vowel are gradually matched by new distinctive features, obtained by a transference of the differentiation between the consonantal and the vocalic axes" (p. 290). See also R. Jakobson and M. Halle, *The Fundamentals of Language*. Gravenhage, 1956.

lack of comments on form in the analytical part of the book – she does discuss in this section some peculiarities of form, such as the pre-sence of the archetype of an arch-form (especially in *Polymorphia* and in *Fluorescences*). These remarks deserve special attention the more so because they reveal some influences coming from outside the "basic system." Among the sources of inspiration, which had an impact on Penderecki's idea of form, the author enumerates visual art, especially that of Paul Klee, and architecture. Whereas, as she argues, "Klee's idea of *carrés magiques* (magic squares) . . . may have supported the concept of the segment as the minimal syntactical unit of Penderecki's sonorism," architecture influenced the composer's formal thinking as far as "the relations among sound masses and the tensions that spring from them" (p. 330) are concerned. Both extra-musical references show that apart from the basic role of the structuralist system itself, there existed also a *personal* factor, the composer's preferences and free choices, which were decisive both for the formal outcome of his works and for their aesthetic effect on listeners.

Another important topic in *Conclusions* is the specific character of Penderecki's sonorism in the context of post-Webernian serialism and other trends in the second half of 20th-century music, such as the sound-mass music of Xenakis, Ligeti, and even Lutosławski. As far as serialism is concerned, the fundamental difference between this technique and Penderecki's music consists in Penderecki applying the rules which govern the sound matter taken *en masse*, whereas in the serial technique the rules apply to discontinuous, *single* sounds of a musical structure. Yet this sound-mass music, although much closer to Penderecki's concept, differs from it in its approach to form, which is, so to speak, not generated by the system itself.[5]

Danuta Mirka's book is certainly the first study of this kind and of this scope, which shows the very nature of Penderecki's avant garde works, both in their systematic character and actual sound-shape, and in a broader musical context of seemingly related styles and compositional techniques. Although the analyzed group of Penderecki's works does not

[5] This is how the author makes her point: "The correspondence in Penderecki's sonorism, between the axiomatic concept of sound matter . . . and the elementary syntactic unit . . . , elicits a coherence between the morphology and the syntax of his compositional system; the syntax forms practically a prolongation of paradigmatic relations, governed by the morphology, on the syntagmatic axis of time in the course of a musical narration. By contrast, the strict regulations of the systems elaborated by Lutosławski, Ligeti, and Xenakis concern only the morphology (that is, how individual sound fields are created), whereas the succession of such fields and their relations with the formal design of a piece are regulated (if at all) by separate rules of a comparatively looser character" (p. 335).

cover all his avant garde explorations, the evidence for which is seen in the compositions of the late 1960s, up to *The Awakening of Jacob* (1974), his early works remain a unique testimony to his sonoristic ideas, displaying them in their full scope, richness and structural consistency. However, what requires criticism in this context, is the disproportion between the presentation of the works of 1959-62 and the those of the late 1960s which are treated in a shortened, if not to say, too generalized a way (this applies especially to Penderecki's choral works and the *St Luke Passion*). And although the author explains this by separating the *sonorism proper,* which refers to the works analysed in the second part of the book, from the *late sonoristic style,* referring - in turn - to the compositions of 1963-73, one would expect this differentiation to be better elucidated and exemplified.

Last but not least, it should be stressed that the author's analyses and interpretations of Penderecki's avant garde works not only throw a new light on their structural properties, but also re-valuate the notion of "sonorism" itself. Its substantial character in the compositions of this Polish master is evidence of the invalidity of those widespread views of sonorism, to quote once again the author, "as a style devoid of any interest in an intellectually organized form, and . . . rather concerned only with the exploration of formless sound matter," and "as anti-intellectual in its attitude towards the problem of artistic creation" or the views of sonoristic works as "catalogues of effects or handbooks of noises . . . rather than genuine works of art" (p. 16). On the contrary, the status and role of sonorism in Penderecki's works, especially the range of new aesthetic qualities it displayed, makes sonorism fully justified as a stylistic category within the output of the avant garde of the second half of the 20th century.

Cindy Bylander
San Antonio

Randolph Foy, *Textural Transformations: The Instrumental Music of Krzysztof Penderecki, 1960-1973*

(D.M.A. dissertation, Baltimore, Peabody Institute of the Johns Hopkins University, 1994)

Randolph Foy chose a rather ambitious project for his dissertation: to analyze compositions previously critiqued as having "impenetrable ideas" and even as being "evidently unanalysable"[1] - namely, Penderecki's instrumental works written between 1960 and 1973. The result: an outstanding study of "texture style," a term coined by Foy to describe Penderecki's treatment of his musical material in these pieces. Foy offered extensive analyses of the *Capriccio for Violin* (1967) and Symphony No. 1 (1973) as examples of texture style in its most sophisticated form, and presented detailed comments on each of the other relevant works as he traced the evolution of this style in Penderecki's music.

Foy defined texture style as "a distinctive combination of timbre, dynamics, articulation and figuration in which global characteristics take precedence over detail. Textures may be used motivically and developmentally such that transformations of a texture may be heard as related to the original presentation." He then described the five basic types of texture found in Penderecki's music: sustained sounds, repetition, moving lines, glissandos and single short sounds. He also acknowledged that "these specific forms often function as motives, undergoing transformations such as augmentation or diminution, registral or timbral variations or changes in dynamics." Although most of these comments are valid, I must register some discomfort with part of them. Specifically, if timbre and dynamics can be varied within a specific textural type - and they certainly are, as illustrated in Foy's numerous musical examples - then these aspects should not be included as integral parts of the definition of texture style. Indeed, my interpretation of Foy's description and examples of each of the five texture types is that articulation and figuration within

[1] Paul Griffiths, Penderecki, *Musical Times* 14, no. 1570 (December 1973), p. 1255.

a "global" setting are the only factors needed to label a "motive" as a particular texture type. Perhaps, then, his definition of "texture style" needs to be refined. Nevertheless, Foy's analyses of Penderecki's music with regard to these texture types are meticulous and insightful. The questions that he poses periodically about Penderecki's compositional techniques are equally appropriate and thought-provoking.

As other writers have done, Foy divided the 1960-1973 works into two smaller periods: those from 1960-1962 (Period I) and those from 1962-1973 (Period II). In his discussion of the Period I works (*Anaklasis, Dimensions of Time and Silence, Threnody, Polymorphia, Canon* and *Fluorescences*), Foy demonstrated how Penderecki handled texture style in conjunction with the pointillism and serialism also present in most of these pieces. Furthermore, he illustrated how Penderecki created a sense of forward motion for these works "by shaping individual textures to serve conventional functions of beginnings, middles, and endings." Another prominent feature of these compositions is the development and recapitulation of texture types, usually within a modified ternary form. Finally, Foy showed how Penderecki moved from using texture as a background component in his earliest pieces to completely discarding the idea of background and foreground layers in most of his later Period I works.

Before discussing the Period II compositions, Foy described the mixture of tonality and texture style in the *St Luke Passion*. This influential piece is the first in which Penderecki used the moving-line texture style, here characterized by half-step/leap/half-step motion. These half-step movements within a moving line are characteristic of Penderecki's use of this texture type throughout Period II; indeed, the moving line is one of the most prevalent texture types seen in the Period II works.

Other features of these works (the Sonata for Cello and Orchestra, *De natura sonoris no. 1, Capriccio for Oboe and Eleven Strings, Partita*, the *Violin Capriccio* and the First Symphony) include an increased emphasis on horizontal lines and pitch centers, although these are still subordinate to the role played by texture style. Greater development of the individual "motives" associated with each texture type in a particular piece is also apparent. Furthermore, a shift from juxtaposing textural types in a quick-cut pattern (as was the case in Period I) to composing a gradual transition from one type to another is also evident in Period II.

Throughout his dissertation, Foy spent much time describing the various ways in which Penderecki developed certain texture styles in his music. In this context, however, the term "development" takes on a somewhat different meaning from that usually used in musical analysis. Here it does not refer to changes of tonality or tonal centers, but instead alludes to changes made to specific texture-type "motives" throughout a piece, such as alterations in dynamics, timbre and tempo. *Threnody*, for example, can be considered a study in the development of sustained clusters.

Foy also elaborated upon the formal layout of each composition discussed. As the composer himself has noted on many occasions, musical form is of utmost importance to him; in fact, it is the first element he decides upon in each of his compositions. Foy touched upon many of the techniques used by Penderecki to create a coherent form in his texture-style works. In the Period I pieces he tended to maintain clear sectional divisions, notwithstanding the presence of overlapping measures between sections in some pieces. Within these sections as well as between them, he created a sense of movement by using opposing forces: for example, static vs. active movement, loud vs. soft dynamics, or sustained notes vs. single sounds. In the Period II works, the composer used these same techniques, but gradually moved toward a more intuitive, organic sense of form, which culminated with the narrative form of Symphony No. 1, described in detail by Foy.

As is the case in most U.S. dissertations, Foy provided the expected biography of Penderecki and references to previous publications about his topic. Regrettably, he did not refer to previous writings on texture studies of 20th-century music, of which there have been several dissertations and articles (see elsewhere in this volume as well as in volume I of this journal for references). He did, however, place Penderecki and his music within the context of his contemporaries, notably Ligeti, Lutosławski and Xenakis, and aptly differentiated among the compositional techniques used by these three in their music. Foy also offered several hypotheses about why Penderecki might have abandoned texture-style music in the mid-1970s, including the general move towards neo-Romanticism by composers at that time, and Penderecki's increased experience with orchestral conducting, which led to his corresponding decision to write more clearly for musicians.

My one remaining regret concerning this dissertation: the quality of its musical examples as reproduced by UMI Dissertation Services is extremely poor. It is literally impossible to discern pitches or distinguish between different texture styles in most of the examples. One must either have the scores to these pieces on hand or trust Foy to provide an accurate description of each example.

Foy ended his dissertation by stating that Penderecki's texture-style pieces had made a major contribution to Western music, since through them, the composer had "successfully challenge[d] the assumption . . . that pitch must be the pre-eminent compositional parameter." This is certainly a valid conclusion. Penderecki's texture-style pieces are all well-designed works, worthy of repeat performances at the close of this century. They bear up well under the analytical microscope and, yes, they pack an expressive punch as well.

Randolph Foy has made a major contribution to Penderecki scholarship. The attention he has paid to detail and his ability to raise and then answer the appropriate questions is commendable. His comprehensive examination of a broad range of Penderecki's avant garde works has yielded important new findings. Hopefully, they will serve as the springboard for future studies of twentieth-century music.

SYMPOSIUMS

Robert Shankovich
Pittsburgh

A Special New York Symposium

Lincoln Center's *Festival 98 Symposium Series* scheduled in conjunction with the "month's (July) programs" provided a unique behind-the-scenes view of the musical world - the music, those who composed it, and those involved in its re-creation. "Creating the *Seven Gates of Jerusalem*" was one such symposium presenting a discussion of the music of Krzysztof Penderecki with a focus on this particular work which had just been given its first United States performance the evening before.

The Kaplan Penthouse in the building adjacent to Avery Fisher Hall (where these events were held) filled up quickly, well before the six o'clock starting time. Judging from the animated conversations I couldn't help overhearing, those who had attended the previous night's extravaganza infectiously spread their enthusiasm to others who had yet to experience it. The distinguished symposium panel consisted of composer Krzysztof Penderecki and conductor Kurt Mazur, moderated by Ray Robinson, without doubt America's foremost Penderecki scholar. It was indeed an imposing trio occupying the dais that afternoon.

Professor Robinson opened the forum with an overview of Penderecki's career, beginning with the composer's first published work from his student days, *The Psalms of David,* progressing to his composing of *Seven Gates of Jerusalem.* According to Penderecki, his first visit to Israel in 1974 left such a strong and lasting impression, that two decades later, when he was commissioned to write a piece in celebration of "Jerusalem - 3000 Years," his inspiration for the work was fueled by those memories.

Mr. Robinson acknowledged questions from the audience, which were generally directed to either Maestri Penderecki or Mazur, although both would contribute to the response from their individual perspective. Mr. Robinson summarized their comments as necessary.

One of the topics had to do with the musical form of *Seven Gates,* its designation as an oratorio, and Penderecki's reluctance to have it categorized as such. It started out as a symphony, and from his comments one could infer that only a fine line separates the two genres ("Mahler's Second Symphony could be an oratorio"). Penderecki went on to explain that the piece we were hearing would eventually be reworked and expanded into what will be his Seventh Symphony. He talked about how Bruckner's Seventh Symphony was the turning point in making him [Bruckner] the great composer as decreed by history. Penderecki further averred that following Stravinsky's era the popularity of the symphonic form dwindled, but he hastened to predict that it will make a comeback in the next millennium.

Some expressed their curiosity about the "new" instrument invented by Penderecki, called the tubaphone, which made its debut in the *Seven Gates* orchestra ("The two tubaphones have a lot to say in the fifth movement"). It is a structure holding various tuned lengths of plastic pipes played by swatting the openings with felt mallets. Not only was the sound fascinating, but the players were fun to watch, too. This led to Mr. Mazur's description of the positioning around the hall, of the instrumental, choral, and solo forces and his task of keeping them together. It was a remarkable and exhausting feat. (In fact, I marveled that Mr. Mazur was giving this time and his energy to the Symposium, with a second performance to conduct only minutes away.) There was a friendly exchange between the two artists about tempi. *Seven Gates* took about 70 minutes in its previous performances; Mazur did it in 52!

One member of the Symposium audience commented (with a question mark) about Penderecki's choice of texts and whether they were specific enough to Judaism. Penderecki explained: recognizing the futility of attempts to incorporate three religions – Judaism, Christianity and Islam – into a single work, he approached the task from his own Christian viewpoint. He chose fragments from Scripture that referred in some way to Jerusalem and set it to music – unmistakably *sacred.* And this is somewhat related to a particular remark from another member of the audience – one that not only defined the impact of *Seven Gates of Jerusalem* on the performers as well as the audience, but that also brought about the most poignant moment of the entire hour's discussion. It was uttered by a member of the orchestra. He described how performing Penderecki's composition had magically united the symphony musicians. He added that although he did not consider himself a "religious person," *Seven Gates* was for him truly a religious experience. And so it was for many!

Cindy Bylander
San Antonio

Oregon Bach Festival Symposium

The second week of July 1998 was a momentous one for Krzysztof Penderecki, one of many such periods in his illustrious career. The culmination of this particular week was the world première of his oratorio *Credo*, given in Eugene, Oregon as part of the Oregon Bach Festival. Accompanying this event was a weeklong series of master classes and symposiums. A panel discussion/press conference on Friday morning, July 10th, served both to introduce the English translation of Penderecki's book *Labyrinth of Time: Five Addresses for the End of the Millenium* to the American public and to allow an opportunity for the exchange of opinions with and about the composer. Sharing the stage at this session were the composer himself, American scholar and conductor Ray Robinson, and Polish musicologist Regina Chłopicka, who, although well-known in Europe and Pendereckian circles for her ground-breaking studies on the composer, was making her American debut as a scholar. Adding a touch of humor to the proceedings was Penderecki's wife Elżbieta, who offered comments from her balcony seat.

Each of the speakers discussed a different aspect of the composer's output. Chłopicka spoke of *Labyrinth*, interpreting its literary symbols as a tree (the unity of past and present), a labyrinth (universal and individual, rational and irrational) and an ark (a sign of rescue and hope that appears at a moment of danger). She also spoke of the composer's Christian roots and his belief, expressed throughout *Labyrinth*, that one should bring the best aspects of 20th century art forward into the 21st century.

Robinson reviewed Penderecki's compositional style, beginning with his avant garde tendencies exhibited most strongly in the early 1960s. Many of the same orchestral techniques still play a role in his music today, albeit to a lesser degree. For the last two decades, Penderecki has discovered a more personal language associated more with beauty than with controversy. He has also intentionally attempted to synthesize the musical innovations of the 20th century, many of which are his own, with some of the traditions of earlier epochs. His recent symphonies

(Nos. 3 and 5) and oratorios (*Seven Gates of Jerusalem* and *Credo*) are a result of this desire for synthesis and interpretation.

Penderecki, of course, was the top attraction at the discussion. Like his wife, he also injected humor into the occasion, making jokes as he answered questions. On the serious side, he spoke mostly about *Credo,* which he had begun two years earlier (1996), shortly after completing *Seven Gates of Jerusalem* (Symphony No. 7), but had finished only a week earlier, on July 4. His original plan, he stated, had been to write a Mass, but by April 1998 he realized that he would not be able to finish it; the *Credo* was already an hour in length. Fragments of the planned *Gloria* and *Agnus Dei* sections appear in the completed *Credo*. The text includes several interpolations along with the traditional words of the liturgy. As he has done in several other works, he connected the piece to his native Poland, here through his use of the Polish equivalent of the Latin "popule meus" and the insertion of two Polish Holy Week hymns. Speaking more generally, he suggested that the formal element was to him the most important part of any composition. For instance, the *passacaglia,* one of his favorite formal devices, has been used in different stages of his career: *St Luke Passion* (1965-66), *Magnificat* (1973-74) and his Symphony No. 3 (1988-95).

The symposium concluded with questions from the audience.

Małgorzata Janicka-Słysz
Cracow

The Cracow Symposium. About Krzysztof Penderecki's Theatre

An international conference on "Krzysztof Penderecki's Music in the Context of Twentieth Century Theatre," organized by the Chair of the Theory and Interpretation of the Musical Work and the Department of Musical Analysis and Interpretation, was held in Cracow from September 18-20, 1998. The symposium was an integral part of the Krzysztof Penderecki Festival being held in Cracow during the jubilee "Krzysztof Penderecki Year."

Two exhibitions were an integral part of the Festival: a showing of Penderecki's sketches and scores, titled *Itinerarium,* at the Artistic Exhibition Bureau "Art Bunker" in Cracow, and *Krzysztof Penderecki* Black Mask: *A Contemporary Dance of Death from Idea to Realization* at the Gallery of the International Culture Center. Regina Chłopicka, whose ideas served as the inspiration for the latter exhibition, said of its major theme that "Penderecki's musical theater is a particular artistic testimony to the anxieties of our era and an impulse to reflection. Death is shown in many dimensions. . . . Krzysztof Penderecki leaves the final choice to each of us."[1] A "musical" supplement to this exhibition was the Cracow premiere of *The Black Mask* at the Słowacki Theater, directed by Krzysztof Nazar, with musical direction by Ewa Michnik.

The symposium sessions were divided into four main thematic sections, organized around Penderecki's four operas, *The Devils of Loudun, Paradise Lost, The Black Mask,* and *Ubu Rex*. "Addresses illuminating the organic context of the issues under consideration" preceded the thematic discussions. Jan Błoński drew attention to the syndrome of the contemporary theatre and the associated reevaluation of theatrical means and aesthetic needs among the audience, while also pointing out that we now find ourselves "at the antipodes" of drama, or even of the dramatic. Robert

[1] R. Chłopicka, "Temat śmierci w teatrze Krzysztofa Pendereckiego" [The theme of death in Penderecki's theatre]. In *Krzysztof Penderecki, 'Czarna maska.' Współczesny taniec śmierci. Od idei do realizacji.* Cracow: Galeria Międzynarodowego Centrum Kultury, 1998, p. 48.

S. Hatten presented a strategy of dramatic distance in relation to Penderecki's genres and themes, and situating his operatic theatre within a range of works of cultural significance, from Berg's *Wozzeck* to Messiaen's *Francis of Assisi*. Krzysztof Szwajgier took up the theme of the avant garde, and advanced the thesis that it is a particular trait of Penderecki's personality and has left a permanent stamp on his artistic evolution.

The remarks prefacing the "opera" thematic sections also included a "presentation of the composer's newest works": *The Seven Gates of Jerusalem* and the *Credo* in a synthetic view by Ray Robinson and the *Hymn "Glory to St Daniil, Prince of Moscow"* in a hermeneutic interpretation by Teresa Malecka.

In the thematic section on "***The Devils of Loudun*** **and the Theatre of Moral Angst**," Edward Boniecki took up the case of Father Urban Grandier - the protagonist of the drama who rises, within the conventions of engaged art to which Penderecki's belongs, to the status of a martyr for a cause. Presenting the issue of the integration of genre, form, and style, Zofia Helman pointed out the work's location at the intersection of various genres of stage music: the opera, musical drama, oratorio, and passion, as well as purely theatrical forms. She also stressed the way that Penderecki remains faithful in *The Devils of Loudun* to the principles of expressionistic theatre while breaking with the ideas of Sartre's existentialism. Stephen Downes turned the spotlight on two categories, laughter, and the grotesque, and proved that they play a decisive musical, dramatic, and psychological role in Penderecki. He also asked whether the character of the possessed woman in *The Devils of Loudun* might not be an echo of the "hysterical" Kundry from Wagner's *Parsifal*. Andrzej Tuchowski compared and contrasted Penderecki's work with *Peter Grimes* and other operas by Benjamin Britten. Remote from each other as they may be geopolitically, culturally, and aesthetically, both composers reveal a similar interest in broadly conceived ethical-social issues in their writing for the stage.

In the thematic section on "***Paradise Lost*** **and the revival of religious theatre**," Pierre Albert Castanet pointed out the origins of Messiaen's religious ethos and the religious opera, Niall O'Loughlin presented Schoenberg's *Moses and Aaron* in the perspective of its meanings for Judaism and Christianity, and Irène Mamczarz discussed the genealogical issues connected with the *sacra rappresentazione* category. Within this same context, Regina Chłopicka examined Penderecki's *Paradise Lost* as a contemporary variant of the biblical "invariant" of the history of salvation and presented the traits of the musical characterization of three fundamental domains: the heavenly, the infernal, and the human. Ray Robinson, in turn, focused his remarks on the issues connected with Penderecki's instrumentation as an expression of the potential of the modern orchestra, with sonoristic techniques foremost - and, at the same time, as a synthesis, an amalgamation of the avant garde and tradition. Ewa Wójtowicz concentrated on listing the harmonic means that are constituents of and significant in the musical language that the composer employs in *Paradise Lost*, from leading motifs and structures to the final D major triad that symbolizes, in the author's view, hope for Adam and Eve after their expulsion from paradise. This thematic section closed with two "posters," by the young musical theorists Agnieszka Draus and Kazimierz Płoskoń, illustrating the connections between the text of Penderecki's work and Milton's epic, and pointing out the differences in the thematic concepts and the approach to the form of *Paradise Lost* in the two works.

Tadeusz Chrzanowski opened the thematic section on "***The Black Mask* and the theatre of extreme emotions**" with a text on "The Theology of Horror," which drew attention to the cultural presence of eschatological themes and the dance of death motif from the dawn of civilization through the baroque, where an intensified interest in the question of death can be observed. Against this background, Regina Chłopicka interpreted Penderecki's *Black Mask* in categories of the contemporary dance of death, accenting the apocalyptic dimension of the work. Anna Łabędzka, on the other hand, viewed Penderecki's opera as a starting point for comparative studies of the baroque and modernism in Central Europe. The text of Hauptmann's that inspired the libretto reveals elements of affinity with Polish literature, and especially Wyspiański's *The Wedding*.

Zbigniew Skowron opened the thematic section on "***Ubu Rex* and the theatre of the absurd**" by examining the poetics of the absurd and the grotesque in the work and their reference to aesthetics in the postmodernist spirit. Iwona Lindstedt interpreted *Ubu Rex* as a game with conventions in which traditional and modern, elitist and popular, and universal and regional codes collide. She also showed how the "multilingual" music of *Ubu Rex* refers to musical styles, techniques, gestures, and idioms from the baroque to the contemporary avant garde. Maria Anna Harley then presented Penderecki's work in the context of the surrealism that is a feature of the Polish musical theatre. Andrzej Chłopecki wrapped up the session with a thesis about "Pataphysical Context in the New Opera," as exemplified by Penderecki's *Ubu Rex*, György Ligeti's

Le Grand Macabre, and John Corigliano's *The Ghosts of Versailles*. He placed *Ubu Rex* in the invigorating current of "hallucinations" on opera, which require a pataphysical perception according to which "what you do not know is what you know."

The symposium closed with ***A meeting and discussion held by producers of Krzysztof Penderecki's operas with the participation of the composer***, chaired by Małgorzata Dziewulska and including Mieczysław Dondajewski, Ryszard Peryt, and Ewa Starowieyska (the producers of *The Black Mask* in Poznań), Marek Weiss-Grzesiński (the producer of *Paradise Lost* in Warsaw and *The Devils of Loudun* in Poznań), Krzysztof Nazar and Zofia de Ines (the director and stage designer of *Ubu Rex* in Cracow), and Andrzej Hiolski (who performed *The Devils of Loudun*).

One of the remarks that Krzysztof Penderecki made about his musical theatre was that "it is hard to make a theatre that is suspended in a vacuum. Theater should be contemporary. . . . I have no wish to influence the staging of my works. When my 'product' is ready, with all the stage directions that I write in the score and that help me to find the form of the work, I leave it to be staged without any interference from me. . . . The most important thing for me is faithfulness to the score."

PERFORMANCES

Ray Robinson
West Palm Beach

Penderecki's *Credo* in America

Of the many works composed by Krzysztof Penderecki that have had performances in the United States, none has had a more enthusiastic reception than *Credo*. Commissioned by the Oregon Bach Festival (Eugene, Oregon) and the International Bach Academy (Stuttgart, Germany), the oratorio was completed in Eugene on July 4th, 1998. Its world première took place on July 11, 1998, with Helmuth Rilling conducting the Oregon Bach Festival Chorus and Orchestra, the Phoenix Boys Choir and soloists Juliane Banse (soprano), Milagro Vargas (mezzo-soprano), Marietta Simpson (contralto), Thomas Randle (Tenor) and Thomas Quasthoff (bass). It was recorded on the Hänssler label on the weekend of the première; the resulting CD was voted best Orchestral/Classical recording in 1999 by the Music Industry (AFIM), best recording by a living composer at the 2000 Cannes (France) Classical Awards Festival, and won a Grammy for Best Classical Performance at the 43rd Grammy Awards Ceremony in 2001. The Oregon Bach Festival première on July 11, 1998 marked the American world premiere of a work by Penderecki.

A second American performance was presented on July 14, 2002 at the Oregon Bach Festival. This production was then taken to Minneapolis, Minnesota, where it was paired with Anton Bruckner's *Te Deum* at the 6th World Symposium on Choral Music, August 8, 2002. The soloists included Amanda Mace (soprano), Milagro Vargas (mezzo-soprano), Marietta Simpson (contralto), Cory Welch (tenor) and Eric Owens (bass). Helmuth Rilling conducted the Oregon Bach Festival Chorus, Minnesota Chorale, San Francisco Girls Chorus and the Symposium Festival Orchestra.

The extended applause at the conclusion of each of the three American performances clearly indicated the audience's approval of the work.

Credo seems to have marked an occasion of special significance in the history of first performances in the United States when a major European composer was commissioned by an American musical organization to compose a full-length (over an hour) concert work for soloists, chorus and orchestra that resulted in an American première. An event of comparable importance has perhaps not taken place since 1946, when Robert Shaw and the Collegiate Chorale commissioned and presented the first performance of Paul Hindemith's *When Lilacs Last in the Dooryard Bloom'd*.

Although commissioned to set the entire Mass text, Penderecki made the decision to compose only the third section of the Ordinary, the *Credo*. At the time of the première, he gave the following reason for this decision:

> Because the *Credo* has gone beyond the dimensions I had planned, the world première will feature only the first [composed] part of the Mass, i.e. the *Credo* (it will be 50-55 minutes long, the time I had originally planned for the entire Mass). I think I will manage to write the successive parts [of the Mass] during the course of the next few years, and the Mass may [eventually] assume considerable proportions (up to 2 hours in length).[1]

When asked why he had confined the musical setting of the new work to the third part of the Ordinary, Penderecki responded: "The *Credo* is the most important text in the entire Mass. Every idea in the Mass is included here."[2] He then went on to suggest that it was not the time factor alone that had forced him to limit its scope, but a more practical reason: he had used up all the *Missa* sketches in the *Credo*: "There was nothing left,"[3] he related with a hint of frustration.

After completing the work, his thoughts about finishing the *Missa* were somewhat different than they had been three months earlier (in March 1998).

> Now I am not sure that I will continue composing the Mass, because this is perhaps the longest *Credo* ever written. Maybe there is a longer one, but I do not know it. No, I do not think I will be able to come back to this idea because everything is now in the *Credo*. All my musical ideas about the Mass have been included in the work. I think it will stay as *Credo*.[4]

---

[1] Krzysztof Penderecki, letter to Ray Robinson, March 29, 1998.

[2] Krzysztof Penderecki, interview given to Ray Robinson, Cracow, Poland, April 10, 1998.

[3] Penderecki, interview, Cracow.

[4] Krzysztof Penderecki, radio interview given to Ray Robinson at KFAX, Eugene (Oregon), July 7, 1998.

And, perhaps, in an attempt to deflect any criticism that might have been forthcoming as the result of his failure to deliver a composition based on the complete Mass, he added:

> But this is the work you compose only once in your lifetime![5]

In terms of its musical materials, *Credo* offers a very different and more accessible style than is heard in composer's earlier works for chorus and orchestra. Because *Credo* was started in December 1996, following the completion of *Seven Gates of Jerusalem,* the musical ideas in the two works are closely related and demonstrate a great contrast in style to the *Passion, Utrenia, Cosmogony, Te Deum* or the *Requiem.* Whereas the musical language of the latter work (the *Requiem*) is built on motives consisting primarily of minor 2nds, minor 3rds, and tri-tones, the linear events of *Credo* are based on the more consonant intervals of 2nds, 3rds, 5ths and 6ths. At certain points, the lyrical lines soar in the romantic tradition as, for example, in the "Credo in unum Deum" theme which opens the work, establishes the tonality of Bb minor, and eventually appears five times throughout the course of the composition to bring formal unity to this seven-movement work.

As he does in *Seven Gates of Jerusalem,* Penderecki follows the opening theme with a rich harmonic texture based on minor third intervals that are doubled at the octave in the divided soprano and tenor parts. This organ-like texture, combining a baroque rhetorical figure and a Bruckner-like romantic symphonic style, first appeared in the composer's musical language in the opera *Paradise Lost* (1978). It is also a musical texture used to great effect in the unaccompanied choral work *Agnus Dei* (1981) and is reminiscent of the kind of scoring one hears in the works of the late-19th century; obviously there is a clear reference to musical tradition.

Finally, the endings in Penderecki's works are usually very interesting. For example, the C major chord that ends the otherwise atonal *Polymorphia* (1961) for string orchestra, the D major chord that concludes *Stabat Mater* (1962), the spread E major tonality that is heard on the final chord of the *St Luke Passion* (1966) and *Seven Gates of Jerusalem* (1996) bring distinctive and surprising conclusions to these works. The ending in *Credo* is a chord with an open fifth: D – A. But then the trumpets, which are behind the audience in the off-stage brass ensemble in the balcony,

[5] Penderecki, interview, Cracow.

play a D major chord quietly, *pianissimo*. You hardly hear them as they sustain the chord like an echo![6]

By the very act of setting the long and difficult *Credo* text, Penderecki is affirming its validity at the end of a millennium that has been generally characterized as post-Christian. He is likewise confirming a personal religious commitment in the manner he knows best, by composing a musical work on a prominent sacred text, a point he strongly emphasized in an interview given on October 26, 1997:

> Since I am a Christian and compose as a Christian, I must write another religious work. I am considered a composer of sacred music. I have [already] written many religious works. Looking at other composers of our time, there is only one - Olivier Messiaen - who has written as much music on sacred texts. This is my task![7]

[6] Penderecki, radio interview.

[7] Krzysztof Penderecki, interview given to Ray Robinson: "Conversations at the end of the Millennium," in New York, October 26, 1997. In *Labyrinth of Time*, p. 89.

Lydia Melnyk
Lviv

Krzysztof Penderecki's *Credo* at the Lviv Opera House

Krzysztof Penderecki appeared in Lviv during the 1999 Contrasts Modern Music Festival. It was not his first visit. Three years earlier, he conducted the *Polish Requiem* in Lviv Cathedral. This year's concert was part of a government exchange program, supported by Polish president Aleksander Kwaśniewski. The Polish first lady, Jolanta Kwaśniewska, attended the concert at the Opera House, and Polish ambassador Jerzy Bar opened the evening. The Carpathian Oil and Gas Construction Company of Warsaw was a sponsor. Speaking before the concert, the firm's CEO noted that this support is based on the the company's rich associations with Lviv. The Carpathian had its home office on St. Mary's Square before the war.

For Penderecki, this concert in Lviv was special. It marked the start of an international tour by the Penderecki Festival Orchestra, featuring the Polish soloists Bożena Harasimowicz-Haas, Izabella Kłosińska, Agnieszka Relis, Adam Zdunikowski and Romuald Tesarowicz. They were joined in Lviv by the local Dudaryk choir and the Dumka choir of Kiev.

Working and making music together is universally recognized as a unifying factor between peoples. This was embodied symbolically in the joint performance of *Credo*, which became a sign of faith and a prayer uttered from the soul. Penderecki's *Credo*, which bears solemn witness to the beauty and immortality of the spirit, became a leitmotif for the whole festival. The Lviv Opera House, one of the most splendid in Europe, was filled to capacity.

Penderecki's increasing emphasis on spiritual themes is no accident. Composed in 1996-98, *Credo* marks another step in the composer's movement away from the extreme innovations of his early work towards an apparently simpler and more accessible mode. This is the sort of simplicity, of course, that is hardly primitive and often demands more artistry than does innovation. The eternal theme of a dialogue with the creator requires a careful choice of methods and melodic sources. Penderecki regards this as especially urgent at a time when "art and religion seldom meet at a high intellectual level."

For listeners who are musically more aware, another criterion of a great work is the sense of time that it embodies. When members of the audience begin glancing at their watches, then the cause is already lost. In the Lviv Opera House, however, the sensation of time was not a factor; an hour passed, but the people listening to the *Credo* did not know it. Then came the recognition of the maestro, the bouquets and the ovation. Time had resumed its normal course, but those in the Opera House knew that there is a master who is able to stop time.

The performance of *Credo* in Lviv on October 12, 1999 was part of the fifth Contrasts International Festival of Contemporary Music.

INFORMATION ABOUT THE PERFORMANCE:

The Lviv Opera (The Operatic Theatre in Lviv)
Performers:
Bożena Harasimowicz-Haas (soprano)
Izabella Kłosińska (soprano)
Agnieszka Relis (mezzo-soprano)
Adam Zdunikowski (tenor)
Romuald Tesarowicz (bass)
The Dumka Choir (directed by Yevhen Savchuk)
The Dudaryk Choir (directed by Nikolay Katsal)
The Penderecki Festival Orchestra
conducted by Krzysztof Penderecki

Robert Shankovich
Pittsburgh

Symphony No. 7 *Seven Gates of Jerusalem*, New York City

Lincoln Center's 1998 Summer Festival offered up an enticing menu of music, theater, dance and film. The piece de resistance was Krzysztof Penderecki's *Seven Gates of Jerusalem,* given its United States premiere on July 7 and 8. The work had been commissioned by the city of Jerusalem for its 3000th anniversary, and was first performed there in January 1997. The New York performances additionally commemorated the 50th anniversary of the founding of the State of Israel.

Seven Gates is a masterwork, a direct descendant of earlier twentieth-century monuments such as Stravinsky's *Symphony of Psalms* (1930) and Honegger's grand oratorio *Jeanne d'Arc au Bûcher* (1938). But with this present work, Penderecki has surpassed even his own *St. Luke Passion* of some forty years ago, elevating the oratorio genre to new heights of grandeur and expressivity. The performance challenges issued by the score were admirably met by the New York Philharmonic Orchestra, the Philadelphia Singers Chorale (David Hayes, Director), five soloists and one Speaker: Christine Goerke and Wendy Nielsen, sopranos; Florence Quivar, mezzo-soprano; Jon Villars, tenor; William Stone, baritone. Boris Carmeli deserves special mention for his impassioned Hebrew narration which intensified the emotional impact of the music - all under the inspired leadership of the Orchestra's famed music director, Kurt Mazur.

Avery Fisher Hall provided the ideal venue for Penderecki's conception of surrounding the audience with sound. Maestro Mazur positioned his musicians on all four sides of the hall. The stage was occupied by a large chorus seated on risers with the massive orchestra in front of them, leaving just enough space for the soloists flanking the conductor's podium. Additional instrumental ensembles were stationed in the back of the hall, one group on the main floor, and a second one in the balcony. Two more forty-voice choirs were located at each side in the highest tier, seemingly touching the ceiling. Waves of music resonated from every direction, blending into a magnificent sonic edifice which enveloped and enraptured the audience. But the separation of musical forces created some difficulties in keeping them all coordinated and synchronized. Mr. Mazur's conducting was televised to the off-stage musicians, but the TV monitor that they relied on was not quite as commanding as the real thing. And so there were a few indecisive entrances by one group or another, not conspicuous enough to impair an otherwise secure performance.

Seven Gates sets fragments from the Old Testament sung in the old-fashioned Latin of the Vulgate Bible. There are seven movements, supposedly one for each of the seven gates. But not according to the composer; he intends to eventually add two more movements to the present work. Nevertheless Penderecki must have kept in mind the special significance of the number seven in Hebrew lore; he ends a prominent recurring bass theme with seven notes.

Music scholars will find the score of *Seven Gates* replete with similar examples of Penderecki's compositional ingenuity, giving them much to theorize about. Likewise, philosophers will no doubt speculate about hermeneutic aspects of the piece. But this music requires no theoretical or philosophical discourse for either grasping its meaning or for justification of its greatness. It communicates clearly and powerfully in its own language, unique in its fusion of opposites - the past with the future, the dramatically complex with pastoral simplicity - extremes of which it is at once neither and both. And to extend the oxymoron even further. *Seven Gates* speaks in a universal vernacular, a musical Esperanto, as it were, its message crossing geographical and cultural boundaries.

This proved to be the case with the New York audiences at both performances. Their reception was exuberant. As a matter of fact, after the second evening's performance I thought to take note of the duration of the final applause. It lasted *seven* minutes!

RELATED INFORMATION

Cindy Bylander
San Antonio

A Selected Bibliography of Books and Articles on Penderecki's Avant Garde Compositions

It is somewhat astounding to realize how much attention Penderecki's avant garde compositions have generated in both the general press and scholarly writings. Articles began to be published in the Polish press almost immediately upon the composer's receipt of three prizes from the Polish Composers Union's Composers Competition in 1959 and they have appeared steadily since then in publications from around the world. Citations of published books and journal articles alone number at least 250 for the fourteen works being examined here - and that includes only those written in Polish, German and English. The number of newspaper articles about these pieces is undoubtedly much larger than that, if one could locate them all.

The publications annotated here include those books and articles that offer analytical information about Penderecki's avant garde works as well as others that offer critical biographical or interpretative details. Books are listed first, while the articles have been separated into several categories: published interviews, general stylistic commentaries about the works, and articles about individual pieces, the latter of which are listed in chronological order from earliest to latest. Within each of these groupings, the annotated items are followed by citations of other relevant publications.

BOOKS

Penderecki, Krzysztof. *Labyrinth of Time. Five Addresses for the End of the Millenium.* Edited by Ray Robinson. Chapel Hill, North Carolina: Hinshaw Music, 1998.

This is an expanded, translated version of the original Polish publication (*Labirynt czasu. Pięć wykładów na koniec wieku.* Edited by Zbigniew Baran. Warszawa: Presspublica, 1997), which is itself a compilation of addresses published individually in *Plus Minus* and *Tygodnik Powszechny.* These thought-provoking addresses collectively form a major statement by the composer on the state of the arts at the close of the 20th century. Among the symbols embraced by Penderecki in these speeches are the tree, the labyrinth, the forest and the ark. The composer's deeply Christian roots also serve as a recurring theme, as does his belief that while contemporary art (especially music) is in danger of decay and self-destruction, it also possesses the ability to resurrect itself in the 21st century.

Included are English translations of the texts for *Dies irae, Cosmogony,* and *Seven Gates of Jerusalem*, a brief biography, and Ray Robinson's twenty-page interview with the composer conducted in October 1997.

* * *

Chłopicka, Regina. *Krzysztof Penderecki między sacrum i profanum. Studia nad twórczością wokalno-instrumentalną* [Krzysztof Penderecki Between the Sacred and the Profane: A Study in His Vocal-Instrumental Art]. Kraków: Akademia Muzyczna, 2000. English expanded edition: *Krzysztof Penderecki: Musica Sacra – Musica Profana. A Study of Vocal-Instrumental Works.* Warsaw: IAM, 2003.

Cf. review, pp. 299-304 (editor).

Erhardt, Ludwik. *Spotkania z Krzysztofem Pendereckim* [Meetings with Krzysztof Penderecki]. Kraków: Polskie Wydawnictwo Muzyczne, 1975.

Erhardt's biography of Penderecki, the first to appear in any language, covers the composer's career through 1973. Citations from published reviews, concise, yet insightful analyses of each work, and detailed information about world premieres are interwoven throughout the biography. Perhaps most valuable – because of its rarity – is the information Erhardt provided about Penderecki's numerous works for puppet theater and short films composed in the early 1960s.

A list of published works, discography, and extensive endnotes are included. Added bonuses are the many photos scattered throughout and the facsimile excerpts from *Capriccio per Siegfried Palm, De natura sonoris no. 2* and *Utrenia.*

Lisicki, Krzysztof. *Szkice o Krzysztofie Pendereckim* [Sketches about Krzysztof Penderecki]. Warszawa: Instytut Wydawniczy PAX, 1973.

This book is, as the author stated in his preface, more a collection of sketches about Penderecki's music than a detailed biography of the composer. After summarizing both the composer's youthful years and the history of twentieth-century music, Lisicki concentrated on Penderecki's compositions, giving general descriptions of his major works and quoting from program notes and concert reviews. Polish translations to the texts of the *St Luke Passion, Dies Irae, Utrenia,* and *Cosmogony* are provided, as are a discography and a list of works and premieres through 1971.

Schwinger, Wolfram. *Penderecki: Begegnungen, Lebensdaten, Werkkommentare* (Mainz: Schott, 1994). [Krzysztof Penderecki. His Life and Works. Encounters, Biography and Musical Commentary]. Expanded edition, translated by William Mann. New York: Schott, 1989. Originally published as *Penderecki: Begegnungen, Lebensdaten, Werkkommentare.* (Stuttgart: Deutsche Verlags-Anstalt, 1979).

Schwinger's biography of Penderecki and analysis of his compositions is the seminal work on the composer and the only full-length one available in English. The author's friendship with the composer lend it an aura of authenticity. This tome, whose German edition is currently the most up-to-date, is a valuable source of information on the dating of Penderecki's pieces - not just their world premieres but also the dates of subsequent performances. Furthermore, its analytical section is the most comprehensive in print. A works list and discography are included, as are numerous photographs and score excerpts.

Świercz, Teresa. *Technika chóralna w dziełach wokalno-instrumentalnych Krzysztofa Pendereckiego* [Choral Technique in the Vocal-Instrumental Works of Krzysztof Penderecki]. Prace Specjalne 9. Gdańsk: Państwowa Wyższa Szkoła Muzyczna, 1976.

Świercz has analyzed the choral writing in five of Penderecki's works: *Psalms of David, Dimensions of Time and Silence, Cantata in honorem Almae Matris, St Luke Passion,* and *Dies Irae.* Among her chief conclusions: aleatoric and traditional techniques are used both simultaneously and separately; the chromatic scale is Penderecki's basic source of pitch material; his polyphonic writing often includes free imitation; meter, tempo, and sometimes rhythm are often undefined in aleatoric passages; and the precise selection of musical means is closely connected to the meaning of the chosen texts.

Tomaszewski, Mieczysław. *Krzysztof Penderecki i jego muzyka. Cztery eseje* [Krzysztof Penderecki and His Music: Four Essays]. Kraków: Akademia Muzyczna, 1994.

The four essays published here are titled "Listening to Penderecki," "Work and Sound in Penderecki's Music," "Absorb All That Has Come to Be," and "Penderecki's Dialogs and Games with Time and Space on Earth." Written over the course of eight years (1986-1993), these essays serve to both document and interpret Penderecki's *oeuvre.* It is Tomaszewski's interpretations that are the most fascinating, for he eloquently illuminates Penderecki's music as a living, viable art that draws on both the past and present (and has always done so) and that often reflects upon the conditions of human existence.

Ćwikliński, Przemysław and Jacek Ziarno. *Pasja. O Krzysztofie Pendereckim* [Passion. About Krzysztof Penderecki]. Warszawa: Polska Oficyna Wydawnicza BGW, 1993.

Jacobson, Bernard. *A Polish Renaissance.* London: Phaedon, 1996.

Malecka-Contamin, Barbara. *Krzysztof Penderecki. Style et Matériaux* [Krzysztof Penderecki. Style and Materials]. Paris: Éditions Kimé, 1997.

Rappoport-Gelfand, Lidia. *Musical Life in Poland. The Postwar Years 1945-1977.* Translated by Irina Lasoff. Musicology: A Book Series, vol. 10. Edited by F. Joseph Smith. New York: Gordon and Breach, 1991.

PUBLISHED INTERVIEWS

"Dyskusja" [Discussion]. *Muzyka* 21, no. 4 (1976): pp. 29-52.

This wide-ranging discussion among Penderecki, Mieczysław Tomaszewski and others took place at the end of a 1975 Kraków seminar on the composer's music. Topics of discussion included Penderecki's composing methods, his ideas about clusters and sonorism (the latter being a term he disliked), his affinity for traditional forms, the reception of his works by both musicians and the public, his sketches for *Psalmus 1961*, and the distinction between sound and murmur in his music. Penderecki freely offered his opinions in this wide-ranging, open-ended conversation among friends.

Dufallo, Richard. "Krzysztof Penderecki." In *Trackings. Composers Speak with Richard Dufallo*, pp. 340-52. New York: Oxford University Press, 1989.

Dufallo's lengthy interview with Penderecki, conducted in February 1987, revolved around several topics: the Darmstadt festivals of the early 1960s, electronic and serial music, the difficulties the composer has experienced in getting performances of his compositions, and the stylistic features of these same pieces. In speaking of his avant garde works, Penderecki cited *Anaklasis* as the first piece for which he developed a new style that was free of the influences of other composers. He also said that he has developed features such as glissando clusters and new playing techniques for string instruments on his own, unaware that composers such as Xenakis, Ligeti, and Stockhausen were experimenting with similar ideas at about the same time.

Felder, David, and Mark Schneider. "An Interview with Krzysztof Penderecki." *The Composer* 11 (1977): pp. 8-20.

Penderecki reflected on his compositional career in this conversation with Felder and Schneider. First, he divided his output into three periods. Prior to 1962, he was concerned with expanding the vocabulary of contemporary music and creating something new in each piece. From 1962-1973, he utilized his own compositional language. Beginning in 1974, he regained an interest in traditional orchestral sounds, pitch and repetition. He also discussed the significance of the notational system used in *Threnody* and other early works, and dismissed reports that some of his music was too difficult to play. Of utmost importance to him were the ideas of tension and release in a composition.

This interview has been cited frequently by other writers as a source of quotes concerning the composer's description of *Fluorescences* as a piece that marked the end of a stylistic period, his attitude towards electronic music, and his background as a composer who lived and worked in communist Poland.

Meyer, Thomas. " 'Man kann nur einmal Avantgardist sein.' Gespräche mit Krzysztof Penderecki" [You Can Only Be an Avant-Gardist Once. A Conversation with Krzysztof Penderecki]. *Neue Zeitschrift für Musik* 150, no. 12 (December 1989): pp. 17-22.

This interview is based on two conversations that Meyer had with Penderecki in Zurich. First of all, the composer noted that 1956 had been a momentous year for all Polish composers. Travel restrictions to the West were finally lifted after more than a decade of closed borders, and the Warsaw Autumn International Festival of Contemporary Music, which brought together composers and music from Poland, Eastern and Western Europe, the Soviet Union, and the United States, also was inaugurated. At last, Polish composers were able to freely discover what had been happening in Western music in recent years.

On a different topic, Penderecki acknowledged that *Strophes* bore the influence of Boulez's *Improvisations sur Mallarmé*. However, he also said that his so-called avant garde works had been written in reaction both to the Darmstadt school of serialist composition and to the conservative music education that he had received. He described himself as a traditionalist who liked the music of Mahler, Bruckner and Sibelius. He also noted that religion had played an important role in his childhood life; this, in turn, had contributed to his lifelong interest in sacred music.

Zieliński, Tadeusz A. "Współczesny kompozytor a tradycja. Rozmowa z Krzysztofem Pendereckim" [Tradition and the Contemporary Composer. A Conversation with Krzysztof Penderecki]. *Ruch Muzyczny* 7, no. 12 (1963): pp. 8-9.

In response to Zieliński's questions, Penderecki expressed his belief that his compositions and those of many other contemporary composers were, at least in part, reflections of their predecessors. However, today's audiences focused more on discovering the modernist aspects of new works than on hearing any of their links to pieces written in earlier decades or centuries. He also contended that the music of Tchaikovsky, to name just one composer, contained many ideas about orchestration, dynamics and texture that were new for his time; thus, the "emancipation of tone color" that some critics had described as an innovative part of Penderecki's own music was not a new idea, but one rooted in the past. Likewise, his expansion of playing techniques and emphases on tone color and texture were not musical novelties, but could be connected directly to the musical practices of earlier composers.

Penderecki's ideas on musical form, counterpoint and 12-tone row technique were also discussed during this interview. Penderecki considered form to be the most important musical element: "Only the medium changes in music: the sound material and the method of making it. The general principles concerning the consistency of style in a work, the logic and economy of its progress . . . remain the same. The concept of what makes a good piece of music is exactly the same today as it was earlier." Finally, Penderecki noted that he taught counterpoint and 12-twelve technique to his students in Kraków because he thought they should learn to be disciplined composers.

Robinson, Ray. "Krzysztof Penderecki: An Interview and an Analysis of *Stabat Mater.*" *Choral Journal* 24, no. 3 (1983): pp. 7-16.

STYLISTIC COMMENTARY

Borris, Siegfried. "Pendereckis Stellung im Synkretismus der 60er Jahre" [Penderecki's Place in the Musical World of the 1960s]. *Musik und Bildung* 7, no. 12 (1975): pp. 609-14.

Borris divided Penderecki's career into four stylistic periods: revolutionary innovations (1957-1959), expansion and consolidation (1960-1963), intensification and affirmation (1964-1967) and retrograde trends (1968-1970, plus 1972). He briefly discussed the compositions that belonged to each category, relating them stylistically to the works of Ligeti, Kagel, Nono, and other contemporaries of Penderecki. His commentary revolved primarily around the instrumentation and timbres used in each piece.

Chłopicka, Regina. "Stylistic Phases in the Work of Krzysztof Penderecki." *Studies in Penderecki* 1 (1998): pp. 51-64.

It is Chłopicka's contention that Penderecki's large-scale vocal-instrumental works form the nucleus of his output. For each of these pieces - specifically, the operas and oratorios - Penderecki created a "cohesive musical language" that served to delineate a specific stylistic phase, while the instrumental works written at approximately the same time as each of these larger works acted "to anticipate, complement or conclude the consecutive stages" of his career. Chłopicka also observed that Penderecki's attitude towards form has remained basically stable, while other aspects of his music have undergone change, with the particular element being altered (sound, intervals, texture, etc.) differing according to the composer's interest at the time.

Having stated this, Chłopicka proceeded to discuss each of the seven stylistic periods that she perceived in Penderecki's output. She emphasized the dramaturgy and rhetorical gestures present in the major pieces of each period as she traced the evolution of his compositional style.

Erhardt, Ludwik. "Krzysztof Penderecki, twórca kultury polskiej" [Krzysztof Penderecki, Creator of Polish Culture]. *Tygodnik Kulturalny* 11, no. 20 (1967): p. 3. Also published in a translated, abridged version in "Krzysztof Penderecki." *Polish Perspectives* 11, nos. 8-9 (1968): pp. 44-46.

According to Erhardt, the originality of Penderecki's music stemmed from the composer's treatment of sound, which has been used "without its traditional melodic and harmonic props, even without any serial arrangement." Penderecki's primary innovations in this field have been the development of non-traditional uses for string instruments and the expansion of vocal sonorities and articulations. Penderecki considered his new string techniques to be "an extension of their natural sounds - just as was once the case with *pizzicato, tremolando . . .*" Regardless of the sound materials used, however, he believed that all successful compositions must embrace a clear, logical form. (Quotes are from *Polish Perspectives*.)

Kałużny, Jan A. "Krzysztof Penderecki and His Contribution to Modern Musical Notation." *Polish Review* 8, no. 3 (1963): pp. 86-95.

Kałużny took as his premise the idea that modern composition had outgrown the limitations of the conventional notational system. Penderecki was one composer who succeeded in reforming that system. His notation is based on divisions of time rather than metrical bar lines. Durations are determined by the lengths of horizontal lines, tone clusters are written graphically as horizontal bars of varying widths and lengths, and vibrato speeds are indicated by sinusoid lines. Kałużny concluded his article by discussing some of the timbral innovations found in *Anaklasis, Threnody* and *Dimensions of Time and Silence.*

Kostrzewska, Hanna. "Zagadnienie sonoryzmu na przykładzie twórczości kompozytorów polskich" [The Question of Sonorism in the Compositions of Polish Composers]. *Muzyka* 36, no. 1 (1991): pp. 83-93.

Kostrzewska defined sonorism as "the domination of a given element [that] causes the emergence of a value of a higher order. (For example, [musical] movement is not a value in and of itself, but the means to creating a [certain] quality of sound). The primary factor in determining sonoristic quality is color, linked here with the source of sound - in other words, with the selection of material used as a point of departure. On the other hand, rhythm, harmony, dynamics, articulation, and tone color [also] can, to an equal degree, create sonoristic structures." She linked the origins of sonorism to Byzantine and Medieval performance practice, then traced its development through the works of Debussy, Schoenberg, and Cowell to Cage, and, in Polish music, to Szymanowski, Panufnik and Bacewicz.

After this introduction to sonorism, Kostrzewska devoted the remainder of the article to a compendium of the sonoristic techniques that appeared in Polish compositions from 1956 to 1980. Penderecki's pieces were cited for their extended instrumental and vocal techniques, extreme dynamic effects, tone clusters and innovative rhythms.

Moor, Paul. "Krzysztof Penderecki. Polens Größter seit Chopin?" [Krzysztof Penderecki. Poland's Greatest Composer since Chopin?] *Der Monat* 22, no. 264 (September 1970): pp. 86-93.

Although Moor never answered the question posed in his title, he did acknowledge his admiration for Penderecki's music and his friendship with the composer. During the course of the article, Moor reviewed Penderecki's childhood, his early influences of Schoenberg and Boulez, his popularity in both Poland and the West, and his methods of composing.

Among the tidbits of information that Moor imparted is the story of why Penderecki had created the graphic notation that appears in his early works, how Penderecki had expanded upon the tone clusters used by Ives and Cowell, and why he had chosen to imitate the sound of a streetcar in *Threnody*.

Müller, Karl-Joseph. "Pendereckis Musik im mobilen Netz trigonometrischer Punkte" [Penderecki's Music in a Mobile Web of Trigonometric Points]. *Musik und Bildung* 7, no. 12 (December 1975): pp. 622-31.

Müller took as his point of departure the concept of a "mobile network of trigonometrical points." In Penderecki's music these points include notation, sound, form, aesthetics, and reception. Müller chose to discuss the ideas of sound and reception in further detail. Using examples from *Anaklasis, De natura sonoris no. 2,* the Cello Sonata, *Dimensions of Time and Silence,* and the Second String Quartet, Müller demonstrated how Penderecki's music differed from Ligeti's, and how it explored the boundary between musical sound and noise.

Müller also quoted the composer as opposing the use of open form, which led to his own discussion of how new music is received by listeners. In his opinion, "the comprehensibility of music is connected closely with its effect and success." Is Penderecki's music comprehensible? Yes, it is, according to Müller, who referred to the First Symphony and its popular acclaim as proof. He also mentioned the *St Luke Passion* and *Utrenia* as examples of pieces exhibiting successful receptive models.

Nikolska, Irina. "O ewolucji twórczości instrumentalnej Krzysztofa Pendereckiego" [The Evolution of Penderecki's Instrumental Compositions]. *Muzyka* 32, no. 1 (1987): pp. 31-53.

In this lengthy essay on the evolution of Penderecki's compositional style, Nikolska touched on several important points. First, she noted that Penderecki's music was intensely emotional and often based on the concepts of the greatness of humanity, the tragedy of war, or other aspects of human life. Next, she stressed the composer's faithfulness to the customary rules of form and drama in composition, even while changing other aspects of his musical style. Finally, she divided his works into three periods (1958-1962, 1964-1973, 1974-) and discussed his stylistic evolution in detail.

Orga, Ates. "Penderecki: Composer of Martyrdom." *Music and Musicians* 18, no. 1 (September 1969): pp. 34-38, 76.

In this extensive article, Orga reviewed the history of socialist realism in Polish music and provided a short biography of Penderecki. He then sketched a line of development and influence in Penderecki's music by exploring the composer's graphic notation, microtonality, innovative sonorities and textures, and dramatic expressiveness.

Rappoport-Gelfand, Lidia. "Sonorism: Problems of Style and Form in Modern Polish Music." *Journal of Musicological Research* 4 (1983): pp. 399-416.

Sonorism in Polish music is a concept first proposed - according to Rappoport - in the 1950s by Józef Chominski. Rappoport defined it as "a special system of musical means, where the sound coloristics functions as the primary factor of a composition. The concept of sound coloristics includes such aspects of musical language as timbre, harmony, register and texture." In her opinion, sonorism has been a major characteristic of Polish music since 1955, particularly in the works of Serocki, Górecki and Penderecki. In the latter's music, sonorism has been used to "create acute, dramatic expression." In *Threnody*, for example, the composer used sonoristic means to evoke a threnody, or funeral chant, while the incorporation of sirens, electric bell and typewriter into *Fluorescences* strengthened the "intense dramatic heat" of that composition.

Robinson, Ray. "Penderecki's Musical Pilgrimage." *Studies in Penderecki* vol. I (1998): pp. 33-50.

Robinson began his discussion of Penderecki's stylistic periods by citing the composer's own opinions on the topic, which have changed several times over the years. Robinson took Penderecki's comments into consideration as he divided the composer's output into six stylistic "phases" (search: 1956-1959, sonorism: 1959-1961, synthesis: 1962-1972, sophistication: 1972-1974, synchronization: 1975-1986, and stabilization: 1986-), then merged them into three "style periods" (search, synthesis, and stability) and, finally, into one over-arching compositional signature. In characterizing each phase, Robinson discussed the following attributes: rhythm, pitch, melody, harmony, tonality, texture, form, instrumentation, and extra-musical influences. He also acknowledged the overlapping that has occurred between phases, since Penderecki has not followed a direct line of stylistic development in his music.

Schwinger, Wolfram. "The Changes in Four Decades: The Stylistic Paths of Krzysztof Penderecki." *Studies in Penderecki* vol. I (1998): pp. 65-82.

Schwinger noted the existence of five stylistic periods in Penderecki's compositional career: preludes (1951-1958), explosions (1959-1961), consolidations (1962-1974), retrospectives (1974-1980) and synthesis (1980-). Sound materials and musical structures in the larger instrumental and choral-instrumental works are the primary focus of his discussion. With respect to the avant garde works, he spoke of their "micro-organic inner life . . . highly complex sound-effect structures . . . [and] noise" that is used to "the pinnacle of excess."

---. "Magische Klanglandschaften - Krzysztof Penderecki und die polnische Avantgarde" [The Magical Land of Sound Creation - Krzysztof Penderecki and the Polish Avant Garde]. *Musica* 22, no. 1 (1968): pp. 4-7.

After describing the explosion of musical activity that occurred in Poland beginning in 1956, Schwinger turned to the compositions of Penderecki, that country's "most brilliant talent." The composer's early exploration of the distinctions between sound and noise led him to write the *St Luke Passion*, whose première has become "a date in music history."

Of particular interest to Schwinger were Penderecki's experiments with sound and noise. Schwinger also saw a line of development between certain elements as they occurred in *Psalms of David* and then reappeared in the *St Luke Passion*. He also described other links between the *Psalms* and Stravinsky's *Les Noces* and *Symphony of Psalms*. In Schwinger's view, *Fluorescences* marked the culmination of Penderecki's research into sound.

Tomaszewski, Mieczysław. "Penderecki's Dialogues and Games with Time and Place on Earth." *Studies in Penderecki* vol. I (1998): pp. 13-32.

This article is a translation of the fourth essay of Tomaszewski's *Krzysztof Penderecki I jego muzyka. Cztery eseje* (Kraków: Akademia Muzyczna, 1994). The author devoted the majority of the article to a discussion of what he perceived as the six stylistic phases of Penderecki's compositions: effective entry (1958-1960), time of trials and experiments (1960-1966), breakthrough and the first synthesis (1965-1971), years of sublimation (1971-1975), dialog with the rediscovered past (1976-1985), and threshold of new synthesis (1985-1993). He described the major works included in each of these phases, emphasizing their links to tradition, their "conceptual program," and their emotional impact.

Zieliński, Tadeusz. A. "Der einsame Weg des Krzysztof Penderecki" [The Solitary Path of Krzysztof Penderecki]. *Melos* 29, no. 4 (September 1962): pp. 318-23.

Zieliński provided a clear summary of Penderecki's musical style to date. In his opinion, the composer abandoned the traditional treatment of melody, harmony, rhythm, and pitch in order to concentrate on tone color and explore the boundary between musical sound and noise.

Zieliński briefly described some of the innovations found in *Anaklasis, Dimensions of Time and Silence* and *Fluorescences*. He stressed that Penderecki did not view the development of new sounds as a goal in itself, but rather as an opportunity to enrich his vocabulary for the purposes of musical development.

---. "Świat dźwiękowy Krzysztofa Pendereckiego" [Krzysztof Penderecki's Sound World]. In *Spotkania z muzyką współczesną*, pp. 68-82. Kraków: Polskie Wydawnictwo Muzyczne, 1975.

In this article, originally written in 1962, Zieliński considered the changes in compositional style and technique already apparent in Penderecki's short career. He began by discussing dynamics and instrumentation in *Anaklasis*, the composer's first piece "in a new style." From there he described timbre in *Dimensions of Time and Silence*, new methods of treating string instruments in *Threnody*, new sound sources in *Canon* and *Psalmus 1961*, and the synthesis of these elements in *Fluorescences*. Finally, he made a distinction between Penderecki's "neoimpressionistic" and "expressive" works. The former, which include *Strophes, Dimensions of Time and Silence*, String Quartet No. 1, and *Fluorescences*, are based on "tender and charming sounds," while the latter (*Anaklasis, Threnody, Psalmus*, and others) are more aggressive in spirit.

---. "Technika operowania instrumentami smyczkowymi w utworach Krzysztofa Pendereckiego" [String Techniques in the Works of Krzysztof Penderecki]. *Muzyka*, no. 1 (1968): pp. 74-92.

Zieliński examined the role of the string instruments in *Threnody*, String Quartet No. 1, *Polymorphia*, *Canon*, *Anaklasis*, and *Fluorescences*. In his opinion, these pieces feature Penderecki's most novel compositional ideas, as the composer abandoned traditional ideas about scales and functional harmony in order to develop a new world of sounds. He took particular advantage of the fact that many different colors could be obtained on the string instruments by using varied means of articulation.

Zieliński divided the main portion of his discussion into the areas of "material," "sound forms" (lines, clusters, and individual points of sound), "layers" (combinations of lines, clusters, and points) and "form." Under the heading of "materials," he elaborated upon Penderecki's notational system. Glissandos, discussed under "sound forms," were used to create the movement of lines and were functional rather than ornamental. Clusters were differentiated according to their thickness and duration, with their internal intervallic structure varying from quarter-tones to whole-tones. Zieliński compared the layering of lines and clusters in Penderecki's music to the different melodic lines in more traditional polyphonic textures. Finally, the form of these early pieces depended primarily on the juxtaposition or opposition of different sounds and layerings, although formal designs following a more evolutionary process were also used.

Linthicum, David Howell. "Penderecki's Notation: A Critical Evaluation." *Choral Journal* 15, no. 4 (1974): p. 32.

Müller, Karl-Joseph. "Traditionnelles bei Penderecki" [Tradition and Penderecki]. *Orchester* 20, nos. 7-8 (1972): pp. 377-80. Also published in *Musik und Bildung* 4, no. 5 (May 1972): pp. 234-37.

Orga, Ates. "Krzysztof Penderecki." *The Listener* (London), May 18, 1967, p. 664.

Pociej, Bohdan. "Krzysztof Penderecki - en traditionell kompositör" [Krzysztof Penderecki - A Traditional Composer]. *Nutida musik* 9, nos. 1-2 (1965-1966): pp. 15-18.

Schiller, Henry. "Po prawykonaniu *Wymiarów czasu i ciszy* Krzysztofa Pendereckiego" [After the World Première of Penderecki's *Dimensions of Time and Silence*]. *Ruch Muzyczny* 4, no. 21 (1960): p. 5.

Wallek-Walewski, Marian. "W kręgu poszukiwań materiałowych - Krzysztof Penderecki" [Krzysztof Penderecki - In Search of Material]. *Ruch muzyczny* 4, no. 17 (1960): pp. 1-2.

Individual Works (in Chronological Order)

Emanations

Rychlik, Józef. "Punktualizm we wczesnej twórczości Krzysztofa Pendereckiego" [Pointillism in Penderecki's Early Compositions]. *Muzyka* 21, no. 4 (1976): pp. 5-21.

Rychlik described the 12-tone technique used in *Emanations* and the pointillist qualities of that piece and *Strophes*. In *Emanations* Penderecki displaced individual pitches of the 12-tone row by one or more octaves in order to produce a pointillist texture. With regard to *Strophes*, Rychlik noted that the entire work was set in a pointillist texture. Penderecki paid particular attention to the text setting of the same piece, with the rhythmic and dramatic accentuations of the music closely matching those of the text. Rychlik also mentioned that nearly every note of this predominantly syllabic text setting had a different dynamic marking.

Psalms of David

Gąsiorowska, Małgorzata. "K. Penderecki - *Psalmy Dawida* na chór mieszany i perkusję" [K. Penderecki - the *Psalms of David* for Mixed Chorus and Percussion]. In *Współczesność i tradycja w muzyce Krzysztofa Pendereckiego*, edited by Regina Chłopicka and Krzysztof Szwajgier, pp. 11-28. Kraków: Akademia Muzyczna, 1983.

Innovation co-exists with traditional means of expression in the *Psalms of David*. This work, which can be sung in Polish or Latin, was the first piece based on a religious theme that was composed by a Polish composer following the end of that country's socialist realist period in 1956. Gąsiorowska delineated the changes that Penderecki made to Kochanowski's poems and expounded on the strong link of the words to their musical setting.

Müller, Karl-Joseph. "Krzysztof Penderecki (1933): *Aus den Psalmen Davids* für gemischten Chor und Instrumental-Ensemble (1958)" [Krzysztof Penderecki (1933): From the *Psalms of David* for Mixed Chorus and Instrumental Ensemble (1958)]. In *Perspektiven Neuer Musik. Material und didaktische Information*, edited by Dieter Zimmerschied, pp. 201-214. Mainz: B. Schott's Söhne, 1974.

Recording information, excerpts from reviews by other writers, and a select bibliography encompass the central portion of this article, which is an analysis of the *Psalms of David*. Here Müller discussed Penderecki's serial technique, his incorporation of jazz and sacred musical elements into an otherwise overtly avant garde piece, and his text setting. Numerous musical examples and a German translation of the text are provided.

Herrmann, Horst Dietrich. "Krzysztof Penderecki: Aus den *Psalmen Davids*" [Krzysztof Penderecki: From the *Psalms of David*]. *Melos* 29, no. 4 (April 1962): p. 127.

Strophes

Orga, Ates. "Early Penderecki." *Musical Opinion* 91, no. 1085 (February 1968): pp. 267-71.

Orga took as his point of departure the February 1968 London performance of Penderecki's *Strophes* and First String Quartet. Before analyzing these two pieces, however, he briefly discussed Penderecki's career, asserting that the composer had chosen not to follow the path advanced by Stockhausen in the 1950s, and had opted instead to explore sound through the use of unusual instrumental and vocal techniques.

Strophes and the First String Quartet were given comparatively lengthy commentary. Orga described their extended playing techniques and novel notational solutions, as well as each piece's lack of conventional melodies and meters. Using score excerpts, he also discussed the relationship between certain melodic figures in *Strophes, De natura sonoris no. 1* and the Sonata for Cello and Orchestra.

Schiller, Henry. "Najmłodsza generacja kompozytorów polskich na III Międzynarodowym Festiwalu Muzyki Współczesnej 'Warszawska Jesień' " [The Youngest Generation of Polish Composers at the Third Warsaw Autumn International Festival of Contemporary Music]. Chapter 2 in *Horyzonty Muzyki*, edited by Józef Patkowski and Anna Skrzyńska. Kraków: Polskie Wydawnictwo Muzyczne, 1970.

In this article derived from an October 21, 1959 radio broadcast, Schiller described *Strophes* as having a serial, pointillist technique. He also mentioned several of its unusual vocal and instrumental techniques and briefly discussed its textual sources. Finally, he made a distinction between Penderecki's modernist features and those employed by Boulez, Stockhausen and Cage.

See also *Emanations*: Rychlik, Józef. "Punktualizm . . . ."

Stein, Leonard. "New Music on Mondays." *Perspectives of New Music* 2, no. 1 (Fall-Winter 1963): pp. 142-50.

Anaklasis

Dibelius, Ulrich. "Polnische Avantgarde" [The Polish Avant Garde]. *Melos* 34 (January 1967): 7-16. Also published in *Orchester* 15 (April 1967): pp. 147-54.

The première of *Anaklasis* at the Donaueschingen Music Days in 1960 caused a minor uproar. After hearing this piece, some in attendance predicted the end of music, while others spoke of its bold breakthroughs and "new humaneness." In Diblius' opinion, the work's success comes from its gradations and development of dynamics, articulation and tone color.

Dibelius also noted with interest that *Anaklasis* was composed after Penderecki began working at Poland's electronic music studio, and that around the same time as *Anaklasis's* emergence, Lutosławski was writing music that sounded similar to Penderecki's, at least superficially.

Gruhn, Wilfried. "Avantgarde - auf der Suche nach einer neuen Form" [The Avant Garde - A Search for a New Form]. *Orchester* 19, no. 1 (January 1971): pp. 5-8. Also published in *Musik und Bildung* 2, no. 10 (October 1970): pp. 481-84.

Gruhn juxtaposed the works of Ligeti and Penderecki in this essay about new means of creating form in music. He described Penderecki as a composer who successfully expanded the available spectrum of musical sounds by exploiting the area of noise. Many consider him to be a revolutionary composer because of the alienating impact of his new instrumental techniques. In Gruhn's opinion, however, these instrumental effects are integrated logically into his music. In *Anaklasis*, for example, both orchestration and thematic distinctions help to determine its form. As Gruhn put it, in this piece "new sounds are consolidated in a traditional form."

Huber, Alfred. "Pendereckis *Anaklasis* für Streicher und Schlagzeuggruppen" [Penderecki's *Anaklasis* for Strings and Percussion Groups]. *Melos* 38, no. 3 (March 1971): pp. 87-91. Also published in *Orchester* 19 (May 1971): pp. 239-43.

Huber presented an almost measure-by-measure analysis of *Anaklasis*. The work is in three large sections, with the first notated for strings alone in durations marked off in seconds. In describing this part, Huber discussed how its tone clusters are divided among the strings. The middle section, for percussion, uses a somewhat more traditional idea of metric notation, but introduces a tremendous amount of rhythmic complexity. The final section, for both strings and percussion, synthesizes both the notational systems and the different types of musical material.

Müller, Karl-Joseph. "Krzysztof Penderecki (1933): *Anaklasis* (1959-1960) für Streicher und Schlagzeuggruppen" [Penderecki's *Anaklasis* for Strings and Percussion Groups]. In *Perspektiven Neuer Musik. Material und didaktische Information*, edited by Dieter Zimmerschied, pp. 215-33. Mainz: B. Schott's Söhne, 1974.

Recording information, biographical data, excerpts from published reviews, and a brief bibliography form the peripheral portions of this article. Müller's main focus is a discussion of *Anaklasis*. Illustrating his points with numerous musical examples, he described the opposing roles of the strings and percussion and the counterpoint of surface sounds versus pointillistic settings. He also delineated the work's various notational devices.

____

Schuh, Willi. "Donaueschinger Musiktage 1960" [Donaueschingen Music Days 1960]. *Schweizerische Musikzeitung* 100, no. 6 (November/December 1960): pp. 370-71.

Stuckenschmidt, Hans H. "Ten Premieres." *Musical America* (January 1961): pp. 34, 148.

Wörner, Karl. "Germany." *Musical Quarterly* 47, no. 2 (1961): pp. 243-47.

Dimensions of Time and Silence

Schiller, Henry. "Z zagadnień faktury chóralnej współczesnej muzyki polskiej" [The Question of Texture in Contemporary Polish Choral Music]. *Ruch Muzyczny* 8, no. 3 (1964): pp. 8-9. Reprinted as Chapter 32 of *Horyzonty Muzyki*, edited by Józef Patkowski and Anna Skrzyńska. Kraków: Polskie Wydawnictwo Muzyczne, 1970.

Schiller's thesis is that contemporary music was moving towards the "automation of sonorities" or, in other words, an emphasis on sonoristic techniques. Penderecki's *Dimensions of Time and Silence* is an example of this trend. In this piece Penderecki introduced clusters of varying thicknesses and intensities, indications for highest and lowest possible pitches, and whistles. He also discarded the traditional metric system in favor of passages divided into seconds, which gave performers some flexibility in their entrances. A score excerpt from *Dimensions* is included.

Thomas, Ernst. "ISCM Meeting." *Musical America* 81 (September 1961): pp. 131-32.

Dimensions of Time and Silence, performed at the 35th ISCM Festival in Vienna, was described by Thomas as being "entertaining in a dangerously nonartistic manner which could end in the noise fetishism of the American dilettante, Cage." In the reviewer's opinion, the piece requires a vocal style that is neither singing nor speaking, and instrumental techniques that result in scraping and scratching sounds.

(ek.) "*Dimensionen der Zeit und der Stille* (Hermann Moeck Verlag, Celle)" [*Dimensions of Time and Silence* (Hermann Moeck Publishers, Celle]. *Melos* 4, no. 29 (December 1962): p. 411.

Olkuśnik, Joachim. "O IV Festiwalu Muzyki Współczesnej i nowej muzyce polskiej." [The Fourth Festival of Contemporary Music and New Polish Music]. *Współczesność*, no. 21 (November 1-15, 1960).

Threnody

Bilica, Krzysztof. "*Ofiarom Hiroszimy - Tren* Krzysztofa Pendereckiego. Próba analizy jednego z aspektów utworu" [*To the Victims of Hiroshima* - Krzysztof Penderecki's *Threnody*.An Attempt at Analyzing One Aspect of the Work]. *Muzyka* 19, no. 2 (1974): pp. 45-71.

This article is extracted from Bilica's Master's thesis, completed at the University of Warsaw in 1972. For this essay the author chose to focus on four features of *Threnody*: its wide range of pitches, its dynamic levels, its tone colors and its durations. Of particular analytical interest are Bilica's discussion of the three-note cells into which Penderecki divided his 12-note rows and the composer's use of hocket technique, which was created with tone colors rather than pitches.

---."Treści *Ofiarom Hiroszimy - Trenu* K. Pendereckiego" [The Essence of *Threnody to the Victims of Hiroshima* by K. Penderecki]. In *Współczesność i tradycja w muzyce Krzysztofa Pendereckiego*, edited by Regina Chłopicka and Krzysztof Szwajgier, pp. 29-40. Kraków: Akademia Muzyczna, 1983.

Bilica differentiated here between the use of symbols and signals in musical scores and performances, particularly with reference to Penderecki's compositions. He defined symbols as concrete signs, such as the names and durations of notes used in traditional notation. Signals correspond to the meanings attached to those symbols - for instance, to many listeners the notes B-A-C-H refer to, or signal, the acrostic spelling of the name of a famous composer.

While Bilica objected to the common perception that *Threnody* is a musical illustration of an atomic explosion, he did admit that the piece contained at least one signal. After describing ancient Greek laments, or threnodies, he suggested that, through its evocation of despair and mourning, *Threnody* was a signal of a musical lament - this despite its original abstract title of *8'37"*.

Gruhn, Wilfried. "Strukturen und Klangmodelle in Pendereckis *Threnos*" [Structure and Sound Models in Penderecki's *Threnody*]. *Melos* 38, no. 10 (1971): pp. 409-11.

In his analysis of *Threnody*, Gruhn examined the work's novel string techniques and notational signs as well as its formal structure. The latter consists generally of sections of clusters alternating with passages of canonic writing.

Rörich, Mary. "Penderecki's *Threnody for the Victims of Hiroshima*: A Case Study in the Dangers of Expressive Aesthetics and the Limits of Formal Analysis." In *Slavic Culture. Proceedings of the First Symposium on Slavic Culture*, edited by I. Masig-Delic, pp. 193-235. Johannesburg: University of the Witwatersrand, 1983.

In the first part of her essay, Rörich offered a brief history of aesthetics in music and discussed the hazards of equating verbal expressions of aesthetic feelings with one's true emotions about music. In her opinion, "music, like every other art, must be understood through its own intrinsic concept and syntax . . . [but] ironically, the same obstacles which impede the communication of the intrinsic expressiveness of the composition may distort the communication of its intellectual content."

The second half of the essay is concerned with *Threnody*. Rörich suggested that "the intrinsic expressiveness of Penderecki's work . . . [is] unquestionable. It is on this expressiveness that the listener should focus rather than the direct reference implied by the title." In order to appreciate the piece fully, both the expressive and analytical qualities of the piece must be "reintegrate[d] . . . into a total perception." To illustrate her thesis, she provided both visual and written analyses of the piece. The visual representation consists of a graph denoting the work's pitches, textures and durations.

Drew, James. "Information, Space, and a New Time-Dialetic." *Journal of Music Theory* 12, no. 1 (1968): pp. 98-99.

Helm, Everett. "Warschauer Herbst 1961 – Die neue polnische Schule" [The 1961 Warsaw Autumn Festival - The New Polish School]. *Neue Zeitschrift für Musik* 122, no. 11 (1961): pp. 467-68.

Spangemacher, Friedrich. "Hiroshima in der Musik. Bemerkungen zu einigen Kompositionen mit dem 'Thema' der nuklearen Bedrohung" [Hiroshima in Music. Remarks about Compositions Having the 'Theme' of Nuclear Assaults]. *Schweizerische Musikzeitung* 120, no. 2 (March/April 1980): pp. 78-88.

(W., K. W.) Ereignisreiche Festkonzerte [Eventful Festival Concerts]. *Musik und Gesellschaft* 15 (December 1965): pp. 855-58.

String Quartet No. 1

Bilica, Krzysztof. "Pozaekspresyjne porządki w Kwartecie Smyczkowym (Nr 1)" [Non-Expressive Systems in String Quartet No.1]. In *Współczesność i tradycja w muzyce Krzysztofa Pendereckiego*, edited by Regina Chłopicka and Krzysztof Szwajgier, pp. 72-77. Kraków: Akademia Muzyczna, 1983.

Bilica's search for mathematical constructs in the First String Quartet led to a discussion of both permutations of 3-note cells and a system of grouping notes under slur marks.

Jarzębska, Alicja. "Sonorystyczne środki wyrazu muzycznego w kwartetach smyczkowych XX wieku" [Sonoristic Means of Musical Expression in 20th-Century String Quartets]. *Muzyka* 26, nos. 3-4 (1981): pp. 47-64.

As part of her essay on sonorism in twentieth-century string quartets, Jarzębska described the various ways in which Penderecki treated timbre as the primary element of a composition. In particular, she mentioned the variety of percussive effects and shimmering atmospheres heard in the First String Quartet and the quarter-tone melodic movement present in the Second String Quartet.

See also *Strophes* - Orga, Ates. "Early Penderecki."

(fm.) "Tage für Neue Musik des Hessischen Rundfunks" [Hessian Radio New Music Days]. *Schweizerische Musikzeitung* 102, no. 5 (1962): pp. 306-307.

Zieliński, Tadeusz A. "Autumn and the Avant Garde." *Musical America* (December 1962): pp. 18-19.

Polymorphia

Joachim, Heinz. "Sind Geigen überholt?" [Are String Instruments Obselete?]. *Melos* 35 (April 1968): pp. 166-67. Also published in *Die Welt*, March 23, 1968.

Bavarian State Opera musicians balked at playing *Polymorphia* because of the piece's unorthodox playing techniques. As a compromise, the orchestra made a tape of the work to be used for its scheduled choreographed performances.

Joachim took the musicians' protest of Penderecki's piece as the starting point for his discussion. He conceded that musicians should not be expected to damage their expensive string instruments, but declared that Penderecki - himself a violinist - was not asking anyone to harm an instrument. He urged musicians and others to be open-minded about the question of sound vs. noise in music, and suggested that composers must be allowed to use their creative imaginations if Western music is to survive.

Kaczyński, Tadeusz. "*Polimorfia* Krzysztofa Pendereckiego" [Krzysztof Penderecki's *Polymorphia*]. *Ruch Muzyczny* 7, no. 22 (1963): pp. 17-18.

Of the five major compositions written by Penderecki between 1960 and 1962, Kaczyński considered *Polymorphia* to be the finest. Although its musical language was not new for the composer, its material was treated in a more "artistically mature manner" than had been the case in his earlier works. Kaczyński gave a brief analysis of *Polymorphia's* form and described Penderecki's use of form as "intuitive" - it did not adhere to a traditional scheme, yet its course of events was well-defined and logical.

Nordwall, Trygve. "Krzysztof Penderecki - studium notacji i instrumentacji" [Krzysztof Penderecki - A Study of Notation and Instrumentation]. Translated by Zofia Stankiewicz. *Res Facta* 2 (1968): pp. 79-112. Originally published as "Notation och Instrumentteknik i Krzysztof Pendereckis Verk samt en studio över Pendereckis' *Polymorphia*." (Trygve Nordwall, 1965).

The first part of Nordwall's essay provides details about notation and instrumentation in *Strophes, Emanations, Miniatures for Violin, Anaklasis, Dimensions of Time and Silence, Fluorescences, Threnody, Polymorphia* and String Quartet No. 1. The central portion is an in-depth analysis of *Polymorphia,* in which Nordwall examined that work's pitch structure, articulations and clock-time notation. In the final section, Nordwall discussed Penderecki's aesthetics, incorporating quotes from an interview with the composer in *Nutida Musik* ("Tonsattaren inför traditionen," no. 1 (1963/64), pp. 14-17). Among other things, the composer asserted that "the emancipation of tone color as an element of composition equal to all others has a long tradition . . . for example the symphonies of Tchaikovsky." He also asserted that a musical form in which "everything is new from beginning to end is not a form at all."

"Viel Staub um *Polymorphia.* Das Bayerische Staatsorchester und Pendereckis Ballettmusik" [Much Ado About *Polymorphia.* The Bavarian State Orchestra and Penderecki's Ballet Music]. *Das Orchester* 16 (June 1968): pp. 283-85. Also published in *Musikalische Jugend* 17, no. 2: p. 3.

Droba, Krzysztof. "Hierarchia czynników formalnych w twórczości Krzysztofa Pendereckiego (na przykładzie *Polimorfii*)" [The Hierarchy of Formal Factors in the Compositions of Krzysztof Penderecki (Using *Polymorphia* as an Example)]. *Muzyka* 21, no. 4 (1976): pp. 22-28.

Canon

Stuckenschmidt, Hans H. "Glissandos, Tontrauben, Elektronenschall in Warschau" [Glissandos, Tone Clusters, and Electronic Sounds in Warsaw].

Melos 29, no. 4 (November 1962): pp. 363-64.

In his review of the 1962 Warsaw Autumn Festival, Stuckenschmidt noted that Penderecki's *Canon* was the "most provocative" of the world premieres given at that event. In his opinion, the music of Varèse and Xenakis had paved the way for Penderecki's own ventures, which in this piece yielded an assortment of knocking, rubbing, and other unconventional means of producing sounds on string instruments. The audience's reaction was a mixture of applause and condemnation.

Zieliński, Tadeusz A. "O polskiej muzyce na Festiwalu. Dobrze i źle" [Polish Music at the (Warsaw Autumn) Festival. Good and Bad.] *Ruch muzyczny* 6, no. 22 (1962): pp. 3-5.

Penderecki's development of musical language has followed a consistent path. Initially, many listeners were shocked by its originality, but they quickly realized that it was also quite expressive. According to Zieliński, *Canon* is more complex and dramatic than *Threnody*. It is to be performed with loudspeakers placed at opposite sides of the room, which allows listeners to discern the work's three layers of sound.

Both *Canon* and String Quartet No. 1 were performed at the 1962 Warsaw Autumn Festival. With the latter piece, the string quartet literature has been expanded to include a work whose sounds were chosen chiefly for their coloristic qualities.

Pilarski, Bohdan. "Dziennik Festiwalowy" [The Festival Chronicle]. *Ruch Muzyczny* 6, no. 21 (1962): pp. 8-12. Also published in Pilarski, *Szkice o muzyce* [Sketches on Music], pp.40-50. Warszawa: Instytut Wydawniczy PAX, 1969.

Rozbicki, Kazimierz. "Na Festiwalu bez zmian" [The Festival, With No Changes]. *Ruch Muzyczny* 6, no. 22 (1962): pp. 9-10.

Fluorescences

Pütz, Werner. "Tendenzen in der Musik der Gegenwart und ihre Bedeutung für den Musikunterricht" [Tendencies in Contemporary Music and Their Significance for Music Education]. *Musik und Bildung* 3 (May 1971): pp. 235-42. Also published in *Orchester* 19, no. 6 (June 1971): pp. 294-301.

Among the pieces discussed by Pütz in this lengthy article was *Fluorescences*. After commenting on both its large, exotic collection of instruments and its non-traditional notational symbols, Pütz discussed its form in some detail. Differences between tension and relaxation and between similarity and variation were created by contrasts in timbre, sound density, rhythm and dynamics. By juxtaposing colors and materials, Penderecki effectively gave a spatial character to this piece. His treatment of rhythm looks back to the music of Debussy and Messiaen. Finally, the score itself is visually appealing.

Schuh, Willi. "Donaueschinger Musiktage 1962." [The 1962 Donaueschingen Music Days]. *Schweizerische Musikzeitung* 102, no. 6 (November/December 1962): pp. 363-64.

Fluorescences marked the continuation of Penderecki's experiments with "organized noise." With its addition of sirens, electric bells, whistles and other non-traditional instruments to a large array of winds, strings and percussion, clear sounds play a subordinate role to those belonging to the category of noise. *Fluorescences* should not, however, be linked to the futurist works of a half-century earlier. In a program note cited by Schuh, Penderecki defended his musical experiments by referring to Odo of Cluny's *Dialogus de musica*.

Zieliński, Tadeusz A. " *Fluorescencje* Krzysztofa Pendereckiego" [Krzysztof Penderecki's *Fluorescences*]. *Ruch Muzyczny* 7, no. 2 (1964): pp. 5-6. Also published in *Spotkania z muzyką współczesną*, 152-59 (Kraków: Polskie Wydawnictwo Muzyczne, 1975).

Fluorescences is "a clear example of Penderecki's revolutionary style." It contains new nuances of sounds, particularly in its treatment of the wind instruments and its use of such non-traditional sound sources as a typewriter and parchment paper. In the last portion of the article, Zieliński described the features of each of the work's six sections.

Joachim, Heinz and Hans Oesch. "Fünf Stimmen über Donaueschingen 1962: Krzysztof Penderecki. *Fluorescences* pour orchestre" [Five Voices about Donaueschingen 1962: Krzysztof Penderecki's *Fluorescences* for Orchestra]. *Melos* 29, no. 12 (December 1962): p. 397.

Lewinski, Wolf-Eberhard von. "Modernität und Qualität" [Modernity and Quality]. *Musica* 17, no. 1 (January-February 1963): pp. 29-30.

De natura sonoris no. 1

Hugli, Pierre. "Penderecki a l'OSR" [Penderecki and the Suisse Romande Orchestra]. *Schweizerische Musikzeitung* 109, no. 2 (1969): p. 95.

The Suisse Romande Orchestra performed *De natura sonoris no. 1* on one of its subscription concerts. Rhythmically and sonorically, the piece is reminiscent of electroacoustic music and Luigi Nono's "post-serial" compositions. Hugli thought the piece deserved a better performance than it received.

Samson, Jim. "Recent Polish Music." *Music and Letters* 62, nos. 3-4 (1981): pp. 478-81.

De natura sonoris no. 1 explores the use of timbre as a major structural element. Samson described the piece as "one-dimensional" but "exhilarating," and one that helped to put Polish music on the musical map.

(jk.) Kański, Józef. "Henryk Czyż i Bronisław Gimpel" [Henryk Czyż and Bronisław Gimpel]. *Ruch Muzyczny* 11, no. 5 (March 1-15, 1967): p. 15.

String Quartet No. 2

Stuckenschmidt, Hans. H. "Westberliner Festwochen zwischen Fracks und Blue jeans" [West Berlin Festival Week, Between Evening Dress and Blue Jeans]. *Melos* 37, no. 12 (December 1970): pp. 512-13.

The première of Penderecki's Second String Quartet was presented by the Parrenin Quartet to "a handful of listeners." The 10-minute piece employs narrow intervals, rough sounds, and "scurrying figures" within a primitive formal plan.

See also String Quartet No. 1: Jarzębska, "Sonorystyczne środki."

De natura sonoris No. 2

Lawton, David. "Krzysztof Penderecki: *De natura sonoris No. 2* (1971)." *MLA Notes* 30, no. 4 (June 1974): pp. 865-66.

Lawton pointed out several of the features that make *De natura sonoris no. 2* a successful work. In particular, he noted that long pedal tones usually indicate a "point of crisis" in the dramatic structure of Penderecki's compositions and that the piece's unusual timbres are not there merely for the sake of creating noise, but have an important musical function.

Symphony No. 1

Erhardt, Ludwik. "I Symfonia. Świadectwo ewolucji" [Symphony No. 1. Certificate of Evolution]. *Ruch Muzyczny* 17, no. 23 (1973): pp. 5-6.

Erhardt began by providing information about the world, Polish, East German, and British premieres of Penderecki's First Symphony. He then noted that critics had greeted the symphony with a full range of opinions, ranging from "contempt, [and] . . . disgust, [to] moderate praise, to praise and enthusiasm." Most criticism was directed towards the fact that a British firm, Perkins Engines, had commissioned a piece from a Polish composer rather than from a British one - a foreshadowing of the controversy that erupted in the United States over the commissioning of *Paradise Lost*.

Admittedly, this piece was quite different from Penderecki's earlier works, particularly in terms of its form and orchestration. This was also Penderecki's first lengthy instrumental piece. According to Erhardt, it is also the first one in which the experiences Penderecki had gained from conducting had played a role in the actual composition of the piece.

Erhardt briefly described the Symphony's form and pitch structure, then commented that this piece exhibited less emotionalism and more intellectualism than had the composer's previous works.

Malecka, Teresa. "I Symfonia" [Symphony No. 1]. In *Współczesność i tradycja w muzyce Krzysztofa Pendereckiego*, edited by Regina Chłopicka and Krzysztof Szwajgier, pp. 176-86. Kraków: Akademia Muzyczna, 1983.

Malecka analyzed Penderecki's First Symphony as a sonata-form movement, complete with two contrasting themes, a development, a recapitulation, and a quasi tonic-dominant harmonic scheme. This form overlays the four sections that Penderecki indicated in the score (Arché 1, Dynamis 1, Dynamis 2, and Arché 2). Malecka devoted the majority of her article to a detailed explanation of the intricacies of this particular sonata-form movement. She concluded by stating that the Symphony was a pivotal work, since it was positioned between two different stylistic periods in the composer's career.

Orga, Ates. "Krzysztof Penderecki." *Music & Musicians* 22, no. 2 (1973): pp. 38-41.

Orga began by mentioning upcoming recordings of Penderecki's music, then briefly reviewed the composer's career to date. The central portion of the article consisted of quotations by Penderecki. The composer refuted the oft-repeated claims that he had been influenced by Xenakis and Stockhausen. In fact, he stated that he did not care for the music of either composer, although he did admire Bach, Tchaikovsky, Berlioz and Renaissance composers Obrecht, Ockeghem and Josquin. He explained his ideas about composition by emphasizing that every piece must have a logical development. When preparing a new work, he plans all the details about its form before writing its actual notes. He also is concerned with "the notion of harmonic tension and the way certain combinations of pitch will react."

With the use of Penderecki's hand-drawn diagrams, Orga described the form of the First Symphony. He then quoted from several British critics who had already reviewed the First Symphony, and commented that "however we may respond to Penderecki's music, we cannot remain unaffected one way or the other. . . . Any composer capable of arousing such attention deserves all our consideration."

Schiffer, Brigitte. "Englische Firmen, englische Orchester und englische Festivals vergeben Kompositionsaufträge." [A Commission for a Composition Is Given Away to an English Company, an English Orchestra, and an English Festival]. *Melos* 40, no. 6 (June 1973): pp. 375-83.

Penderecki's First Symphony, commissioned by Perkins Engines, was premiered at the Peterborough Cathedral. In one movement, the piece moves through five [*sic*] sections, using material derived predominantly from sound effects. These effects, which to some critics signified a link with the Perkins factory, were similar to those used by Penderecki in *Anaklasis* and *Fluorescences,* among other works. According to Schiffer, the piece is enjoyable more on a sensual level than on a technical one. The London Symphony Orchestra's performance was met with lengthy applause.

Griffiths, Paul. "Penderecki." *Musical Times* 114, no. 1570 (December 1973): p. 1255.

Orga, Ates. "London Premieres." *Music and Musicians* 22, no. 4 (December 1973): p. 68.

Peterson, Melody. "Los Angeles Philharmonic: Penderecki Premiere." *High Fidelity/Musical America* 25, no. 5 (1975): MA22.

Sandow, Gregory. "Faking It." *Village Voice,* July 3, 1984: pp. 88-89.

Index of Penderecki's Works

Index of Names

S

T

List of Penderecki's Works

1953* Sonata for Violin and Piano (No. 1)

1955 Two songs for voice and piano: *Cisza* [Silence], *Niebo w nocy* [Sky at night], text by Leopold Staff (unpublished)

1957 String Quartet (unpublished)

1956 *Three Miniatures* for clarinet and piano

1958 Two songs for voice and piano: *Oddech nocy* [The Breath of Night], text by Leopold Staff; *Prośba o wyspy szczęśliwe* [A Plea for the Happy Isles], text by Konstanty Ildefons Gałczyński (unpublished)

1958 *Epitaphium Artur Malawski in memoriam* for string orchestra and timpani (unpublished)

1958 *Psalms of David* for mixed choir and percussion

1958 *Emanations* for 2 string orchestras

1959 *Strophes* for soprano, speaker and 10 instruments

1959 *Miniatures* for violin and piano

1960 *Anaklasis* for 42 strings and percussion

1960 *Dimensions of Time and Silence* for mixed choir, strings and percussion

1960 *Threnody to the Victims of Hiroshima* for 52 strings

1960* String Quartet No. 1

1961 *Fonogrammi* for flute and chamber orchestra

1961 *Psalmus 1961* for tape

1961 *Polymorphia* for 48 string instruments

1962 *Air and Two Minuets* for string orchestra

1962 *Canon* for string orchestra and 2 tape recorders

1962 *Fluorescences* for orchestra

1962 *Stabat Mater* for 3 mixed choirs *a cappella* (later incorporated into the *St Luke Passion*)

1963 *Brigade of Death* for speaker and tape

1964 *Cantata in honorem Almae Matris Universitatis Iagellonicae sescentos abhinc annos fundatae* for mixed choir and orchestra

1964 Sonata for Cello and Orchestra

1964 *Capriccio* for oboe and 11 strings

1966 *Passio et mors Domini nostri Iesu Christi secundum Lucam* for soloists, speaker, boys' choir, 3 mixed choirs and symphony orchestra

1966 *De natura sonoris No. 1* for symphony orchestra

1967 *Dies irae oratorium ob memoriam in perniciei castris in Oświęcim necatorum inexstingubilem reddendam* for soloists, mixed choir and orchestra

1967 Concerto for Violino Grande and Orchestra (unpublished)
(later incorporated into Concerto for Violoncello and Orchestra No. 1)

1967 Concerto for Cello and Orchestra No. 1 (revised 1971-72)

1967 *Pittsburgh Overture* for Wind Orchestra

1967 *Capriccio* for violin and orchestra

1968 *Capriccio per Siegfried Palm* for violoncello solo

1968 String Quartet No. 2

1969 *The Devils of Loudun*, opera in 3 acts; libretto by the composer based on Aldous Huxley with the stage play by John Whiting

1970 *Utrenia I. The Entombment of Christ* for soloists, 2 mixed choirs and orchestra

1970/1 *Utrenia II. The Resurrection* for soloists, 2 mixed choirs and orchestra

1970* *Cosmogony* for soloists, mixed choir and orchestra

1971* *De natura sonoris No. 2* for symphony orchestra

1971 *Prelude* for winds, percussion and contrabasses

1971 *Actions* for free jazz orchestra

1972* *Partita* for concertante harpsichord, electric guitar, bass guitar, harp, contrabasses and orchestra (revised 1991)

1972 *Ecloga VIII* for six male voices

1972 *Ekecheiria* for tape

1973 *Canticum canticorum Salomonis* for 16-part vocal ensemble and orchestra

1973 Symphony No. 1

1973 *Intermezzo* for 24 strings

1974 *The Awakening of Jacob* for orchestra

1974 *Magnificat* for bass solo, 7 male voices, 2 mixed choirs, boys' choir and orchestra

1977 Concerto for Violin and Orchestra (No. 1); revised in 1988

1978* *Paradise Lost – sacra rappresentazione*, opera in 2 acts; librettto by Christopher Fry based on John Milton

1979 *Adagietto* from *Paradise Lost*

1979 *Prologue, Visions and Finale* from *Paradise Lost*

1980*. Symphony No. 2 "Christmas Symphony"

1980 *Capriccio* for tuba solo

1980 *Te Deum* for soloists, 2 mixed choirs and orchestra

1980 *Lacrimosa* for soprano solo, mixed choir and symphony orchestra (later incorporated into the *Polish Requiem*)

1981 *Agnus Dei* for mixed choir *a cappella*

(later incorporated into the *Polish Requiem*)

1981 *Czyś ty snem była?* [Were you but a dream?], song for baritone and piano (unpublished)

1982 Concerto for Cello and Orchestra No. 2

1983 Concerto for Viola and Orchestra

(version for viola/violoncello/clarinet, strings, percussion and celesta, 1984)

1984 *Cadenza* for viola solo (violin version by Christiane Edinger , 1986)

1984 *Polish Requiem* for soloists, mixed choir and orchestra (composed 1980 to 1984; *Sanctus* movement added in 1993)

1986 *Die schwarze Maske* [*The Black Mask*] opera in one act; libretto by the composer and Henry Kupfer based on Gerhart Hauptmann

1986 *Per Slava* for violoncello solo

1986* *The Song of Cherubim* for mixed choir *a cappella*

1987 *Prelude* for clarinet solo

1987 *Veni Creator* for mixed choir *a cappella*

1988 *Der unterbrochene Gedanke* for string quartet

1988 *Passacaglia and Rondo* for symphony orchestra

1989 *Adagio*. Symphony No. 4

1991 *Ubu Rex* [*Ubu King*], opera buffa; libretto by Jerzy Jarocki and Krzysztof Penderecki based on the play *Ubu roi* of Alfred Jarry

1991 String Trio

1991 *Sinfonietta* No. 1 for string orchestra (version of the String Trio)

1992 *Benedicamus Domino* for 5-part male choir *a cappella*

1992 Symphony No. 5 "Korean"

1992 Concerto for Flute and Chamber Orchestra (version for clarinet and chamber orchestra, 1995)

1993 *Benedictus* for mixed choir *a cappella*

1993 Quartet for clarinet and string trio

1994 *Musik from Ubu Rex* for symphony orchestra

1994 *Sinfonietta* No. 2 for clarinet and string orchestra (version of the Quartet for clarinet and string trio)

1994* *Entrata* for brass instruments

1994 *Agnus Dei* (from the *Polish Requiem*); setting for string orchestra

1994 *Divertimento* for violoncello solo

1995 Concerto for Violin and Orchestra No. 2 "Metamorphoses"

1995 *Agnus Dei* from the *Requiem der Versohnung* [*Requiem for Reconciliation*] for soloists, mixed choir and orchestra

1988-95 Symphony No. 3 (incorporating the movements of the *Passacaglia* and *Rondo*)

1996 *The Seven Gates of Jerusalem.* Symphony No. 7 for soloists, speaker, 3 mixed choirs and symphony orchestra

1996 *Passacaglia* per archi

1997 *Hymn to Saint Daniil* for mixed choir and orchestra

1997 *Hymn to Saint Adalbert* for mixed choir and orchestra

1997 *Serenada* for string orchestra

1997 *Credo* for soloists, mixed choir, boys' choir and orchestra

1998 *Luzerner Fanfare* for 8 trumpets and percussion

1998 *De Profundis* (from *Seven Gates of Jerusalem*); setting for string orchestra

1999 *3 Cadenzas* to the Concerto for Trumpet and Orchestra in Eb of Franz Joseph Haydn

1999 Sonata for Violin and Piano No. 2

2000 Sextet for clarinet, horn, string trio and piano

2000 *Musik* for block flute, marimbaphone, percussion and strings

2001 *Concerto grosso* for 3 cellos and orchestra

2002* Concerto for Piano and Orchestra "The Resurrection"

2002 *Benedictus* for equal voices *a cappella*

2003 *Largo* for cello and orchestra

*Works that received a premiere performance in the United States

Contributors

Michelle Biget-Mainfroy, Professor at the University of Tours (France), is a musicologist and pianist specializing in 19th-century music. He has published *L'écriture pianis-tique romantique, Musique et révolution française : la longue durée,* and *Le rêve et la fureur* (romantic musical writing). Co-editor of the journal *Les Cahiers du CIREM* (International Center for Research on Musical Aesthetics).

Cindy Bylander received her Ph.D. in musicology from The Ohio State University and now resides in San Antonio, Texas. Her research specialty is post-World War II Polish music, particularly the Warsaw Autumn Festival and the music of Krzysztof Penderecki. She has published in *Fontes Artes Musicae, Ruch myzyczny,* and *American Record Guide.* Her book on Krzysztof Penderecki: *A Bio-Bibliography* is forthcoming from Greenwood Press.

Pierre Albert Castanet, a composer and musicologist, is Professor at the University of Rouen (Normandy) and the Conservatoire National Supérieur de Musique in Paris. He has published numerous books (on Scelsi, Dufourt, Louvier, and Levinas), as well as hundreds of articles on the history and analysis of post-1945 music. Director of the European Laboratory for the Social History of Contemporary Music and editor of the journal *Les Cahiers du CIREM* (International Center for Research on Musical Aesthetics), he won the "Prix des Muses" for his book *Tout est bruit pour qui a peur; pour une histoire sociale du son sale* (Paris: Michel de Maule). In March 2003, he interviewed Krzysztof Penderecki at the Polish embassy in Paris for the *Décibels* program on France Culture radio (Radio France-Paris).

Ĺubomír Chalupka, Slovak musicologist, is Professor at the Department of Musicology of Comenius University in Bratislava, Slovakia. As a teacher and researcher, he focuses on music theory and the development of and style problems of Slovak music of the 20th century. Participant of international musicological conferences in Slovakia and abroad. Publishes analytic studies in Slovak ("Hudobný zivot," "Slovenská hudba"), Czech ("Hudební veda") music periodicals and Congress reports. Book: *Dejiny slovenskej hudby* [History of Slovak music], Bratislava 1996 (joint-author).

Andrzej Chłopecki, a musicologist and music critic. Since 1976, with a break from 1982 to 1991, he has programmed contemporary music on Polish Radio. Since 1994, he has represented that broadcaster on the International Composers' Tribunal of the UNESCO International Music Council in Paris. He has commissioned more than 100 works by Polish and foreign composers as head of contemporary music at Polish Radio, a board member of the Polish section of the International Contemporary Music Association, a staff member at Polish Music Publishers in Cracow, and a member of the Warsaw Autumn festival program commission. Over 20 works have been dedicated to him. From 1987 to 1993, he worked with DeutschlendFunk radio in Cologne, and he has belonged to the program board of the journal MusikTexte in the same city since 1989. He was a member of the jury of the Masterprize composers' competition in 2002, and has published over 500 texts in Poland and elsewhere.

Regina Chłopicka, music theorist, is Professor at the Academy of Music in Kraków, Poland. Her publications, which number over 50 (e.g. *Krzysztof Penderecki: Musica sacra-Musica Profana. A Study of Vocal-Instrumental Works,* Warsaw: IAM, 2003), span three research fields: Polish contemporary music in the context of European music (the oeuvre of Penderecki, Lutosławski), topos of death in music (the Passion and Requiem genres), and 20th-century musical theatre in the context of history and theory of the theatre. Her articles were published in collaboration with such research institutions as CNRS Paris, *Les Cahiers du CIREM* Tours, Duquesne University Pittsburgh and University of Leipzig. She participated in numerous international conferences and research projects (e.g. sponsored by European Science Foundation) and has been Co-Editor of *Studies in Penderecki* research series (1998 Princeton). She has been Dean of Faculty of Composition, Conducting and Theory of Music; lecturer running seminars both in Poland: e.g. Warszawa, Poznań, Lublin and abroad, e.g. École Normale Supérieure in Paris, Université F. Rabelais Tours, International Bach Academy Eugene, Oregon; member of e.g. Polish Composers Association, Société Française d'Analyse Musicale, Société Internationale d'Histoire Comparée du Théâtre, de l'Opéra et du Ballet.

Erik Christensen is a Danish musicologist, specialized in music listening. He works for the Danish Broadcasting Corporation as an editor of contemporary music programs and is currently active as a guest lecturer in universities and music academies in Europe and America. In 1996, he published *The Musical Timespace. A Theory of Music Listening.*

Michał Głowiński is a literary theoretician and historian, and a Professor at the Literary Research Institute of the Polish Academy of Sciences. Main research interests: the history and theory of the narrative form (e.g. *Gry powieściowe* [Novel games], 1973); issues of literary communication (e.g. *Style odbioru* [Styles of reception], 1977); the fate of the signs and symbols of European culture in 20th-century literature (*Mity przebrane* [Myths dressed up], 1990); the analysis of the deformation of language and art within the sociopolitical reality of "real socialism" (e.g. *Nowomowa po polsku* [Polish newspeak], 1990, *Marcowe gadanie* [March talk], 1991, *Rytuał i demagogia* [Ritual and demagogy], 1992). His *Collected Works* appeared in five volumes between 1997 and 2000. He is also the author of *The Black Seasons,* a Holocaust memoir (to be published in English in 2003).

Rūta Goštautienė is Lecturer in Music History and Aesthetics of Music at the Lithuanian Academy of Music in Vilnius. Her research interests lie at the intersections of reception of music, cultural theory and 20th-century music. She has published fairly widely on these issues in Lithuania and abroad. She is editor of collection on music semiotics (*Baltos lankos,* Vilnius, 1997) which earned her the Award of the Association of Art Unions. A collection of essays on postsoviet Lithuanian art and cultural changes she is co-editing with Lolita Jablonskienė entitled Mapping Territories is forthcoming in 2003.

Robert S. Hatten is Professor of Music Theory at Indiana University and author of *Musical Meaning in Beethoven* (Indiana University Press), a co-recipient of the Wallace Berry Publication Award from the Society for Music Theory in 1997. His article, "Krzysztof Penderecki's Music in the Context of 20th-Century Opera" appeared in a collection of essays edited by Teresa Malecka (Cracow: Academy of Music, 1999). Dr. Hatten is general editor of a new book series with Indiana University Press entitled "Musical Meaning and Interpretation," and he recently submitted a manuscript for the series, "From Synthetic

Interpretation to Emergent Meaning: A Theory of Musical Gesture, Topics, Tropes, and Continuity."

Małgorzata Janicka-Słysz, music theorist, Ph.D., Assistant Professor at the Department of Music Theory and Interpretation of the Musical Work, Academy of Music, Cracow. Her publications include *Vytautas Bacevičius i jego idee muzyki kosmicznej* [Vytautas Bacevičius and His Ideas of the Cosmic Music] (Cracow: Academy of Music, 2001); "Charles E. Ives: *II Sonata fortepianowa "Concord"*: portret amerykańskich transcendentalistów" [The Second Piano Sonata "Concord" of Charles Ives: Portrait of the American Transcendentalists], in: *Muzyka w kontekście kultury* [Music in the context of culture], edited by M. Janicka-Słysz, T. Malecka and K. Szwajgier (Cracow: Academy of Music, 2001); and "Vytautas Bacevičius' *Poème "Contemplation," Poème Mystique, Poème Astral*: an Anticipation of 'Cosmic Music,' " *Lietuvos Muzikologija*, 2 (2001).

Alicja Jarzębska is Professor and the current Director of the Institute of Musicology at the Jagiellonian University. Her principal research interests are the theory of music from the eighteenth to the twentieth centuries, methods for the analysis of the musical work, and the history and aesthetics of 20th-century music with particular emphasis on the works of Stravinsky, Polish composers (including Penderecki, Lutosławski, Panufnik), and American and British composers. She has lectured at universities in the USA (Department of Music, the State University of New York, Buffalo) and Germany (Institut für Musikwissenschaft, Universität Regensburg). She is the author of the books *Idee relacji serialnych w muzyce XX wieku* [The Idea of Serial Relations in Twentieth-Century Music] (Cracow, 1995), *Z dziejów myśli o muzyce* [From the History of Thought on Music] (Cracow, 2002), and *Strawiński. Myśli i muzyka* [Stravinsky: His Thought and Music] (Cracow, 2002), and numerous articles in periodicals in Poland and other countries. She is working at present on a book titled *Wprowadzenie do muzyki XX wieku* [An Introduction to the Music of the Twentieth Century]. She also contributed several major biographical entries to the PWM (Polish Musical Publishers) Music Encyclopedia and the *Encyclopaedia Britannica.*

Primož Kuret, Professor of Music History at the Music Academy in Ljubljana, is president of the Slovenian Society of Musicology, a member of the Fachkommission Musikgeschichte im Johann-Herder-Forschungsrat Marburg an der Lahn, an honorary member of the Accademia Filarmonica di Bologna, and has been chairman of the annual international musicological conferences in Ljubljana since 1986. His books include *Glasbeni inštrumenti na srednjeveških freskah na Slovenskem* [Musical Instruments in Medieval Frescoes in Slovenia] (Ljubljana,1973), *Glasbena Ljubljana 1899-1919* [Musical Ljubljana 1899-1919] (Ljubljana, 1985), *Umetnik in družba* [The Artist and Society] (Ljubljana, 1988), *Mahler in Ljubljana* (Ljubljana, 1997), *Mahler in Laibach* (Vienna, 2001), and *"Immortality to the Spirit": From the Academia Philharmonicorum to the Slovenska Filharmonija (1701 - 2001),* (Ljubljana, 2001, in Slovenian and English), as well as numerous articles in musicological reviews at home and abroad.

Iwona Lindstedt is an Assistant Professor at the Institute of Musicology, University of Warsaw. She specializes in the history, theory, and analysis of 20th-century music, with particular emphasis on Polish music. She has published on the work of Józef Koffler, Bogusław Schaeffer, Karol Rathaus, and Krzysztof Penderecki, as well as articles on computer aided analysis of twentieth-century music. She is author of the book *Dodekafonia i serializm w twórczości kompozytorów polskich XX wieku* [Dodecaphony and Serialism in the Work of Twentieth-Century Polish Composers] (Lublin: Polihymnia, 2001).

Lidia Melnyk was born in Lviv. She graduated from the Łysenko Academy of Music in 1999 with a degree in musicology and is now an Aspirant Lecturer there, working on a doctorate on "The Neo-Baroque in Twentieth-Century Music" under Professor Yarema Yakubiak. Since 1999, she has also been press director of the Contrasts International Festival of Contemporary Music in Lviv.

Niall O'Loughlin is an English musicologist who specializes in the 20th-century music of Central and Eastern Europe. He has given conference papers on Mahler in Utrecht, Ljubljana and Keele, on Schoenberg in Ljubljana, Uppsala and Cracow, on Stockhausen in Loughborough and Ljubljana and on Panufnik in Cracow. He has written numerous pioneering papers and articles on Slovene music of the 20th century, in addition to his book, *Novejši glasba v Sloveniji*, which was published in 2000.

Maria Piotrowska is a Professor at the Catholic University of Lublin. Her graduate studies were concentrated on the problems of aesthetics in the field of 20th century music with particular interest in the area of music and hermeneutics. She is also the author of two books: *Neoklasycyzm w muzyce XX wieku* [Neoclassicism in 20th century music] (Warsaw, 1982) and *Tezy o możliwości hermeneutyki muzycznej w świetle stu lat jej historii* [Theses about the possibilities of the hermeneutics of music in light of the 100 year history of music] (Warsaw, 1990). She published also numerous articles, e.g. "Chopin i Uhland" [Chopin and Uhland], in: *Muzyka Chopina jako źródło inspiracji wykonawczych* [Chopin's Music as an inspiration for performers] (Warsaw, 1999); "O regułach hermeneutycznych" [On hermeneutic rules] in: *Muzyka sztuką przezwyciężania czasu* [Music as an art of conquering time] (Warsaw, 2003).

Leszek Polony, musicologist, musical critic, and publisher, joined the faculty of the Academy of Music in Cracow in 1972 and became a Professor in 1993. He was also vice-rector for student affairs from 1991 to 1993. He was music reviewer and culture editor of *Gazeta Krakowska* newspaper from 1970-81. At the Polish Musical Publishers (PWM), he was editor in chief from 1991-2001 (with a break in 1994-95), became managing director in 1995, and is now president. He has contributed articles to *Ruch Muzyczny, Muzyka, Tygodnik Powszechny*, and *Życie Literackie*. His scholarly interests extend to the aesthetics of music, music of the Romantic and modern periods, 20th-century Polish music, and the performing art of eminent pianists. His books include *W kręgu muzycznej wyobraźni* [In the Circle of Musical Poetics] (Cracow, 1980), *Poetyka muzyczna M.Karłowicza* [The Musical Poetics of Karłowicz] (Cracow, 1986), and *Polski kształt sporu o istotę muzyki* [The Polish Shape of the Controversy over the Essence of Music] (Cracow, 1991).

Ray Robinson is Senior Professor of Music at Palm Beach Atlantic University in West Palm Beach, Florida. He has written extensively on Krzysztof Penderecki and his music, including numerous articles and two books. Professor Robinson is Chair of the Editorial Board of *Studies in Penderecki*, and he has contributed regularly to The Choral Journal, Opera News, Ovation and various publications of the Cracow Academy of Music.

Svetlana Savenko is a Professor at the Moscow State Conservatory and the author of some 100 publications mainly connected with twentieth-century music (Stravinsky, Ligeti, Stockhausen, Schnittke, Silvestrov and other Russian composers).

Tom Service is a Ph.D. student at the University of Southampton working on the music of John Zorn. He writes about music for The Guardian, and teaches at Trinity College in London. He contributes regularly to Tempo, Opera, the BBC Magazine, and appears as presenter and broadcaster on BBC Radio 3.

Robert Shankovich is Professor of Music at Duquesne University. He serves as Chair of the Musicianship Department, and is also the Director of the Graduate Division of the School of Music. His teaching specialty includes courses in counterpoint, analysis and philosophies of music history and theory.

Zbigniew Skowron is Professor at the Institute of Musicology, University of Warsaw. He graduated in Polish philology and musicology at the University of Warsaw, and in music theory at the Academy of Music in Warsaw. In 1987-8 he studied with Leonard B. Meyer at the University of Pennsylvania on an American Council of Learned Societies fellowship. Among his scholarly interests are aesthetic and historical aspects of XXth-century music, history of musical aesthetics, and Chopin's biography. He is the author of *Teoria i estetyka awangardy muzycznej* [Theory and Aesthetics of the Musical Avant-Garde] (Warsaw, 1989) and of the monograph *Nowa muzyka amerykańska* [Modern American Music] (Cracow, 1995). He is also the editor of *Lutosławski Studies* (Oxford, 2001) and the editor-in-chief of *Przegląd Muzykologiczny* [Musicological Review] - a yearbook of the Institute of Musicology, University of Warsaw.

Milan Slavický is a composer, lecturer, writer on music, and recording producer. He graduated in musicology from the Charles University in Prague (1970) and holds a Ph.D. from the same institution (1972). He also studied composition under Jan Kapr at the Janaček Academy of Performing Arts in Brno (1968-1972) and music theory at the Academy of Performing Arts in Prague (1970-1972). He is a senior recording producer at Supraphon. He has lectured at the Charles University since 1990 and taught composition at the Prague Academy of Performing Arts since 1994. Aside from books and articles about twentieth-century music (including a study of Gideon Klein, the "Theresienstadt composer"), he has produced over 500 LPs and CDs. His writing about orchestral and choral music won him the Carl Maria von Weber Prize in 1976 and 1979 and the Czech Music Critics' Prize in 1993.

Andrzej Szczerski is a member of the faculty of the Jagiellonian University Art History Institute and the recipient of stipends from the Foundation for Polish Learning and the Brzezia Lanckorońskich Foundation. He has held scholarships at Oxford University and the Zentralinstitut fur Kunstgeschichte in Munich. His research interests include the history of nineteenth- and twentieth-century art in central Europe, twentieth-century Polish art, and the history of design. He is the author of *Wzorce tożsamości. Recepcja sztuki brytyjskiej w Europie Środkowej około roku 1900* [Patterns of Identity: The Reception of British Art in Central Europe around 1900] (Cracow: Universitas, 2002). He has contributed numerous articles to periodicals and exhibition catalogues in Poland and abroad, including *Studia*

Waweliana and *Apollo*. He is a member of the academic board of the exhibition *Der neue Staat. Polnische Kunst 1918-1939 zwischen Experiment und Repräsentation* at the Leopold Museum, Vienna, 2003) and of AICA, the International Association of Art Critics.

Mieczysław Tomaszewski is a Polish musicologist and Professor (and doctor *honoris causa*) at the Academy of Music in Cracow, where he heads the Faculty of Music Theory and Interpretations. For many years he served as Director of the Music Publishing House, Polskie Wydawnictwo Muzyczne (PWM). He has written extensively on the ontology of musical works, problems of the Word-Tone relationship in music, and Polish music of the 19th and 20th centuries. He is author of the following books, e.g.: *Krzysztof Penderecki i jego muzyka* [Krzysztof Penderecki and his music] (Cracow, 1994), *Muzyka Chopina na nowo odczytana* [Chopin's music read anew] (Cracow, 1996), *Chopin. Człowiek, dzieło, rezonans* [Chopin: the man, the work, the resonance] (Poznań, 1998), *Nad pieśniami Karola Szymanowskiego* [On the songs of Karol Szymanowski] (Cracow, 1998), *F. Chopin und seine Zeit* (Laaber, 1999), *Interpretacja integralna dzieła muzycznego. Rekonesans* [The integral interpretation of the musical work: A reconnaissance] (Cracow, 2000), *Fryderyk Chopin. Życie twórcy.* Leksykon multimedialny, CD-ROM [Frederyk Chopin: the life of the artist], 2000, *Chopin i George Sand* [Chopin and George Sand] Warsaw 2003.

Tadeusz A. Zieliński, theoretician, critic, and writer on music, graduated in musicology from Warsaw University in 1957. His interests center on 19th- and 20th-century music and harmonic and scale-melody issues. He is the author of studies of Chopin (published in France and Germany), Bartóka (published in Switzerland and Germany), Szymanowski, and Serocki, as well as a general study, *Style, kierunki i twórcy muzyki XX wieku* [Twentieth-Century Styles, Trends and Composers], the brief theoretical treatise *Problemy harmoniki nowoczesnej* [Problems in Contemporary Harmonics], a treatment of *Die modalen Strukturen im Werks Bartóks* (Jahrbuch Peters, 1981/82), and the article on "Harmony and Counterpoint" in *Dutton's Dictionary of 20th Century Music* (New York). He has written on Polish contemporary music in the journals *Melos* (Mainz), *Musical America* (New York), *Nuova Rivista Musicale Italiana* (Rome), and *Nutida Musik* (Stockholm). He is also author of the forthcoming book *Dramat instrumentalny Pendereckiego* [Penderecki's Instrumental Drama]. Aside from music, he also publishes on philosophical issues under the pseudonym Antoni Domaniewski (*Byt i względność* [Being and Relativity], Warsaw 2002).